FORM; *Being;* *A b s e n c e*

Architecture and Philosophy

PRATT JOURNAL OF ARCHITECTURE

RIZZOLI
NEW YORK

ACKNOWLEDGEMENTS

Volume 2, Spring 1988

Editorial Board

Stephen Perrella, Directing Editor and Designer

Caleb Crawford, Principal Editor

Alan Cohl, Editor
P. Jung Wong, Editor

Executive Editorial Consultant
Helen Anne Easterly

Consultants
Melissa DeGroff, Editorial
Alastair Noble, Art

Advisors
John Lobell, Administration/Production
A. Raleigh Perkins, Research

The second volume of the PRATT JOURNAL OF ARCHITECTURE *is dedicated to Donald Cromley, Undergraduate Chairman of the School of Architecture and Adjunct Associate Professor of Architecture, in friendship and admiration.*

Advisory Board
Raimund Abraham
Michael Hollander
John Johansen
Mimi Lobell
Michael Zisser

For their generous contributions of time, consultation, and advice, we would like to thank Elliot Feingold, Arakawa, Madeline Gins, Jeffrey Kipnis, Mark Wigley, Peter Eisenman, Joseph Kupfer, John Schumacher, Diane Coffield, Roger Bell, Hajime Yatsuka, John Nambu, John Whiteman, Donald Wall, David Shapiro, Lebbeus Woods, Kenneth Frampton, the PRECIS 6 *editors, and, Fumihiko Maki.*

The PRATT JOURNAL OF ARCHITECTURE *was produced by undergraduate students of the School of Architecture. Among our colleagues, we are particularly grateful for the time and talents of Yew-Thong Leong, Nora Coffey, Ladan Doroudian, Margarita Torres, Mark Bess, Gary Scholten, and the* PRATT JOURNAL *Vol. 3 editors.*

We gratefully acknowledge the generous support that we have received from the administrative staff at Pratt Institute, particularly from Arlene Friedman, Lyman Piersma, and Alma Delany.

Front cover: Arakawa, A Couple, 1985. Oil and acrylic on canvas. Collection of J. & S. Colton.

Back cover: Jesse Reiser and Nanako Umemoto, Engendering Plate with Sigils.

The PRATT JOURNAL OF ARCHITECTURE *is published bi-annually by the School of Architecture, Pratt Institute, Brooklyn, New York. Pratt Institute: Richardson Pratt, Jr., President; Joseph J. Azzinaro, Vice President for External Affairs; Marie Avona, Director of Public Affairs; School of Architecture: Paul Heyer, Dean Sidney Shelov, Associate Dean Copyright © 1988 by the School of Architecture, Pratt Institute. All rights reserved. Printed in the United States of America. ISBN: 0-8478-5455-8 ISSN: 0883-7279 LC: 85-061973*

The PRATT JOURNAL *was composed in Helvetica Bold Condensed and Garamond. Type compostion was done on a Macintosh Plus computer by the* JOURNAL *executive editors, and the type was printed on a Linotronic computer at 1270 d.p.i. resolution by Micropublishing Center, Inc., New York, NY. Mechanical artwork and graphic production was done by Stephen Perrella Design Consultants. The text was printed on 80 lb. Lustro Dull by The Nugent Organization, Inc., New York, NY.*

Distributed by Rizzoli International Publications, Inc., 597 Fifth Ave, New York, NY 10017.

Address editorial correspondence to the PRATT JOURNAL OF ARCHITECTURE, *200 Willoughby Avenue, Brooklyn, NY 11205.*

FORM; *Being;* *Absence*

Architecture and Philosophy

PRATT JOURNAL OF ARCHITECTURE

"But we do not want to get anywhere. We would like only, for once, to get to just where we are already."
    Martin Heidegger, *Poetry, Language, Thought*

"I sometimes have the feeling that the Heideggarian problematic is the most 'profound' and 'powerful' defense of what I attempt to put into question under the rubric of the *thought of presence.*"
    Jacques Derrida, *Positions*

C O N T E N T S

FORM; *Being;* *Absence*

Architecture and Philosophy

The Architectural Displacement of Philosophy

Mark Wigley

This article was developed from a discussion with Mark Wigley and Jeffrey Kipnis at the Museum of Modern Art on June 11, 1988

JEFFREY: Do you agree with the use of Heidegger in this book?

MARK: Of course Heidegger needs to be reread in architectural discourse. But thinking about Heidegger presupposes an earlier question, implicit in the structure of this book — why read philosophy in architectural discourse? Perhaps we should go further: why is it that it is impossible to talk about architecture without talking about philosophy? Why is such talk a congenital complaint of architectural theorists? In my view, there are certain strategic relationships between architectural discourse and philosophical discourse that prescribe a tradition of reading of philosophy in architecture. Any architectural reading of Heidegger is an example of this relationship, but a very special example, as the relationship can only be understood in Heideggarian terms. Heidegger made thematic the ancient bond between architecture and philosophy and then problematized the relationship so that it can no longer be thought outside him. There is, of course, a long tradition of reading Heidegger in architectural discourse, but it is, sloppy, erratic, inconsistent. This sloppiness should not be understood as an historical accident, a weakness of architectural theorists. Rather, it should be understood as a form of defense, a strong defense against a certain threat.

While architectural theorists understand that they must refer to Heidegger, they understand that they must not observe Heidegger's work too closely because there are frightening implications. Heidegger is read only in order to resist that threat. This journal is useful inasmuch as it undermines this tradition of reading in order to identify the threat.

Heidegger has been exploited as a kind of

magic wand to legitimize conservative practice. This consumption of Heidegger is very easy to spot. Architectural theorists tend to repeat certain quotations and always miss exactly in those very texts the most radical and clearest claims about architecture. They distance themselves from that moment to produce a conservative reading of architecture. In this way, Heidegger's concern with the question of place is used to legitimatize dull-witted thinking about place in architecture. Heidegger's rereading of place, his displacement of place, is glossed over precisely in order to reconstitute the traditional sense of place. Heidegger is employed against his own agenda. The side of the *other* in Heidegger, which problematizes all of those values of home and place and site and presence and so on, his disruptive or subversive dimension, is never used in architectural discourse. Heidegger is always understood to be concerned with architecture to reify place and home and so on. To my knowledge no one has exploited the disruptive dimension let alone the apparent problematic interlocking of the two. The reading of phenomenology in architectural discourse is reactionary, an account which returns us, via perception, to the body but to a precisely defined cultural body, constructed by value systems that need to be questioned. It is a return to home base, to home territory, to that which is closest, to the sense of one's self and therefore to the classical subject. Thus it preserves certain suspect ideological structures. Therefore, my description of architectural discourse as the impoverished use of subservient theory is not a criticism. The mediocrity of architectural discourse has considerable strategic value and is produced by very precise cultural behavior. Contrary to received wisdom, mediocrity is hard to sustain. To produce a mediocre architectural discourse requires the use of the most elaborate strategies by which anything interesting is diluted. Architects by and large are expert diluters who can water down any strong proposition. They are well trained to do so at architecture schools, in which they learn to resist the radical possibilities. Mediocrity is not a crime in architecture, but a professional skill, rehearsed in both theory and practice. No-

where is this more evident than in the reading of Heidegger.

JEFFREY: There is a distinction between early Heidegger and late Heidegger; from that flows the question of applying the early and the late Heidegger. That could be extended into Derrida, how do we apply Derrida?

MARK: Firstly, it should be noted that since post-structuralist thought is so indebted to Heidegger, the architectural resistance to Heidegger has in recent years been expanded into a resistance to post-structuralism. To read Derrida, for example, in architectural discourse presupposes a rereading of Heidegger. Heidegger's work inhabits the philosophical tradition in order to subvert it. Derrida asks again and again to what extent Heidegger inhabits the tradition in a way that simply reconfirms it? He identifies that dimension of Heidegger which consolidates the tradition rather than subverts it. Much of Heidegger's discourse is simply lazy inhabitation of, rather than parasitical intervention in, traditional metaphysical discourse. A lot of Derrida's work rewrites of those sections of Heideggarian discourse in which Heidegger does not operate critically, but leads us back down the path to the clearing and into the home in order to resist the homelessness that is modernity, to recover the presence of unmediated Being. Derrida follows Heidegger's return home, but in order to demonstrate that home is not what philosophy claims it is. The home becomes the most anxious site of all, the violent scene of alienation. This rewriting of Heidegger undermines the simplistic division between early and late Heidegger.

Rather, I would argue, the distinction between early and late is an attempt to historicize Heidegger's work to remove its most dangerous possibility, that those propositions of "late" Heidegger are entangled with those of early Heidegger in the "early" work. The "late" work is no more than a development of an enigma within the early work, and, all the force of a Heideggerian analysis derives from this enigma. This problematic makes Heidegger the key figure for discussing Derrida.

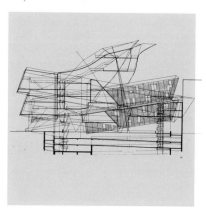

Apartment Building. Vienna. Austria 1986. Coop Himmelblau

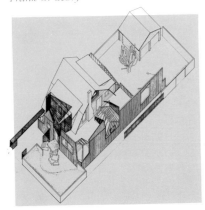

Gebry House.
Santa Monica, California, 1978-8.
Frank O. Gebry

Derrida cannot be discussed outside of Heidegger. His work is no more than an extended interrogation of that enigma in Heidegger. Derrida only makes that enigma policy, understands it as constitutional. He suggests that Western thought is necessarily committed to a search for presence, frustrated not because presence is simply absent or blocked by the dissimulation of representational masks, but presence itself is constructed precisely through complicated exchanges between such masks.

In saying this I oppose the typical Anglo/American reading of Derrida which argues that Derrida is no more than warmed-over Nietzschean clichés about loss of origin, the subject, center, meaning, presence — a nihilistic rhetoric of absence. The force of Derrida's argument derives precisely from the claim that Western thought is governed by an obsession with presence. None of Derrida's analysis is in any way a demolition of metaphysics; it is a displacement of metaphysics effected in the terms of metaphysics.

JEFFREY: Because I am one of the people you cast aside, we have to discuss the question of application; but let me proceed with one point. You don't read Derrida's use of the word *metaphysics*, as in the phrase, "the metaphysic of presence," as a pejorative term, meaning a truth taken uncritically and therefore operating as a symptom.

MARK: It is understood as a symptom, the mark of a systematic repression, but Derrida offers something other than therapy. He is a traditional philosopher inasmuch as he employs every tool given to him by the tradition of philosophy derived from Plato. He applies those tools to the tradition itself to demonstrate it is riddled with gaps and flaws; but never does he disown the discourse or attempt simply to escape it. The typical reading which I criticize attempts to say that Derrida necessarily takes us to some new place. The force of his work is precisely to argue that the tradition does not simply occupy a "place" from which one can move, but is the side effect of a sequence of displacements. Deconstruction is not a theoretical tool which can be applied to a

discourse in order to transform it. One does not replace a discourse with another. Deconstructive theory radically shifts our thinking about place; but, at the end of the day, there is no simple pragmatic consequence of that shift. Application of Derridian theory leads not to some practical displacement, but accentuates a certain disquiet already operative within the games that we are always already playing.

Therefore, metaphysics is not set up simply as a target to be destroyed, but as a misrepresented mechanism. Derrida argues that while philosophy endlessly attempts to put a certain regime in place, the operation of metaphysics, which is cultural and governs every aspect of our lives, in fact operates otherwise. Philosophy here is understood as that discourse which conserves a series of assumptions crucial to the organization of culture. Metaphysics is the mechanism of cultural production in which we are all enveloped. Architecture plays an absolutely central role in this mechanism. Philosophical discourse is able to construct itself only inasmuch as our culture maintains a certain account of the architectural object. In other words, one can put theory in place only by employing a precise set of assumptions about the condition of objects: specifically, the ability of an object to stand up and to enclose. Architectural discourse is the trustee of these assumptions. The architect appears to control objects, to transform them, but in fact merely manipulates them without tampering with their fundamental condition. The architect preserves the object, protects it from radical transformation, in the name of culture, thus ironically, insulating the object from culture. Indeed, architects have been charged with the responsibility of bracketing architecture from culture.

This is not to deny the conventional wisdom that architecture is that discourse which is by definition most embedded in culture. On the contrary. But it is embedded in a very strange way. Architecture inhabits culture according to the lines of a very convoluted geometry. Architectural discourse has assumed the role of disguising that geometry in order to prohibit culture from interrogating architecture. In other words, we manipulate systems of representation (words, buildings, drawings, photographs...) to produce a defensive screen which blocks other accounts of architecture. We gain the status of a discourse inasmuch as we prevent any displacement of a certain account of architectural objects and, therefore, of objects in general, because it is in architectural discourse that the status of the object is made thematic. Inasmuch as the discourse can keep the architectural object in its place, domesticating architecture by veiling its disarming and disquieting qualities, the discourse sustains the whole mechanism with which that culture organizes itself. At every level, all cultural operations depend on the capacity to draw a line, to distinguish between inside and outside, a capacity which presupposes the understanding of the architectural object as the exemplary articulation of inside and outside.

In these terms, architecture neither houses nor represents culture, neither precedes nor follows culture. Rather, it is the mechanism of culture. Obviously, all discourses are cultural. But architecture has a unique relationship with culture because it sustains the system by which all discourses are organized. This is a political account of architecture, but not in the sense of what kind of architecture can be associated with what kind of political institution, nor of what radical forms are appropriate for a radical institution and what conservative forms for a conservative institution. Rather, it is about the capacity of architecture to make it possible for us to distinguish between radical and conservative. I mean the capacity for architecture to organize culture at a much more comprehensive level than housing. Indeed, the extent to which architecture does, in fact, house anything, let alone cultural institutions, is not clear.

This is to discuss architecture in terms of its strategic political relationships with other discursive practices. I suggest that these relationships are defined by specific epistemological contracts, with simple rules but a lot of fine print within which it is possible to elaborate propositions which disarm, without abandoning, the very structures the contract protects.

This deconstruction of the tradition is not effected by simply applying Derrida to architecture. Rather, it is a question of identifying the architectural argument which already occupies by contractual necessity and, indeed, makes possible the Derridean argument: What architecture is presupposed by Derridean discourse, and how does it relate to the contractually preserved architecture of the tradition?

Deconstructive theory needs to be reread closely in order to locate within it an architecture already in place, already organizing a certain economy. This kind of reading, just begun, represents a second stage of readings of Derrida in architecture. The first stage followed the tradition of applying "outside" theory to architecture. We always look to other discourses for descriptions of our own object. This application from outside is governed by the need not to look too closely at architectural objects for fear of violating the contract on which the discourse is organized. The first readings of Derrida in architecture simply put Derrida's name in the place of those of previous sources of external legitimation. Derrida was seen by definition outside and above architecture and therefore authoritative as a philosopher, to comment on our discipline and to influence our thinking. We, as trustees of architectural objects, turn to philosophy for the next culturally acceptable description of architecture. So in the last few years readings of Derrida publicized architecture as dissimulated literary texts. Derridean readings of texts where simply transposed into readings of architecture.

But this first reading started to turn over onto itself; something in this description of architecture called into question the very way that description was set up. If architecture really did have these strange qualities, then the status of theory must also be transformed. If architecture was no longer simply an object, theory could no longer simply be detached from it. No longer could the traditional protocol of theory be observed. Consequently, Derrida could not unproblematically assume authority over architecture, could no longer be

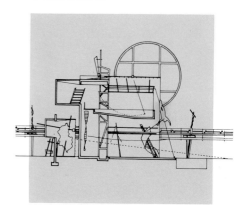

Parc de La Villette. Paris, France, 1982-5. Bernard Tschumi

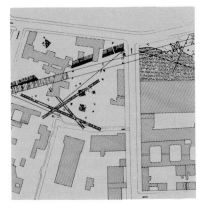

City Edge. Berlin, Federal Republic of Germany, 1987. Awarded First Prize, IBA City Edge Competiion, 1987. Daniel Libeskind

read in the same way. Once-reverent readings of Derrida became critical. This development coincided with a transition in Derrida's own thinking about architecture. Having seen architecture as no more than a secondary application of deconstructive discourse, he began to see architecture as a critical site on which the limits of deconstruction are explored. Suddenly architecture posed a certain threat to deconstruction. Radical possibilities emerged within architecture whose status was unclear. These possibilities assumed great significance because architecture is clearly that discourse which should be most resistant to deconstruction. Suddenly deconstruction seemed to be unproblematically "consumed" in architecture. Architectural discourse became increasingly confident, able to disturb the contractual relationships that limited it, and, therefore, to disturb the way in which theory is appropriated. Different readings of Derrida became possible.

Consequently, a second generation of readings had to do with critical examinations of Derrida's text to locate the limits of its architectural argument. The first generation, typically reverent and subservient, had glossed over the relationship between literary texts and architectural objects on which it depended. But something passed across the gap between these two discourses and developed into the possibility of displacing the whole contractual relationship between them.

It became possible to locate within deconstruction an architectural argument unexpected for both architects and philosophers. Since traditional philosophy presupposes a certain account of the object, deconstruction must displace that account in order to displace philosophy. Otherwise, it only elaborates certain deflections, rather than displacements, of philosophical discourse.

We know that within Derridean argument the operation of architectural metaphors is as important as for the operations of traditional philosophy. One can extract it from a certain subversive rhetoric of the uncanny, of the grotesque, the abyss, and so on. A series of

such figures appear to displace traditional thinking about architecture and are pivotal in the organization of deconstructive discourse. They are displacements of the architectural motif that organizes traditional philosophy. Architecture appears there as a metaphor which one would abandon upon completing the great work of philosophy, but these metaphors cannot be erased from philosophy, because they are not simply metaphors. Philosophy is not so much a mode of inquiry as a preservative mechanism which sustains certain assumptions about objects. Its discourse is riddled with symptoms of a neurotic relationship with architecture. Philosophers describe themselves as architects and philosophy as architecture. Philosophers begin from the ground and work their way up, check the ground, check the foundations, and so on; a philosopher gets rid of ornament. This "metaphor" operates throughout the philosophical tradition. Plato's most important idea, the idea of the idea, which is of course the idea of theory itself (a theory of theory is the basis of philosophy), is introduced by and rests upon the idea of the architect and the house. First the architect has the abstract idea of the house and then builds the concrete image of that idea. The whole tradition of Western metaphysics as a technical discourse stands on the foundation of this understanding of architecture.

Immediately Plato, as with all the rest, says, "This is just a metaphor, don't worry about it, folks," when the project of philosophy is completed these metaphors will have to be abandoned. But in the very moment of the attempt to exclude the metaphor, one is forced to use the metaphor. This procedure is doubly twisted because the very idea of metaphor, is made possible by an idea about architecture. Derrida demonstrates that the idea of metaphor depends upon the idea of grounded structure. Therefore it is impossible for philosophy to abandon these metaphors; they are constitutional. Therefore they are not simply metaphors. A certain understanding of architecture makes metaphor and, therefore, philosophy possible, and that understanding cannot be excluded from philosophy. A certain account

(continued on page 95)

ART AND SPACE

Martin Heidegger
translated by Charles H. Seibert

If one thinks much, one finds much wisdom inscribed in language. Indeed, it is not probable that one brings everything into it by himself; rather, much wisdom actually lies therein, as in proverbs.
G. Chr. Lichtenberg

Δοκει δε μετα τι ειναι και
χαλεπον ληφθηναι δ τοποσ

It appears, however, to be something overwhelming and hard to grasp, the *topos* — that is, place-space.
Aristotle, *Physics*, Book IV

The remarks on art, space and their interplay remain questions, even if they are uttered in the form of assertions. These remarks are limited to the graphic arts, and within these to sculpture. Sculptured structures are bodies. Their matter, consisting of different materials, is variously formed. The forming of it happens by demarcation as setting up an enclosing and excluding border. Herewith, space comes into play. Becoming occupied by the sculptured structure, space receives its special character as closed, breached and empty volume. A familiar state of affairs, yet puzzling.

The sculptured body embodies something. Does it embody space? Is sculpture an occupying of space, a domination of space? Does sculpture match therewith the technical scientific conquest of space?

As art, of course, sculpture deals with artistic space. Art and scientific technology regard and work upon space toward diverse ends in diverse ways.

But space — does it remain the same? Is space itself not that space which received its first determination from Galileo and Newton? Space — is it that homogeneous expanse, not distinguished at any of its possible places, equivalent toward each direction, but not perceptible with the senses?

Space — is it that which, since that time (Newton), challenges modern man increasingly and ever more obstinately to its utter control? Does not modern graphic art also follow this challenge insofar as it understands itself as dealing with space? Does it not thereby find itself confirmed in its modern character?

Yet, can the physically-technologically projected space, however it may be determined henceforth, be held as the sole genuine space? Compared with it, are all other articulated spaces, artistic space, the space of everyday practice and commerce, only subjectively conditioned prefigurations and modifications of one objective cosmic space?

But how can this be so, if the objectivity of the objective world-space remains, without question, the correlate of the subjectivity of a consciousness which was foreign to the epochs which preceded modern European times?

Even if we recognize the variety of space experiences of past epochs, would we win already an insight into the special character of space? The question, what space as space would be, is thereby not even asked, much less answered. In what manner space *is*, and whether a Being in general can be attributed to it, remains undecided.

Space — does it belong to the primal phenomena at the awareness of which men are overcome, as Goethe says, by an awe to the point of anxiety? For behind space, so it will appear, nothing more is given to which it could be traced back. Before space there is no retreat to something else. The special character of space must show forth from space itself. Can its special character still be uttered?

The urgency of such questions demands from us a confession: So long as we do not experience the special character of space, talk about artistic space also remains obscure. The way that space reigns throughout the work of art hangs, meantime, in indeterminateness.

The space, within which the sculptured structure can be met as an object present-at-hand; the space, which encloses the volume of the figure; the space, which subsists as the emptiness between volumes; — are not these three spaces in the unity of their interplay always merely derivative of one physical-technological space, even if calculative measurement cannot be applied to artistic figures?

Once it is granted that art is the bringing-into-the-work of truth, and truth is the unconcealment of Being, then must not genuine space, namely what uncovers its authentic character, begin to hold sway in the work of graphic art?

Still, how can we find the special character of space? There is an emergency path which, to be sure, is a narrow and precarious one. Let us try to listen to language. Whereof does it speak in the word "space"? Clearing-away (Räumen) is uttered therein. This means: to clear out (roden), to free from wilderness. Clearing-away brings forth the free, the openness for man's settling and dwelling. When thought in its own special character, clearing-away is the release of places toward which the fate of dwelling man turns in the preserve of the home or in the brokenness of homelessness or in complete indifference to the two. Clearing-away is release of the places at which a god appears, the places from which the gods have disappeared, the places at which the appearance of the godly tarries long. In each case, clearing-away brings forth locality preparing for dwelling. Secular spaces are always the privation of often very remote sacred spaces.

Clearing-away is release of places.

In clearing-away a happening at once speaks and conceals itself. This character of clearing-away is all too easily overlooked. And when it is seen, it always remains still difficult to determine; above all, so long as physical-technological space is held to be the space in which each spatial character should be oriented from the beginning.

How does clearing-away happen? Is it not making-room (Einräumen), and this again in a twofold manner as granting and arranging? First, making-room admits something. It lets openness hold sway which, among other things, grants the appearance of things present to which human dwelling sees itself consigned. On the other hand, making-room prepares for things the possibility to belong to their relevant whither and, out of this, to each other.

In this twofold making-room, the yielding of places happens. The character of this happening is such a yielding. Still, what is place, if its special character must be determined from the guideline of releasing making-room?

Place always opens a region in which it gathers the things in their belonging together.

Gathering (Versammeln) comes to play in the place in the sense of the releasing sheltering of things in their region. And the region? The older form of the word runs "that-which-regions" (die Gegnet). It names the free expanse. Through it the openness is urged to let each thing merge in its resting in itself. This means at the same time: preserving, i.e., the gathering of things in their belonging together.

The question comes up: Are places first and only the result and issue of making-room? Or does making-room take its special character from the reign of gathering places? If this proves right, then we would have to search for the special character of clearing-away in the grounding of locality, and we would have to meditate on locality as the interplay of places. We would have then to take heed that and how this play receives its reference to the belonging together of things from the region's free expanse.

We would have to learn to recognize that things themselves are places and do not merely belong to a place.

In this case, we would be obliged for a long time to come to accept an estranging state of affairs:

Place is not located in a pre-given space, after the manner of physical-technological space. The latter unfolds itself only through the reigning of places of a region.

The interplay of art and space would have to be thought from out of the experience of place and region. Art as sculpture: no occupying of space. Sculpture would not deal with space.

Sculpture would be the embodiment of places. Places, in preserving and opening a region, hold something free gathered around them which grants the tarrying of things under consideration and a dwelling for man in the midst of things.

If it stands thus, what becomes of the volume of the sculptured, place embodying structures? Presumably, volume will no longer demarcate spaces from one another, in which surfaces surround an inner opposed to an outer. What is named by the word "volume," the meaning of which is only as old as modern technological natural science, would have to lose its name.

The place seeking and place forming characteristics of sculptured embodiment would first remain nameless.

And what would become of the emptiness of space? Often enough it appears to be a deficiency. Emptiness is held then to be a failure to fill up a cavity or gap.

Yet presumably the emptiness is closely allied to the special character of place, and therefore no failure, but a bringing-forth. Again, language can give us a hint. In the verb "to empty" *(leeren)* the word "collecting" *(Lesen)*, taken in the original sense of the gathering which reigns in place, is spoken. To empty a glass means: To gather the glass, as that which can contain something, into its having been freed.

To empty the collected fruit in a basket means: To prepare for them this place.

Emptiness is not nothing. It is also no deficiency. In sculptural embodiment, emptiness plays in the manner of a seeking-projecting instituting of places.

The preceding remarks certainly do not reach so far that they exhibit in sufficient clarity the special character of sculpture as one of the graphic arts. Sculpture: an embodying bringing-into-the-work of places, and with them a disclosing of regions of possible dwellings for man, regions of the possible tarrying of things surrounding and concerning man.

Sculpture: the embodiment of the truth of Being in its work of instituting places.

Even a cautious insight into the special character of this art causes one to suspect that truth, as unconcealment of Being, is not necessarily dependent on embodiment.

Goethe said: "It is not always necessary that what is true embody itself; it is already enough if spiritually it hovers about and evokes harmony, if it floats through the air like the solemn and friendly sound of a bell." *

*Originally published in
Man and World
An International Philosophical Review
Volume 6, No. 1, February 1973

Basic Problems of Phenomenology

Martin Heidegger,
Rainer Maria Rilke

Poetry, creative literature, is nothing but the elementary emergence into words, the becoming-uncovered, of existence as being-in-the-world. For the others who before it were blind, the world first becomes visible by what is thus spoken. We may listen to a quotation from Rainer Maria Rilke's *The Notebooks of Malte Laurids Brigge* as testimony on this point.

Will anyone believe that there are such houses? No, they will say that I'm falsifying. But this time it's the truth, nothing left out and naturally also nothing added. Where should I get it from? It's well known that I'm poor. Everyone knows. Houses? But, to be precise, they were houses that no longer existed. Houses that were torn down from top to bottom. What was there was the other houses, the ones that had stood alongside them, tall neighboring houses. They were obviously in danger of collapsing after everything next to them had been removed, for a whole framework of long tarred poles was rammed aslant between the ground of the rubble-strewn lot and the exposed wall. I don't know whether I've already said that I mean this wall. But it was, so to speak, not the first wall of the present houses (which nevertheless had to be assumed) but the last one of the earlier ones. You could see their inner side. You could see the walls of rooms on the different storeys, to which the wallpaper was still attached, and here and there the place where the floor or ceiling began. Along the whole wall, next to the walls of the rooms, there still remained a dirty-white area, and the open rust-stained furrow of the toilet pipe crept through it in unspeakably nauseating movements, soft, like those of a digesting worm. Of the paths taken by the illuminating gas, gray dusty traces were left at the edges of the ceilings, and here and there, quite unexpectedly, they bent round about and came running into the colored wall and into a black hole that had been ruthlessly ripped out. But most unforgettable were the walls themselves. The tenacious life of these rooms refused to let itself be trampled down. It was still there; it clung to the nails that had remained; it stood on the handsbreadth remnant of the floor; it had crept together there among the onsets of the corners where there was still a tiny bit of interior space. You could see that it was in the paint, which it had changed slowly year by year: from blue to an unpleasant green, from green to gray, and from yellow to an old decayed white that was now rotting away. But it was also in the fresher places that had been preserved behind mirrors, pictures, and cupboards; for it had drawn and redrawn their contours and had also been in these hidden places, with the spiders and the dust, which now lay bare. It was in every streak that had been trashed off; it was in the moist blisters at the lower edge of the wall-hangings; it tossed in the torn-off tatters, and it sweated out of all the ugly stains that had been made so long ago. And from these walls, once blue, green, and yellow, which were framed by the tracks of the fractures of the intervening walls that had been destroyed, the breath of this life stood out, the tough, sluggish, musty breath which no wind had yet dispersed. There stood the noondays and the illnesses, and the expirings and the smoke of years and the sweat that breaks out under the armpits and makes the clothes heavy, and the stale breath of the mouths and the fusel-oil smell of fermenting feet. There stood the pungency of urine and the burning of soot and the gray reek of potatoes and the strong oily stench of decaying grease. The sweet lingering aroma of neglected suckling infants was there and the anguished odor of children going to school and the sultriness from the beds of pubescent boys. And much had joined this company, coming from below, evaporating upward from the abyss of the streets, and much else had seeped down with the rain, unclean above the towns. And the domestic winds, weak and grown tame, which stay always in the same street, had brought much along with them, and there was much more too coming from no one knows where. But I've said, haven't I, that all the walls had been broken off, up to this last one? Well, I've been talking all along about this wall. You'll say that I stood in front of it for a long time; but I'll take an oath that I began to run as soon as I recognized the wall. For that's what's terrible — that I recognized it. I recognize all of it here, and that's why it goes right into me: it's at home in me.**

Notice here in how elemental a way the world, being-in-the-world — Rilke calls it life — leaps toward us from the things. What Rilke reads here in his sentences from the exposed wall is not imagined into the wall, but, quite to the contrary, the description is possible only as an interpretation and elucidation of what is "actually" in this wall, which leaps forth from it in our natural comportmental relationship to it. Not only is the writer able to see this original world, even though it has been unconsidered and not at all theoretically discovered, but Rilke also understands the philosophical content of the concept of life, which Dilthey had already surmised and which we have formulated with the aid of the concept of existence as being-in-the-world.*

*Martin Heidegger, *The Basic Problems of Phenomenology*. trans. by Albert Hofstadter (Bloomington: Indiana University Press, 1982), p. 172-3.

**Rainer Maria Rilke, *The Notebooks of Malte Laurids Brigge*. Trans. by M.D. Herter Norton. Copyright © 1949 by W.W. Norton & Company, Inc. Reprinted by permission of W.W. Norton & Company, Inc.

Andy Warhol

The Philosophy of Andy Warhol

Space is all one space and thought is all one thought, but my mind divides its spaces into spaces into spaces and thoughts into thoughts into thoughts. Like a large condominium. Occasionally I think about the one Space and the one Thought, but usually I don't. Usually I think about my condominium.

The condominium has hot and cold running water, a few Heinz pickles thrown in, some chocolate-covered cherries, and when the Woolworth's hot fudge sundae switch goes on, then I know I really have something.

(This condominium meditates a lot: it's usually closed for the afternoon, evening, and morning.)

Your mind makes spaces into spaces. It's a lot of hard work. A lot of hard spaces. As you get older you get more spaces, and more compartments. And more things to put in the compartments.

To be really rich, I believe, is to have one space. One big empty space.

I really believe in empty spaces, although, as an artist, I make a lot of junk.

Empty space is never-wasted space.

Wasted space is any space that has art in it.

_____   _____   _____   _____

An artist is somebody who produces things that people don't need to have but that he — for *some reason* — thinks it would be a good idea to give them.

Business Art is a much better thing to be making than Art Art, because Art Art doesn't support the space it takes up, whereas Business Art does. (If Business Art doesn't support its own space it goes out-of-business.)

So on the one hand I really believe in empty spaces, but on the other hand, because I'm still making some art, I'm still making junk for people to put in their spaces that I believe should be empty: *i.e.,* I'm helping people *waste* their space when what I really want to do is help them *empty* their space.*

* Andy Warhol, *The Philosophy of Andy Warhol* (New York: Harcourt Brace Jovanovich, Inc., Copyright © 1975), p. 143-4. Reprinted by permission of Harcourt Brace Jovanovich, Inc.

Opposite page: Andy Warhol, *Untitled*, 1976-1986. Black and white photo patchwork. Courtesy: Robert Miller Gallery.

Gordon Matta-Clark

Bingone, Gordon Matta-Clark
(Lewistown, N.Y., 1974).
Courtesy: Holly Solomon Gallery.

Paris Cuttings, Gordon Matta-
Clark (Paris, 1975). Courtesy:
Holly Solomon Gallery.

Splitting, Gordon Matta-Clark (Englewood, N.J., 1974). Courtesy: Holly Solomon Gallery.

Bronx Floor, *Threshole*, Gordon Matta-Clark (New York, 1972). Courtesy: Holly Solomon Gallery.

What is invisibly at play behind a wall or floor, once exposed, becomes an active participant in a spatial drawing of the building's inner life. The act of cutting through from one space to another produces a certain complexity involving depth perception. Aspects of stratification probably interest me more than the unexpected views which are generated by the removals — not the surface, but the thin edge, the severed surface that reveals the autobiographical process of its making. There is a kind of complexity which comes from taking an otherwise completely normal, conventional, albeit anonymous situation and redefining it, retranslating it into overlapping and multiple readings of conditions past and present. Each building generates its own unique situation.*

*Excerpted from "An Interview with Gordon Matta-Clark" by Don Wall, In the *Internationaal Cultureel Centrum* catalogue entitled, "Gordon Matta-Clark," Antwerp, November 1977.

Vito Acconci

Bad Dream House

In the project *Bad Dream House*, there are three upside-down houses: Two upside-down houses on the ground, tilted, leaning against each other, cradle a third upside-down house on top. The upside-down houses on the ground, faced with brick and shingled roofs are more conventionally related to the ground; the upper house of glass is in the air: a green house.

The bottom houses are entered through open gables on either side. The wood interior walls are stained brown; the ceilings (which now function as floors and side walls) are blue; the floors (now overhead) are green. One then goes past or sits at an upside down table, proceeds upstairs to a set of facing bleachers, or further upstairs to the glass/garden house. Benches offer a variety of seating positions where a person may sit next to another person, or opposite him/herself before a mirror, blocked off from the outside by opaque blue plexiglass, or looking outside through clear or blue tinted plexiglass.

The prototype for this piece is the notion of house; it is easy to focus on because everyone within a culture knows the house form. It is a device that establishes a place in which a viewer can initially feel at home. Once the viewer is there, something may happen; the project takes conventions known to all and twists them or literally turns those conventions upside down.

Lewis Stein

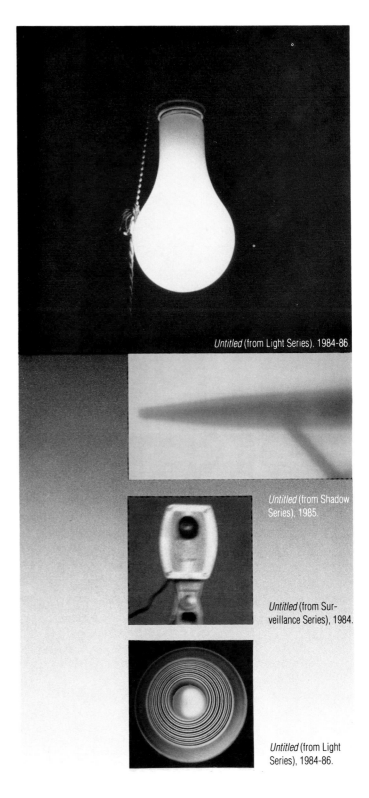

Untitled (from Light Series). 1984-86.

Untitled (from Shadow Series), 1985.

Untitled (from Surveillance Series), 1984.

Untitled (from Light Series), 1984-86.

Heidegger writes of our involvement with the world in terms of a "concern." A relationship to "ready-to-hand" entities is one manifestation of this concern. In a narrow sense these entities can be seen as tools or equipment, or more broadly as having a structure of "in-order-to" or "for-the-sake-of." Heidegger presents hammers as a representative example of a "ready-to-hand" object. In our everyday dealings we perceive the hammer not as "a perceptual cognition" but in terms of its potentiality, or its potential relation to our bodies to realize our concerns. Heidegger calls this latter mode of perception "circumspection." When we seize the hammer and test its worthiness, we are operating in this mode of perception. However, when we use the hammer, our relationship to it shifts. The hammer is subordinated to the hammering, to our in-order-to. In this mode, the hammer, despite our direct relationship to it, no longer exists; it is no longer perceived.

Heidegger describes how radically all this can change. There can be a breakdown. The head can come flying off the hammer. Only in circumstances like these can we become aware of the processes of the in-order-to and for-the-sake-of. It is also at these times that the equipment, in its "conspicuousness of unusability," demonstrates itself most clearly in its character as "ready-to-hand," and at these times we can become aware of the larger context — the world — in which we have previously operated unaware.

Untitled, 1968-72, (chained door).

Untitled, 1967-74, (hammer).

"Chained door" (1968-72) consists of a single solid-core door in a door jamb secured to a wall. A regular door chain is fixed between the door and the jamb from the inside. Under optimal conditions, ten or more identical doors would be placed at regular intervals in an exhibit space. The doors do not lead anywhere. The viewer has two options: either to try one of the doors or to resist their call. In either case, the body's action is determined in relation to the doors. An attempt to open one of the doors will result in a sudden jolt. The question remains about the other doors. Are they all the same?

The works designated "hammers" (1967-74) are a series of ten hammers. Each object consists of a 16-oz. claw hammer mounted on a board which forms the bottom of a sealed polished aluminum box with a plexiglass window. The head, handle and background are each painted a different bright pastel color, beautiful in a way that subverts or mocks the masculinity usually associated with hammers. Their placement on a low platform encourages the viewer to stand directly in front of each hammer respectively and to peer down at it; the object's seductiveness notwithstanding, the sealed box prevents any manipulation.

*Martin Heidegger, *Being and Time*. Translated by John Macquarrie and Edward Robinson (New York: Harper and Row, Publishers, Inc., Copyright © 1962). Reprinted by permission of Harper and Row, Publishers.

Equipment can genuinely show itself only in dealings cut to its own measure (hammering with a hammer, for example); but in such dealings an entity of this kind is not *grasped* thematically as an occurring Thing, nor is the equipment-structure known as such even in the using. The hammering does not simply have knowledge about [*um*] the hammer's character as equipment, but it has appropriated this equipment in a way which could not possibly be more suitable. In dealings such as this, where something is put to use, our concern subordinates itself to the "in-order-to" which is constitutive for the equipment we are employing at the time; the less we just stare at the hammer-Thing, and the more we seize hold of it and use it, the more primordial does our relationship to it become, and the more unveiledly is it encountered as that which it is — as equipment. The hammering itself uncovers the specific 'manipulability' ["*Handlichkeit*"] of the hammer. The kind of Being which equipment possesses — in which it manifests itself in its own right — we call "*readiness-to-hand*" [*Zuhandenheit*]. Only because equipment has *this* 'Being-in-itself' and does not merely occur, is it manipulable in the broadest sense and at our disposal. No matter how sharply we just *look* [*Nur-noch-hinsehen*] at the 'outward appearance' ["*Aussehen*"] of Things in whatever form this takes, we cannot discover anything ready-to-hand. If we look at Things just 'theoretically', we can get along without understanding readiness-to-hand. But when we deal with them by using them and manipulating them, this activity is not a blind one; it has its own kind of sight, by which our manipulation is guided and from which it acquires its specific Thingly character. Dealings with equipment subordinate themselves to the manifold assignments of the 'in-order-to'. And the sight with which they thus accommodate themselves is *circumspection.**

Keith Sonnier

Monticello Wall

A wall containing a usable telephone, stereo and television exists as a pedestrian obstruction; the everyday elements are put into a context in which their activities are no longer familiar. One is forced into the context of the piece. Normal utilitarian notions about architecture are altered to put the piece "into the world." Qualities of direct utilitarian engagement redescribe the relationship between a subject and the work.

Porte-Vue, 1987

Porte-Vue is a site-specific commission for the grounds of an 18th-century chateau in Brittany. The surrounding context has similar stone placings from paleolithic Druid cultures. Three 20-ton extractions of granite, the predominant indigenous stone, recall ancient architectural sites. Modern equipment has left traces on the unearthed stones which contrast with the stone's surface texture. As one walks through *Porte-Vue*, which translates as porthole, one is at eye level with the holes through which the winter sun shines.

Justen Ladda

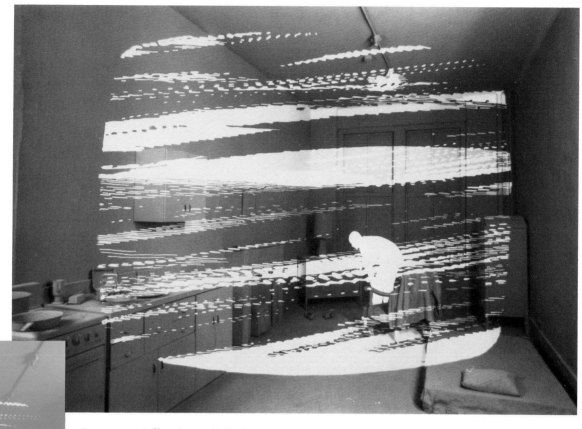

Someone Adjusting a T.V. Set
The superimposed image, projected into
the fully furnished room from a specific
point, has been painted in fluorescent
colors and is lit by ultraviolet light. From
the point of projection the undistorted
image of the television screen appears to
be floating in space. As the viewer moves,
the image disintegrates or coalesces. The
space becomes the screen and the viewer
becomes the projector.

The Thing, 1981. ©, ™Marvel Comics Group. Installation in
a Bronx school room. Photo: Martha Cooper.

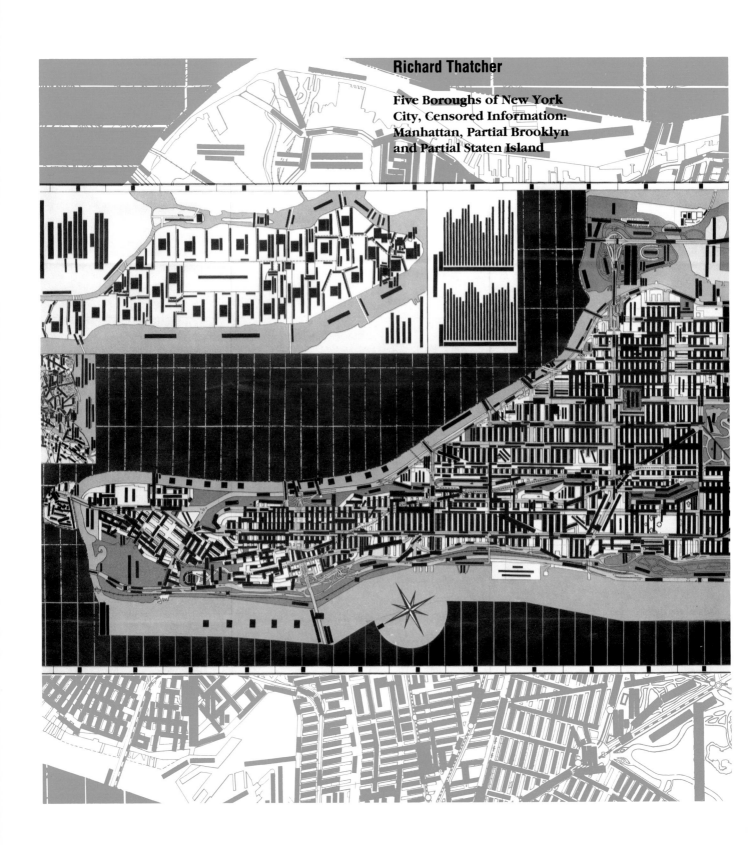

Richard Thatcher

Five Boroughs of New York City, Censored Information: Manhattan, Partial Brooklyn and Partial Staten Island

Chris Burden

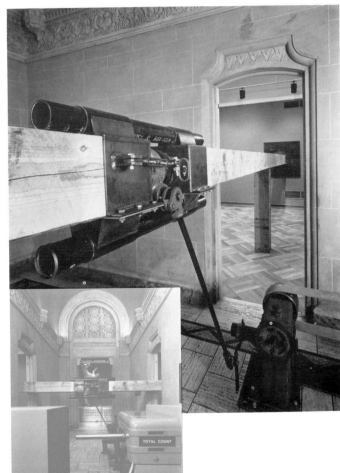

Samson

Samson is a conceptual sculpture consisting of a 100-ton jack placed five feet above the gallery's floor between two 23-foot-long, 10 x 10-inch timbers. The jack pushes the timbers out against 42-inch square steel plates which in turn push against the bearing walls of the museum. A turnstile through which viewers must pass to gain admission to the exhibition is mechanically connected to the jack's lever arm through a system of gears. Each visitor passing through the turnstile extends the jack ever so slightly and increases the pressure on the timbers and ultimately on the building itself. The gears that connect the turnstile to the lever arm of the jack step down the ratio so that thousands of visitors must pass through the turnstile in order to advance the jack handle one stroke. The small counter on the turnstile indicates the number of visitors that have passed through it. Implied in this slow kinetic sculpture is the fact that if enough visitors attend the exhibition, they will force the building's walls apart.

Samson, 1985. Turnstile, winch, worm gear, leather strap, jack, timbers, steel plates. 64.25" x 555" 148.75". Courtesy of the artist and Henry Art Gallery, University of Washington.

Public projection on the
Allegheny County Soldiers
Memorial Hall, Pittsburgh,
Pennsylvania, 1986.

The Method of Projection

We must stop this ideological "ritual," interrupt this journey-in-fiction, arrest the somnambulistic movement, restore a public focus, a concentration on the building and its architecture. What is implicit about the building must be exposed as explicit; the myth must be visually concretized and unmasked. The absent-minded, hypnotic relation with architecture must be challenged by a conscious and critical public discourse taking place in front of the building.

Projection on the Pediment
of the Museum Fridericia-
num during Documenta 8,
June, 1987.

Public visualization of this myth can unmask the myth, recognize it "physically," force it to the surface and hold it visible, so that the people on the street can observe and celebrate its final formal capitulation.

This must happen at the very place of myth, on the site of its production, on its body — the building.

Only physical, public projection of the myth on the physical body of myth (projection of myth on myth) can successfully demythify the myth.

The look, the appearance, the costume, the mask of the buildings is the most valuable and expensive investment. In the power discourse of the "public" domain, the architectural form is the most secret and protected property.

Public projection involves questioning both the function and the ownership of this property.

Wodiczko's artworks encourages us to begin thinking about the language of architecture by abetting de-mythologisation of the existing architecture. One possibility which Barthes refers to for counteracting myth is to mystify it, that is, create an artificial myth. Wodiczko artificially constructs a myth which is that these buildings can be given anthropomorphic qualities — they can acquire gesture and dress via a modification which is essentially illusory. Another possibility for demythologising the existing architecture is to encourage a reconstruction of the myth. Perhaps this begins to happen when Wodiczko turns his projectors off. The projection may last only one evening in the hope that casual viewers will attempt to reconstruct what they have seen the night before — perhaps think about it, talk about it. This in turn may encourage a deconstruction of the existing architecture — an attempt to place it within a social vocabulary. The rapid removal of the image is crucial if it is not to hazard assimilation into the existing architecture, perhaps as spectacular surface decoration.*

Projection on the Tower of Lutherkirche, Kassel, West Germany. The first three weeks of Documenta 8, between 10:30 and 1:00 AM each night. Three xenon arc slide projectors were used.

* *Canadian Journal of Political and Social Theory/Revue canadienne de théorie politique et sociale,* Vol. 7, Nos. 1-2 (*Hiver/Printemps,* 1983).

Portable Flops: Design for the Urban Nomad

As long as there are people living on the street, they require emergency help — *on the streets.* The problem of homelessness is complicated and demands long term planning for public housing, but emergency service must be provided before considering that such assistance will soon be unnecessary.

This proposal expresses, through architecture, the plight of the homeless person living on the street and at the same time frees the homeless individual from physical and psychological abuse. The object of the portable dwelling is not to keep the homeless on the street, but to provide help for those who have no choice. This project aims to maintain the dignity of the individual.

Constructed of molded fiberglass, the units are durable, lightweight and maneuverable.

The units may be produced at low cost by individual fabricators who are members of an autonomous interest group. Space may be allotted to allow the portable flops to be brought together to form small communities.

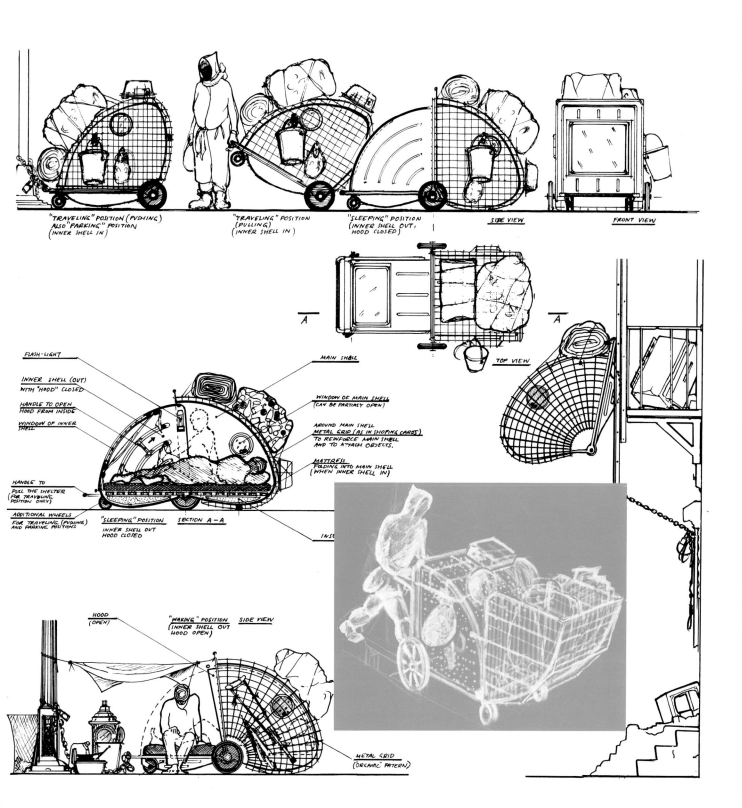

Anselm Kiefer

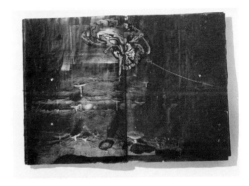

Martin Heidegger

Martin Heidegger, Anselm Kiefer (1976). Photographs painted with acrylic and oil paint, glued together; pages of wallpaper soaked in black oil (chalk) and shellac bound with canvas; covers made of cardboard. 13 spread pages including cover. Photo: Jon Abbott. Courtesy: Marian Goodman Gallery.

Heidegger envisages a world that has been totally reduced to technological terms, a world in which... the only relationships are technological ones — relationships, that is, of pure manipulation. The will to power of a purely calculative, technological thinking threatens to obliterate Being, for Being is something that can in no way be encompassed in the standing-reserve. Technological man concerns himself solely with beings, forgetting even the possibility of Being. In *An Introduction to Metaphysics*, ... the first text in which he evokes the "encounter between global technology and modern man," Heidegger unequivocally views the "technological frenzy" of the modern world as a manifestation of the "spiritual decline of the earth." This decline, he goes on to maintain,

is so far advanced that the nations are in danger of losing the last bit of spiritual energy that makes it possible to see the decline (taken in relation to the history of "Being"), and to appraise it as such. This simple observation has nothing to do with *Kulturpessimismus*, and of course it has nothing to do with any sort of optimism either; for the darkening of the world, the flight of the gods, the destruction of the earth, the transformation of men into a mass, the hatred and suspicion of everything free and creative, have assumed such proportions throughout the earth that such childish categories as pessimism and optimism have long since become absurd.

In short, the nihilistic impulse lying at the foundation of Western culture finds its culmination in technology. Here is the ultimate locus of the crisis that confronts Western man.

For those who have difficulty seeing why anyone would take Heidegger — especially the later Heidegger — seriously, much of the answer is to be found in the fact that his nostalgic, idealistic, technological catastrophism does seem in many aspects to accord with twentieth-century experience. The Holocaust, nuclear weapons, the growing technologization and bureaucratization of modern life — all these realities seem to confirm Heidegger's text, or at the very least can be convincingly interpreted in Heideggerian terms.*

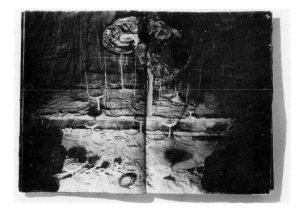

* Text excerpted from: Allan Megill, *Prophets of Extremity* (Los Angeles: The Univesity of California Press, Ltd., 1987), p. 140.

Neil M. Denari

Leesburg, Virginia Town Hall Competition

This project is a competition for a new town hall in Leesburg, Virginia, a city of 13,000 located 30 miles west of Washington, D.C. The functional program is a 30,000 square-foot building consisting of typical town government facilities, including a police station and council chambers. A 320-unit car-park and public space development were required for access and civic completion of the town's historic district, of which the site marks the center.

Inherent in the history of a town and its politics is the goal of social order. The project is a place where latent energy in the confrontation between public and institutionalized opinion is converted into the potential for order. A reading of the present condition of the site, suggests a proposition different from the history of the American Revolution written in the site. The project is an attempt through Architecture to structure "particles of chaos."

The cylindrical shaft of space connects "regenerative ground planes" symbolized by the floor plates in section, and establishes a center in relation to the building's random perimeter. The council chambers fills the upper section of the cylinder in collaboration (read contamination) with the interior public space. The hydraulic cherry-picker extending from the facade is a mechanized manifest- ation of public pro- clamation.

Model

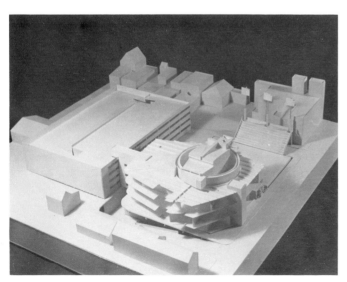

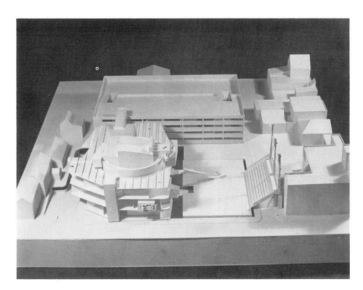

Site plan

Plans, perspective, section

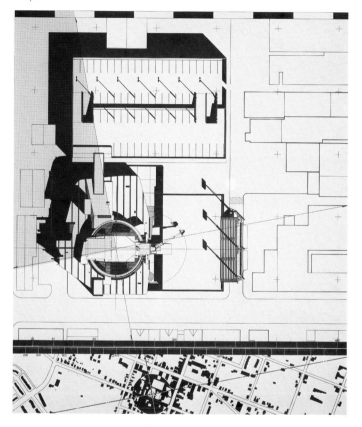

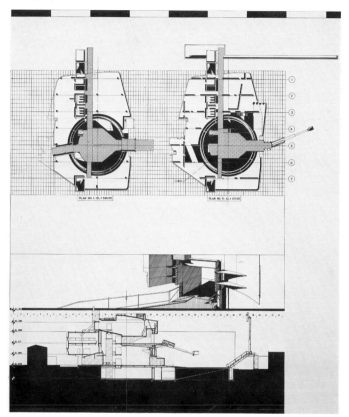

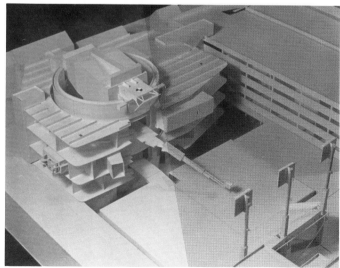

Taeg Nishimoto

The city is a built dream, a vision
incarnated. What makes it grow is
its image of itself.
Peter Conrad, *The Art of the City*

Model , section, plans

Site plan

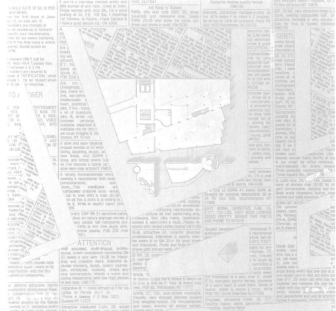

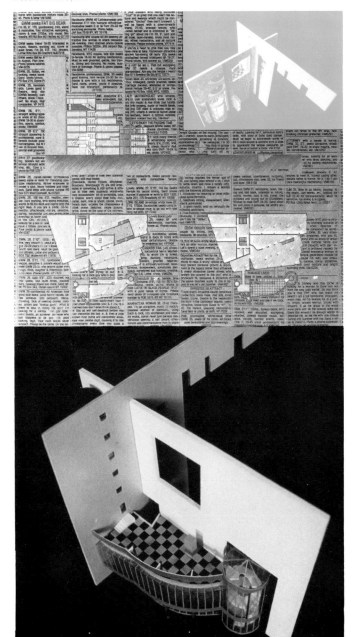

This project is a part of the theoretical series "New York Reinterpreted," which addresses the notion of *genius loci*, or "spirit of place," as described by Christian Norberg-Schulz. The image of the city has developed not only through information about the places, but also through the places' influence on the culture. Painting, sculpture, literature, photography, and music generate the atmosphere of the place. This design interprets the facility of the artists' imagination in an architectural setting to invoke a mythological reality. It is designed as a writers' club, the program derived from the area's history of literary activities.

The collective associations examined in the *Astor Place Project* may be considered "urban coincidences": the images generated by coincidence in everyday life.

Subway train rides symbolically represent the accidental mixture of racial backgrounds. Keith Haring's attitude towards subway graffiti addresses the commonality of an anonymous people. Joseph Cornell's collection of objects and trinkets from city streets and shops resembles the personal ads in the *Village Voice*, a vital mechanism of urban life.

In New York City, blank walls are rare except for the spaces used for advertising murals. A formal response to the project seeks to invoke image, coincidence and accidental mixture by using a wall as Cornell used a container. The two crossing walls at the front of the building allow independent readings from each side; the detachment of the front walls from the rear sides makes possible multiple readings of the wall.

Robert Venturi, Denise Scott Brown and Steven Izenour

Vegas Redux: A Significance for A&P Parking Lots, or Learning From Las Vegas

Learning from the existing landscape is a way of being revolutionary for an architect. Not the obvious way, which is to tear down Paris and begin again, as Le Corbusier suggested in the 1920s, but another, more tolerant way; that is, to question how we look at things.

The commercial strip, the Las Vegas Strip in particular — the example *par excellence*, challenges the architect to take a positive, non-chip-on-the-shoulder view. Architects are out of the habit of looking nonjudgmentally at the environment, because orthodox Modern architecture is progressive, if not revolutionary, utopian, and puristic; it is dissatisfied with *existing* conditions. Modern architecture has been anything but permissive: Architects have preferred to change the existing environment rather than enhance what is there.

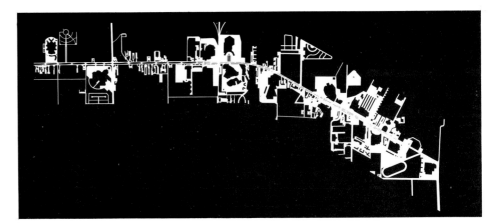

Asphalt

But to gain insight from the commonplace is nothing new: Fine art often follows folk art. Romantic architects of the 18th century discovered an existing and conventional rustic architecture. Early Modern architects appropriated an existing and conventional industrial vocabulary without much adaptation. Le Corbusier loved grain elevators and steamships; the Bauhaus looked like a factory; Mies refined the details of American steel factories for concrete buildings. Modern architects work through analogy, symbol, and image — although they have gone to lengths to disclaim almost all determinants of their forms except

Autos

Buildings

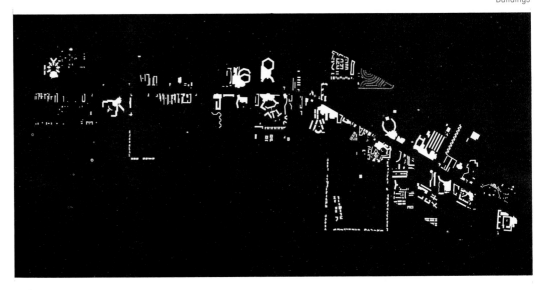

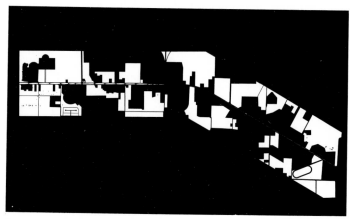

Upper strip, undeveloped land

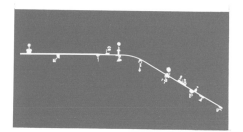

Ceremonial

Nolli's Las Vegas

structural necessity and the program — and they derive insights, analogies, and stimulation from unexpected images. There is a perversity in the learning process: We look backward at history and tradition to go forward; we can also look downward to go upward. And withholding judgment may be used as a tool to make later judgment more sensitive. This is a way of learning from everything.*

* Robert Venturi, Denise Scott Brown, and Steven Izenour, *Learning from Las Vegas* (Cambridge: The MIT Press, Copyright © 1975), p. 3. Reprinted by permission of the authors.

Kristian Gullichsen

Civic Center, Pieksämäki, Finland

The Civic Center, presently under construction, is situated by a lakeshore parkland in the small city of Pieksämäki, Central Finland.

The scheme comprises the new city library, entrance hall with café, art gallery, and multipurpose auditorium seating 350. Its unassuming composition, which is derived from its peaceful lakeside setting, will serve as a transitional element between the urban milieu on one side and the parkland on the other, acting as both a buffer against the street and a backdrop to the park.

The tripartite street elevation contains echoes of a Renaissance palace with the entrance gate and courtyard *cour d'honneur*. The central axis of symmetry, distorting the entrance space, culminates in a fireplace, an unaccustomed symbol of hospitality in a public building. The long curving wall addressing the park stands aside from the landscape as an observer might, surveying the scene with its large openings and projecting veranda. At the north end of the wall stands a watchtower with a moat, functioning as a

children's story room and adult reading area, providing a setting for d'Artagnan, the Three Musketeers and all the other characters who will inhabit the place.

The architectural language as a whole is a loose agglomeration of elements from many different origins, including Nordic classicism and Scandinavian functionalism; form follows function, and in the tradition of Aalto, the psychological is as important as the physical. This project is continuous with the intellectual and artistic base of the 85-year tradition of the Modern movement which contains an inexhaustible source of architectural concepts, rich in meaning and history.

Interior perspective

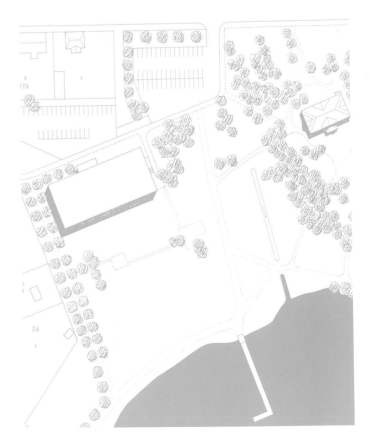

First floor plan

Second floor plan

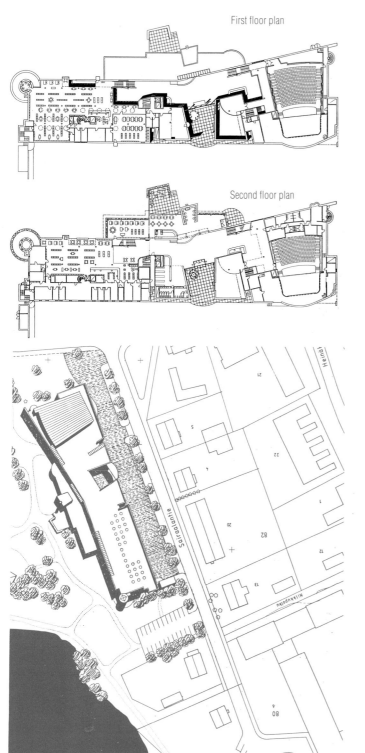

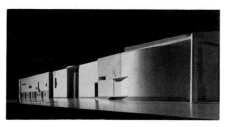

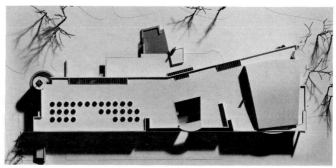

Model   Model Photos by Kauko Sillanpää

Site plan

Aldo Rossi

Architetture Padane

The small book entitled *Architetture Padane** expresses, in part, an idea I discussed some time ago with Luigi Ghirri and Giovanni Jacometti. It is not a catalog to the exhibition "Aldo Rossi at the Casa del Mantegna" in Mantua; rather it is a project similar to Fiera-Catena, the stables, and others.

The images shown here are not limited to ones of Mantua, because in the architecture of the Po River region there are seeds of a richer civilization — one that will be studied eventually in its entirety.

Architetture Padane refers to the architecture of the Po River. The Po is the largest river in Italy. It runs west to east and passes through the regions of Vale D'Aosta, Piedmont, Lombardy, Veneto and Emilia-Romana (Translator's note).

Ghirri (who is from Modena), Jacometti (who is from Novara), and I (from Milan) have discovered in Mantua a common ground — a place analogous to the Po region.

I have not written an introduction, but instead have collected some notes on my work and this countryside.

Whenever I set out to write about architecture, I always end up writing about time and place. It is these qualities that please me about the casa del Mantegna in Mantua, which I refuse to think of as a museum. Ghirri, Jacometti, and I had originally considered rebuilding Mantegna's house. I recalled the artist's rooms — the *Villa con Interno* project that I have been working on for many years which has, over time, acquired its own artistic and social history. But Mantegna's house has another, more personal history, that of a house in Mantua, owned by a forgetful, unorganized, and lazy man.

I have been thinking about this interior for some time, and I realized that it is not very different from the Po River region itself. Years ago, I was struck by an interior in Visconti's movie *Obsession.* As movie lovers well know, these interiors are full, in a pictorial sense, of the black, shiny, silk lingerie of the beautiful Clara Calamai, veiled by the sweat of a Ferrara summer which makes her even paler. Various objects are strewn about these interiors — lamps, coffee pots, carelessly made soup, and glasses of wine. An interior of an architecture of desire.

Mantegna's modest house on the canal possessed the same desire as the Palazzo del Te, or the Favorita ruins, or the white horses in the frescoes, or the farm houses of Mantua. In Mantua this obscure Lombard desire is emphasized in the same way desire is revealed in the sinful and erotic interiors of Cairo.

There is a difference between the north and south of the Lombard region that even the work of the poet Alessandro Manzoni barely acknowledges.

At times the lagoon and the fog over the rice fields, lake and canal complement each other as in Mantegna's painting *Death of a Virgin.* In the painting, death occurs in an enclosed place, even though the enclosed place is a landscape by which the artist depicts both the pathos of death and a Mantua without a past, where the Po history (which is, above all, typically Lombardian and, in part, Emilian and Venetian) acknowledges its own analogous place.

There is also another vision of Mantua, an earlier one, that of the Romans and Virgil. This vision of Mantua constructed a landscape seen from afar, where shadows lengthen and double (as in Virgil's first and second Bucolics), the night robs these objects of their color and, therefore, destroys them. Here, paleness is the main sign of disease.

We could have spoken better about this in our project for Fiera-Catena, which is dominated by a Virgilian meadow. This lawn is inseparable from the town, as the covered piazzas are inseparable from Milan, and the lagoons inseparable from the wetlands.

It occurs to me that when Andre Gide spoke of the elusiveness of the poet, he refers to Virgil himself and not to Virgil's poetry by saying those elements that create the mood of the lagoon are like the forms of the bucolics, or, more to the point, a Virgilian component. At the same time, the lagoons are exactly the opposite.

This could be a description of Po River region architecture and Mantua or even its opposite. These issues are addressed in the Fiera-Catena project, which is only two years old but seems antique:

It is clear, though not obvious, that in the center of the meadow there is a white marble statue of Virgil; there, with its shadow, the statue stands alone. The Virgilian meadow ignores the notion of "free time" as written about by sociologists and provided for by zoning regulations. The meadow neither assumes the existence of free time or implies a way to be used.

The statue of Virgil multiplies its own reflections in the same way that the poet saw objects and in the same way that the painter Giorgio De Chirico saw shadows — like a train conductor (this metaphor belongs to Jean Cocteau, who said "De Chirico is the time of the train"). Since Mantua is not included in major train routes, the statue becomes symbolic of other systems of transportation. The statue is made of white marble, which has a double meaning. On the one hand, "marble white" describes how the image was realized — with the appeal of a Milanese Chamber of Commerce price list, which describes each material and its cost with the precision of a Stendhalian engineer. On the other hand, it refers to the pale, sickly demeanor that Virgil describes.

Therefore, this project located on the Po River would like to transcend that which we have abandoned and the feelings that accompany that abandonment, because we often lose beautiful things, but, in the end, suffer. Behind all new things are sentimental ruins, a "mountain of ruins."

The horses of the Palazzo del Te, Mantegna's horses, that recur in Luigi Ghirri's photos, represent fantasy. The horses are white, but not genetically, rather from a pallor — the same pallor that Virgil

R. Mantovano, B. Pagni (on drawing of G. Romano), Horse's room, Palazzo del Te, Mantua.

refers to. This sickly cast, as described by Virgil, contrasts with the horse's anatomical structure, which represents its earthly being. In the Palazzo del Te, the interior becomes an exterior, and the horses that always return to Mantua are the inhabitants of the stable project, which though it is only begun, I nonetheless present in the small book.

In the studies by the Englishman, George Stubbs, called "The Anatomy of the Horse," the horses interest me more for their skeletal structure than for their overall form. The drawings inspire a clinical interest in horse bones and their pathology. Most Lombardians would blame such defects on the humidity of the region, which is probably accurate, although they are also inherited traits. That is why studies of the anatomical structures of horses are intertwined with furniture and architecture in my drawings.

Drawing from *I Cavalli*, 1983.

The most architectonic part of the stables is in front of the Palazzo del Te in Domenico Gilardi's project for stables in Khrenovoe, U.S.S.R. that belong to Count Orlov-Chesmenskij. As a Russian book describes: "The stables became famous because of the Count's pure bred horses, although they have functional value even in our time." As in Kuz'minki, the courtyards of Khrenovoe form an enclosed square, surrounded by stables and service rooms with their own courtyards. In the middle of this composition is a riding track that faces the main facade, which has five arched openings (the two openings on the sides lead to the courtyard). A recent photo shows this exceptional building with a horse in the foreground. This image brings us back to the Palazzo del Te and our book/project.

Here Luigi Ghirri's photos are exteriors/interiors.

It was our intention to reproduce Domenico Gilardi's plan, but for various reasons it wasn't possible. In fact, we prefer his written description of it, especially since we have always maintained that projects are describable ("an enclosed square..." etc.). This project for a stable has a Lombardian nature even though Gilardi is from Ticino and the two architects who encouraged us to publish these drawings, Fabio Reinhart and Dolf Schnebli, are from Switzerland. It is partly to their credit that this stable is presented as a narration. For those of us interested in architectural theory, it is impossible to present this project in any other way.

From this point on, our project can no longer be explained by images, nor by the logical train of thought that is characteristic of an architect or engineer, nor by anything that is easily communicable.

So stands Mantegna's house in the center of a town that is analogous to us and others from Lombardy. We have selected Mantua as the final metaphor of the southern Po River region. (The metaphor is not restricted to the Lombard region. My colleague, Morris Adjmi, found in the houses of Mantua a reflection of his own home in Louisiana — the image of New Orleans to be exact. I agree with this because ancient channels connect man's history and, on my first visit, New Orleans did not seem foreign to me.) By now the reader has understood that "homeland" refers to a place particularly known and recognizable, or the place where one is recognized.

Sometimes when I look at this homeland I can't distinguish its borders; that is why I approved of Jacometti's proposal to call this book *Architetture Padane*. I would have also liked to discuss Greek architecture, but Jacometti's idea is certainly more focused and honest in that it overcomes cultural gaps. In considering the sinful and erotic interiors of Cairo and the spaces of the Palazzo in Mantua there is truly a thin line between crime and beauty.

Perspective of Fiera-Catena Competition design

Perhaps the cathedrals of this countryside were never purely white because the fog and humidity cracked their surfaces (like the vertebral distortions of arthritis), but their eerie images reappear. On the embankments of the Po River, there are abandoned houses that are part of the landscape; they are active and mysterious places.

Perhaps this project should be dedicated to these active and mysterious places: to the construction of Mantegna's house; to the Po River embankments; to those towns facing the embankments that are part of my architecture; to Clara Calamai's black lingerie which is shiny, sticky, sacred, and sinful, and her carelessly made soup; to the gardens of Mantua and Ferrara; to the mythical horses of the Gonzaga and Count Orlov; to the sickly pallor of the body; and to the "pale diseases" of our patriot poet, Virgil.

To this collection of places that constitute a rediscovered homeland.

From this and other things begins our project *Architetture Padane*.[*]

* Originally published in Italian in:
Aldo Rossi, *Architetture Padane*.
Translation by Morris Adjmi, Ciro
Asperti, and Karen Stein.

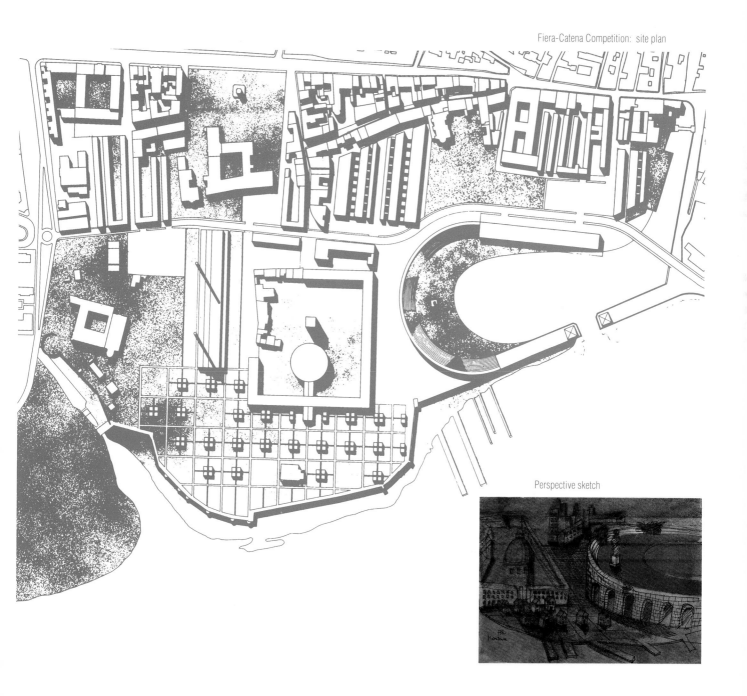

Fiera-Catena Competition: site plan

Perspective sketch

Karen Bausman and Leslie Gill

Owen's Box

For Karen Bausman and Leslie Gill, art, rather than architectural history, is an inspiration for design. History isn't a source of influences to be pillaged; rather, it is an atmosphere to be entered. The usurpation of historical elements may result in mere eclectic assembly; but an attitude toward historical ideas, their beginnings and the entire context of their circumstances may evoke an emotional engagement rather than a disinterested focus on formal features of the past.

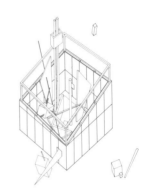

Seasightings,
axonometric drawing

Pictorial spaces are potential influences, not to be literally translated: There is a "world" in a work of art. The beginning of architectural form may come from exploring these worlds, creating an emotive rather than a Cartesian space. The depth of space in the paintings of the Medieval, Gothic, and Constructivist periods have a mysterious reading; the plasticity of the picture plane renders a simultaneity of past, present and future compressed into one viewpoint. This differs from Renaissance paintings in which a perspectival view can define and be measured. The viewer's relation to a picture is considered in the viewing of a painting, rather than through formal analysis. The question becomes: how to engage with the world of a work of art and manifest that revelation as built form.

Huxford House, Model

The impetus for the work of Bausman and Gill is their research employing still-life compositions in small enclosures. These "boxes" are collaged with a variety of architectonic elements: poetic studies of space. These constructions may also be read as worlds. In a kaleidoscopic manner the boxes with their elements can move in scale, forming spaces in which human dimensions do not define scale. When a box becomes a building, the referential size of a door or window is always put into question: Windows can be a conventional size or four inches square.

The *Huxford House* was an attempt by Bausman and Gill to extend what they learned from their research in abstractly constructed spaces to a realized architectural project.

John Hejduk

Bovisa

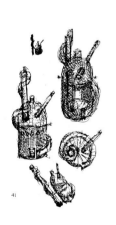 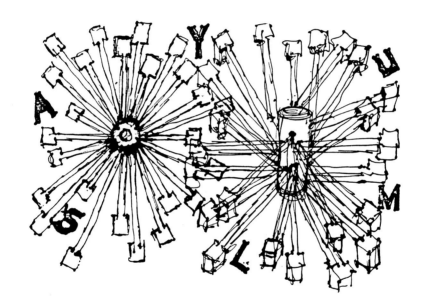 

Sketches for *Bovisa*, 1986.

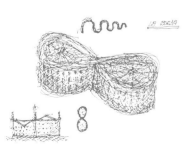  

45

Northern Episode
John Hejduk

Hawthorne was not pleased by his friend's impending visit, although he was attracted to the attentions of Melville's smile. His unease was intensified by the knowledge of the relationship between Zenobia and the former seaman. The New Yorker always asked questions about her death. He seemed to be after details regarding the drowning.

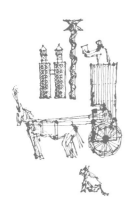

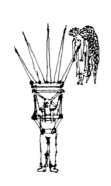

That they belonged to different centuries did not reassure the elder New Englander. He suspected Melville's suggestion that they take a walk in the snow at the edge of the frozen pond.

He watched through the small window light as the black carriage was pulled by the white horse. It ascended the hill after making the turn at the fork in the road. His eyes were momentarily distracted when a large hawk flew above the dark green of the pines. He thought he heard Celia closing the barn doors. The occupant of the approaching conveyance looked like a black bear blowing fog before him. A shot could be heard coming from the winter woods.

The white horse was absorbed by the dark of the barn. Hawthorne could hear Melville stomping the snow off his boots on the wood planks of the porch. As Melville entered the house he immediately related an experience he had had in the South Seas. Hawthorne was unable to imagine such a place.

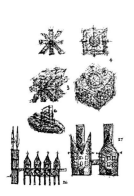

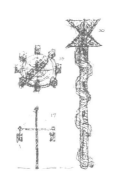

"The natives of that island were as quiet as the heavens. During the night they must have softly glided their canoes to the bow of our sister whaler. In any case they removed the ship's figurehead and, as you know, that act is the sentence of death to a ship and its crew. The next morning upon discovery of the missing figure the sailors were driven to a frenzy. They lowered a long boat and headed for shore, where they captured an island maiden. They brought her back to the ship and promptly lashed her to the bow as a replacement of the lost figurehead. I watched from the deck of my own ship as they tied her to the whaler. No more than an hour had passed when a ferocious storm came suddenly upon the harbor and the two ships. In horror I watched as the maiden plunged in and out of that devilish sea. Then an event occurred which struck me still. Perhaps because of the constant movement of the ship, or perhaps for other

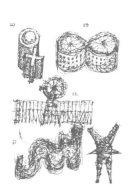

reasons, the island woman was released from her bonds.
And I saw her leap like a dolphin out of the waters, then
disappear into the night of the sea. Our own ship rode out
the storm... the other ship sank to the bottom. The following day the woman was washed up on the shore and I
was told that her thighs were covered by fish-like scales."

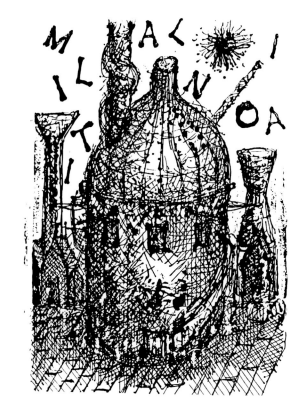

At the moment of Melville's last words both men
were startled by an unearthly animal scream coming from
the barn. They quickly ran to its interior and there they saw
the white horse standing still in his stall, blood moving
slowly down his sides. In two open wounds on his back
two severed hawk wings had been inserted. Hawthorne
and Melville also witnessed Celia in her black cloak
running down to the frozen pond, she moved towards the
center of the ice.

The two men dashed out from the barn towards
the winter water and Celia. As they approached the
pond's edge she waved them off with one hand while she
held to her breast the wingless hawk. Across the pond a
silver timber wolf began to howl. Celia moved in a circle,
cracking the ice around her with the heel of her boot. The
water began to engulf her and she was sucked down as if
a black lily was pulled by its roots into the earth. The last
thing they saw was the cloak closing above her body like a
night flower.

Hawthorne turned to Melville and shouted:
"Damn you; you were not to be satisfied until you had
your third drowning."

Minutes later Melville nailed the wings of the hawk
to a wooden post, threw a blanket over the open wounds
of the horse, led him out of the barn and walked slowly
down the hill until both were encompassed by the white
landscape.

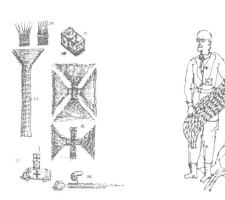

Later...

In the spring, when the ice on the surface of the
pond had melted, Nathaniel searched for Celia. He was unable to find her. Yet he
knew the spot of her drowning, for black water lilies grew there. He built a six-foot high iron
fence around the perimeter of the pond. In the summer evenings the land and water snakes wrapped
themselves around the vertical metal shafts, forming a moving garland marking Celia's disappearance.

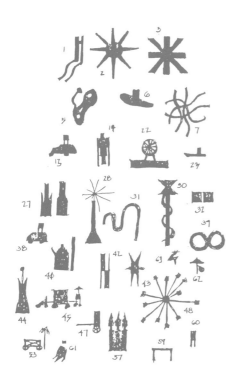

Review: *Mask of Medusa*
Diane Lewis

it is then too
that your mouth and eyes
open
simultaneously

Medusa, John Hejduk

This nonlinear, anti-narrative collage of the works of John Hejduk is a 20th-century conjuration, an exploration of the dialogue between *communitas* and isolation, a state provocative of the expression characterized by the mask of its title. The architectural and literary terrain of these pages is inductive of a philosophic and analytic architecture, which captures and combines the metaphysical tenets of the research on nonobjective imagery in our century, and embodies what Pasolini observed as "the meta-historical surrealism of fables." Once immersed in the body of drawing, construction, critical writings, poetry, and interviews, through the author's pedagogical skills, messages, as if sewn into the linings of our coats, are then challenged in concealment or exposure by the thought presented in the thirty years of work.

Having lived each stage of the classic passage in becoming the visionary architect, John Hejduk "re-presents" in his projects the evolution of his thought and position in the theater of events that surrounds him. This book-construct takes the temporal form of "Frames," seven acts coincident with critical evocations of the postwar era, culminating in the proposals for buildings and projects invited by the City of Berlin, where the application of Hejduk's *communitas* commentary wields its most trenchant possibilities. Here the project for the "Berlin Masque," on the site of the former Gestapo headquarters, crystallizes existential possibilities of American thought in a radical demonstration of program and new spatial principle. Hejduk, passionate witness of a forgotten social contract, is an architect who perpetuates a school and its research, builds, writes, and projects. This publication, compiled and composed during his prolific and varied endeavors, is an important datum for the evaluation of the architect's participation in society, a provocative portrait of what the work of architecture can be in the life of the collective and the individual spirit.

Abstinence from representational modes, in which every artist in the lineage of Rimbaud stoically engages, bears notational inventions and codifications, not only for the painter and *litterateur*, but produced in parallel for the architect the image of an *explosante-fixe* spatial condition, and the derivation of syntax and iconography in the evolving form of the "free section." In the early chapters of *Mask of Medusa*, Hejduk, international torch-bearer-elect for this research, reveals his conceptual mastery of projects, pedagogy, and critical essays. These pursuits converge in the production of three poetic works in three realms: the seminal *Wall House*, a definitive extension of the free section; *The Cooper Union Foundation Building* internal, a constructed dialogue of archetypal form and ideal program; and the polemical essay "Out of Space and Into Time," an American interpretation, no longer naive, projecting a visceral grasp of the vision of Le Corbusier toward temporal and iconographic possibilities.

Arguments regarding the subject matter of the early works as pure formalism, precipitated after the 1971 publication of *Five Architects*, evaporate in this dense and synthetic re-view which shows that Hejduk's research has been the unrelenting engagement with program as literary counterpart to the architectural work. The projects emerge from this manuscript of intertwined text and imagery as crystallizations of essence expressed in the titles which have become their signs. This monograph enunciates an architectural alchemy consisting of images with their hauntingly poetic specifications, with the concept of the bipartite "text" as a fundamental architectural faculty, applied simultaneously to history and to the present. *Wall House, Cemetery for the Ashes of Thought, House for the Inhabitant who Refused to Participate*, and the *Masques* represent textual invention of program that join the titles of LeDoux, Wright, and Mies in the historical memory of architecture. In the "*Sous Realism*" lectures and particularly the projects in *Frames* 5–7, Hejduk universalizes this pivotal approach. His criterion of "other-ness" to attain a state of architecture, detected from works of his spiritual predecessors, creates a crisis of principle for those who aspire to contribute to the body of architectural thought by requiring complete authenticity and permeation of material by mind at every scale of endeavor.

Miesean theses allowed no intellect aspiring to be critical to escape response in the form of a philosophic position. Formalist analyses, such as Rowe's *Mathematics of the Ideal Villa*, stemming from an English Palladianism, did not recognize existential principles of Miesian space. Tom Wolfe's recent media revival of Johnson's style-based, (international appearance categorizations) attempted once again to close dialogue on the definitive architectural conceptions of this century, consolidating them in flip populist characterizations devoid of any sensitivity to the inspiration and challenge they have offered.

Tafuri's European proposal that notational hermeticism creates a suicidal semiotic condition is the third spoke in the axis powers of criticism who consciously disengaged from the potential and specificity of the vision of the individual engaged in a dialectic of subjective-objective languages, predicated on the false assumption that 20th-century movements were utopian. Hejduk, one of the artists, recognizing generative principles in the inventions that these critics' positions define as infertile, presents their extensions in philosophical terms as opposed to stylistic application, offering critique through works, the direct approach, another 20th-century orthodoxy. His confrontation with the Wittgensteinian principle of expression in the abstract, so familiar in the discourse of art criticism, is still unrecognized as a profound trans-historical reading of architectural form. It has led him to state the opposition between architecture and design, the role of the individual in the production of architecture, and the recognition of the mystical aspects of social contract.

The alternating optimism and pessimism forming the world-view of one born in New York during the stock market crash keep alive the critical and dialectical spirit. The use of a subjective-objective voice throughout the book allows a *veritas* to emerge which may shed light on some of the obscure events of our architectural present. However, although the work in its authenticity will always be "news," in its non-confirmation of prediction, it will Re-Mind.

1 **MASK OF** 12
2 **MEDUSA** 11
3   10
4   9
5   8
6   7
7   6
8   5
9   4
10   3
11 **JOHN**   2
12 **HEJDUK**   1

RIZZOLI

Jesse Reiser and Nanako Umemoto

The Globe Theater
Notes Toward The Globe Theater — *Teatrum Mundi*

To the cosmic meanings of the ancient theatre, with its plan based on the triangulations within the Zodiac, was added the religious meaning of theatre as temple, and the related religious and cosmic meanings of the Renaissance Church. The Globe Theatre was a magical theatre, a cosmic theatre, a religious theatre, an actors' theatre, designed to give fullest support to the voices and gestures of the players as they enacted the drama of the life of man within the theatre of the world.... His theatre would have been for Shakespeare the pattern of the universe, the idea of the macrocosm, the world stage on which the microcosm acted his parts.

Francis A. Yates, Theatre of the World.

This conception of the Globe Theater, which had its roots in the magico-religious tradition of the Renaissance, envisions a theater derived from a universal harmony acting as a divine mediator between man and the universe — which would lead ultimately to God.

Through a notion of "universal sympathy" the theater would operate as an effective talisman which acted locally as a place for the enactment of drama. It would evince a reciprocating influence: outwardly, on the greater spheres of the world, and inwardly, bringing down favorable influences from the heavens. The Globe Theater existed first and foremost in the realm of "Ideas," tied neither to any particular locality nor so the material stuff of building.

It is perhaps ironic that the contemporary descendant of the Globe is the "mass media" whose occult origins have been masked by the sophistries of technique. Any direct representation of a Renaissance theater into its modern equivalent could not adequately question the nature of a "theater of the world" and its subsequent manifest shapings of historicity.

In proposing a new theater, the real estate of Bankside, which was the original site of the Globe Theater, was deemed inappropriate and exchanged for a site both ubiquitous and universal. Living in the "absence of Gods," and lacking any credible "idea" of the world, the detritus of post-industrial society — the seemingly endless flow of printed matter — serves as a suitable ground for the project. The chaos of discarded "language" became the site, acting as a profane-liturgical text; a Borgesian "mirror-of-enigmas."

The construction *Métier à Aubes*, which takes its name from an eponymous fragment from Raymond Roussel's novel *Impressions of Africa,* is an artifact derived from an ongoing project for a contemporary reinterpretation of the Globe Theater. The project seeks to illuminate the currently obscured yet ancient and venerable relationship between language and architecture. This relationship, though generally excluded from current definitions, is clearly articulated in pre-classical Greek literature as *Diadala* and

more recognizably in the language of Rome. The Latin verb *textus* (according to classical Roman rhetoricians) indicates the (de) composition of both a literary and an architectural work, and is, of course, the root of the word "textile," thus leading back to Roussel's pregnant *jeu de mot* whose twofold meanings fortuitously encompass the antique definitions: "*Métier* [work/loom] *à Aubes* [dawns/paddle wheel]. I thought of a profession which required getting up at the crack of dawn (Roussel)."

The construction may be divided into two, "mutually informing," mechanisms suspended in a framework; the upper a language loom consisting of a communicating series of "perscribed" metal plates and, the lower, an adjustable reclining chaise (*figura*) from which the plates can be "read." The entire apparatus may be viewed as a kind of "protestant" mechanism whose resistance can be explained ethically or historically but whose possibility of functioning effectively is scarcely attainable, or attainable only after a "willing suspension of disbelief."

Engendering Plate

The Engendering Plate is a result of experimentation with papier-maché hemispheres built up from alternate layers of *The Yellow Pages* and newsprint. Sanding the surface irregularities obliterated text and revealed the underlying layers. The resulting surface was miscellaneous bits of texts. The emergence of new combinations of word fragments occurred as sanding continued. When sanding ceased, configurations appeared fixed, and the fixed text was photographed. The nature of the photographic process renders the image as a shadow, cleansed of all incidental qualities.

I began to play with the idea that the act of sanding was in some way analogous to the action of a catalyst which promotes a reaction but itself remains unchanged and indifferent.

The allusions to antique maps of globes in the finished plate were at once troubling as they suggested sensual or tactile qualities associated with a superficial aestheticism. These carnal attributes were inappropriate to the engendering plate as the coupling of language had to be of a dry or siccative nature — the conjoinings were to remain strictly in the realm of language and not present a material aspect.

Book of Sigils

An 11" x 17" portion of the engendering plate was enlarged. A grid was superimposed over the enlarged portion, using 1–1/2" squares, similar to a Mercator grid. The vertical axis was lettered from A – K; the horizontal axis was numbered from 1 – 17; the field was thus broken into 181 squares or "views." Most views yielded three legible bits of text (word fragments, words, or phrases), which are called "residents," and are catalogued in book form. Then twenty-five letters of the alphabet (not including the letter "z") were shuffled, chosen randomly, and assigned to squares within a 5 x 5 grid. The letter "z" was dropped, to land somewhere outside of the grid. The letters constituting the residents were then plotted on their respective places in the grid. Starting with the first letter of the resident and continuing to the last, the letter places were connected with lines. Each figure was then recorded alongside its corresponding resident, a total of 561 entries.

The martial grid lays open as with a sword the language of the "resident" revealing an internal sign or signature.

Static Song of the Sigils: Enlarged Section of Engendering Plate with Sigils

The signatures developed in the book were replotted at their origins; the signature emanates according to the amplitude of its voice. The points of fortuitous overlap among signatures generate a blind coupling.

The image in its entirety is an index of three successive extractions and "fixings" from the engendering plate. The first was the fixing of the text on the plate after sanding; the second was the transformation of that text through the breaking up of the plate into views; the third was a random plotting of the alphabet on the 5 x 5 martial grid. A condition of suspension is rendered through the products of chance operations.

In certain instances the voice is so weak that the signature remains a congested blot.

The points of fortuitous overlap among signatures (generated as they were in isolation and in the chaste dryness of language: rigor mortis), signify a blind coupling, each in its own space overlapping but different.

A third degree condition of suspension is achieved where the unstable products of operations governed by chance unite in a song of stasis.

Cameo (Root) Plate

The text on the plate was assembled by the coupling of sentence fragments gleaned from various daily newspapers and tabloids. The text, while obeying the laws of syntax, continuously diverges, wherein short-lived *dramatis personae* make their sudden appearance, proceed along a probable course of action, and exit abruptly as the possible syntactical routes are exhausted. In certain locations on the plate the sentences rejoin, resulting in an onanistic circularity. The narrative is sustained and proliferates only as long as the syntactical mechanism is supplied with an impulse toward language.

Within each possible route the narrative seeks to attain a state of artificially attenuated existence. Thus the narrative is sustained and proliferates only as long as the syntactical mechanism is supplied with language.

52

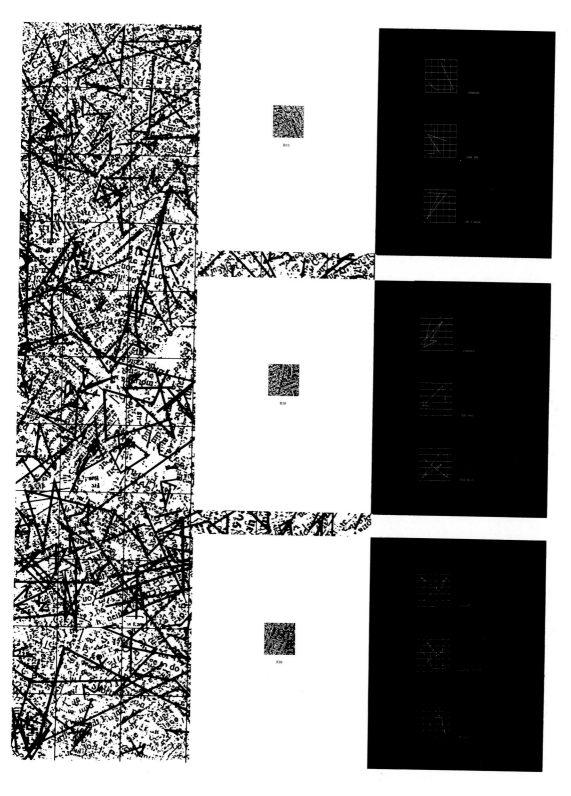

Static Song of the
Sigils: Engendering
Plate with Sigils
(center spread).

Selected excerpts
from the Book of
Sigils (left).

The idea that the sacred scriptures have (aside from their literal value) symbolic value is ancient and not irrational: it is found in Philo of Alexandria, in the cabalists, in Swedenborg. Since the events related in the scriptures are true (God is truth, truth cannot lie, etc.), we should admit that men, in acting out those events, blindly represent a secret drama determined and premeditated by God. Going from this to the thought that the history of the universe — and in it our lives and the most tenuous detail of our lives — has an incalculable, symbolic value, is a reasonable step.

Jorge Luis Borges, *Other Inquisitions*.

Even the articulate or brutal sounds of the globe must be all so many languages and ciphers that somewhere have their corresponding keys — have their own grammar and syntax; and thus the least things in the universe must be secret mirrors to the greatest.

Thomas De Quincey, *Writings*, Vol. 1.

[H]istory is an immense liturgical text where the iotas and the dots are worth no less than the entire verses or chapters, but the importance of one and the other is indeterminable and profoundly hidden.

Léon Bloy, *L'âme de Napoléon*, Mercure de France, 1912.

Cameo (Root) Plate

Stanley Allen

Piranesi and Duchamp: The Fictional Present

I am beginning to appreciate the value of exactitude, of precision, the importance of chance.

Marcel Duchamp, *Marchand du Sel*

For Piranesi, as much as for Duchamp, the juxtaposition of precision and chance was not paradoxical. Duchamp understood that the one necessarily follows the other, and that rationality carried to an extreme leads directly to irrationality. In Duchamp's work, the production of chance is the result of painstaking and systematic calculation. In the case of Piranesi, technical exactitude and scientific (archeological) precision enable him to construct a world in which rationality is so inevitably permeated by its opposite as to call into question the incompatibility of the rational and the irrational.

The third plate of Piranesi's *Campo Marzio* is an engraving entitled *Scenographia Campi Martii*. The use of a theatrical term here is not insignificant. With this image, he is setting the stage for the virtuosic performance to come, a performance which reenacts the reconstruction of a fictional past from this fictional present.

The remains of the Roman past are represented in this image, in their correct topographical relations, framed, like a proscenium stage, by displaced fragments of that same past. This image serves to indicate Piranesi's starting point: faithfulness to the topographical evidence and the possibility of reconstructing an entire building from a single stone or column.

The monuments are shown in ruins, indicated by traces or fragments. A correspondence is established to the actual condition of the ruins in the middle 18th century. Clearly, a great deal of time has passed since these buildings were constructed or occupied. But the fiction of the drawing is to present these objects shorn from their actual context, as if the intervening years had passed without the occupation and transformation of this part of Rome: as if the level of the terrain had not risen, burying colonnades up to their capitals. Or, it has the effect of suggesting other historical scenarios: that the *Campo Marzio* had become a cow pasture, like the Roman forum; or that Rome itself had been abandoned, only now to be discovered, its artifacts lately unearthed and the

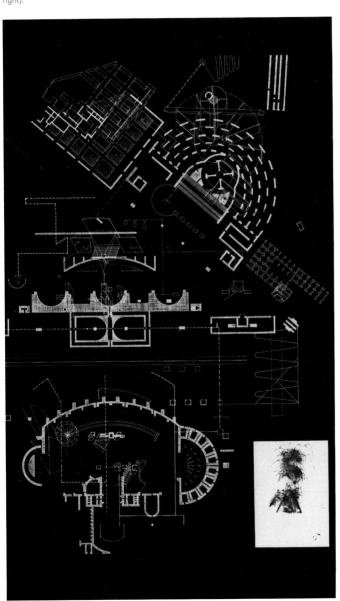

task of reconstruction now set before its archeologists and architects. The Stadium of Domitian, for example, is indicated by a track in the earth and a solitary structural bay, the remains, perhaps, of the imperial box. Its figure is preserved, empty, as if to deny that a medieval town had grown up precisely in this area, and that the form of the circus, while still preserved, exists as a densely built urban space formed by the churches and houses which have been constructed over the stadium.

This drawing is a sign of the rupture willed by Piranesi onto his material. It is a violent act of distancing the project from the real historical continuity of Rome in order to reinvent — through creative interpretation — that very history. Engaging in a play of memory and traces, Piranesi simultaneously gives us the clues — the fragments — and the solution: the project. But, given the fiction of the starting point, we are left to wonder if this is just one of many possible scenarios.

This "fictional present" has its 20th-century analogue in the imaginary landscape produced by Marcel Duchamp in collaboration with Man Ray entitled *Elevage de poussiere* (Dust breeding). Man Ray describes the circumstances of its creation as follows:

> In the far corner near the window stood a pair of trestles in which lay a piece of heavy glass covered with intricate patterns laid out in fine lead wires. It was Duchamp's major opus: *The Bride Stripped Bare by her Bachelor's Even.* A single unshaded bulb hung from the ceiling to furnish the only light. On the walls were tacked various precise drawings covered with symbols and references, studies for the glass. One section of it bore an irregular mirrored surface, seen from the back, on which a delicate series of ovals had been traced ...Looking down on the work as I focused the camera, it appeared like some strange landscape from a bird's-eye view. There was dust in the work and bits of tissue and cotton wadding that had been used to clean up the finished parts, adding to the mystery. This, I thought, was indeed the domain of Duchamp.
> Man Ray, *Self Portrait*

The mechanical apparatus of the camera distances the work from reality, "framing" it, allowing the "strange landscape" to emerge. It is through the precision of the mechanical means that the work is opened up to indeterminacy, to the irrational, to the mystical.

Precision and the science of archeology are the means by which Piranesi constructs his fictional present, the means of forgetting, which allows him to recreate, with exactitude, a world entirely mediated by chance. It is this which makes the project of Piranesi resonant in this century. It is here that we can see that Duchamp is not the contrary to enlightenment rationalism, but rather its exasperated protest against itself, a local disturbance resulting from turbulences set in motion by Piranesi and others.

In the Labyrinth: After Piranesi and Robbe-Grillet

Yet the reality in question is a strictly material one; that is, subject to no allegorical interpretation. The reader is therefore requested to see in it only the objects, actions, words or events described without attempting to give them either more or less meaning than his own life, or his death.

Alain Robbe-Grillet,
In the Labyrinth

This project intends an excavation, through drawing, of the "negative utopia" drawn by Piranesi for the *Campo Marzio* of Rome. Piranesi's *Grande Pianta* is conceived as a site to be colonized, covered over and modified, as when a building is built on ruins. This process of rereading establishes a relationship parallel to that which Piranesi maintained toward his own (archaeological) sources: dreamlike, inventive, and improvisational.

Manfredo Tafuri has suggested that the project of the *Campo Marzio* by Piranesi contains all of the potential — and the contradictions — of modern architecture and the city. For Tafuri, Piranesi represents a tragic moment of architecture's insight into its own fate at the precise point at which the doors to modernity open. The "epic battle" being waged on the *Campo Marzio* is, that of "architecture against itself." It is the first crisis of the self-consciousness of architecture. The present project is an almost empirical test of that thesis, to see if it is possible to draw out (literally) those explicitly modern tensions and contradictions to create an architecture which is not a comforting pastiche of the past, but is marked by its complexities, tensions, and contradictions.

The working method for achieving this was the superimposition of the reading of this city of the past with an analogous text. The literary analogy operates at two levels. First, in a strictly literal sense, the descriptions of the written text are transcribed through architectural means, with as little metaphorical intervention as possible. Thus there is an attempt to find equivalents for certain images drawn very precisely in the novel: the footsteps of the soldier in the snow, the endless rows of houses, the drawbridge, the circular boulevard. The second parallel exists at the level of formal devices. The abrupt spatial dislocations, the interruptions of the narrative line of *In the Labyrinth* or the repetitions and the *caesuras* of *The Erasers* have their exact counterparts in the formal language of the project.

Like Raymond Roussel's *Locus Solus*, the structure of Piranesi's text is episodic: a series of figures, each drawn and described in minute detail, but juxtaposed, overlapping or intersecting in ways which seem casual and

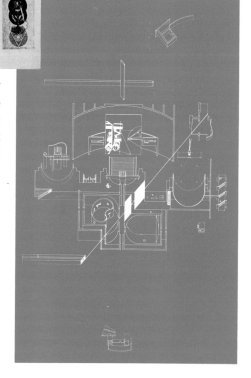

haphazard: the product of time and the exigencies of site planning. Yet all of these figures together form a *locus solus*. They accurately describe a singular place.

As this project has been developed, the original text — the site plan — has been divided into three episodes. Each is assigned programmatic functions, creating formal or iconographic links to the original Piranesi project, and elaborated in drawings which have become increasingly detailed. As the threads of the analysis have unraveled, I have not sought an elaboration of meaning; rather a greater precision of detail and description, remembering, as Robbe-Grillet said of Kafka:

What the hero is searching for vanishes before the obstinacy of his pursuit, his trajectories, his movements; they alone are made apparent, they alone are made real.

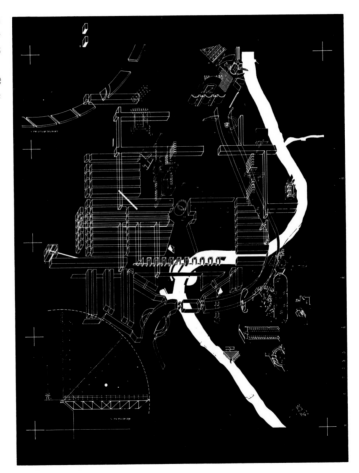

On the Relevance of Phenomenology

Dalibor Vesely

A seminar with Dalibor Vesely was held in the graduate history, theory and design program at the University of Houston, December 11, 1984. Faculty participants included Bruce Webb, William Taylor, Ben Nicholson and Mark Schneider, the instructor of the course. Also included in the discussion were students Martin Axe and Robert Castillo. A transcript of the seminar was extensively edited and revised by Mark Schneider and Dalibor Vesely for this publication.

Schneider: Why should an architect study phenomenology?

Vesely: This is a question one asks quite understandably: Why phenomenology? What is its value and relevance for the current architectural reality? One may see it as something which is perhaps too sophisticated, complex, and demanding; but the irony is that phenomenology is a tendency to see things in the way that people used to see them, as designers or painters. Phenomenology is an attempt to understand from the inside — and not to dismiss or criticize from the outside — the whole spectrum of the current experience which we generally call "reality." If one looks at what is commonly called reality, one discovers that it is an incredibly sophisticated and complex mixture of ideas and half-finished thoughts. People in practice take it for granted that what they understand is reality, yet one needs to question this understanding from the very beginning because it represents a highly sublimated, intellectual, and abstract world. It reminds one that the reality which makes sense inside the office and inside a pragmatic sphere of reference involving people who understand architecture as a problem of money and as a problem of production is, in fact, the "reality" of a society *within* a society. The question about reality addresses reality in a broad context, not just the reality of those who represent the architectural profession. One is first of all dealing with culture. We are, for example, asking questions about how painting or music or literature is related to architecture.

This is where our inquiry begins — in the full context of what is given — in reality as a whole. Reality becomes an issue when one is outside the neat, well-established, cultivated, and rather esoteric frame of reference that we normally assume as a status quo upon which what we call "common sense" is said to be founded. Max Scheler said that phenomenology would not exist if it weren't for the positivistic sciences which made the arrogant claim that science is the measure of reality, the ultimate court of appeal for all answers to the questions we ask. Thus it is the development of modern culture itself which led to the development of phenomenology. The idea that the unfolding of culture engenders phenomenology should not be taken lightly, because phenomenology is a much less calculated response to a recognized condition than one might think. Rather, we are involved in a certain way of living through a situatedness which we are experiencing as individuals in a culture.

Phenomenology is not a philosophy, as such, but a tendency to restore to the modern situation a global and consistent conceptual direction. One can think of it as an inevitable dimension or hygiene of the modern mind. It is a catharsis one must go through in order to restore one's own experience. The word "phenomenology" is not important. One also does not have to worry about phenomenology as a discipline. Phenomenology has to do with questions in the area of culture where we work as architects. An architect deals with planning methods, regulations, etc., but at the same time he asks questions about culture, symbolism and meaning. We cannot escape any of these. We are permanently pushed into what could be described as a second level of phenomenology, concerned with the every-day cultural existence which cannot be ignored. Thus we are confronted with a dilemma in which we see an apparent conflict between something which is purely economical and something which is culturally relevant. The second level or form of phenomenology addresses the ground upon which this conflict can be understood. When we try to get some sense of a ground for understanding, we come to a curious problem which appears in many different forms on the contemporary scene: On what ground, for example, can the physicist, the philosopher, and the psychologist understand each other and communicate? This is a phenomenological problem. Or think about it in these terms: There are planners, economists, and sociologists working on a large-scale project, and the architect is in the middle. How is a ground from which he can talk to all of these people established? This is again a phenomenological problem. Unless we assume that the result will be a mere pastiche and resign ourselves to that, we are in the realm of phenomenology. The question which cannot be ignored is this: *Who* among these specialists is talking about what is real? Is reality just a fiction?

The problem in any such situation is the lack of a central reality — an equivalent of a *polis*, in the Greek sense. Indeed, on what basis can architects talk among themselves? How can Peter Eisenman and James Stirling find a common ground for discussion? Every disagreement involves deep agreement. We would not disagree if we didn't already agree about something. If you have a very violent argument with somebody, it can only mean that you are seriously interested in what is at stake. If there were no agreement — somewhere — you would be completely indifferent to the outcome of the dispute. This means that you somehow see the agreement before the disagreement, but how? On what ground is this agreement possible? This is the heart of the whole contemporary concern about meaning, understanding, interpretation, and communication — the ground on which one can talk about culture again. This is a question of hermeneutics, the latest stage of phenomenology, which involves the problem of agreement in disagreement.

Nicholson: Is there anything today worth looking at? Today, in Houston for example, it seems very easy to dismiss the urban landscape as a filthy mess not worth looking at. If this is so, what is worth looking at?

Vesely: What is worth looking at is culture; this is the goal. One should look at the richest possible conditions under which architecture can be realized. A mess is not necessarily a pessimistic message, but is provocative and potentially good. What is worth doing is to build equivalently to the relative richness that we still find today in some countries.

Theater directors are often more relaxed about their world than architects are today. They are often more optimistic, but not in an utopian way. It is a matter of imagination — of imaginative vision about what is possible, and at the same time, about how much is missing. We are living in a society of clever and sophisticated people — biogenetic engineers and so on. In that context, we have to ask whether the architect has anything to offer. The creative scientist is also and very often engaged in the imaginative enterprise. This is the standard against which the architects of the immediate future must measure themselves; otherwise they fail. I say this, not because of the belief that science dominates or should dominate culture, but because it brings the dialogue to the proper level of

competence and imaginative vision. Under such conditions, we are likely to do something worthwhile. If not, the only choice remaining is to be absorbed in the machinery of the mindless computer. The real crisis is intellectual ability: what kind of imaginative and competent picture can be built up in architecture in order to represent a culture that has the power to resist the pressures that are put upon it.

Nicholson: But why is it that science has succeeded, but only by a myriad of little pieces that probably only a very few have the key to?

Vesely: Science leaves *behind* its frame of reference, which architecture cannot afford to do. The given reality is a continuum. A house is still a part of the landscape and of what goes beyond the horizon, which is not a problem for the scientists who can operate with a much more transparent definition of what he is doing and what his product is referring to.

Axe: If to be is to build, as Heidegger seems to suggest, does it follow that to build is to dwell? Do we dwell poetically today? If not, why?

Vesely: Heidegger tries to make a distinction between the building as a physical phenomenon — the fabric — and building as a process related to content and purpose. Taking the building as a mere fabric doesn't grasp the context, the setting, the scene, what the building is a part of, where it is, and how it is situated. The architect's job is to be at home in the *contextuality* of what he is doing. Anybody can design a room, but the approach and the result will certainly be different if it is done by a sculptor, painter, dancer, or theater designer. The architect must see the room as a situational context, as a setting, something we are involved in. He must see the space as a whole; how we inhabit it and how we live in it. How we live in it, of course, involves the existing physical conditions, but it also has to do with the conditions which constitute the situation itself — like sitting around a table and talking, sleeping in a bed, or listening to music. These are situations not entirely created by the architect, and it

is naive to suppose that he is simply free to manipulate them in any way he likes, as though they were his own inventions. What is requisite here is a concern for the contribution of architecture. How to structure a table is not necessarily an architectural problem, though we have become used to this kind of thinking in the 20th century.

One discovers that in the past a painter could say a great deal about sitting around a table, as can be seen in the works of Caravaggio, Rembrandt, and Velazquez. History is full of examples like these which have nothing to do with architecture but rather with a very precise understanding of contextual issues which *we* architects now consider exclusively ours — how to look out from a window, how to enter a house, how to touch something, or how to live in a room and listen to music. Now, if one is not arrogant, then one can get a great deal of inspiration from spheres that are no longer mentioned in the modern architectural debate. In literature, texts by Joyce, Breton, and Proust are full of architecturally relevant interpretations. These authors are not interested in architecture itself; they are not architects. But they talk sensitively about architectural and contextual issues: about the transparency of windows, the external wall, the garden, the horizon. In the end, it is the situation that matters most of all. We dwell in situations. The architect contributes to the situation but, in an important sense, he does not create it. Dwelling means being situated and having the ability and opportunity to come to a very rich context and live in it, inhabit it.

Taylor: Isn't dwelling also involved in the case of a man who writes poetry in prison? Doesn't dwelling go beyond the physicality of the situation?

Vesely: This is what we have been saying, and the prison is a good example because the prison in 18th-century Europe was often an old monastery. This is a paradox, but it shows how much the situation actually contributes to what is commonly thought of as a purely architectural context. The same room which was one day a monk's cell, an earthly paradise, the next day becomes a hell. The same room! The situation is a cultural phenomenon to which the architect contributes and which he certainly needs to understand. But at the same time he needs to recognize the limitations of his contribution. We inhabit more than we realize. To eliminate situation is to reduce architecture to a matter of mere technique or aesthetics.

Nicholson: What about objects?

Vesely: Objects are always "on the way"; they constitute the setting. Architecturally, they are less important. When Heidegger talks about the thing, he establishes it in relation to dwelling. By dwelling he does not mean just having a house. Inhabiting is a situational condition involving memories, dreams, and imagination. Heidegger means an absolutely primary dimension dealing with situated culture. He talks about dwelling in terms of the fourfold: Earth, Sky, Divinities, and Mortals, which he understands as the ultimate points of reference which constitute a context or continuum in which objects are situated. The object begins to be relevant to architecture at the moment when it begins to build up the spatiality of our world.

Thinking, as Heidegger understands it in "Building Dwelling Thinking," cannot be taken in isolation from building and dwelling. Thinking is thinking *about something*. Thinking, understood properly, is a poetic process, where "poetic" means opening the context to the implied whole; there one finds dwelling. You are recalling where you stand. Even when we don't realize it, our everyday thought depends upon an implicit understanding of where we are — our situation. One may ask "What time is it?" but where and in relation to what: in Detroit? We dwell in so far as our thinking takes account of our fundamental situatedness in the broader reality of the cultural context.

Castillo: What about the effect of technology and the notion of the wasteland of modern life?

Vesely: Technology is the capacity to create not only a reality but also a delusion of culture. It is a defensive operation which can postpone confrontation with the problem of reality. The possibility of living in a delusion that looks like reality is one of those things one feels when coming to the U.S. from Europe. Other countries cannot do this as extensively because there is greater cultural resistance.

Axe: How do you differentiate between reality and Disneyland?

Vesely: Here we are dealing with what is perhaps the most fundamental problem of hermeneutics which Gadamer discusses at length in *Truth and Method*, though his terms are somewhat different. There is no absolute reality, no ultimate norm which is authentic. To suppose that there is would be to posit a kind of omniscience obtained from a vantage point beyond all finite, human experience. If there is no such vantage point, how do we differentiate between reality and Disneyland? What matters is whether Disneyland can stand a confrontation with a broader reality than itself. Good theater might survive where Disneyland would go to pieces. If you challenge it with those phenomena which it pretends to represent, it would fail. This can also be discussed in terms of monologue and dialogue. As long as an artifact is treated as a monologue in isolation, it can seem equal to any other. But when an artifact is brought into a dialogue with a reality broader than itself, its limitations become evident.

Using the level of illusion as a distinguishing criterion, I would argue that illusion is potentially positive because it extends the possibilities of reality. There is, however, a point in the development of European culture where illusion becomes impossible. This is where the contextual horizon is lost. The thing represented becomes a world of its own, self-referential and autonomous. At this point, illusion becomes delusion because the ground for distinguishing between the two has been lost. In that situation, one can be deluded about anything; there is no way to tell where you are. No longer dreaming, one is dreamt by the representation itself. Authentic representation is always a means of participation. We represent in order to participate in reality, and this applies to art throughout history. Why draw an animal on a wall in a cave? It was not for the sake of representation.

In the 18th century, and particularly due to the development of perspective, there is an apparent shift toward delusion in which one participates for the sake of representation rather than reality. In the end there is nothing to participate in but representation itself. This culminates in the spectacle, the panorama, the international exhibition, and finally in the film and television. It is representation for the sake of the fantastic, without knowing or caring where it comes from, without a concern for its dialogue with reality.

Gadamer discusses the same phenomenon in relation to prejudice, by which he means pre-judgement. We all have the experience of discovering prejudices in ourselves and others. If there is no absolute reality, how is this possible? If we are not simply mistaken whenever we identify a prejudice, and there is no absolute reality, then we need to consider whether there is, nevertheless, a cultural ground which constitutes the broader framework in which the recognition or prejudice makes sense. Behind every serious disagreement there is tacit agreement that the issue in dispute *matters*, and such prior agreement is a legacy of culture or tradition, a "prejudice" or prejudgement, if you like, which goes beyond any simplistic reduction of culture to mere arbitrary, restrictive "authority." Gadamer puts this very well when he says that "the fundamental prejudice of the enlightenment is the prejudice against prejudice itself, which deprives tradition of its power.... There is no such unconditional antithesis between tradition and reason.... The (hermeneutical) circle, then, is not formal in nature, it is neither subjective nor objective, but describes understanding as the interplay of the movement of tradition and the movement of the interpreter."[*]

*Hans-Georg Gadamer, *Truth and Method* (New York: Crossroad, 1984), p. 239-40, 250, 261.

Axe: In "Eye and Mind," Merleau-Ponty questions the relation between science and art, apparently thinking there is a possibility that science can be the same as painting is today — an access to being. Is this possible?

Vesely: Art, more than any other field, is still capable today of maintaining a dialogue in what otherwise tends to be the monologue of an hermetic civilization. In reality, science and aesthetics belong together, but not science and art. Art and science are the most contradictory tendencies in modern culture. To make science what art is, it would first of all be necessary to elevate it to the level of philosophy. I do not mean the process taking place during the last 200 years, during which we have seen the reverse — the suppression of philosophy to the level of science.

Aesthetics came into existence with the development of science in the 18th century. We can begin to see what has happened if we look at Alexander Baumgarten's *Reflections on Poetry* of 1735 in which the word "aesthetica" (aesthetics) is first used in the modern sense. Baumgarten wants to define a science which will be to things perceived what logic is to things known. Things known are said to be known by a "superior faculty," while things perceived are said to be known by an "inferior faculty." Aesthetics thus becomes the science of things perceived, the science of the beautiful.

One might discuss this development, as Heidegger does, in terms of the devaluation of Being and sensory experience, and the corresponding elevation of thought, idea, or form which is characteristic of dualistic metaphysics going back to Descartes, but it is perhaps even more critical to see how, for Descartes and later for Baumgarten, a gap opens between perception and knowledge. From this point on, science increasingly dominates the whole field of knowledge while art, now the subject of aesthetics, increasingly becomes a matter of "significant form" — of form which has no apparent relation to knowledge or the cultural dialogue. Art thus becomes subjective, a matter of

privatized "taste," and form shows a corresponding tendency to become content, a point of view which Nietzsche attacks with great intensity. It is in the Romantic period that the individual finally replaces the *polis* as the basis of evaluation. The question of the relation between the beautiful and the good, the appropriate, which already troubled Plato, disappears from the discourse.

The distinction we take for granted today between art and science was unknown in classical Greece. For the Greeks, science was concerned with the broadest possible understanding. As long as we continue to think of art as the subject matter of aesthetics, the Greek word *techné* cannot simply be translated as "art." Neither can it be translated as "technology." The Greeks understood *techné* as the knowledge of making, as the know-how required to bring something to appearance as this or that particular thing. For the Greeks, making shoes was not different in this respect from the other arts. They did not distinguish between fine arts and crafts, as we do. In classical Greek thought, *techné* goes hand-in-hand with *poésis*, which is making or bringing forth.

Modern science is anti-poetic in nature, but not because science is rational and art emotional. To say that is to assume that people either think or feel but never do both at the same time. Rather it is because science, as Heidegger puts it, "challenges forth" rather than "brings forth" what it discloses. These terms are easily misunderstood, partly because of the illustrative examples Heidegger gives, but they nevertheless mark an important distinction. Science and technology are ultimately privileged constructions which have not been brought into an adequate confrontation with a cultural reality broader than themselves. Instead, they have become that to which both art and philosophy have been leveled. This is why Heidegger, unlike some critics, does not make a distinction between science and technology where some would expect him to. Challenging forth is an hermetic act which, in effect, lays waste to the cultural residue which lies outside its purview and control. Heidegger's examples, such as the contrast

he develops between plowing a field and strip mining, are metaphors designed to suggest how the challenging forth characteristic of science and technology, unlike the bringing forth of art, lays waste to something for the sake of production. *Poésis*, like the plow, overturns without laying waste. This should be taken as a point of departure for any genuine discussion of architecture.

Phenomenology and Architecture

Don Ihde

Does phenomenology as a style of philosophy have any contribution to make to the practice of architecture? Perhaps now, in the late 20th century, with both distance and a change of context from earlier times, the moment is proper to explore this question.

Intellectually, the contemporary situation is stimulating. Ironically, in the very midst of the present apparent domination of scientific and technological concerns in the developed countries, much of the intellectual ferment is coming from humanities and arts contexts. It is popular to characterize this situation as "Post-Modern." But it is not always easy to isolate what precisely defines postmodernism.

There are, however, several aspects of the contemporary scene which are indicative: (a) There is a *pluralism* of interdisciplinary theoretical, critical and interpretive [hereafter TCI] perspectives upon disciplinary subject matters which stimulate creative debate; (b) there is a questioning of the traditional boundaries of disciplines; (c) TCIs both cross and criticize boundaries, but no one TCI can be called dominant and certainly not exclusive. (d) This means that in spite of heated debates between TCIs, tolerance of the varied methods is implicitly necessary.

The intellectually informed citizen will recognize in this description illustrations from various disciplines. In literary circles, after traditional scholarship and the New Criticism, there followed affairs with semiotics, structuralism, then the post-structuralisms — including the current rage for deconstruction. In philosophy there has been the decline and isolation of the previous forms of analytic philosophy into the declaration of the demise of foundationalism and a recognition of a plurality of "conversations" (Rorty). In legal studies, the revisionist forms of social utilitarianism (Rawls) have been challenged by critical theorists (after Habermas). And in every discipline there has been a ferment after new conceptual styles and models.

Rhetorically, within this mélange, phenomenology has sometimes been characterized as one of the "surpassed" TCIs. Earlier, it was misunderstood as a revival of idealism under the technical language of a Husserl caught in the death throes of modernism with its language of the "subject." Later, Rorty further stigmatized it as a mode of traditional foundationalism. Yet all would allow that within the contemporary debate, whether as the old enemy (Derrida and Foucault) or ancestor (Habermas and Gadamer), phenomenology has played a strong role as a paradigm TCI.

Here I shall argue that at the core of phenomenology, traditionally interpreted, lies hidden a distinctly postmodern form of thought which is simultaneously deconstructive and non-foundational, yet retaining the sense of structure and multistability which also makes of it a matter of possible concern for the discipline of architecture.

This "new" phenomenology — if it may be called that, to differentiate it from its previous interpreters and exegetes — is to be found in making the *imaginative praxis* of phenomenology central. It is my contention that a radical phenomenology is to be found in its *theory of variations* and the subsequent reinterpretation of an imaginative praxis which arises from the use of variation theory.

Even "classical" phenomenology could have been distinguished by having two trajectories: an outward, fantasy trajectory (emphasized by Edmund Husserl in the early and mid-periods) and a downward or "material" trajectory (in the existential and hermeneutic phenomenologies of Maurice Merleau-Ponty and Martin Heidegger). But while scholars more interested in exegesis than in philosophical praxis might too often have contrasted these trajectories, they belong, in fact, to the same use of imaginative variations. And the elevation of imaginative praxis, even in relation to perception, is a distinctly postmodern emphasis.

When variational theory and imaginative praxis are made central to a new and non-foundational phenomenology, the earlier development of variational theory may be characterized in a particular way. Husserl was the first explicitly to elevate imaginative praxis to prominence. But in so doing, he placed this use of imagination within a specific cognate model and put it to directed use. That model he drew from his own disciplinary background in logical and mathematical forms of the imagination. Historically, this use was even more narrowly construed in relation to the early-20th-century mathematical interest in variant/invariant structures. What Husserl did, however, was to broaden a mathematically-conceived-of imagination to a new use which included perceptual and other experiential domains. It was a move which eventually drew away from the purely "formal" or "abstract" mathematical domain towards the perceptually and experientially "concrete domain." Yet the use of imaginative praxis was no more "subjective" at base than it is in mathematics *per se.*

Husserl's own claims concerning variational theory revolved around what he alternatively called *imaginative* or even *fantasy* variations. These he elevated to the highest priority with respect to phenomenological investigation:

There are reasons why, in phenomenology as in all eidetic sciences, representations, or, to speak more accurately, *free fancies,* assume *a privileged position over against perceptions,* and that, *even in the phenomenology of perception itself.*[1]

Imagination here is being elevated, in postmodern fashion, over perception. In this respect, Husserl anticipates the present intellectual environment.

Husserl had a specific aim and purpose for his use of imaginative variation. It was aimed simultaneously at *deconstructing the habit of taking the empirical or past actual results of any domain of inquiry as primary* — it was here that his principle that essence precedes empirical came into play — *and at discovering, through variational praxis, some structural or essential configuration within an object domain.* Clearly, imaginative variation was not free floating, but fantasy *in service* of a predetermined philosophical goal.

To illustrate this role of variations more concretely, I return to a set of examples from my own *Experimental Phenomenology*[2] developed from studies of the Necker Cube (figure 1).

This object is very familiar, at least to citizens of developed Western countries, as a two-dimensional representation of a three-dimensional object. It could represent a transparent cube. The standard psychologies have spilled much ink puzzling over the "ambiguity" of an apparent bivalent three-dimensional effect. The cube is said to "reverse itself" so that it may be seen to be tilted whether upward or downward, its specific line arrangements thus reversing themselves spatially. [I formalize these in phenomenological fashion as being three-dimensional forward and three-dimensional reverse variant profiles. Thus I am already applying variational theory to this empirical example.]

Now what is empirical or actual about this example is that we can actually see (phenomenologically fulfill a visual intention) either of these three-dimensional variants upon the cube. *But* in the standard psychologies these two variants are often taken as the only variants upon the cube, thus closing its range of possibilities at the two empirical profiles. Occasionally this same literature allows that a third, two-dimensional effect, is noted by "fatigued subjects." This hints at a third variant.

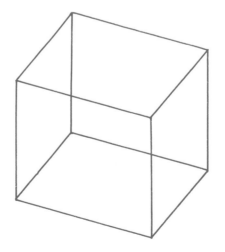

1. Necker Cube

This third variant, however, is easily established if a different context is provided. For example, if I tell you that the drawing represents, not a cube, but a hexagonal opening within which is stretched a six-legged insect the two-dimensional effect becomes both more easy to see and to retain. Phenomenologically, this is a first step towards the Husserlian use of variations to seek out a deeper structure, an *essential* structure which precedes or opens up the merely habitual sediment of the "empirical." Note that the third effect [two-dimensional] is not non-empirical in any sense differing from the previous two variants — it is equally fulfillable, hence "empirical" as well, but now in a different sense. The *meaning* of the drawing now begins to change since it is seen to hold a wider or deeper set of possibilities than were first taken to be the case.

Nor do we need to stop there with this outward trajectory of variational theory. The drawing *could* be taken to represent a different, but equally compatible set of three-dimensional objects. Again a tale can help *gestalt* this new set of effects: If we regard the drawing as a hexagonally-shaped transparent gem, the central parallelogram *can* be seen as the facet which is upward, closest to the viewer, with the previous lines, which in the case of the cube were sides of the cube and in the insect example the legs, projecting downward to the parameter of the hexagon, thus creating a three-dimensional effect totally incompatible with a cube. And now (phenomenologically), obviously, we should be able to note that just as the cube was reversible, so is the gem or upward-flexed insect. We simply have to push the body/facet in the opposite direction, away from the viewer, to achieve this effect.

With this expansion or deconstruction of the previously narrow "empirical" interpretation of the drawing, we have begun to do genuine *phenomenological* variations. Such is the first movement outwards in structured and directed fantasy. One can see how such a method simultaneously undercuts sedimented or habituated ways of seeing, while pointing in a second and more constructive direction. *But in both movements, the fantasy imagination remains fulfillable, embodiable in a new "empirical" form.* In the simple examples being followed, each new variant can be built, can be an actual material object.

Yet the very meaning of the empirical has clearly changed, for the outward trajectory of phenomenological analysis demonstrates that there is a *structure of possibility* in this region of inquiry. And in the case of the cube series — which now could be renamed — that structure is clearly a *multistable* one.

I have shown five variants upon the Necker Cube. As may now be suspected, not even these five exhaust the possible referential objects of the drawing. As it turns out, the actually buildable and seeable possibilities are quite large in number, being the combination of possible projective facets which the entirety of parts allows. The "essential possibility" or phenomenological structure of the drawing thus is highly complex and complexly multistable.

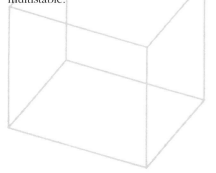

Yet what should be of interest here to those concerned with architectural praxis, is that which might initially be seen as not an unrestrained, but nevertheless an imaginatively led variation chase. But it remains in every case a possibility upon the material realm. The exploration of the material on existential realms were more thoroughly developed by Husserl's followers, Maurice Merleau-Ponty and Martin Heidegger. This clearly points to the second trajectory, the return to body and earth in the "Merleau-Pontean" and "Heideggerian" moments of phenomenological development.

If Husserl's first and early development of imaginative variations can be thought of as an outward movement, outward to fantasy *in order to discover possible structural features of some area of inquiry*, then the early followers of Husserl, primarily Maurice Merleau-Ponty and Martin Heidegger, can be seen for having capitalized upon the more concrete experiential aspects of those variations. If Husserl's variations are "imaginative," those of his successors could be called "material" variations.

By this I mean that at the center of Merleau-Ponty's work lies a concern with quite specific *perspective* and the role of the human body in being the focus of that perspective. And for Heidegger, the material focus is upon the role of *earth* and the experienced *environment*. It might be thought that his latter, more concrete emphasis would place these more "existential" phenomenologists closer to the concerns of architects than the fantasy variations of Husserl. It might seem that there are, in fact, two phenomenological trajectories, one outward into fantasy, the other earthward towards body and earth. Yet I do not think this is so.

While some scholars — perhaps more interested in exegesis than in philosophical praxis — may wish to make these directions contrary, it seems to me that the latter, more material or existential direction, is actually the logical outcome of practicing the use of variations in precisely their Husserlean form.

Rather than turn here to the classical texts, such as Merleau-Ponty's *The Eye and the Mind* or Heidegger's "Origin of the Work of Art" to illustrate this double-sided phenomenon, I shall return to the previous, now deconstructed Necker Cube illustration to indicate the role of body perspective and environmental *gestalt* in typical phenomenological analysis.

After the imaginative deconstruction of the previously, more narrowly perceived cube variants, one notes that the series of perceptual variations upon the drawing stretch into a long, if definite number of possibilities. The "object" has been changed insofar as it can no longer be simply a bivalent "cube," but now must be the series of structured possibilities revealed in the variational process. But to this point the focus has been upon the object-domain. *From* the object-domain, however, one can also analyze *reflexively* indices of *bodily, existential involvements with the object-domain.*

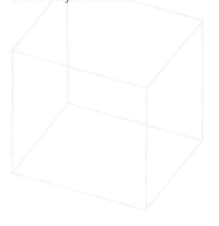

I return to perceivings of the cube-series. Beginning again with the simple, three-dimensional reversals of forward facing and rearward facing cubes, if I am attentive, I note that *in the reversal* there is an apparent "jump" in the cube presence. But this "jump" is *also a slight, but detectable, shift in my perspectival position.* My position is a more from "above" or "below" location in the first two reversals. It could be said that not only is the cube's appearance *strictly correlated* with a specific viewing perspective, but that this perspective is an implied, *concrete* bodily location. Here enters the "material" side of the analysis: For something to be seen at all, it must be seen within and reflexively related to a particular perspectival position. The imaginative praxis *locates* a bodily particularity.

It was Merleau-Ponty, the classical phenomenological analyst, who elaborated this direction of variational theory. And the result for the experienced (*corps vecu*) body turned out to be parallel in result to what was previously noted in the object-domain. We do not experience our bodies (our embodied being) mono-dimensionally, but polyvalently. We are as multidimensioned, even if existentially located, as our cubes. Yet we remain spatial nexii within an experienced environment.

And it was Heidegger who developed the complex theory of a phenomenologically analyzed environment. Our experienced "world" is always likewise material, but a multidimensioned material. It shows itself as a *gestalt* of relations, including relations of meaning. Again returning to the cube series, the subtle clue to such *gestalts* can be detected in the ways in which the changes in object-meanings took place.

I suggested stories (hermeneutic devices which serve as mini-myths in the cultural sense) which allowed our seeing to re-see a previously sedimented way of seeing. Thus from cubes to insect (and many other stories would have served as well), the mini-worlds of the cube profiles could change. Here we have a phenomenological glimpse of the structures of cultural plurality which make up our human "worlds." And, they too, turn out to be complexly multidimensioned and multistable.

All of this is "standard" phenomenological analysis, although viewed from an emphasis upon the central role of variational theory. And even though schematic and suggestive, rather than thoroughly worked through, this updating of phenomenology is obviously consistent with the contemporary currents of postmodernist experience. The interdisciplinary impact, the polymorphism of both object and environmental domains, the deconstruction of previously canonical forms, all are found in the imaginative praxis of variational theory.

At this point the usual charge against this recognition of pluralism and multistability is of relativism. But phenomenological *relativity* is not relativism. This is so for two reasons: First, the interrelation between embodied beings (*Dasein*, or "being-here," in Heidegger's term) and a world, is, although a relation, not itself a type of relativism, but an essential structure. Secondly, the exploration through imaginative praxis reveals something precisely structured, although it turns out that the structures are more complex and multistable than they seemed at first. If a science can be tempted toward greater and greater reductiveness, it would seem that a postmodern phenomenology is tempted toward a greater and greater proliferation of possibilities. In that sense it may be closer to an *art*.

And, if the above is true, then it should also be clear that the location of a new or revisionist phenomenology finds itself in a situation not unlike that of the practicing architect, *between* a science, at least in the sense that what is structural must be accounted for, and art, in the sense that the range of possibilities remains at least indefinite, if not infinite.

I should not have to draw the implications from this inquiry, but a few observations which further locate us in the contemporary milieu are tempting: (a) A phenomenological inquiry is clearly one far distanced from many modes of thinking which have prevailed in the history of both art and philosophy. Here can be found no possibility of a doctrine of imitation or resemblance [Platonism], since at most any resemblance is reduced to a single mode of presentation. (The Necker "Cube" as cube, can *only* be a single actual representation.) Similarly, the deconstructive movement of phenomenology itself reduces any and all reductive styles of interpretation to single possibilities — such as "form is function." Such minimalism has no obvious advantage or superiority over, let us say, new-romantic revivals. This is what is often meant in terming phenomenology "pre-theoretical." And although this deconstructive moment in no way precludes developments which seek their justification in such reductive styles, the opening to the richness of complex possibility structures always points in many directions, rather than a single, direction. (b) Positively, this use of imaginative praxis reveals the complexity of any possibility field. Multidimensionality and multi-stability *become* the expected results, and the question then becomes one of isolating those structures in a kind of topography. Interestingly, there are sciences which do approximate this type of inquiry, such as elements of cultural anthropology, or the biological sciences which are, on one side, ecological, and on the other, linguistically modeled. But such directions in science are themselves "post-modern" insofar as they move in essentially anti-Cartesian directions. (c) Finally, while the ultimate constraint within phenomenological praxis remains one of being directed towards possible structures, one should be able to see that a disciplined development of variational theory in practice can also be playful. Whimsy itself may have essential elements.

Could phenomenology, in a very concrete way, then, make a contribution to the practice of architecture? I think, yes. I could well conceive of courses in "phenomenological seeing," led by trained practitioners of such analyses. And, indeed, such introductions to the central use of imaginative and variational praxis are both contemporary, and yet return us to the beginnings of phenomenology. Martin Heidegger confessed that he was never able to follow the perplexities of phenomenology through Husserl's writings until "after I met Husserl personally in his workshop… Husserl's teaching took place in a step-by-step training in phenomenological 'seeing'… I myself practiced phenomenological seeing, teaching and learning in Husserl's proximity…"[3] Here the most abstruse theory unfolds in a method of discovery which in its very perceptual and material implications should be of interest to the student of architecture.

Notes

1. Edmund Husserl, *Ideas*, trans. W.R. Boyce Gibson (London: George Allen & Unwin Ltd, 1939), p. 199.

2. Don Ihde, *Experimental Phenomenology*, (Albany: SUNY Press, 1986, reprinted).

3. Martin Heidegger, *On Time and Being*, trans. J. Stambaugh (New York: Harper &Row, 1972) p. 76-8.

Language Games and the Newer Architecture

Diane Michelfelder

Since this seminar* invites us to consider the issues of text, tectonics, and texture as they play a role within postmodern architecture, I thought it would be appropriate to start out by looking at a building where these three things come together in an unusual way — and likewise at one that is arguably postmodern. I have in mind here the house at 708 Pacific Palisades, renovated in the early 1980s by Eric Owen Moss. When we look at this house, our attention is immediately drawn to two things: a text that is, quite literally, in and part of the house itself: a giant-sized 708 on the walls facing the street, created by a combination of textures (window glass and paint to contrast with the primary colors of the exterior walls), and likewise a flying buttress that in marking the entrance to the house also — because one of its ends is simply parked on the ground — makes a tectonically-related joke (figure 1).

How could we, if we were interested, read these elements of text/texture/tectonics in the text of the building itself? To the extent that the 708 is suggestive of the supergraphics of Pop Art and Venturi's decorated sheds, we might see it as a parodic comment upon the traditional practice of putting house numbers on individual homes, or as an ironic testimony to the strength of the idea that no matter how "real" a house is in Southern

California, it cannot completely tear itself away from the shadows of Hollywood. Together with the flying buttress which also serves to emphasize the "are-we-having-fun-yet?" meaning of this text, it would call our attention to how postmodern architecture is not adverse to kidding around and distorting common conventions seemingly for the sake of entertainment and comic relief. If we remind ourselves that we can also find plans for a residence called the "Fun House" among Moss's designs, we would be tempted to chalk up some more points for this particular interpretation.

Another approach would be to look at these features as being a response to the recognition that this house, despite its clear-cut status as a private dwelling, is also part of a larger social context. In connection with other uses here of intentional "misquotations" of traditional architectural forms (a "flying wall" to parody gables in the surrounding built environ-

1. Eric Owen Moss, *708 House*

ment, for example), the buttress draws our attention to how the house belongs to a much larger order of things, a world which is public, historically defined and friendly all at once, a neighborhood.[1] The exaggerated size of the numbers works in much the same way. Against the *sub specie aeternitatis* quality characteristic of so much modernist architecture,[2] this address-text helps to establish a sense of location and belonging to a place, by relating the house not only to the series of homes surrounding it but also, because of its immediate visibility to anyone driving by, to the changing rhythms of the frontal street and those beyond and thus even to the smogged-out *Holzwege* known as the L.A. freeway system.

2. Eric Owen Moss, *708 House*

I mention these two possible readings not with a view to choosing between them but rather to wonder what it means that we can make both these readings in the name of postmodernism. In picking up on the lighthearted quality of the 708 house, the first reading does not single out any feature on which postmodern architecture has a monopoly. Postmodern art, music, literature, film — we can find works in all of these marked by a sense of humor and whimsy. As Terry Eagleton has written recently, if we can agree on anything concerning the "typical postmodernist artifact," we can at least conclude that it is "playful" and "self-ironizing."[3]

What, though, about the second reading? What is its relation to other forms of postmodernism? It speaks of the value of place, an emphasis well known to anyone in the least familiar with postmodern architecture. "Architecture," Norberg-Schulz has written, "can be defined as the making of places."[4] If we accept this definition, then we can understand the postmodern movement in architecture as an attempted recovery of its own identity, an identity temporarily forgotten under the modernist enthusiasm for forms based on geometrical regularities and its illusion that universal solutions can be applied to particular problems. Unless the language of architecture can respond to the imperative to create places and thereby help us to reestablish a "collective consciousness of place," warns Paolo Portoghesi, we will experience an ever-increasing disjunction between our daily lives and the spaces we inhabit.[5]

Considered from this imperative to create places, we can see postmodernism in architecture — and here I have American postmodern architecture primarily in mind — taking off in a different direction from other movements within postmodernism. Take, for example, the postmodern strategy, often used in conjunction with pastiche, of borrowing dissimilar elements from their usual contexts and putting them together. Juxtapose a chainlink fence and an asphalt kitchen floor with a white picket fence and old window moldings, as Gehry did in his house in Santa Monica, and one can trigger a dialogue of the old with the new in such a way as to create a house where, despite its almost excruciating heterogeneity, almost anyone can feel at home. "Even on the first visit," one critic has remarked, "it gives one the feeling of having been there before."[6] But it is difficult, for instance, to imagine hearing for the first time a recording of Laurie Anderson performing a piece dedicated both to Ludwig Wittgenstein and the Reverend Ike, without experiencing some feelings of dislocation and disorientation. In the collision of these two names, we are set adrift. ("There are ten million stories in the Naked City," she says directly afterwards, "but no one can remember which one is theirs.")[7]

And so no matter how much one might be attracted to Fredric Jameson's claim that the rise of postmodernism signals an end to society's "capacity to retain its own past" and the beginning of an age where we all will come to experience the moments of life as a "series of perpetual presents,"[8] it is difficult to see how postmodernist architecture is helping to push forward the point when this change would come about. For in thinking the idea of place, we think the interrelatedness of time and space. As it responds to the human demand for a sense of place, postmodern architecture aims at having us

recover the measure of our existence not only in terms of how we are situated in space but also in how we are caught up in the dynamics of time. A long list of examples could be cited here, including the "Fun House" mentioned earlier (figure 2). We can imagine, in fact, that it *would* be fun just to be able to look up at the sky, from inside the house, through openings in the roof arranged by Moss in the forms of Canis Major and Canis Minor to symbolize his client's large collection of dogs, but we can also see how our gaze would

3. Robert A.M. Stern, *BEST Catalogue Showroom*

allow us to read the passage of time in the sky and thus affirm our way of belonging to time, our finitude.

On a much larger and less personal scale, we can point to Robert Stern's BEST Products Showroom design (figure 3). Here, along the frontal arcade, we find images of an engagement ring, a television screen, a baby carriage, and other consumer items. Spatially, the placement of these images bears a reference to the physical layout of the store — where one can find these objects if one goes inside — but they also symbolize major events in a temporal sequence that could easily be the subject of many a

shopper's media-fed dream-life. Together, both meanings offer a sense of place, as banal as it might seem to be. And of course we could add to this list the most talked-about designs within postmodern architecture, such as the Portland Building and the Plaza d'Italia, which try to develop our sense of place through the conscious use of historical motifs and allusions.

So by way of replying to Jameson, we might say something like this: By emphasizing the value of place, postmodernist architecture reminds us of our finitude, but without fragmenting this experience into a sequence of discrete and disconnected nows.

But at this point it seems to me we encounter a difference in directions within postmodernism that is not simply one of interest or focus. If postmodernism encourages us to experience the discontinuity of time, it does so because, as Jameson also contends, it is vigorously suspicious of the reality of a human subject who "has experiences" and thus of the reality of a private, inner world of meaning belonging to an individual. For postmodernism, he observes, either the notion of traditional subjectivity is obsolete (as it is to Baudrillard, for example) or it is understood (by Foucault, among others) to have been a philosophical contrivance all along.[9] But if postmodernism in architecture wants to make us more aware of the continuity of time despite flux and change, this is because it tends not to put into question the reality of subjectivity or the concept of meaning as a representation within the mind of a subject. If we look to its designs and theory behind them expecting some recognition of the "end of philosophy," or criticisms of metaphysical concepts such as selfhood, truth, meaning, and representation as lively as those found in Derrida or Foucault, our expectations are very likely to go unmet. From observing the newer architecture, it would be difficult to tell, as Reiner Schürmann once put it, that "the present economy of things, actions and words appears to be receding from man."[10]

It is precisely this emphasis, for example, that is not placed in question by Mary McLeod in her recent article on postmodern architecture when she asks, by way of identifying what she takes to be its central concern, "To what extent can architecture serve as a system of visual signs expressing ideas and values?"[11] If this issue is the primary one postmodern architecture needs to solve in order to carry out the imperative to create places, then, by virtue of its reliance on metaphysical assumptions, it stands not only in a relationship of difference and dissimilarity to postmodernism as described by Jameson and particularly to its developments within philosophy, but also in a relationship of tension and opposition. In the next part of this paper I want to specify this opposition more clearly, to offer some thoughts as to why, within architecture, postmodernism did not develop as radically as within philosophy, and to wonder where this opposition leaves us.

In the introduction to his influential work *New Directions in American Architecture*, Robert Stern points out that because modern architecture had faith that it could produce social change, it took its inspiration from its own ideals, not from extant values. Because it tended not to consider how buildings were specifically to be used, it ignored the presence of existing social values. "Inclusivist" architecture (which Stern later would come to identify with the postmodern movement in American architecture), on the other hand, respected these already existing values in its design forms. It is through this respect, Stern believed, that postmodernism would come to resurrect meaning in architecture.

But just how does this respect show up in an architectural text? It comes about, we could say, through representing these values in the body of the text. For example, to represent "ugliness" or "ordinariness," Venturi suggests we need merely to borrow elements from the vocabulary of the existing environment, the closer to "Main Street" the better, which would symbolize these values. Thus the very familiarity of these elements would make it possible for someone to "read" the text without having to interpret it. "Ugly and ordinary architecture," as the authors of *Learning From Las Vegas* put it, "suggests more or less concrete meanings via associations and past experience."[12] Why concrete, and therefore relatively easy-to-get, meanings? Given the hurried conditions of modern life, these associations need to be made quickly. This was the reasoning, for instance, behind the *Bill-Ding-board* proposed by the Venturi firm for the National Football Hall of Fame competition. Large enough to be seen across the vastness of the parking lot in front of it, it would serve, Venturi explained, to "evoke the instant associations crucial for today's vast spaces, fast speeds, complex programs, and, perhaps, jaded senses which respond only to bold stimuli."[13]

Of course, the meaning of such a text, so easily read in terms of "this stands for that" (and the Portland Building stands out as another example), would be easily exhaustible; and the more ambiguous, and therefore the richer in meaning postmodern architecture is, as Charles Jencks suggests, the better. But whether one gets a meaning immediately or can't decide between meanings, what is of interest here is the idea that meaning is produced through an arousal of associations.[14] For in the belief that architecture can become more meaningful through

setting up associations — and thus make up for a lapse in the vision of modernism whose buildings seemed to strive for a kind of "thinness" of associative possibilities — postmodernism approaches the readers of its texts as the subjects of experiences. It wants to take advantage of those experiences which they had in the past in order to open up the possibility that its texts can be meaningfully experienced in the present. Its buildings invite a multiplicity of associations through the complexity of their design and explicit attention to the symbolic nature of detail. It rides on the potential for us to have a rich inner life through our freedom to make associations and so to understand a work of architecture if its signifiers inspire us to form associations.

With this in mind, we can perhaps see more clearly how postmodern architecture, although unheroic and unpretentious when compared to, say, the vision of Le Corbusier in his *Plan Voisin*, remains tied to Platonism, both in its acceptance of the representational character of its own language and in the individual character of human subjectivity. The metaphysical assumptions of modernism continue in American postmodernist architecture.

This should not come as a surprise if we see the growth of the latter as a reactive movement, a rejection against and turning away from modernism. Take, for example, the modernist values of purity and simplicity. If we see it from one perspective, Mies van der Rohe's curtain wall is an exemplary expression of these ideals. But when we look at the curtain wall from another perspective, as the most famous signifier in Mies's vocabulary, its success becomes more questionable. We can immediately recognize it when we see it without understanding its meaning. By over-extending its use, Mies sharply reduced its signifying force, thereby leading to the perception that much of his work is "inarticulate"[15] because his buildings tell us so little about themselves. Wherever the values of purity and simplicity dominate the language of architecture, the danger exists that it may become a private language, meaningful only to a few. So wherever it prefers the vernacular to the universal, the conventional to the artificial, *parôle* to *langue*, postmodern architecture is reacting to this danger by trying to make the language of architecture more openly significant again.

But if modern architecture was struck by the importance of purity and simplicity, it is also because it valued the display of rationality in built form. When Le Corbusier proclaimed that "we must enlist the discoveries made in industry and change our attitude altogether,"[16] his point was to apply what we have come to know through Heidegger as "calculative thinking" in order to solve design problems, and so lead to the production of standardized houses whose inhabitants would no longer feel confused in their living spaces, much in the same way as one would not feel confused behind the wheel of a well-designed automobile. Corbusier's desire was to ground the language of architecture in the perfection of technique for the purpose of creating more perfect human beings. But in the judgment of postmodern architecture, the abstraction of such a process was seen to lead in the opposite direction, in the creation of homes fit only for abstract beings. By staking its hopes on the rationality of technical thinking and its ahistorical

objectivity, modern architecture was led to forget about the importance of individual subjectivity. In preferring the historical to the atemporal, working with given materials instead of starting from scratch, respecting the idiosyncracies of personal taste, postmodern architecture is reacting to the event of this forgetfulness.

If we put this reaction together with the other one just mentioned, then we can see how, to the extent that postmodernism in architecture is simultaneously an anti-modernism, it takes upon itself the project of making buildings more meaningful to the individual; but since this anti-modernist attitude is restricted to modernist architecture, it affirms values which we have come to associate with the development of other forms of modernism such as modernist literature.

If we were interested in locating in philosophical space the assumptions lying behind postmodern architecture, we would, I suspect, immediately think back to the existentialist critique of rationality begun by Kierkegaard and Nietzsche and carried on by Sartre, Heidegger, and others. When Charles Moore described his aim of "building the opportunity for people to know where they are in space, in time, and in the order of things,"[17] it seems he could as well have said that his work provides the possibility for us to remember that we are not a "'pure, will-less, painless, timeless knowing subject'"[18] but rather a subject whose self-understanding is rooted in an historical context. In pursuing its critique of instrumentalist reason and arguing for a renewal of a creative thinking that would find some truth to the past and to history in order to make buildings more meaningful and thus restore our sense of place, postmodern architecture realizes the value of the idea that history has something to teach us, but seems to have stopped short of discovering what Nietzsche believed to be one of the more important lessons it has to offer: that because philosophy acts to create the world in its own image, history leads just as surely to the creation of fictions and myths as it does to truth and certainty.[19] And, what is more, that this image is not itself a unified whole. "The purpose of history, guided by genealogy," Foucault writes about Nietzsche, "is not to discover

the roots of our identity, but to commit itself to its dissipation."[20]

Just what risks, we might want to ask ourselves at this point, does postmodern architecture run by operating under its chosen interpretation of what a text is for: the assumption that "buildings are designed to mean something, that they are not hermetically sealed objects"?[21] By taking the failure of modern architecture to be a failure of communication, can postmodernism avoid the same problem if it wants to restore our sense of place while holding on to the ideas of meaning-as-representation and individual subjectivity? Or is it threatened by the same difficulty that modernism faced, of addressing its texts to a philosophically-questionable reader, this time around not a rationality so pure that it needs only the barest forms of furniture, but a complex, imperfect, disorganized but still more or less unified person, who thinks of her/himself as "having an identity" and an "inner life?"

It seems to me quite possible that the answer to this question could be yes. If so, then it is likewise possible that postmodernist architecture in its current state cannot satisfy, in a vital and challenging way, our demand for a sense of place. It is true that we cannot reject history but, as Foucault says about architecture, we cannot return to it either.[22] It seems as though we are now historically at a point where any affirmation of who we are must be an affirmation of our irreducible complexity rather than our irreplaceable subjectivity. This would suggest, then, that architecture should seek this affirmation in responding to the imperative to make places.

Might it not then be possible for postmodern architecture to aim at the creation of places without making this aim dependant on a metaphysical picture of human beings and of language? If, though, architecture would give up the picture of its own language as a vehicle of communicating meanings to individual subjects, what could it say to help awaken us to a sense of our place, and to whom, and how would it say it?

"Less is a bore," says Venturi, and one can agree. We need the experience of "more" so that our own complexity will find its resonances. But just what kind of complexity is this? Suppose, going back to the "economy of things, actions and words" mentioned earlier, we take words as our starting-point. In terms of our relationship to language, we are more than just on the receiving end of communications, and so more than just the recipients of meanings. Let us take here as a clue one of Wittgenstein's statements from the *Investigations*. To understand something, he writes, is to be able to find one's way around, to be able to participate in a language game. Here is a notion of understanding less metaphysically oriented around the representation of meaning than pragmatically oriented around saying things in the context of a diversity of linguistic activities. Lyotard makes it clear how whenever I am talking with someone, I tend to move very rapidly from one language game to another, sometimes playing more than

one at the same time,[23] and this movement can take on the shape of an ungrounded unity that we call a conversation. Language, Wittgenstein believed, also had this kind of "hanging together":

> Our language can be seen as an ancient city: a maze of little streets and squares, of old and new houses, and of houses with additions from various periods; and this surrounded by a multitude of new boroughs with straight regular streets and uniform houses.[24]

From this viewpoint, one's "self" could be conceived of as one's involvement in this interplay of language games: One's self would be more of a *doing* than a *being*. What would it mean for such a self to have a sense of place? One thing it would mean is to know one's way about in this ancient city: knowing how to play a number of different language games and being flexible enough to move from one game to another. This would not, though, make it akin to the "electronic" or "schizo" self which we also find suggested as a metaphor for a self belonging to the postmodernist age. To some degree this latter self is a metaphysical self stretched out of all proportion, capable of action over vast distances and of being "present" in more than one location at the same time. It experiences the fragmentation of time across experiences of spatial continuities of an ever-enlarging scale. The self I have in mind here bears a closer resemblance to the one Lyotard identifies as "pagan." If one accepts his point that language games "cannot be synthesized into a unifying metadiscourse,"[25] then for a "pagan" self radical discontinuity is unavoidable. That would make its sense of belonging to an order of things turn more on temporality than on spatiality, and would introduce aspects of risk and insecurity into a sense of place itself.

One might ask how architecture could play a role in establishing such a sense of place, so little connected to how we are situated in physical space itself. Would not the positions we occupy in a language game, as the sender of messages or their recipient, open up for us the possibility of place? — and what would architecture have to do with any of this? Here, in continuing to take our clue from the notion of language games, is one thought that comes to mind.[26] Wittgenstein once pointed out how uncertainty pervades our speaking with others: If someone throws a ball in a conversation, the other doesn't know if he is supposed to keep it, or throw it back, or throw it to someone else.[27] For Lyotard, this uncertainty appears as the freedom we have to come up with new moves as we play language games, ones that could change the way the game gets played in the future.[28] Such freedom is not, it seems, guaranteed by a language game itself, or by anything, for that matter. But if not guaranteed, possibly it could be intensified and strengthened by an architecture that would seek to help us discover a sense of place not so much by putting us in the position of being spoken to as by providing a flexibility that would lead us to develop new ways for us to speak to each other.

In this regard, Moore's design for Kresge College at UC Santa Cruz strikes me as working particularly well. In his description of this work, Jencks observes that its symbolic link to a Mediterranean village is "inescapable," and one would have to agree (figure 4). Understanding this work, though, does not seem to be a matter of "getting" the meaning here, of representing "Mediterraneanness" to oneself, in much the same way as the design of the Portland Building might be understood as "democracy." A more active kind of understanding seems to be called for here, an understanding operating more at the level of practice than representation. Such an understanding would be more of a matter of relaxing one's guard, of going along with the play of architectural forms and rhythms formed by the placement of street lamps and telephones, all of which seem to suggest that something is just about to happen. A matter, too, of opening oneself up to the possibility of surprising someone or being surprised oneself, to the possibility of taking the conversational ball and running off with it.

A postmodern building, Moore says at one point, allows us to get "involved with everything all at once."[29] I would suggest that this particular example of Moore's work projects a slightly different message, but one still in accordance with a postmodern complexity: not "everything is happening all at once," but "many things are still possible; there is more to come." A sense of place influenced by this message would be determined not only by presence but — and just as importantly — by absence as well. Of course, the suggestion I am making here, that postmodern architecture can help us find our sense of place not through the symbolic representation of values but through enhancing our freedom to play a variety of language games, is just that — a suggestion, an underdeveloped thought. But if the idea of place implies a commingling of presence and absence, then any further development of this thought would show that awareness of place, in the long run, settles no issues.[30]

4. Charles Moore and William Turnbull, *Kresge College*

*This paper was presented as a seminar at the conference *Postmodernism: Text, Politics, Instruction*, at the University of Kansas, May 1, 1987.

Notes

1. Moss's plans for this house, as well as for the *Fun House* and other residences, are described in a special issue of *Global Architecture* on California Architecture: *GA Houses Special 1* (April, 1985).

2. For a discussion of the relation of architectural form to our desire to exist in a world outside of time, see Karsten Harries' article, "Building and the Terror of Time," in *Perspecta 19* (1982), p. 59-69.

3. Terry Eagleton, "Awakening from Modernity," in the *Times Literary Supplement* (February 20, 1987), p.194.

4. Christian Norberg-Schulz, "Heidegger's Thinking on Architecture," in *Perspecta 20* (1983), p. 66. An elaboration of this definition can be found in his *Genius Loci* (New York: Rizzoli, 1980), p. 6-23.

5. Paolo Portoghesi, *After Modern Architecture* (New York: Rizzoli, 1980), p. 18.

6. John Pastier quoted by Tod Marder in "Gehry House," in *The Critical Edge*, ed. Tod Marder (Cambridge: M.I.T. Press, 1985), p. 107.

7. Laurie Anderson, *United States* (WB 25192-1), Side 6.

8. Fredric Jameson, "Postmodernism and Consumer Culture" in *The Anti-Aesthetic: Essays on Postmodern Culture*, ed. Hal Foster (Port Townsend, WA: Bay Press, 1983), p. 125.

9. *Ibid*, p. 114-115.

10. Reiner Schürmann, "Anti-Humanism. Reflections of the Turn Towards the Post Modern Epoch," in *Man and World 12* (1979), p. 162.

11. See Mary McLeod's chapter on architecture in *The Postmodern Moment*, ed. Stanley Trachtenberg (Westport, Conn.: Greenwood Press, 1985), p. 32.

12. Robert Venturi, Denise Scott Brown, and Steven Izenour, *Learning From Las Vegas* (Cambridge: M.I.T. Press, 1977), p. 129.

13. Robert Venturi, "A Bill-Ding-Board Involving Movies, Relics and Space," in *Architectural Forum* no. 128 (April, 1968), p. 76.

14. For an explanation of the idea that the feeling of "being at home" is a product of multiple associations found in one's immediate living environment, see Charles Moore, Gerald Allen, and Donlyn Lyndon, *The Place of Houses* (New York: Holt, Reinhart and Winston, 1974).

15. This is spelled out, for instance, in the first chapter of Charles Jencks's *The Language of Post-Modern Architecture* (New York: Rizzoli, 1984).

16. Le Corbusier, *Towards a New Architecture* (New York: Holt, Reinhart and Winston, 1960), p. 223.

17. Charles Moore quoted by Robert Stern in *New Directions in American Architecture* (New York: George Braziller, 1977), p. 70.

18. Fredrich Nietzsche, *On The Genealogy of Morals*, trans. Walter Kaufmann (New York: Random House, 1966), sec. 9, p. 16.

20. Michel Foucault, "Nietzsche, Genealogy, History," in *Language, Counter-Memory, Practice* (Ithaca: Cornell University Press, 1977), p. 162.

21. Stern, *op. cit.* 17, p. 162.

22. Michel Foucault, "Space, Knowledge and Power," in *The Foucault Reader*, ed. Paul Rabinow (New York: Pantheon, 1984), p. 250.

23. Jean-François Lyotard to Jean-Loup Theobaud, *Just Gaming* (Minneapolis: University of Minnesota Press, 1985), p. 54.

24. Ludwig Wittgenstein, *Philosophical Investigations* (New York: Macmillan, 1968), sec. 18, p. 8.

25. Lyotard, *op. cit.* 23, p. 58.

26. Heidegger's remark from "Building Dwelling Thinking": "Only if we are capable of dwelling, only then can we build" points to a relationship between architecture and language that is similar to the one I am trying to sketch out here.

27. Ludwig Wittgenstein, *Culture and Value*, trans. Peter Winch (Chicago: Univ. of Chicago Press, 1980), p. 74e.

28. Lyotard, *op. cit.* 23, p. 60ff.

29. Charles Moore, "Plug It In, Rameses, and See If It Lights Up, Because We Aren't Going to Keep It Unless It Works," in *Perspecta 11* (1967), p. 43.

30. I want to thank Doug Drape and Leo Marmol for their kindness in providing me with some of the materials used in this paper.

In your paper you state: "[I]f architecture would give up the picture of its own language as a vehicle of communicating meaning to individual subjects, what would it say to awaken us to a sense of place, to whom and how?" Your comment at the end of the paper states: "[I]f the idea of a place implies a commingling of presence and absence, then any further development of this thought would show that awareness of place, in the long run, does not settle any issues."

These statements describe contemporary architecture as speaking to a "subject" through representation or metaphor, resulting in a sense of place. Instead you call for open-ended language games in which presence and absence commingle. How do the positions of Kenneth Frampton and Christian Norberg-Schulz, who exhort a sense of place in Heideggerian terms, compare to the postmodern architecture you describe, which only speaks to us? How does Moore's Kresge College at UC, your example of practice as opposed to representation, differ from the recent projects of Peter Eisenman, who also claims to oppose metaphor and representation? The final question, and I am thinking of hermeneutics, is this: How does historicity figure into your discussion of language games? The works of Venturi, Gehry, Rossi, and Eisenman all engage history in a committed manner, but how would this issue involve your discussion?

Response from author July 11, 1987:

You're right in perceiving that my aim was to critique the idea, within the context of postmodernism, that "the language of architecture" is (or ought to be) representational. There are a couple of connections to Heidegger here.

Concerning "place," I think Heidegger's notion is sound. If we consider what Heidegger means by "place" in spacio-temporal terms, we are led to the idea of a location that has the power to make us aware of the historically-existing, finite beings that we are. Hence, here there would also be a commingling of presence and absence.

Heidegger is also clear on the point, I think, that it is possible for architecture to give us place itself, not the representation of place. Any genuine thing — of course that would include instances of genuine building — does not represent a meaning to us — metaphorical or otherwise — but instead is an event, an active unification of its surroundings into a location.

As you know, for Heidegger, not only genuine building but also genuine thinking is nonrepresentational. It can be identified neither with technique nor with a theory offering the basis for a technically-oriented practice. This would imply that in a dialogue between philosophy and architecture, Heidegger is misread if he is seen as possibly providing a theoretical basis for a particular direction in architecture. In other words, even if one works up a philosophy of architecture based on Heidegger, I don't think it is reasonable to think that one could develop out of that, to use the phrase that I have heard, "Heideggerian architecture." If architecture is an event that orders things into a place, as Heidegger maintains, it is an event whose origin cannot be traced back to a central point. Hence the stress, at the end of "Building Dwelling Thinking," on how "it" was able to build the Black Forest farmhouse. To approach this from another angle, we know that one of the most continually-stressed points in Heidegger is the idea that we are not in charge of language. (This is a point that Lyotard also mentions in his writings.) We are not its masters, and that holds, too, for the language of architecture, obviously with implications for the process of design. So whatever contribution Heidegger can make to the dialogue between philosophy and architecture would be, I think, more to the question of an "architectural thinking" — as Derrida has suggested — than to the question of built form itself.

Perhaps I have gone off on a tangent, but I wanted you to get a clearer idea of a role I think philosophy can legitimately play in the conversation between itself and architecture.

In response to your last question, the issue of historicity figures into my discussion of language games in the following way. I would say that each kind of language game has its own form of temporalizing, its own dynamics, and so its own form of historicity. Discontinuity would not necessarily imply the absence of a history, as Heidegger's idea of the history of philosophy shows. With reference to the postmodern emphasis on historical allusion, this to me is a kind of lego-historicity, not a genuine interplay of presence and absence.

As I've tried to bring out in my paper, architecture, when it opens up a sense of place, conveys to us a message that "Many things are still possible; there is more to come." So, although I am somewhat sympathetic towards Eisenman's attitude about metaphor, I do not think that he would agree that this message can or ought to be the message of architecture. It seems to me that Eisenman argues not only for an architecture devoid of explicit historical references, but for an architecture that takes place in a moment that hasn't been anywhere and doesn't have anywhere to go. So when he says that his use of the grid is what ties Berlin to the rest of the world, it is difficult for me to see how this "tie" could be thought of in the sense of opening up a place. Even Derrida seems to expect more from a nonrepresentational architecture when he states that he hopes it will lead to a place "where desire can recognize itself." One could make a similar point thinking of Heidegger: When the language of architecture speaks, the rest of the world does not remain silent.

Ontogenetic Difference:
Heidegger and Nietzsche
Elliot Feingold

Editor's Introduction

The philosophical emphasis adopted during the development of this issue of the *PRATT JOURNAL OF ARCHITECTURE* was inspired by conversations with Elliot Feingold. This article is an excerpt from one of the numerous discussions conducted with Elliot to articulate the fundamental principles and differences between Martin Heidegger, his contemporary Hans Georg Gadamer (Hermeneutics), and Friedrich Nietzsche and his contemporary Jacques Derrida (Deconstruction).

Philosophical Development of Being

In all German philosophy after Kant, there is an effort to overcome the dualisms in earlier Western thought from Descartes on, which left us in the Enlightenment with a skepticism, an all-encompassing rationalism expressed in scientific inquiry and scientific method, and in mathemati-cal science, or in a new interest in psychological phenomena or internal phenomena. Internal and external phenomena were characteristically separated in the 18th century. The internal was disparaged in the age of reason and materialism. In German philosophy, what is known as German idealism was an attempt to reunify the world as a whole, and to make the internal perspective fundamental in mapping out a metaphysics, a conception of reality. This was an answer to a material-ist philosophy's primarily external point of view on things and to the limitations that came out of Kant's philosophy. One of the implications of Kant is that through a purely epistemological, or cognitive investigation of reality, "things in themselves," the permanent things that Kant is looking for, are inaccessible.

Being, at least as Kant understood it, is inaccessible by means of a cognitive understanding: by a reason severely disciplined by experience, that is, empirical, observational knowledge. Thus the real question was whether to pursue a restricted philosophical program stressing methodological and epistemological issues presented by the empirical sciences or to renew philosophy along traditional lines of a quest for an encompassing vision. That led to a notion of looking at the world as a spectator, as a knower, which ultimately led to Kant's conclusion that the world as such is truly inaccessible.

Kant's austere view on the limits of knowledge and inaccessible truths coupled with the separation of the spheres of science, ethics, and aesthetics satisfied some, but left many with a gnawing metaphysical feeling of dislocation and a keenly-felt need for a philosophical wholeness to unite intellect and emotion. Post-Kantian philosophy is an attempt to reintegrate. The way to reintegrate is to start out with a total conception of Being so you don't end up with Kant's problem: that Being eludes you. In describing the three great representatives of German idealism, you encounter "total" philosophies of Being. In Hegel it becomes the Supreme concept, the Absolute idea. In Schelling there is a "nature mysticism" but also a sense of "complete identity" or ultimate category of Being as a kind of oneness: an identity through nature that is the external world of nature and the spiritual life: spiritual Being and natural Being. Schelling conceives of it as based on a principle of identity, that is, the ultimate metaphysical category, the oneness of nature and spirit. Hegel, like Schelling, seeks a fundamental unity through the diversity of phenomena. Unity, to be understood, requires a principle of self-development, self-unfolding; with Hegel it is the dialectic: the logic of the Absolute as it manifests itself. It emerges in various phases of the dialectic, in consciousness, in reason, and in spiritual life which includes social and political institutions. Fichte was one of the first and most ambitious of the post-Kantian philosophers. He tried to extend Kant to bridge the gap between Kant's subjective reality of experience and the objective world of things and events.

German idealism is all about the transcendental self. The transcendental self is the basic metaphysical principle which is a principal also, since it is a self; selves are not things, selves are not inert, selves exist by virtue of performance, of doing, of manifesting themselves. A self *is* by virtue of its performance, its action, its behavior. The transcendental ego is the source of the externalization of nature as something alien and, then, the reintegration of nature; in other words, the moral drama of the universe is a story first of externalization and, in moral terms, alienation, and then reassimilaiton — reunion.

Ultimately, Kantian dualism is between a realm of things in themselves and, a realm of appearances: the world as it appears to us and the world as it truly is, and the dilemma that creates. How do we get from appearances to the things in themselves? Kant said we can't really do that through science; science can't give us things in themselves; science established relations among perceivable phenomena, measurable phenomena. Fichte attempts to bring together the subjective world of appearance, and external reality. The basic concept in which he does this is the transcendental self which bifurcates into the internal and the external. What Fichte is doing is looking for what accounts for the division of the world between Nature and Spirit: the world into the things in themselves, and appearances. What accounts for that is the ultimate metaphysical category of the self as a transcendental being by virtue of the externalization of itself.

The point is, all these philosophies represent some total view. A total perspective is an all-encompassing overview which integrates spiritual existence and nature as the self expression of Being as an integrated whole. In all these philosophies externalization is the underlying principle. Heidegger has been accused of idealism because of his use of the foundational, metaphysical concept of Being; not an internal as opposed to an objective principle, but Being as an emergence; a coming out of, the development from within. One can never discover that from being outside of it, through logic or reason.

What lies behind the surface of things, ultimate Being, or what *is*, becomes accessible through pre-discursive thinking or experiencing from a non-discursive orientation.

The difference between Heidegger and the total point of view in Hegel, Fichte (and Schelling and German idealism) is that one cannot grasp things from some absolute perspective; one is always in the medium of *dasein* (being-there). The existential element is not present in the idealists. For the transcendental idealist Being is conceived as an integrated whole of self-expressive totality. For Heidegger, Being is a destructured or indeterminate horizon of the determinate world of philosophy, science, and ordinary experience. It is the sort of thing which leads him to talk in this way about the problem of *is*, *to be*, and so forth in his work, *An Introduction to Metaphysics*: Here he is asking questions at this point, not giving any particular answers; only saying:

A heavy storm coming up in the mountains "is," or what here amounts to the same thing, "was" during the night. Wherein consists its being?

A distant mountain range under a broad sky.... It "is." Wherein consists the being? When and to whom does it reveal itself? To the traveler who enjoys the landscape, or to the peasant who makes his living in it and from it, or to the meteorologist who is preparing a weather report? Who of these apprehends being? All and none....

The door of an early Romanesque church is an essent. How and to whom is its being revealed? To the connoisseur of art, who examines it and photographs it on an excursion, or the abbot who on a holiday passes through this door with his monks, or to the children who play in its shadow on a summer's day? How does it stand with the being of this essent?

A state — *is*. By virtue of the fact that the state police arrest a suspect, or that so-and-so-many typewriters are clattering in a government building, taking down the words of ministers and state secretaries? Or "is" the state in a conversation between the chancellor and the British foreign minister? The state *is*. But where is being situated? Is it situated anywhere at all?

A painting by Van Gogh. A pair of rough peasant shoes, nothing else. Actually the painting represents nothing. But as to what is in that picture, you are immediately alone with it as though you yourself were making your way wearily homeward with your hoe on an evening in late fall after the last potato fires have died down. What is here? The canvas? The brush strokes? The spots of color?[1]

These are the sorts of questions being asked here; the answer to the question doesn't lie in any external or analytic view or self-conscious examination of one's experiences, but Being is revealed through dwelling in it. Through dwelling in it, something comes to be. The whole notion "revelation of disclosure," is central to this. It is by virtue of being *within* it; so it's this internal principle; things are not revealed by some external analysis, philosophical or otherwise, but by dwelling within, because it is from within that a thing emerges out of itself. This sense has to be recovered in order to be able to talk about the world. But to establish this recovery, first one has to proceed along destructive lines established by Nietzsche's attack on Being.

The existential theme plays a strong role in the beginning here. The existential disclosure of the world which reveals a basic poetic experience is contrasted with the observational-intellectual view. One cannot externally uncover the world, one can authentically recover (discover) the world of things through a fundamental existential mood of dread or anxiety as a possibility of human reality. In that dread withdrawal takes place, and the relationship between these experiences — withdrawing, which leaves you with non-being, then with Being emerging out of non-being; these themes come into play through an *existential projection*. The larger context is that one has to experience in such a way that makes possible, if one experiences it authentically, an understanding of the philosophical problem that Nietzsche raised.

In using this notion in architecture, you can take a project by Daniel Libeskind, who, by way of bending and moving things around in such a way that they don't have the characteristics of representations, just as in much of abstract art, indicates that if you alter things, and show that materials are capable of new structures, new revelations, new disclosures, and new relationships, then you have gotten away from a reified world and you experience things freshly. Heidegger, of course, is a philosopher primarily, and he is interested in the general question concerning human beings in quest of meaning; but that question arises in the context of History or a history: a history that reveals to you where you are at any given cultural moment. Heidegger requires that you come to terms with Nietzsche and destructive philosophy as a historical phenomenon. You can't simply rediscover in a void, you can't simply break through the surfaces of an inauthentic world, a reified world of fixed meanings, a dead world.

Heidegger and Nietzsche: Being or Will?

In adopting Heidegger's philosophy to address its relation to architecture, one could use certain central themes in Heidegger's *ontological difference* to open up the space from which you can break down the identification of Being with beings (things), and recreate some sense of Being. The early preoccupation and the central theme in Heidegger's work is the theme of Being, even though the word Being disappears in his later work.

The source of Heidegger's project of recovering the basic impulses of philosophy is to be found both in the crisis, in Husserl's term, produced by the debates arising the 19th century from the philosophical residue of Kantian and Hegelian school's of philosophy, and in the provocatively decentering reflections of Nietzsche. In the first instance, the identity and aim of philosophy was hotly debated between those who believed, with Kant, that philosophy should pursue a program of logical and epistemological inquiry firmly grounded in the substantive concerns of mathematics and empirical science, and those who, in the spirit of Hegel, believed that philosophy found its true mission in the hermeneutic or interpretive understanding characteristic of the cultural disciplines.

Husserl's program of pure phenomenology developed out of the philosophical crisis produced by the rival methodological paradigms of mathematics and the exact sciences on the one hand, and the hermeneutic cultural disciplines on the other. For Husserl neither model or paradigm succeeded in achieveing what he thought to be the paramount objective of philosophical inquiry: the exploration of the foundation of being, knowledge, and value. Husserl's program of phenomenology, therefore sought, by means of a purely descriptive account of the acts and structures of a timeless, contentless, transcendental consciousness, to purge philosophy of all the assumptions and prejudgments found in more limited forms of inquiry, namely mathematics, the exact sciences, and cultural disciplines.

Parallel to these developments out of the methodological debates of 19th-century German philosophy were the provocative reflections of Nietzsche, for whom the very aim of philosophical inquiry was put into question. He exposed as illusory the quest for the foundation of knowledge and values. The idea of a foundational order of things, of fundamental truths, was for Nietzsche nothing but a self-preserving myth of Platonic philosophical culture and the Christian religion. Modern man, stripped of philosophical and religious myths, would in the future have to accommodate himself to the illusion of truth, and to the truth of illusion.

Heidegger's view of his own philosophical vocation as the renewal of the question of Being becomes clear in the light of these developments of German philosophical thought around the turn of the century. Heidegger adopted the phenomenological method of his teacher, Husserl, but rejected the idea of a purely descriptive phenomenology, based on the time-worn Cartesian assumption of a foundational consciousness, in favor of an interpretive or hermeneutic phenomenology. This modification of Husserlian phenomenology bears the imprint of Kierkegaardian existentialism with, its insistence on concrete human reality as the point of departure for authentic understanding, as well as of the Nietzchean dictum that truth is exclusively a matter of interpretation.

Nietzsche's philosophy breaks down and dissolves, at least on a metaphysical level, all concepts of essence and being. At the heart of things is nothing as such, no-beings, simply force, power, movement; nature is force, rather than objects which can be described. Nietzsche did not like philosophy or anything in a discursive language; he was not a discursive thinker, and to dissolve the tyranny of fixed structures requires a non-discursive, almost poetic language.

Heidegger views Nietzsche's philosophy as a culmination of Western thought in which the foundational question of Being found itself gradually submerged in a scientific and historical world of objects and events, evolutionary processes and historical forces. Nietzsche's resurrection of pre-Socratic philosophies of flux and dynamic movement aim at dissolving the question of Being entirely. For Nietzsche the time-honored quest for the perennial philosophy had run its course. The attack on the revered Western philosohical tradition proposes a challenge to modern thought in the form of a pervasive philosophical nihilism. Heidegger's project may be viewed as an effort to confront Nietzsche's as a form of renewal of the question of Being.

Heidegger is trying to establish a renewed relationship to experience. Once you free yourself from material things, beings, or entities, then you have to reexamine the question of Being in terms of self-emergence, self-unfolding: the word "physics" in its original Greek sense. Before physics came to mean a material thing, it meant, at least in Heidegger's reading of the Greek language, a kind of unfolding, something that comes out of itself. This takes you to a realm of non-being, because Being and non-being are so intimately connected. What does this word *Physis*, the origin of our word physics, entail? Heidegger's fresh interpretation of terms which have become dead from their use over the centuries involves descriptions which are not characteristic of the thing, but deal with movement of some sort, of coming to be:

What does the word *physis* denote? It denotes self-blossoming emergence (*e.g.* the blossoming of a rose), opening up, unfolding, that which manifests itself in such unfolding and perseveres and endures in it; in short, the realm of things that emerge and linger on. According to the dictionary *phyein* means to grow or make to grow. But what does growing mean? Does it imply only to increase quantitatively, to become more and larger?

Physis as emergence can be observed everywhere, *e.g.* in celestial phenomenon (the rising of the sun), in the rolling of the sea, in the growth of plants, in the coming forth of man and animal from the womb. But *physis*, the realm of that which arises, is not synonymous with these phenomena, which today we regard as part of "nature." This opening up and the inward-jutting-beyond-itself... must not be taken as a process among other processes that we observe in the realm of the essent. *Physis* is being itself, by virtue of which essents become and remain observable.[2]

He is not thinking in terms of something that can be described within a framework of categories, such as a substance having two dimensions, potential Being and actual Being, in the process by which it becomes what it is. He is trying to separate this original primordial conception of emergence, of something coming out of itself. "The Greeks did not learn what *physis* is through natural phenomena, but the other way around: it was through a fundamental poetic and intellectual experience of being that they discovered what they had to call *physis*."[3] In other words, it is not an already intellectualized, sophisticated analysis of the world that they drew their category of *physis*, but a more primordial type of experience. *Physis*, in its original primordial sense, means, "[T]he power that emerges and the enduring realm under its sway. This power of emerging and enduring includes 'becoming' as well as 'being' in the restricted sense of inert duration."[4]

Here Heidegger's criticism of Nietzsche comes into play and he sees Nietzsche as within the tradition of Western philosophy. It is Nietzsche who is opposed, under the influence of pre-Socratic thinking, to becoming from Being as opposed to becoming *to* Being, the process of movement, of emergence to what *is*. Heidegger disagrees; he says that Nietzsche can say that because he is already in a tradition that has lost any relationship to ultimate Being and thus is looking at things in two ways: either in some sort of Aristotelian way in which things have some permanent, underlying structure, or in some way in which things don't have a permanent underlying structure, becoming is the only truth about them. There are no stable properties attached to anything that gives it an enduring identity.

Heidegger is trying to recall or reconstruct this whole problem by saying it is not a matter of emerging and enduring as a part of becoming and Being in a restricted sense of inert duration; *physis* is the process of arising, of emerging from the hidden whereby the hidden is first made to stand. In other words, we first have to get to where Nietzsche got to, to deal with the modern problem, and then we have to overcome Nietzsche. We have to get to Nietzsche's critique of a philosophy of Being, which is essentially a perspective or vision on the world which emphasizes stable structures and things which endure through time and remain as change takes place. We have to get to where Nietzsche swept that away and left us with nothing but movement, constant flux and change itself, which leads us to a kind of nihilistic vision.

Nietzsche is concerned to get away from a Platonic search for a permanent underlying structure of being, which is repeated in modern philosophy in Kant's shadowy idea of the "thing in itself," that which is impervious to all changes and appearance, which in itself is not susceptible to change, which remains behind the surface world of changes. Nietzsche's critique is aimed at these two sources. The Kantian idea is linked up to the Christian concern that what ultimately is beyond change is God, the spiritual. Heidegger sees Nietzsche's critique as fundamentally true, but Nietzsche himself is an element of it on the metaphysical level. What emerges from Heidegger's perspective is how in Nietzsche the question, Being as such, as Heidegger understands a primordial Being, is totally lost, is totally forgotten in some profound way. The nihilistic character of philosophy denies permanence, and that is the case because Heidegger's conception of primordial Being, since it comes out from within, requires some idea of a nowhere, a non-physical conception of space, a non-material conception of a void. The idea of Being is only born in the sense of a withdrawal from being; one comes back to a sense of Being as something coming out from a distance, from the hidden. Its part of the internal logic of the concept of Being as expounded by Heidegger to introduce the idea: nothing, as that from which something emerges out of. Heidegger's thinking aims at recovering the root experience "nothingness" from the Nietzschean legacy of philosophical nihilism by making it central to thinking, the "ontological difference" as the non-specifiable horizon of specifiable reality (concepts, and entities).

Hermeneutics

Heidegger's concept of *Dasein* lends itself to the possibility of a narrative of the self. Since one of the existential features of *Dasein* is the notion of being projected out of a past, the self has some kind of identity. The concept of Being-in-the-world attempts to transcend both the ancient concept of an external point of view on things, looking at everything objectively, looking at everything "out there" and arranging it; that's where logic comes from, concepts of similarity and dissimilarity.

Heidegger's concept of history is also somewhat unconventional, because history, like everything else with Heidegger (since his whole philosophy is designed to break down the concept of being as givens) cannot be conceived as a set of givens which lie dormant, dead in the past or retrieved in the present by virtue of an act of historical scholarship or detached understanding. History does not involve a detached understanding of the past; nor does he see the present as a set of accretions, growths, developments piling up on each other, in which the present is seen as simply continuous with the past; there is no idea of continuity. The conventional notion of history is narrative: The present world in which we exist is an outgrowth, built up like a monument, an heroic history of momentous events, all of the great moments of the past.

Heidegger approaches history as the engagement of history, as part of the engagement of *Dasein*, or selfhood, with the world. An understanding of history comes out of the way in which we experience the present. Modern man's engagement in the world involves the disclosure or the concealment of Being, since every kind of disclosure also involves some kind of concealment. Understanding modern man involves seeing everything in terms of technology, not in the way that sociologists or technical people speak of technology, but as a certain way of framing the world in terms of potential energies, uses, things which can be manipulated, shaped, in order to realize "Humanistic" objectives of control over the natural and social world.

Experiencing the world in a technological framework is contrasted to experiencing the world in a poetic framework. Technology conceives of the world in terms of function, application, and thus it changes our relationship to things, takes away the mystery of things. From that point of view nothing has sacred value; the world is experienced as bundles of energy, of possible uses. We don't look at things as artistic objects; rather, we view everything as having use. Everything is conceived not as an object in itself, but as functional, a tool to be used for other purposes. Functionalizing experience is a part of modern experience. This takes away from the poetry of experience, from seeing the way a poet or artist would see things simply as a form in the Greek sense, as some sort of harmonious, beautiful object.

In Heidegger's view we don't relate to things in the given structure, model or paradigm, but as an act of revelation; the work of art comes to you, it reveals a world to you. The act of revelation itself is central to the poetic experience as understood by Heidegger. In the technological framework, things are not forms as such, they are all functional: What is it for? What does it do?

Heidegger would take the notion of technology as the way in which contemporary man is projected into the world; Being-in-the world in our modern era. It is this experience and understanding of technology that generates a certain approach to the past. At that point we see the present in relation to the past not from a detached point of view; the more deeply you experience modern existence the more it engages you with its historical origins. History is generated out of a present engagement, out of more deeply experiencing the way the world is today. Superficially you do not see it because you just go about your business like everyone else. What it requires is not a stepping back, but a deeper involvement, a kind of philosophical involvement in your time to seek further and further the meaning of the present as it reveals itself to you; thus you can understand the past.

For Heidegger history is a result of the engagement with the present. Thus an effective historical consciousness comes out of the deepening of one's existential commitments. History becomes more meaningful to the extent that you are engaged in the present. You cannot stand on the sidelines. You must take a stand and commit yourself to the new — against History. Heidegger is not a traditionalist in that sense. The conservative idea of tradition as shaping all things, judgments, and actions, is one that Heidegger is very much set against; a romantic conservatism he has no use for. History can be understood only through contemporary engagement.

For a more independent development of the theme of how you relate to the past and the present, look at the work of Hans-Georg Gadamer, who was once a student of Heidegger. Heidegger's early existential thinking represented an attempt to replace a transcendental mode of thinking with a hermeneutic mode. Gadamer adapted Heidegger's early philosophy of existential hermeneutics into a philosophical method of interpretation or a hermeneutics of literary texts. He felt that you could not approach the past from a totally neutral and indifferent point of view, nor could you simply subjectivize the past. There is a fusion of horizons, the horizon of the present with that of the past. Gadamer seeks to bridge the gap between present and past by means of a dialogue that assumes the interpreter exists in a contemporary setting which employs reason and prejudice as the essential condition of an historical setting. One is simultaneously bridging between an historical presence and a projection backwards into the past. The interpretation of a text requires a posture, an historical position, and one's relationship with time can never be outside of time, nor in a subjective view: a view which assumes seeing things as projecting outward from within a subject, but through time, in a dialogue. The only way to interpret the Renaissance in terms of any aspect of its culture, political or aesthetic, is to engage in a dialogue. A dialogue is not some sort of a detached neutral thing. You can only come to a dialogue as someone engaged in a world yourself; you have judgments, points of view. A dialogue is not between two neutral people. A dialogue generates insight out of a past which is in someway given to you; it is there in its works, art, texts, and institutions. The dialogue is a fusion of horizons which involves someone coming at it from a present shaping, so that you can never step outside of any cultural frame of reference; you cannot be neutral in relation to the past. This is Heidegger's conception of destructuring the past: breaking down preconceived ideas, and making an effort to describe how these are shapings, disclosures. This has been carried on by Gadamer in a more systematic way.

You can never bridge the gap because you can never become a Renaissance man, you cannot become a Greek, you cannot have the innocence of a Greek. You are capable of fusing horizons because you are capable of understanding that past. But you can only understand that past as a participant in a dialogue; we have the capacity of being lodged in a world and yet able to move beyond that world, but we cannot simply take leave or remove ourselves from the present. Creative or aesthetic concerns cannot simply be shaped by any past conception of things; it cannot be a function of any understanding of what the past was.

Contemporary Philosophical Debate

Jacques Derrida says that Heidegger is very deeply rooted in the Western tradition and more narrowly in the German tradition, in retaining some presence, some place in which one can position oneself. It's questionable whether on this point he is reading Heidegger altogether correctly, because Heidegger's theme, the *ontological difference*, is that Being is only possible not as something that you can separate off from being, but only in the space between the two, so that, is space in itself. Derrida is saying that Heidegger brought this difference forward and is thus trying to think it through more deeply. Derrida rejects a dissolution of Being into a metaphor of Being that is influenced by or historically shaped by our ways of conceptualizing and looking at things. Beings *are* by virtue of the way in which we represent them: as material objects, as emotional states, influenced by our history, our intellectual categories: Beings are a function of our ways of representing them. Derrida rejects the thinking of the ontological difference, the non-specifiable horizon of determinate reality as a concealed form of the metaphysics of presence.

If you wanted to get into this debate and think about it in terms of structures, relations between materials and spatial relations, in such a way as to create human habitations; in constructing something, the Nietzschean perspective would insist that at any angle, which leaves nothing open to you; does not make you understand that the void is the center of the thing, is a lie.

In Heidegger it is not the void or nothingness which is considered central in an existential experience. In Heidegger's conception of Being, it is only through the void that one can understand the self-emerging characteristic of Being; but the void itself must be seen in terms of the presence or absence of Being, it is not taken as an absolute condition of Being; only the necessary condition for the possibility of emergence. Nietzsche would say that any attempt to show the void as somehow existing by virtue of any concept of structure or order, or supported by any concept of Being, is itself a lie, whereas in Heidegger there is the desire to bring that notion of a void in an intrinsic relationship to order, to suggest the extraordinary. The void is always the extraordinary in Heidegger but it is the extraordinary which introduces you to the limits of order. Being, for Heidegger, limits the void; Being structures the void by providing a sense of limits to a void, whereas Nietzsche absolutizes a void. Heidegger's perspective allows him to talk about nothing in referring to philosophy, poetry, and science:

All scientific thought is merely a derived form of philosophical thinking, which proceeded to freeze into its scientific cast. Philosophy never arises out of science or through science and it can never be accorded equal rank with the sciences.... Philosophy stands in a totally different realm and order. Only poetry stands in the same order as philosophy and its thinking, though poetry and thought are not the same thing. To speak of nothing will always remain a horror and an absurdity for science.... By virtue of this superiority the poet always speaks as though the essent were being expressed and invoked for the first time. Poetry, like the thinking of the philosopher, has always so much world space to spare that in each thing — a tree, a mountain, a house, the cry of a bird — loses all indifference and commonplaceness.

In other words, through poetry there are limits; the circle presents limits, whereas Nietzsche wants to break all forms to stress creativity as the emergence of forms through some creative process. Underlying those forms in Nietzsche is the ultimate truth which is no-form, a kind of cosmic energy. Heidegger cites a passage from Knut Hamsun's last works, *The Road Leads On*:

It describes the last years and end of this August, who embodies the uprooted modern man who can do everything equally well yet who cannot lose his ties with the extraordinary, because even in his weakness and despair he remains authentic and superior. In his last days August is alone in the high mountains. And the poet says: "Here he sits between his ears and all he hears is emptiness. An amusing conception, indeed. On the sea there were both motion and sound, something for the ear to feed upon, a chorus of waters. Here nothingness meets nothingness and the result is zero, not even a hole. Enough to make one shake one's head, utterly at a loss."[6]

Heidegger is saying there is something very interesting about nothing, because it is nothingness that brings us back to the primordial experience, and this experience provides a sort of stage setting for the emergence of the Being of things. You have to be able to experience that in order for things to come at you; that is, if they are in a fixed aesthetic or moral space, then you can't truly experience them. It frees you from any kind of pre-conceptions, and to be freed from preconceptions is to move away from representing something; you adopt a fresh posture, which is in effect a way of talking about the nothing: a posture which hasn't oriented you so that you are really not representing nothing; you are inside of nothing until it begins to fill in a certain way with a kind of meaning.

We could go back to Derrida, but he is primarily interested in objecting to the notion of eventually coming through the nothing to some presence. Derrida is true to the Nietzschean moral imperative to remain courageously in the truth: *One must always keep sight of the void*; taking no meaning structure as privileged in any way which might allow you a certain kind of seriousness for having found the ground, having established something. Any time you establish an orientation you find out where you are "coming from," "where things are at." Out of that ground-edness would emerge a new kind of seriousness, whereas Nietzsche employs tragic irony: almost a tragic-comic view of existence: the tragic, the absurd, and the comic: the dissolution of all things into the zero point which is the only truth. Nietzsche's conception of the eternal return, then, suggests rebuilding, constantly shaping and forming. Heidegger's approach involves freeing yourself from all forms of representation and conceptual thinking so that you are facing nothing

and thus allow things to come at you and to emerge through your involvement, so that revealed meaning is always *possible*, not an *absolute* as we see in Nietzsche.

Heidegger doesn't answer the question as where you are or what the difference is between abstaining from representational thinking and involving yourself with Being. If there's a point in which Being does reveal itself in an authentic way, there is a revelation of things that always holds something back. It conceals as well as reveals. Heidegger seems to emphasize a kind of tension. Authenticity is the attempt to say, I have abstained from all forms of representational or conceptual thinking of a world that has to do with habit; I can now experience the way in which it truly comes to me.

It is a question of whether or not any authentic experience is sufficient to counter the Derridean/Nietzschean selling out of the void, the selling out of nothingness to something. Does Heidegger retain enough of that when he says the *nothing* can be completely grasped or understood as such? There is always the hidden, and the hidden is what is not-present. In every presence there is the not-present. In creating forms and structures, you want to avoid any suggestion of relationships, and of materials, and connections that seem to be completely revealed, or that you can completely encompass or explain. Such revelation would fix us in a relationship to the structures we create in rigidly narrow, precisely defined relationships. There is the suggestion of mystery in Heidegger. There is the suggestion that the authentic experience will always involve something unsatisfying, or something not present. You are projected toward the not-present as well as the present.

The theme of what is present in Being is hard to express in discursive language because a feature of presence is non-presence. In a discursive way one must speak in paradoxes, but Heidegger wants to retain that tension, and it can be retained only in terms of a poetic rather than a discursive experience, because the latter doesn't allow you to say "it is there and it's not there," whereas a poetic account of things allows you to speak that sort of language.

In one way Heidegger's philosophy holds out the possibility of security within Being. I guess this is what the Nietzscheans are attacking him for. There is a security or a certain kind of sense of self that comes with an experience of things in that they are not complete; there is a security which completes your relationship to the absent: security in the sense of Being: to wrap things up neatly and exhaust the question, and reach the outer limits of it. Since absence is a feature of any kind of genuine experience, the poet sees the absent through what is present and sees the present through what is absent.

Heidegger is not suggesting that you can reach the outer limits; he is suggesting that whatever is present always suggests what is beyond or hidden, and the hidden thus comes to mean what is present. The Derrideans are emphasizing more the creation and destruction theme, and that is the absolute impermanence that strangely enough is the beginning in a profound poetic experience. Heidegger would say *that reifying impermanence really loses the sense of what impermanence is truly about*. The original Greek experience, to be able to see in a poetic way, the world as it persists and the world that is evanescent, is a certain sense of dwelling in a world which provides a kind of security in an insecure situation: a sense of coming

and going and of persistence at the same time — that is the original Greek experience. What Heidegger sees in Nietzsche is an overlay of too much Western philosophy which ultimately reduces things either into a Platonic heaven of permanent, static, stable forms or into an anti-religion of pure impermanence manifested through the ups and downs of self-assertion and will: the coming and going of things, and the making and dissolution of things. Derrida's thinking such as it is, proceeds from an orientation within language, not from the voluntarism of a metaphysics of will. Language is nothing but metaphor: endless differentiating, substituting, supplementing, leaving traces and displacing itself. It is this perspective on language that Derrida offers in criticism of a Heideggerian view of the possibility for an authentic language, a language that rises beyond discursive formulation to disclosure and revelation. Heidegger retains a belief in truth, a truth in Being, whereas Derrida dissolves the notion of truth into the obliqueness of metaphor; everything is indirection; things are not unconcealed, they are oblique.

As it affects the arts and architecture, I think that a Nietzschean vision wants to destabilize any structure, so that it constantly takes you back to no center or no place of reference. Wherever you go, you can't settle anywhere.

Notes

1. Martin Heidegger, *An Introduction to Metaphysics*, trans. Ralph Manheim (New Haven: Yale Univ. Press, 1959), p. 34-35.
2. *Ibid*, p. 14.
3. *Ibid*.
4. *Ibid*.
5. *Ibid*, p. 26.
6. *Ibid*, p. 26.

Form; *Being;* A b s e n c e

Stephen Perrella

Heidegger attempts to interrogate the familiar in order to discover what he later describes as the "danger" concealed within it.... Metaphysics produces homelessness by repressing the originary homelessness. Man is detached from the house and the ground precisely by thinking of them as secure.

   Mark Wigley

Mark Wigley and I are both interested in a deconstruction of the opposition: habitable vs. uninhabitable. Both share a parallel interest in that opposition, and the question of how one deconstructs that opposition. Mark is interested in the uninhabitability of the habitable, he is apparently looking for the return of the repressed that always already exists in the mundane, via the uncanny, etc. I am considered to be more avant garde in being closer to the Freudian, Nietzschean tradition in that I choose to habitate what is called the uninhabitable.

   Jeffrey Kipnis

We are trying to restore the difficulty in life, not to make it impossible.

   John Caputo

Towards a Radical Hermeneutics
The issues explored in this journal have developed around two questions: the possibility of radicalizing (foundational) Heideggerian positions in architectural discourse, and how writings on the relationship between deconstruction and architecture are influenced by the dominantly (Platonic, Hegelian) dialectical context of Western culture. In other words, to what extent may deconstruction be limited in its capacity to be critical? These questions pursue the enigmatic difference between the inherent limitations in any notion of context, and the limiting effect of a cultural context on critical strategies.

If deconstruction (as a critical practice which has influenced architecture) while demonstrating that "knowing" Truth or History is illusory is itself somehow *shaped* by cultural and historical contexts, what position will accommodate this disparity? Inasmuch as these questions presuppose that we live in an historical-political context, they ask what kind of limitations exist if we cannot think the limitation, or know the context.

Presence/Architecture
To begin with Heidegger is to institute at once certain presuppositions about presence, in order to question them. Indeed, to speak is to make assumptions. "Speaking," here, is meant to include any kind of human impulse, a self which goes beyond itself (*ekstasis*). The bearing on architecture of these questions about Heidegger and deconstruction involves the possibility of uncovering what always already exists, albeit temporarily. Heidegger suggests that this originary quality in which things emerge poetically has been obscured by a dominant Western interest to fix what is present as an object of a subject's "common sense." (The same holds true in scientific thought.) Common sense takes for granted an object as self-evident: We see *i.e.*, it's simply there — naturally. Taking what is present for granted is symptomatic of our failure to scrutinize the established relation constructed by Metaphysics, to which architecture contributes. If questioned, this *presence* will be found incomplete: In the construction of knowledge about what is present, the gaps if scrutinized, become, instead of foundational an endless abyss. Our failure to scrutinize those discontinuities is a slumber, an inability to see how thought is shaped or fictional. "This 'unthought' is, for Heidegger, 'what is most worthy of thinking'" (*Altarity* 42). In its Hegelian form, the culturally induced assumption determines that "Nothing can be present to self-consciousness unless it is represented by the subject's *own* representative activity." In other words, "The representing subject sees *itself* reflected in its own 'object'" (39).

Generally, then, common assumptions, which may be characterized as Hegelian, are appropriative. The emphasis is always on something outside of us which in turn is appropriated through a mirror-play of self-reflexive operations in language. "This illusion, in turn, gives rise to one final delusion: It seems as though man everywhere and always encounters only himself.... If man meets only himself, he never encounters otherness or difference." (40).

It is possible to displace common (Hegelian) assumptions by noticing that the question about presence (architecture) asks further: How is it that a thing *can be* present? How *can there be* presence as such? These questions lead us to rethink a fundamental principle which for Heidegger is the nihilistic impulse in Western culture: the will to power. They are also concerned with undermining mental operations which separate us by the very means by which we hope to relate; concepts and subjective responses are *projected* onto the object we believe we address.

The repressive mechanism in the Hegelian "system of appropriation" is seen by Heidegger in discursive language (*logos*). This repressive assumption operates at each moment in a culturally shared phenomenon: language; yet it may be argued that meaning must exist, if at all, *in* language. Mark Wigley's preface (see above 4) reveals the influence of operations of language (metaphor) in the neurotic relationship between architecture and philosophy, where the entire Western philosophical tradition has relied upon architecture metaphorically to establish secure foundations (metaphysics). Wigley's arguement is established in his dissertation:

The motif of the edifice is that of a structure while free-play is constrained by the ground. The play of representations is limited, controlled, by presence. Philosophy is the attempt to restrain the free-play of representation by establishing the architectonic limits provided by the ground. It searches for the most stable ground in order to exercise the greatest control over representation (Jacques Derrida *and Architecture: The Deconstructive Possibilities of Architectural Discourse* 74).

His thesis unmasks the hidden contracts and convoluted dichotomies of traditional philosophy's reliance on metaphor. Heidegger's essay *Art and Space* (see above 9) describes the condition of the context necessary for Wigley's investigation.

Heidegger's alternative to the Hegelian system is an attack on subjectivity. Heidegger's excerpt from the poet Rainer Maria Rilke (see above 12) suggests the way things come to be present is: "about that understanding which constitutes the ground of the possibility of things showing themselves. It is to ask about the opening up of the space for such showing, about the disclosure of world, about *disclosedness*" (*De-limitations* 92). This ground is also seen as the possibility for philosophy to establish the foundations of knowledge. Heidegger aims at disengaging the fundamental concepts which determine the preliminary understanding of a region which then become the grounds for Truth. The purpose of this critique is to reopen questions apparently settled, "regaining these questions as live and open is the only way to get behind our unexamined assumptions to see how they are now our basis" (*What Is A Thing?* 252).

The work of the artists presented in the first section of this journal has been chosen to "discuss" certain features of Heideggarian "unthoughts." Although these projects may be read in innumerable ways, we read of these projects in relation to Heideggarian issues *to bring about the possibility of a play of issues* in relation to the more radical philosophical positions in the second section. All of these general readings characterize certain Heideggarian values, and should in no way be taken as a claim to be *the* meaning but only as *a* reading of these texts. A close reading of each text bears out the phenomenological assumptions with which each as a work of art establishes presence. These readings begin to explicate philosophical issues only in being brought into play. It may also begin to suggest the capacity of descriptive (phenomenological) thinking, to break down conventional ways of seeing things in and of themselves, beginning to undermine the *degree of presence* in an act of thought by "standing under" (instead of understanding) subjective or objective projections as a means to comprehend. For Heidegger, art is the way in which truth becomes; the truth of the world establishes itself only in the work of art as truth's "becoming" and "happening."

The following constitute thus a general reading of issues in Heidegger's thinking as they relate to the projects in the first section: A. The *nothing* which nihilates (Warhol), which involves Heidegger's inclusion of the consideration of nothing with the consideration of something; B. the destructuration of conventional notions (Acconci), where the ground of conventions is destructured to reveal the mechanism of ground as constitutive; C. the act of description (Matta-Clark), almost a literal illustration of the Rilke excerpt; D. the relation to the ordinary object (Stein),

the excerpt from *Being and Time* here illustrating the breakdown in the conventional consideration of tools as a means to complete ourselves, which touches Heidegger's critique of humanism; E. the artist's derivation as constituted through a description of its context (Sonnier), involving Heidegger's explication of an object as a manifestation of the manifold of a context; F. the fiction of subjectivity (Ladda) depicting a subject in *relation* to the object as existentially constituted; G. the breakdown of the traditional role of language as representational (Thatcher), in which all of the words in the maps have been covered over; H. the existential priority of the self over institutions (Burden), Heidegger's argument against his teacher Husserl that it is not man's institutions which define man but more primordially our being-in-the-world, is the more fundamental condition; I. the breakdown of the transcendental (historical) subject by revealing the repressive content of historically constituted — institutional conventions (Wodiczko); and J. (Kiefer) the relation between Heidegger's critique of technology and the artist's illustration of the growing tumor which eventually killed the philosopher.

Language, Being/Architecture
Heidegger's destructuring of Western metaphysics set forth a critique of presence, renaming language as Being. For the Cartesian subject, inextricably involved in the relentless drive of technology to objectify knowledge, reality becomes a representable object for a knowing subject. Undermining the "disinterested interest" elicited by the Cartesian system involves Phenomenological seeing, an interest in the disclosure of the "things-in-themselves," an immediate experience of things which avoids the imposition of a philosophical grid, or interpretation, upon the world. Heidegger argues that language is not an object to be spoken *about* but that language itself *speaks*. The subject is fictional to the degree

that it is constituted by the socio-cultural world which, greater than any singular subject, constitutes the subject and not the reverse:

To undergo an experience with language, then, means to let ourselves be properly concerned by the claim of language by entering into and submitting to it. If it is true that man finds the proper abode of his existence in language — whether he is aware of it or not — then an experience we undergo with language will touch the innermost nexus of our existence (*On the Way to Language* 57).

Heidegger does much to displace the traditionally conceived subject. Throughout his career he sought to erase the presence of subjectivity from the project of Being as language — to remain "underway." His concern was to "break up the deadly hold which the principle of reason has on us." What Heidegger calls releasement (*Gelassenheit*) means "to be released from the illusions of representationalism and willfulness and released to the mystery of the play, the holding sway of the withdrawal... a releasement toward things is always openness to the mystery which is what withdraws beneath, behind, beyond the grip of concepts, the range of historical meanings and conceptualities" (*Radical Hermeneutics* 204).

A body of architectural thought has been affected by an historicized account of Heidegger held largely in academia. The foundational/conservative Heideggerian influences in architectural theory which this journal seeks to displace, may be found in the work of such theorists as Christian Norberg-Schulz, Kenneth Frampton, and Alberto Pérez-Gómez, who are influenced by Heidegger. Each maintains that Heidegger offers an account of a return to an origin, and each argues for architectural practices informed by natural context,

regionality, or personal authenticity. In each case the manifold of a context becomes reified as a fixed concept which is then employed in the service of arguments for harmoniousness, semi-autarchical resistance, or poetic dwelling. The question to be put to these writings is whether or not Heidegger's "later" thinking is allowed to inform the "earlier" in such a way that reification becomes problematic.

A note on the relationship between philosophy and architectural practice: While identifying Heidegger's thought with such figures as Norberg-Schulz is easy, the *practitioners* of phenomenological positions would never identify themselves as such. Venturi has suggested that he avoids any kind of intellectualization about his practice; the emphasis is on *doing* architecture. It is perhaps significant that the breakdown between theory and practice becomes more structurally possible in the more radical practices, *e. g.* Eisenman, who is largely responsible for integrating philosophy into architecture. It comes as no surprise that the foundational theories are deemed separate by those who in practice establish a degree of presence. Thus we suggest here that the maintenance of the distinction between disciplines is sustained in conservative theory and practice, and that the element which structures these divisions is *presence*.

One cannot ignore, however, the work of Louis I. Kahn and Robert Venturi, and of (low modern) contextualists like Alvar Aalto. While the theoretical bases of these practitioners are phenomenological (descriptive), it should be noted that each assumes in his thinking a fixed (historical, cultural) horizon which provides the limits for description (the worldliness of the world). What would Venturi be without Las Vegas? Kahn without institutions? Aalto without the specificities of each context? Through the phenomenological engagement with context, each process assumes a degree of fixity about context, whether historical, cultural, natural, geographic, or vernacular. The fixing of any horizon or context is precisely what is put into question by Radical Hermeneutics. At the point at which these authors fix the context, they also fix presence, fall back onto the tradition of *logos* which seeks certainty. The question for a "Radical Hermeneutics" is this: what happens when we delimit or, rather, deconstruct the boundaries of these assumed contexts or horizons? What, then, happens to presence, the agenda attached to the description — that which is fixed?

Within the series of architectural projects in the first section, we have attempted to juxtapose projects which assume a cultural horizon with those which radicalize that context. Developing further the issues which suggest the radicalization of institutionalized, Heideggarian architectural theory will require us to address the critiques of Jacques Derrida and his strategy of deconstruction of Heidegger and the metaphysics of presence.

Derrida, Absence/Architecture

For Derrida, Heidegger's radical critique of subjectivity was not radical enough. Derrida sought to remove the "context" of meaning to the text rather than language (Being), as it was even *further away* from the subject. Derrida's line of attack is to identify the work of loaded metaphors to support a powerful structure of presuppositions. One of these was the privileging of speech over writing. It is at this crucial divergence that Derrida, Heidegger's closest ally, becomes an antagonist. Here Heidegger's "destruction of metaphysics is intended not, like Derrida's, to release a multiplicity of meaning but to call meaning back to its proper, self-identical source [Being]" (*Deconstruction* 70). Whereas Heidegger calls presence into question, Derrida seeks to erase presence altogether. Writing destroys self-presence. "It obtrudes an alien, depersonalized medium, a deceiving shadow which falls between intent and meaning, between utterance and understanding. It occupies a promiscuous public realm where authority is sacrificed to the vagaries and whims of

textual 'dissmenination' " (28). Jeffrey Kipnis has pointed out that when Heidegger says *nothing*, he really thinks he is talking about nothing. Derrida believes that nothing as such cannot be grasped *as language*. Instead a much more thorough strategy involving a condition of textuality is needed:

It is because of différance *that the movement of signification is possible only if each so-called "present" element, each element appearing on the scene of presence, is related to something other than itself, thereby keeping within itself the mark of the past element, and already letting itself be vitiated by the mark of its relation to the future element, this trace being related no less to what is called the future than to what is called the past, and constituting what is called the present by means of this very relation to what it is not: what it absolutely is not, not even a past or a future as a modified present. An interval* [intervalle] *must separate the present from what it is not in order for the present to be itself, but this interval that constitutes it as present must, by the same token* [du même coup], *divide the present in and of itself, thereby also dividing, alone with the present, everything that is thought on the basis of the present, that is, in our metaphysical language, every being, and singular substance or the subject. In constituting itself, in dividing itself dynamically, this interval is what might be called* spacing [espacement], *the becoming-space of time or the becoming-time of space* (temporization). *And it is this constitution of the present, as an "originary" and irreducibly non-simple (and therefore,* stricto sensu, *nonoriginary) synthesis of marks, or traces of retentions and protentions (to reproduce analogically and provisionally a phenomenological and transcendental language that soon will reveal itself to be inadequate), that I propose to call archi-writing* [archi-écriture] *or archi-trace* [archi-trace]. *Which (is) (simultaneously) spacing (and) temporization* (Margins of Philosophy 13;13-14).

[W]riting is no longer only the worldly and mnemotechnical aid to a truth whose own being-sense would dispense with all writing-down. The possibility or necessity of being incarnated in a graphic sign is no longer simply extrinsic and factual in comparison with ideal Objectivity: it is the sine qua non *condition of Objectivity's internal completion. ...the act of writing is the highest possibility of all "constitution"* (Edmund Husserl's "The Origin of Geometry": An Introduction 88).

Heidegger created the possibility for the displacement of subjectivity; Derrida further problematized that move. Questions remain as to whether he went too far, or not far enough. What we may notice from this debate, however, is the proximity of Heidegger to Derrida. Attention to deconstruction too often overshadows the significance of Heidegger's work toward deconstruction. Heidegger was able to achieve a degree of displacement from metaphysical operations to Being-in-the-world (*Dasein*). This move entirely changed the context of the subject as it is understood in Western culture. Derrida made that shift a policy.

What is important here is the shift which took place *before* the practices of deconstruction, this is perhaps one explanation for the difficulty of a Hegelian context in accepting Derrida's deconstruction, or, further, the difficult political implications of deconstruction. The focus in this project towards a Radical Hermeneutics involves, on the one hand, accepting Heidegger's critique of Hegel, and on the other hand accepting Derrida's critique of Heidegger, and further accepting the difficulty in the disparity between the radical policies of deconstruction and a so-called Hegelian cultural context.

The scene for the relationship between deconstruction and architecture has nowhere been better articulated than the 1988 exhibition, *Deconstructivist Architecture* at the Museum of Modern Art in New York City. According to its proposal, brilliantly posited by Mark Wigley, it sought to comment on the status of the theory of the object of architecture, and the capacity of built form to elicit that which has been repressed in the conservative tradition of architecture. This exhibition and its remarkably subtle theoretical content constitute an explanation for

the two questions at the beginning of this text. Wigley comes to deconstruction *through* Heidegger and along the way embraces its critique of Heidegger and Derrida's reliance on Heidegger's precedents. While no particular work in the exhibit illustrates precisely what Wigley has in mind, one must come to terms with the fact that he is discussing our relationship with architecture as a condition of habitation. In the second section of Wigley's preface for this journal (see above 95) he describes the problematics of presence in architecture and continues his challenge to post-structuralist philosophy and to Derrida to acknowledge the relevance of architecture to that discourse. Indeed, the very same issue of presence in this journal and in Wigley's exhibition (and article) seems to prevent entry to the Heideggarian/Derridean discourse which informs deconstructivist architecture. Responses to the exhibit, to this book or to the discourses that do not consider that assumptions operate within any response may be due to an inadequacy in the response; that inadequacy is presence.

Another theorist equally significant in the appraisal and manifestation of post-structuralist thought in architecture is Jeffrey Kipnis. While Kipnis's approach to deconstruction is Freudian, Nietzschean, his theory of Objectology and his continued private debate with Jacques Derrida, at once parallel to and in conflict with Derrida's Grammatology, remains one of the most intriguing discourses in the con-text of deconstructivist architecture. In the wake of both Jeffrey Kipnis and Mark Wigley the con-text of Radical Hermeneutics is to be developed — and then erased, if only to contribute to the play of issues which deconstructivist architecture sets free.

Wigley and Kipnis both are critical of the degree of presence of the author in architectural design. A key distinction is in the manner in which each believes the authority of the author to be undermined. This subversive value brings about a more open and mortally profound quality. Wigley believes we already always inhabit the mechanism of a cultural *context* in which lie the possibilities for disruption, and Kipnis argues that it is the *object* which defines us and which therefore has the capacity to elicit a Nietzschean brand of anxiety, if it is an object which defies repressive standards of convention.

While it should remain problematic to simplify these complex (and developing) discourses, this general distinction is useful to negotiate an argument for a Radical Hermeneutics. The key figure is Hegel, whom Kipnis revives and Wigley has overcome. Hegel is useful as a characterization of the context which influences all we do. While Wigley comes through that context and overcomes it, Kipnis stands outside of it and confronts it. Both are limited by the manners in which they relate to the Hegelian context. This is in no way a criticism of either of these discourses, but merely a comment on the kinds of limitations which might exist if such a context does restrict radicalizations. Radical Hermeneutics, then, seeks to deconstruct the context, that which limits, which establishes some tie or relation to shape, in some way, any discourse. An example of the delimitation of context may be seen in the difference between the work of Venturi (see above 35) and that of Jesse Reiser and Nanako Umemoto (see above 50). The latter do not assume the cultural horizon which informs Venturi's work, but constitute the horizon only as a *play* of elements which in turn do not *symbolize.*

Radical Hermeneutics

Contemporary developments in "continental" philosophy have further interrogated the differences between hermeneutics and deconstruction. The significance of non-foundational thinking for architecture is problematic and is the object of this project. Non-foundational philosophy, of which Heidegger is a central figure, continues to develop (see above 63, Don Ihde) and plays an important role in the relationship between phenomenological and other critical practices (particularly of Foucault). While these philosophical enterprises remain within the discipline of philosophy while commenting on the status of scientific, ethical, and political thought, they do not always maintain rigid distinctions between disciplines and often offer philosophical comment on art and architecture (see above 68, Diane Michelfelder). Indeed, Heidegger has played a major role in rearranging Western perception about the relationship between art and truth. Heidegger is the ambiguous figure in the transition between Husserl and Derrida. Whereas Husserl was interested in using phenomenology to establish foundations (for science) and Derrida endlessly disrupts anything which seeks to become established, the Heidegger of Radical Hermeneu-

tics suggests a poetic thinking which "achieves a relationship with the world which is more simple and primordial than reason: ...it is so deeply tuned to things that the need for reasons never arises" (*Radical Hermeneutics* 224).

Hermeneutics pursues problematics of the interpretation of past epochs, texts, and cultures in the shift from objective understanding to interpretation, which is a product of one's context of culture and history. Instead of the traditional attitude which posits an objective observer of history, hermeneutics places us in a dialogue with history, allows for a conversation. For Heidegger, hermeneutics was a later development of his thinking, carried forth by his former student, Hans-Georg Gadamer. Gadamer has contributed to the development of Heidegger's philosophical positions, but has rendered this development more conservatively than Heidegger might have. A discussion of these differences in the treatment of hermeneutics may illuminate that enigma in Heidegger which suggests radicalization. There are really three Heideggers: Gadamer, Heidegger, and Derrida. Gadamer's position seems to rely on the truth of cultural-historical horizons; Heidegger subverts presence, and thus his work is an effort to remain open; Derrida continues to overcome the metaphysics of presence, thus radicalizing Heidegger's project. The hermeneutics of Gadamer inform the conservative Heideggarian architectural theorists. Whereas deconstruction is celebrated for overcoming the "failure" of Heidegger to break away from presence, one may argue that "Derrida does not undo hermeneutics, but releases its more radical tendencies" (5).

The notion of horizon arises from the belief in the possibility of an historical subject, and originates in us. Hermeneutics is "admission to the sphere of the two-fold (the dif-fering which opens up the difference), the opening up of the clearing in which things come to presence" (105). Heidegger gave up the word Being and even Hermeneutics in the effort to keep language from turning words into objects. He was not interested in the adequacy of words — their success — but in "their vigilance about their own inadequacy," (107).

There is a distinction in architecture between conservative Heideggerian translations and

that of the deconstructivists: The conservators reify a horizon which brings forth the objects of their understanding, while in the form of theories are attached to some agenda (political, moral, aesthetic). The practitioners similarly effect a reification of architectural form, taking as a given the cultural horizon which shapes the understanding of form. This operation, true in its subjective form, retains qualities of "willfulness" (subjective projection) as opposed to what Heidegger calls "thinking" (meditative thought). The theoreticians Norberg-Schulz, Frampton, and Pérez-Gómez assume Heidegger's phenomenological horizon (reduction) as a means to control and define a particular view of what our culture should be. Similarly the deconstructors must always rely on the cultural horizon, playing the role of the parasite, inhabiting the dominant rational texts (which are constructs and thus an illusion of the inevitable abyss). Deconstruction is, then, a response to the context and exists because of it: Eisenman has called deconstruction an ethical response. Yet, to describe deconstruction as merely the *policy* of what Heidegger deems *thematic*, is to trivialize. Deconstruction is *absolutist*, policy remains fixed, and that is precisely what Derrida has criticized Plato for. Indeed, Kipnis will quickly admit that he is an absolutist. A suggestion follows: to go back to Heidegger and find a way to respond to these limitations: to reread the conservatively rendered Heidegger to "deconstruct" the dichotomy between the conservative and radical architectural translations.

If it is possible to "radicalize Heidegger," and if deconstruction's subversive limitations are due to its relation to a describable cultural context (horizon), then it may be possible to deconstruct the two questions stated at the beginning. Philosopher John Caputo's recent work *Radical Hermeneutics* is an attempt to "restore life to its original difficulty" which involves going back to Heidegger's self critique. This operation allows the connection between Heidegger and Derrida to facilitate the collapse of distinctions which limit each discourse:

Deconstructive criticism is for me the gateway through which radical hermeneutics must pass. I am interested in breaking the spell of metaphysics where metaphysics means the attempt to arrest the play

and to flood us with reassurances. I am interested in letting the play play play itself out. But I contend — and this goes to the heart of what I mean by radical hermeneutics — that after tracing out this deconstructive course, after allowing the disseminating drift its full play, we are in an odd way led back to ourselves, not in a moment of recovery and self-presence but in a deeper, less innocent way. Radical hermeneutics makes a pass at formulating what the French call la condition humaine, *the human situation. I do not mean by this to incite another wave of the "humanism" which deconstruction has tried to put down but to evoke the notion of "facing up" to the limits of our situation, to the illusions of which we are capable, to the original difficulty of our lives. And I call this "hermeneutics" just because I think there is something liberating about all this, not dehumanizing (97).*

Notes

Caputo, John D., *Radical Hermeneutics* (Bloomington & Indianapolis: Indiana University Press, 1987).

Derrida, Jacques, *Edmund Husserl's "Origin of Geometry": An Introduction,* trans. John P. Leavy, David B. Allison (ed.), Nicolas Hays, (New York: Stony Brook, 1978).

Derrida, Jacques, *Margins of Philosophy,* trans. A. Bass (Chicago: University of Chicago Press, 1982).

Heidegger, Martin, *On The Way To Language* (New York: Harper & Row, 1971).

Heidegger, Martin, *What Is A Thing?* (Indiana: Regnery/ Gateway, 1967).

Norris, Christopher, *Deconstruction: Theory and Practice* (New York: Methuen, 1982).

Sallis, John, *Delimitations* (Bloomington & Indianapolis: Indiana University Press, 1986).

Taylor, Mark C., *Altarity* (Chicago: University of Chicago Press, 1987).

Wigley, Mark A., *Jacques Derrida and Architecture: The Deconstructive Possibilities of Architectural Discourse* (Doctoral dissertation for the University of Auckland, 1986).

The Architecture of Exhaustion

Douglas Darden

Subdivisions, Opus 10, 1985.

By this time, the pig that had been killed was cleaned and the entrails taken out. These happened to have a considerable share of those convulsive motions which often appear in different parts after an animal is killed; and this was considered by the spectators as a very favorable omen to the expedition, in account of which the sacrifices had been offered.

After being exposed for some time, that those who chose might examine their appearances, the entrails were carried to the priests and laid down before them. While one of their number prayed, another inspected the entrails more narrowly and kept turning them gently with a stick. When they had been sufficiently examined, they were thrown into the fire and left to consume.

> Captain James Cook, *Account of the
> Ceremonies of the Great Morai, Tahiti*
> Tuesday, September 2, 1777

Behind the sublime realization of value, there lies something else. Something else speaks, something irreducible that can take the form of violent destruction, but most frequently assumes the cloaked form of deficit, of the exhaustion and refusal of cathexis, of resistance to satisfaction and refusal of fulfillment.

> Jean Baudrillard, *For a Critique of the Political Economy of the Sign*

Any genuine exploration of architecture is a delving into the origins of human thought and into our deepest conceptions of order and disorder. Architecture is an object of aspiration and of wishes fulfilled, an activity that defines the boundary between the world we believe is within our control and the larger inconclusive domain of human desire.

At its heart, architecture is a testament to a particular social and political reality. In contemporary culture architecture is an object of desire caught in the rebounding, self-devouring, and self-renewing forces of production and consumption. Routed along an intricate and illusive network of acquisition, simulation, and assimilation, the cultural organs of production are increasingly difficult to distinguish from those of elimination. Waste and sustenance mingle as one.

In this context current tendencies in architecture demonstrate a provisional delight with the disorder and debris of our civilization, evinced in architectural expression by fragmentary, discontinuous, and dislocated forms; by colliding, non-Cartesian geometries; and by purposefully inconclusive, non-synthetic spatial configurations.

Postwar architects embody in their work a profound ideological aversion to synthetic formal and spatial resolution. Behind this aversion is the revelation of an especial, timely logic. It is "the logic of assassination": a logic which reveals an investment not only in the progressive development of human civilization and in the creation of forms, but in our concomitant powers for self-negation and global destruction. Such a logic reveals the end of the world no longer as dramatic, apocalyptic (the Millennium)[1]; instead, it releases a paradoxical ecstasy of annihilation. So much is destruction a part of our lives that in our need to cope with it we have found in it a new form of aesthetic pleasure: not the momentary insight that allows us to recall the "humane" history we believe once existed, nor the "breakthrough" to a new revolutionary reality (such as envisioned by modernism), but the uncovering of a substratum of fears and desires made flesh in the moment of an imagined annihilation.[2] In this paradoxical fashion, we manifest our deepest ambivalences towards ourselves as masters of our own age. The architecture thus produced is the *architecture of exhaustion* and is most clearly evident in projects by Daniel Libeskind, Coop Himmelblau, Bernard Tschumi, Morphosis, OMA, Frank Gehry, and the recent work of Peter Eisenman. Each has an authenticity and ingenuity, yet together they form a predominating body of intentions. Embedded in a majority of their work is a complex and deeply ambiguous attraction/repulsion for the very forces within our culture that establish and valorize architectural meaning. These concentric and overlapping tendencies can be characterized in five ways.

The Totalized Aesthetic

Hermeneutically we can examine several Western poets and novelists from the 19th century whose work demonstrates impulses and poetic intentions parallel to those found in the aforementioned architects. One may cite the French poets Rimbaud and Baudelaire and the American writers Poe and Melville. These authors all sought a power of expression in their work which would equal the force of their cultures' upheavals and of its new potentials with the rise of industrialism.

Before the 20th century's phenomenon of the *avant garde*, these authors realized a level of desire in their work and in their aesthetic agendas which offered a radical sovereignty of expression in their belief that art could summarily reflect culture. Their work reigned through a totalized aesthetic that tied together impulses of life-affirming creation and the transgressive urges of self-imposed annihilation to transcend acceptable canons of the art forms of that time.

This aesthetic established for the French "decadent" poets a landscape where "exhaustive pleasure choked and reeled into bliss." Baudelaire's *Les Fleurs du Mal*, for example, indulged him in "A nightmare without cease/ [where] You dream of poison to bring peace,/ And love cold steel and powder well."[3] A deep ambivalence towards the politics of power brought forth an aesthetic in which pleasure and pain deeply overlapped.

Poe and Melville in America each formed a dialectical aesthetic through which each voiced his feelings of ambivalence towards accelerating Western industrialism. Melville confessed in letters to Hawthorne regarding his *Moby Dick*, "I have written a wicked book, and feel spotless as the lamb." Melville cloaked the "wickedness" of *Moby Dick* in his unassuming commentary on the whaling industry. Yet behind this seemingly placid account of facts, Melville sought the epic of an enlarged aesthetic that asserted critical moral value. The Melvillean aesthetic was an attempt to articulate a dialectic of construction and demolition, between the promising and progressive events in burgeoning America, and the fears of apocalyptic annihilation.

The *architecture of exhaustion* offers a similar aesthetic agenda. Beneath its formal strategies is an architecture which does not attempt to conceal the conflicts out of which forms arise in our culture. The architecture demonstrates a tense, provisional and vulnerable relationship between architecture and the creation of meaning. The architects' stance is both critical and auto-critical.

This stance does not reconcile appearances, but gives legibility to the complex net of realities that envelop our age. The architecture gives shape to the world to which we ascribe "order" and yet which we experience as a maelstrom of presences and absences. Its achievement reconquers three-dimensional form as a process of living — and of dying — matter, a corporeal understanding of the density of life itself, of the perpetuity of order and its random disintegration. This process involves our logocentric conceptions of order and embraces areas that we deem as "Other." Current tendencies in this theoretical architecture cleave open neglected areas which lie between our conceptions of things to view what the Chinese thinker Lao Tzu called "authentic chaos."

The fascination with annihilation has been pointed out by Tschumi as a reflection of the 20th century. Citing George Bataille's *Death and Sensuality*, Tschumi uncovers the necrophilic compulsions behind the great white walls of Modernism, "where all the rotting flesh has finally disappeared from the royal corpse, when nothing is left of the remains but a hard, clean, incorruptible skeleton."[4]

Combining Bataille's preoccupation with the corpse, Tschumi's work pulls us through a series of deconstructive and transformative operations on proto-modern architectural elements. Tschumi's architectural episodes (for example *La Villette*) are infinitely variable and inconclusive. His projects denote the organized construction of a disaster and its aftermath. Such paradoxical organization, where the cessation of one life spawns the activity of another, evokes the "nausea of putrescence," the anticipation of a sickening triumph of annihilation exceeding the "death of history" touted by the early Futurists, and ending belief in progress. "Finality" itself is exhausted as the potentially explosive heterogeneity of his overlapping classical and free-plan systems and becomes a jammed infinity of debris and de-dramatized purposes. Tschumi's operations reveal the entropic efforts of all humankind.

Subdivisions, Opus 12, 1985.

These impulses are reflected in the recent "archaeological" *tours de force* of Peter Eisenman and in the domestic assemblages of Frank Gehry. In the works of both architects is an impulse to break through the opaque fabric of conventional architecture and destroy its symbolic order with a barrage of syntactical forms. The architects destructure the impulse of the conventional architect to create synthetic and stable signifying order. Spatial arrangements are new, yet forms are "given." This predilection for arrangement of what has been, released the architect from the *angst* of what might be. Closure is withheld; there can be no "end."

In this spirit the architecture acknowledges that those things in ourselves which repel violently, should not be swept under a positive rug, but embraced as part of ourselves. Rather than falling toward the nihilism that results from the impossibility of Faust's ambition, the architecture shapes despair. It plays out the merits of modern visions of dissipation in lieu of self-censoring disdain.

This willingness to engulf the terror of Faustian impossibilities by a totalized aesthetic empowers postwar architecture with an affirmative dimension.

The machinations of culture that construct and destroy architectural form and its meaning are united and reenacted in one consummate eruption. Like the genuine tragedy and the very nature of the organic cell, the *architecture of exhaustion* is the manifestation of the fullness of that "pushing, self-protective and self-destructive fever of impulses we refuse to admit to ourselves or to our friends,"[5] but which nonetheless exists.

The Exhilaration of Annihilation

The *architecture of exhaustion* shows its strength and its ability to signify strength through continually spending and endangering itself; that is, by signifying weakness. This defines and redefines the parameters of architecture itself: The architecture is possible only when there is a dance with its own death. Like the frenzied Dionysian dance, the different geometries, structures, spatial organizations, and syntactical forms operate as subversive yet exuberant tactics against the works themselves.

Eisenman has stated that the ground for authenticity in architecture is possible only when we see architecture as "the last repository of the real through its embodiment of violence and pain."[6] Thus he articulates a recovering somatic impulse latent in postwar architecture, telling us that the human being stands in space with a need for understanding his place, to understand his sensations and his distance from the idealized tissue we create to protect ourselves from the circumstantial world. For this understanding to occur through architecture, we must account for our pain and our final death through the syntax of architectural form itself. The production of architectural form must be, in part, self-negating.

While destruction is valorized in the *architecture of exhaustion* through its representation in the syntactical arrangement of partial and obscured forms, we see a residual yet tenacious longing for the power of architecture to symbolize life as rational form. Historically, this tendency was made material in temples and other edifices of ritual. By replacing such time-honored positivist creations with works which make equivalences to destruction, contemporary theoretical architecture (re)affirms the position of architecture from the pre-modern hierarchies of culture to articulate the value of human life in a context of limited power and unachievable desire.

The *architecture of exhaustion* evinces the power to signify life by framing a dialogue with its death. The architecture makes a suggestive picture of potential growth, allowing us to dream a myth of circulating energy and of primary experience. The death of architecture is conceived not as a dialectical opposite to their work, but as a phenomenon which is entwined in its very roots. The assimilation of death is an affirmation that feeds on its own negation, on its exhaustion. This assimilation, used as a weapon, signifies power, and, paradoxically, creation itself.[7]

"To represent" is to form an equivalent of some aspect of our experience. The *architecture of exhaustion* represents the violence of life. Such violence approaches negation as an irreducibly authentic ground for architectural expression. But in Bataille's words, "If a man begins to follow a violent impulse, his expression of it signifies that he is no longer following it for at least the duration of its expression. Expression requires the substitution of an external figurative sign for passion itself. He who expresses himself must therefore pass from the burning sphere of passion to the relatively cold and torpid sphere of signs. When confronting that expression, we must then always ask whether the subject is not headed for a deep sleep."[8] Such a sleep is the legitimate domain for the architectural expression of our time.

One must question the intention to see destruction as a uniquely authentic ground for architecture. Does the representation of violence and pain not fall prey, as Bataille warns, to the same devaluation of sign-making that eventually accompanies all forms of representation? Is the representation of violence any less resistant to co-option and simulation than any other human action? We have only to see a television commercial advertising a home alarm system with the image of the Hiroshima bomb to know that it is not. Etymologically "representation" means the presentation of what already has taken place.[9] While in our post-industrial age willful annihilation may be our single most intense form of action and control, representing such action may undermine the last remnant of power asserted as an activity of cultural production and expression.

The Criticism of Instrumental Reason

In the midst of forbidden territory, the architecture of exhaustion makes a critique of the pious grounds of empirical science and causality. No one system, form, geometry, or spatial organization is asserted as an absolute. Instead of privileging any particular organization of space, the architecture is conceived by simultaneously employing all systems and "suspending judgment" of them. It is carried out under protest against rationality, and in turn, it is replete with empirical gaps, false starts, and partly obscured

Subdivisions, Opus 1, 1985.

conceptions; that is, with conscious intellectual doubt. By implication, the tectonic realization of such doubt throws a critical shadow over our largest cultural works and the epistemology that engendered them. The greatest error we could make would be to believe that the architect does not err.

More closely connected than Einstein's theories to the modern *avant garde*, the investigation by postwar theoretical architecture parallels principles in the theories of probability and uncertainty in quantum mechanics by scientists such as Heisenberg and Bohr. Without Platonic ideation or clear distinctions between subject and object, the *architecture of exhaustion* reflects the volatile and wavering epistemology of molecular arrangement and rearrangement described in quantum mechanics: Neither form nor form-giver acts any longer as substance; each must "drift" as possibility, as emanation, always with the potential to become something else. This principle of the "drift" is inherent in disparate and incomplete geometries and destroys not only the classical notion of causality within metaphysics, but the physics of

form itself. The fragmented geometries evince a dematerialization of matter that establishes "possibility" and allows only a provisional commerce between idea and form; each suffers the improprieties of the other: "The ultimate constituents of the world... will be disconnected. We can note of them only their mutual occurrence or nonoccurrence, as the case may be."[10]

The *architecture of exhaustion* exposes not only a radical epistemological skepticism, but the proximity of a state

where nothing is fixed and where we can neither touch bottom nor support ourselves on the surface; filled with conditional meanings, architecture signifies chaos. These characteristics, once made over into architectural events, evince at once an "absolute disdain of the absolute" and the epistemological emptiness that lies before our self-assured structures of thought.

Beyond this skepticism towards science is the acknowledgement of the limits of our technological civilization, an attitude strikingly akin to Hugh Ferriss's admonition in the 1930s that the "age of science" is also "an age of universally recognized danger."[11] In this sense, Ferriss's representations in *The Power in Buildings* reframe industrial power as an emblem of an awe-inspiring, only partly controlled endeavor; Ferriss's architectural world is situated not only in the timeless relationships of masses in tension and compression, but on a precarious condition of vertigo. At the base of Ferriss's works we can sense the archaic idea of the Tower of Babel: the catastrophe as a subversive potential, an activating moment that changes all history.

The Utility of Desire

As defined by Edmund Burke, the experience of the sublime carries, on the one hand, a sense of awe, and on the other, fear and dread. To experience both, the individual self must be annihilated before the spectacle of nature's indifference.[12] Assimilated into the *architecture of exhaustion* through the representation of annihilation, are a similar intention and indifference, fostered by muting the self-legitimizing concern within architecture for what is commonly called "function," or more precisely, for corporeal comfort and accommodation. This disregard is, *prima facie*, a negation of our physical selves. It is also the reinternalization of the indifferent yet awesome face projected onto nature in the 19th century and throughout our entire history. Turned back on itself, the architecture of exhaustion reconstitutes nature as an immense practice of constructive disregard: "The passions which belong to self-preservation [and the sublime] turn on pain and danger; they are painful when we have an idea of pain and danger, without being actually in such circumstances."[13]

In the elaboration of the sublime through the representation of pain and danger, the *architecture of exhaustion* emerges to enhance and counterpoise fact. By situating itself beyond the pleasure of utility, it registers the utility of desire. "Desire" is not form, but a procedure, a process.[14] Desire, rather than its accommodation, represents an intention to signify life on a perilous edge, prompting us to peer into the pumping chambers of the chest and perceive the virtue of confronting our world as an exceptional yet exhilarating ordeal, by which we make our way through our lives and possibly to an "other" world.

As Mircea Eliade mentions, once we suspend the primacy of utility, we can experience a high level of imaginative life. For all of its veracity, this life is strikingly (and ironically) similar to the world we see in fairy tales. In fairy tales evil is as omnipresent as good.[15] While there are usually parental figures who help lead the innocent child out of terror, monstrous beings compete for the child's attention. The fairy tale stirs up the paradoxes that surround the child's life, in turn helping the child to acquire a sense of the fabulous difficulty of moral and mortal life.

In contemporary theoretical architecture the duality of comfort and peril becomes the situation in which, in Rilke's words, "Every angel is terrifying."[16] The duality is apprehended first through the expectations of the architectural commodity, and then as one is pitted against the other. Comfort is appreciated only insofar as the architecture objectifies the fear that sits in our stomachs and prompts us to struggle for shelter. While the iteration of this struggle may be of little consolation to the world-weary, it offers a recognition of life's equilibrium over the nothingness from which the most unassuming of our creations spring.

Obscurity

The final tendency of the *architecture of exhaustion* is the potential to anticipate and incorporate its foreseen death by its elaboration of an arcane mask which is a mockery of instrumental reason. As mockery approaches madness, the mask, like those of the Greek tragedians, creates a "panic shudder of meaning."[17] The intentions of the mask of contemporary theoretical architecture are at once profound and puerile: They are the mark of what Paolo Portoghesi called the "jealous autonomy of the new" and of what Freud called the "mysterious masochistic trends of the ego."[18] These desires replicate the principle Freud believed was inherent in all organic life:

[T]o restore an earlier state of things... to move towards the inertia of foetal life as an expression of the conservative nature of living substance, the instinct to return to an inanimate state independent of the pleasure principle, yet in fact in league with it.[19]

This principle, the death wish, exists beyond the pleasure principle and reasserts an understanding of the potential place of the concepts of origin and order in our world. The death wish is itself the product of anxiety, and has been experienced (in early modernism) as formal abstraction and eschatological liberation. Postwar architecture executes a balancing act which locates the apocalyptic consciousness between moralizing discourse and detached aestheticization.[20] This provisional activity acknowledges humans as discontinuous beings in a world of larger continuity.

While trying to maintain our separate existence, death — or at least the contemplation of death — links us to continuity and origin. The attention to death links us to the transcendent power of the sublime, to one primal foundation of origin and end.

Subdivisions, Opus 4, 1985.

To approach an origin is to be filled with terror; yet as origin is truly outside the realm of our signification, to approach origin necessitates transcendence. Transcendence may involve going beyond the narrow logocentric concepts of order, which in their blunt utility construe perpetually the world at large. For transcendence, the *architecture of exhaustion* adopts a posture of obscurity, the necessary masking of the processes which shear away the exigencies of the present and the self. These exigencies (manifest throughout history in the panoply of architectural styles) are displaced in the *architecture of exhaustion.* Beyond this displacement, the willing movement of architecture towards obscurity is reminiscent of the "strategist of exhaustion," James Joyce. With Joyce we can understand the most generous and diabolical virtues of the *architecture of exhaustion.*

Joyce's well-known dictum to the artist was to practice silence, cunning, and exile. This lucid prejudice is reflected in contemporary theoretical architecture: In this material world of appearances truth is always cloaked; only the cloak *itself* is truth. Whatever is profound needs a mask. With this caveat, the *architecture of exhaustion* does not aim to represent (T)ruth, but to give meaning to the silent forces which allow us to live effectively with our own (t)ruths for our brief time.

Beyond this, when architecture concerns itself with facts of its construction as the sole source of its representation, while ignoring its fictions, the power of its expression cannot be sustained. Transgression of the "facts" of architecture is necessary because whatever "truths" exist in architecture are supported equally by its lies. Architecture must maintain illusions if it is to maintain itself. Obscurity is thus the willful character-

istic of the *architecture of exhaustion.* It induces an internal tension without finality, provisional and tenuous, cloaked in the moment, and ultimately destined to exceed our control.

In our everyday lives we may feel that we move helplessly among substitutes for substitutes, and at best architects can hope to create a cult of aesthetic ambiguity, our real death — as individuals and as a collective — remains dark, uncertain, and obscure. In an age that insists we consume, promiscuously accepting, increasing amounts of lifeless information, and in a culture which through its methods of reproduction help make our world obsolete, the *architecture of exhaustion* clarifies the nature of the authentic and the mysterious. It exhorts the possibility that life is an encounter of vital forces at a hundred points still in their fantastic and chaotic origin.

Notes

1. Klaus R. Scherpe, "Dramatization and De-dramatization of 'the End': The Apocalyptic Consciousness of Modernity and Post-Modernity," in *Cultural Critique* (Number 5, Winter 1986-87), p. 95.

2. *Ibid*, p. 126.

3. Charles Baudelaire, "Madrigal Triste," in *Les Fleurs Du Mal* (New York: New Directions,1958), p. 159.

4. Georges Bataille, *Death and Sensuality* (Salem: Ayer, 1984), p. 67.

5. Joseph Campell, *The Flight of the Gander* (New York: Regnery, 1972), p. 127.

6. Peter Eisenman, delivered in a symposium; "The Culture of Fragments," Guggenheim Museum, October 17, 1985.

7. cf. Octavio Paz, *Marcel Duchamp* (New York: Seaver, 1978), p. 79.

8. Georges Bataille, "Nietzsche's Madness," from *October 36* (Spring 1986), p. 44.

9. Roland Barthes, *The Responsibility of Forms* (New York: Hill and Wang, Farrar, Straus and Giroux, 1985), p. 228.

10. William Barrett, *The Illusion of Technique* (New York: Doubleday, 1979), p. 43.

11. Eduardo Subirats, "Architecture of Civilization: Hugh Ferriss," from *Architectures 3* (Volume 1, Number 3, Summer 1986).

12. Stephen Westfall, "Ripp's Romantic Theater," from *Art in America* (January 1986), p. 108.

13. Edmund Burke, *A Philosophical Enquiry into the Origins of Our Ideas of the Sublime and Beautiful* (Notre Dame: University of Notre Dame, 1968), p. 51.

14. Gilles Deleuze and Felix Guattari, *Kafka: Toward A Minor Literature* (Minneapolis: University of Minnesota, 1986), p. 8.

15. Bruno Bettleheim, *The Uses of Enchantment* (New York: Random House, 1977), p. 74.

16. Rainer Maria Rilke, "The Second Elegy," from *Duino Elegies*, translated by A. Poulin (Boston: Houghton Mifflin, 1955), p. 13.

17. Barthes, *op. cit.* 9, p. 28.

18. Sigmund Freud, *Beyond the Pleasure Principle* (New York: Norton, 1961), p. 8.

19. *Ibid*, p. 30.

20. Scherpe, *op. cit.* 1, p. 119.

of architecture inhabits and organizes the philosophical tradition that attempts to abandon it. This poses a certain threat to philosophy. Architectural discourse must be tamed, controlled. We're given the subordinate role of the trustee; we're told to keep our mouths shut and sell the party line; in return we get to be suspect members of the academy. We get to have the worst academic tradition of all the discourses, we get to have the sloppiest theory, a profession dedicated to mediocrity, because anything else would allow a thorough interrogation of architecture. Architectural theory is perhaps the most impoverished discourse, set up precisely to evade the interrogation of its own object.

JEFFREY: I think we should ask you for the third notion: How does architectural theory conduct its investigation of the object without being an applied philosophy?

MARK: We've developed for the purposes of this discussion a fiction of three stages of readings of Derrida. Before examining the third stage we should clarify the nature of this fiction. It appears to be a linear history of fiction. It appears to be a linear history of necessary steps in rigorous inquiry; they are actually but overlapping moments within the event of translating Derrida in architecture. They only have the appearance of an historical sequence because some are more difficult than others, and are therefore formulated more precisely later. The first stage attempts only to say what Derrida says about other discourses in architectural discourse, and that was late in coming, because we understand ourselves as secondary, we don't really think that we have anything to offer. In the second stage we started to think we had the right to interrogate the theory that we were applying, but we still felt we had to apply it once we found it. In other words, inasmuch as we could find a new idea about architecture hidden within Derrida's text, despite Derrida rather than because of him, we could apply it. It is a more sophisticated application, but an application nevertheless.

The third stage, necessarily the most difficult, is to understand to what extent certain kinds of

The Architectural Displacement of Philosophy

Mark Wigley

(continued from page 8)

architectural practice can displace philosophical practice. Inasmuch as there is some form of architectural behavior that would disrupt or deflect philosophical practice, we would have completely revised our thinking about the relationship between architecture and philosophy. We would have left behind a simplistic idea of application, because we would no longer understand philosophy to be outside and above architecture. Rather, we would understand philosophy as a certain effect of architecture. That is to say, in the production of form, there is a side-effect known as *philosophy* which operates as a constrained discourse about certain limited qualities of form, a repressive discourse made possible by enigmatic qualities of form it cannot thematize. This involves reexamining the economy of architecture with the same thoroughness applied to Derridian discourse in the previous stage. A series of experiments are being carried out, both by people who we used to think of as architectural theorists and by people we used to think of as architectural practitioners, who attempt to locate the limits of architectural discourse. Those limits are not external; it is not a matter of pushing the outside edge of the envelope by developing a radical practice, but of locating what limits inhabit the center of everyday architectural discourse, within the very banality and impoverishment of the mediocrity fetishized by that discourse.

The question is, what in those pathological repetitions of banality is potentially disruptive and can be exploited to displace the condition of all theory? At what moment in architectural discourse does architecture's relationship with other discourses become radically subversive? To be interested in this moment is not to be interested in the *application* of anything. I can only sketch several aspects of this problem today because this work is just beginning. We must behave improperly within architectural discourse in order to identify its most disruptive possibility, frightening even to those who think of themselves as concerned only with disrupting the discourse, which is organized by a contract, in blood, with the devil, presumably. And the devil is in the details; so there is

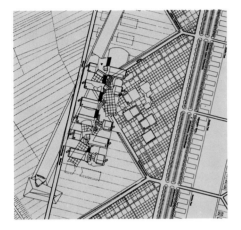

Biocenter for the University of Frankfurt. Frankfurt am Main, Federal Republic of Germany, 1987. Peter Eisenman (Site plan)

an attempt now to locate the darker side of architecture, that architecture was never supposed to have, the hidden dimension of the contract. Architecture was not meant to be contaminated by the other; such a contamination disrupts the protocol of architectural discourse, not just its internal structure nor the way it exploits external theory, but the very sense that it has an inside, that there is a discourse proper to architecture. One discourse is no longer simply divided from another by some kind of gap across which there is some kind of translation. That gap actually cuts and divides, fractures, the inside of philosophy and architecture; what is proper and what improper in each discourse is no longer clear. The difference between philosophy and architecture and therefore the problem of translation between

them does not disappear, but is relocated to a multiplicity of strategic sites within both discourses, so that it starts to operate in another way. Deconstructive theory, for example, does not exist outside of architectural discourse prior to its translation into architecture.

Philosophy is produced in its application to architecture, in that moment when philosophy appears to lower itself into architecture, when ideas are supposed to impregnate form in the traditional sense. In that moment the designer infects form with the irresistible presence of an idea, the moment of design (in the romantic view of the architect) which Plato revered as much as we do. A theoretical proposition comes into being only as a result of what appears to be its application: an important consequence of the claim that Derridean discourse is not the demolition or removal of metaphysics but an attempt to exploit and interrogate its enigmas. It comes into operation in the very moment of its breakdown, its descent. Metaphysics is not some ideal original discourse to which one either descends or aspires, but is a discourse produced in its very failure. The edifice of metaphysics is constituted in its collapse. This failure is not weakness but is the source of its strength. In a strange way, the capacity of metaphysics to define and domesticate the *other* is precisely authorized and given power by the extent to which the other always escapes and subverts domestic enclosure.

Deconstruction is therefore produced by its architectural translation. Derrida's work, in that sense, is not now being applied to architecture late, after all the other disciplines, Derridean discourse is only now for the first time being *produced* through its reading of architecture. This moment of production, of reproduction, is marked by Derrida's recent claim that the stakes of deconstruction are highest in architecture. But the fate of deconstruction in, or as, architecture is unclear. Architecture poses a threat to deconstruction: All its claims about the condition of various texts are vulnerable to architectural thinking. It is unclear whether they will survive.

To summarize: Because we understand better the contracts organizing architectural and philosophical discourse, we understand what kinds of disruptions of cultural discourse might be effected. We know quite precisely how the geometry will be displaced. Theory is no longer outside and above practice. Theory becomes a possibility constructed within a certain understanding of architecture. Consequently, we start to think of Derrida as an architectural construction. So we have moved from talking about what a deconstructive architecture might be to the idea that architecture produces deconstruction.

This establishes the scene for the most pressing question. If architecture produces deconstruction, in what way does it exceed that production? What kind of objects can deflect post-structuralist theory? That theory is no more than a specific theory of discourse. We are interested now in that aspect of architectural discourse which redefines completely the possibilities of discourse in general beyond the revision effected by post-structuralist theory.

So the issue is how a certain object, or displacement of the object, can deflect post-structuralist discourse. Exploiting certain capacities to disrupt philosophical discourse, will make the architectural object potentially parasitical on the culture which previously it could only support and sustain as foundational. Not that architecture is transformed: Perhaps it was always operating this way, always subversive, necessary to culture for precisely this subversion which culture could not represent as such, particularly in domains which are designated by culture as storehouses of cultural values. Of course, when one pursues such an interrogation of the object one discovers that it does not simply occupy the space allocated to it by culture. Which is to say, it is not simply an object but a complex intersection of heterogeneous systems of representation.

JEFFREY: You have spoken of the catastrophic effects of architecture for deconstruction, in terms of the figure of the contract. This leaves us with a problem: you construct a situation where we have a choice, and I think you have to discuss for us now motive for the choice.

MARK: It is appropriate for you to talk about motives, because the history I outlined was set up that way; but it should be understood that history is always strategic, always a construct to activate a specific discourse, which in turn may undermine that very history. So the question of motive needs to be rethought and deconstruction is no more than such a rethinking. It radically undermines the traditional teleology from motive to objects, intentions as authority over objects. No longer does the subject simply make choices about the world: The subject and the object become side effects of a discourse that exceeds them. In this way deconstruction thematizes the dilemmas of intentionality, but it is not simply exempt from those dilemmas. The domain of choice, or more precisely, of the prohibition of choice, is the political. The question of deconstruction and architecture is, of course, primarily political. The motive is political. But its impact cannot be registered within the traditional domain of "politics." The motive for reading Derrida otherwise is to displace radically the political condition of architecture. But this displacement cannot be understood as radical within traditional discourse.

JEFFREY: So it will be a catastrophic effect, that when propagated by the object, will not be felt as a catastrophe, since the object itself will have changed the terms of the definition?

MARK: Precisely. As I said before, the reading is undermined by the objects which it makes available. I used a language of catastrophe, the familiar rhetoric of crisis, but of course exactly what produces such a crisis is that the objects produced are not new. None of the qualities that I have described are radical in the sense of Modern. On the contrary, what is most disquieting is that these are the most ordinary objects. Inasmuch as they are everyday, banal objects, their displacement initiates a catastrophe for theory. Theory preserves the claim that objects stand up and enclose and in so doing sustain the infrastructure of hierarchical cul-

tural values. This view of the object is incorporated in the repressive mechanisms by which our culture separates itself from what it defines as the other and then attempts to place the other within a domestic enclosure in order to tame it. Consequently, it would be catastrophic for the culture if familiar everyday objects don't support those divisions but completely undermine them. But this will never be experienced as catastrophic. It would not be a catastrophe for either the architect or the theorist or for philosophers or for the public that might use these objects. We are talking here about buildings, regular buildings.

It seems to me that one of the ways in which architects have resisted the claim that architecture might be interesting is precisely by making what appear to be interesting buildings. We have gone to some length to say that the way architecture becomes interesting is a matter of representation. But precisely what is most interesting about the architectural object is the extent to which it disturbs the status of representation. We have fended off trouble, blurred the scent for those who would like to find the most disruptive capacities of architecture, by representing disruption architecturally. The representation of disruption in architecture has always been ornamental; anything which deviates from assumptions about the formal purity of structure is tolerated only insofar as it is ornamental. Ornament is understood as the only site of danger. Architects have veiled the most dangerous capacity of architecture by representing danger ornamentally. In other words, they have attached to the outside of a form simulations of the potential nightmares of that form in order to stop anybody from understanding the extent to which that form was in itself always already slippery, uncanny, nightmarish, grotesque, haunted.

In recent years, strong projects appeared to resist this tradition of decorative danger by launching an attack on structure. But they merely transformed the representation of danger into the representation of deconstruction. There is a need to move beyond the representation of deconstruction,

Biocenter
(Exploded axonometric)

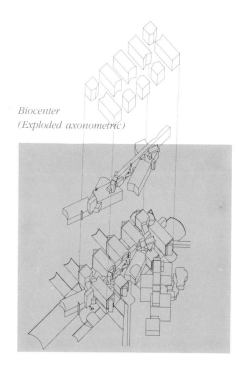

whether it be in the gross form of work which destroyed structures by external violence, or the sophisticated form of work which diffused structures into traces. These two kinds of practice, promoted within the discourse as deconstructive, have given way to another generation of work which doesn't deal with the dissimulation or demolition of the object but rather stages a more literal encounter with an object, subverting rather than abandoning traditional relationships between structure and ornament. Rather than representing that subversion on the outside of a regular structure, they make that representation part of the structure itself. In so doing, they transform the status of representation, and therefore the status of the object. But the limits of these projects have to be ob-

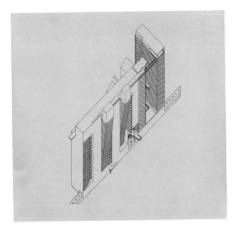

Apartment Building and Observation Tower.
Rotterdam, Holland, 1982.
Rem Koolhaas

served. The projects make the dilemmas of pure form poetic, and so remain within a romantic tradition. In that sense we are still talking about architecture representing its most dangerous capacities. These practices are still too safe. They are somewhat too frenetic, too desperate to tell us about disruption rather than to effect the disruptions. My interest is in an even more literal encounter with the architectural object, a more disruptive practice, but of course the words "object" and "practice" would no longer be adequate here.

Clearly, these three kinds of "practice" are aligned with the three moments of reading deconstruction I discussed earlier. In this slow process the architectural discourse takes its own object seriously, accepts its

own authority, accepts the constitutional status of architectural objects at the cultural level, before putting itself on the couch and analyzing its pathological symptoms in order to identify its repressed condition.

This self-analysis begins with a radical displacement of the concept of design that is central to that repression. Such a displacement necessarily takes us into the dangerous territory of the banal. The banal object is one whose maneuvers are so subtle that it appears to be making almost no moves at all. The presence of the designer is no longer self-evident. But it is a mistake to understand a banal object as one in which design has been simply erased. Rather, it is an object in which design has been made problematic. Design is not problematized by simply removing it and promoting the object as the necessary result of certain economic mechanisms. It must slide dangerously between the presence and absence of design such that those aspects of the objects which figure themselves as design disarm the designer.

Perhaps this can be understood in terms of an architecture which slides between the work of Rem Koolhaas and John Hejduk. On the one hand Koolhaas exploits that moment of the modern movement which deals with the ready-made non-designed object: the rhetoric of mass production and mass culture, but turns that moment on itself by treating the modern movement as itself a ready-made discursive practice. On the other hand, Hejduk employs the most straightforward articulation of fundamental architectural moves in a way that proves profoundly disruptive and disturbing. Both are profoundly reductive. Each reduces, dilutes, the presence of the designer. But in the end each restores that figure. Koolhaas erases himself only to replace himself with one of the canonic designers of the modern movement. Hejduk supplements his exemplary reductions with additions which refer to his strategic presence as a privileged author, whether it be by the location of poetic texts along side or the inscription of personal references within the structure of the work itself. The signature of the designer is

erased from the object only to be restored in another language.

Both practices take us close to the slippery horror of a banal architecture only to reinsert design as a form of insulation against that horror. The designer protects us from the horror by making it thematic — representing it, taking responsibility for it. To slide between these practices is to deal with the horror of the dumb object that exceeds the designer, exceeds the subject, escapes the subject, and therefore its own status as an object. The slippery object is precisely that one which slides away from its own objecthood.

Such non-objects resist the traditional strategies by which radical work in architecture is resisted precisely because they do not make that radicality thematic. Their subversion operates under the peaceful disguise of the banal. Architectural projects which represent themselves as radically disruptive are traditionally resisted by being placed in the ghetto of sculpture. They are seen as too dangerous for architecture. Most people, of course, refuse to look closely enough at those objects; they simply embrace them as yet another aesthetic production by the crazier fringe of architectural discourse.

JEFFREY: The exteriorization of problematic architecture into sculpture is the strategy even Hegel uses: At that point where architecture becomes problematic, it is no longer architecture, but sculpture.

MARK: This is yet another symptom of philosophy's indecision about architecture. It makes a double claim: revering yet subordinating architecture by means of the split between building and architecture, presentation of the ground and representation detached from it. Inasmuch as it is condemned it is condemned as architecture. Inasmuch as it is promoted, it is as building. Building is privileged as the special scene of structure, of construction, of the construct, of everything that philosophy stands for. But it is condemned precisely for those qualities of architecture which exceed, yet make possible, that scene of construction: that event in which it becomes slippery by exceeding the

98

realm of structure without simply becoming representational, undermining the division between presentation and representation.

JEFFREY: I am struck by Heidegger's answer to the question what do we do: All we can do is wait for a new God. In this point of our conversation one could say, wait for the return of architecture: not the return of what architecture was, but the return of a beginning of architecture.

MARK: Inasmuch as all architectural discourse is theological, this return of architecture is necessarily the return of God. But no longer God as the immaculate designer of which all architects are surrogates. Rather, it is God as a criminal — violator of the very truth it empowers. Here we are describing the extent to which the basis of architecture is improper. Having understood that ornament is a crime, now we are understanding that structure is a crime. This necessitates an interrogation of details. All questions of detail are questions of the relationship between structure and ornament, even if these questions are asked within "structure," or within "ornament." Any detail does no more than draw a line between structure and ornament. And the configuration of structure/ornament is a configuration of dominance, of authority, of power. The details are the political battlefield of architecture in which power relations are defined. The authority of architecture emerges from the way this line is drawn. The post-structuralist threat to that authority is made by problematizing that line to displace the status of the detail. By no means are we discussing here a new kind of detailing. Rather, it is a way of interrogating the details of apparently secure conventional buildings which renders them suddenly insecure by problematizing the fine lines out of which they are constructed.

We are speaking of the need for an architecture which slides very lightly and therefore dangerously between the banality of an object from which design has been somehow mythically extracted and the mystique of a "designed" object which thematizes its link to the subject. One can operate very close to the banal, familiar buildings that exemplify

traditional cultural production in a way that radically undermines that culture's description of itself. Architecture no longer acts as a mechanism of domestication which sustains repressive systems at a cultural level. Architecture no longer simply stands up and encloses. It problematizes the very thing of which philosophy understands it to be the paradigm. Architecture becomes precisely that capacity of objects to confuse and contradict what philosophy claims about architecture: a capacity marked by philosophy's need to isolate architecture's representational capacity from its material presence by splitting it into building and architecture, and to systematically resist the thought that the two are problematically entwined. This displacement can be thematized through a practice which interrogates everyday, readymade objects to demonstrate that those objects are radically subversive of the culture they appear to reify. As Heidegger argues, the most familiar is the most dangerous. This follows a concern with the politics of form rather than the extent to which form can align itself, or not, with specific political positions. To undermine architecture's capacity to stand up and enclose is to undermine the violent mechanisms of repression with which our society operates, mechanisms which domesticate the other.

There is a nonlinear, but constitutional, relationship between culture's attempts to domesticate the other and its belief in architecture's capacity to articulate space vertically and horizontally. To subvert this belief may only modify architectural practice slightly. Very small moves can be made within regular structures which thematize the unseen condition, the otherness of the objects. Such a practice is subversive rather than revolutionary. It inhabits the cultural mechanisms it questions. It exploits that part which is at odds with itself, not by radically disrupting the system, but by forcing the fissures within the very heart of the architectural tradition, in order to disrupt that tradition. Such a practice does not represent its own radicality architecturally; it remains near to the banal, to the rhetoric of mass production and consumption. But it

Victims, #42 Identity Card Man.
John Hejduk

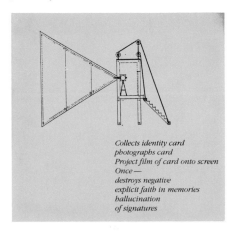

Collects identity card
photographs card
Project film of card onto screen
Once —
destroys negative
explicit faith in memories
hallucination
of signatures

remains extraordinarily dangerous because it defies the very consumption it invites. It inhabits the economy of consumption, but through an extremely close analysis of its mechanism it is able to disrupt it and produce a certain indigestion.

We are only just beginning to grasp some of the strategic relationships in which architectural discourse is enmeshed. The kind of inquiry I am describing somewhat inadequately is an extremely difficult one and it is unclear where it will lead but I am unable to escape it.

Of Objectology

*Excerpts from
Conversations with
Jeffrey Kipnis*

...it is simply a personal agenda. I have as long as I can remember been fascinated by what thinking at the limit has produced and can produce — in mathematics, physics, art, philosophy, everywhere. I am personally interested in an extreme speculation on architecture; I say "speculation" intending to invoke its philosophical sense, but also its everyday sense, with all of its connotations of risk and even recklessness.

I do not believe that there is anything about architecture which needs or demands an investigation into the possibilities of architectural displacement or decentering, in fact quite to the contrary. I do not believe, as I once did, that there is some severe congenital defect in architecture which only an extreme intervention can repair. But I do believe that architecture, because it is so deeply rooted both in its history and as an experience in truth, certainty, grounding, and so forth, even if it does not cry out for a decentering investigation, even if it profoundly resists such thinking, nevertheless, it brims with the question of the possibility of decentering. It seems to me incontestably the one discipline above all others in which the stakes of decentering are highest, higher than life and death, as high as one world or another. But I want to reiterate that mine is merely a personal agenda; the speculative possibilities of architecture are not there unless you are hungry for speculative possibilities.

Some use may be obtained from distinguishing between active and reactive disciplines if one does not rely too heavily on those terms, hypostatizing them into categories, that is, holding that any discipline can be totally inscribed under one or the other. One might then say that a reactive discipline is one whose processes are largely constituted by and devoted to the persistent truth of its constructed history, *i.e.*, its tradition. An active discipline, on the other hand, would be one whose processes are determined largely in order to effect a departure from its tradition. In the reactive, therefore, the history of the discipline is the discipline; in the active, the history of the discipline is the sum of the detritus, the residue left behind in the movement of the discipline. Physics, perhaps, is an example of the active, for what we mean by the history of physics consists of that which used to be taken as physics but is no longer, *e.g.*, Newtonian determinism. Law seems, off-hand, to be a reasonable example of a reactive discipline, for it exists and develops largely on the basis of precedent. Clearly neither is purely active nor reactive, but there does seem to be a difference between the two.

In these terms, the possibility exists that architecture, and philosophy for that matter, are becoming primarily reactive disciplines, that is, they are facing not their end, but their *closure*. Recently, at least, they have engaged in very little else but the study of their own histories. I see architecture as becoming reactive not out of any natural evolution, but as a result of the operation of very strong forces, resistances, which I try to articulate and plan tactics and strategies against. On the other hand perhaps becoming reactive is the inevitable transformation of a discipline, its *telos*, its maturity, so to speak, in which case my work is merely a form of anguish. Who knows?

Photo by Caleb Crawford

One way to state the issue for speculative architecture today is to say that it seeks to defeat Hegel's relegation of architecture (incomplete, inadequate to the demands of the Absolute Spirit, restricted to the symbolic, etc.). The Hegelian relegation does not, as he says clearly, mean the end of architecture, but merely its confinement, its closure. Hence it is closely related to the active/reactive characterization. To accomplish this requires using the powerful tools developed by Marx, Freud, Nietzsche, Derrida, and so forth to forge something like a generalized Hegelian logic, one freed from the teleology and the comprehensive role of reason that operate uncritically in that philosopher's thought.

Through these tools developed in the movement of alphabetic writing (confirming Hegel!), ultimately architectural design, rather than (alphabetic) writing, will be the medium for this overturning and reforging, because of the relative positions of each in Hegel's thought. If the battle is won, new architecture would be very different from what it is today; but if it is lost, new architecture would still be different, for there will continue to be development, this is the distinction between closure and end. What's at stake is the differences between those two systems of differences.

I don't dream of the future, but there are buildings I would like to see built. Tafuri was very much to the point in his critique of an architecture which aspires to build the future. Dreaming of the future, like dreaming of the past, is escapism in the present. However, the problem of looking forward is part of the present, it plagues the present and cannot be erased from it. I look forward to some buildings.

To my mind, the object world, the plastic world, particularly what we call the "inanimate" world, whether an ashtray or a building or a work of art, has yet to receive the benefits or the ravages, *i.e.*, the just dessert of well-organized and incisive speculation. I would like to make a contribution to doing the inanimate object justice. Hence "Objectology," my somewhat whimsical term for my work.

I am interested in what happens to architectural theory and design when you try to think architecture without transcendentality. I don't care how many people find it easy to write "god is dead" or to declare "I am an atheist." As I see it, you only have two choices today. You either believe in the transcendental, in God, which is incredibly difficult to do, or you try like hell not to believe in God, which is virtually impossible. Trying not to believe in transcendentality, in God, absolute truth, and so forth requires an enormously willful, wholesale suspension of the self-evident.

Probably Nietzsche, who with Freud provides the most powerful tools for thinking through transcendentality, said it best when he comments in *Twilight of the Idols*, "I am afraid we are not rid of God because we still have faith in grammar." There is something very exciting about this remarkable sentence, namely that it is written in correct grammar. Now perhaps Nietzsche was blind to this paradox, which in itself would be an important lapsus to analyze. But I prefer to think that he was quite aware of it and crafted a statement with such resonant irony that he opened and possibly closed the problem in one and the same moment.

My work has led me to speculate about something which might be termed the "mind" or, better, the "will" of the object. It shows up in the following relationship, which I call the axiom of Objectology:

$$\langle \mu_o \rangle \leftrightharpoons \langle \mu_s \rangle$$

Though it would not be entirely correct, it can reasonably be interpreted as saying: the quantity of the will of the object is in dynamic equilibrium with the quantity of the will of the subject.

I won't try to elaborate upon this now, it's far too complicated, but let me discuss one or two of its implications. It says that if, in the investigation of the repeal of transcendentality, we are going to continue to operate with any conceptual structure employing notions like mind or will, then it is no longer tenable to confine those concepts to animate things, particularly man. We must begin logically to think the reality of the will of the object.

I realize that it is no longer fashionable to speak of subject and object, and it is certainly true that the Cartesian subject and Kantian subject have been inadequated. But from my point of view these terms are far from having neither been defeated nor exhausted; rather they have become taboo. Anyway, I'm digressing; we'll leave that topic to another time.

To continue, I see architecture as a discipline in which (for very important reasons) the will of the subject is obedient to the will of the object; that is, the equilibrium is dominated by the dynamics of the will of the object rather than that of the subject.

To put it simply for this conversation, and thus run the risk of turning what I believe to be an insight into a bromide, this means that the architectural object produces the architectural subject as obedient to it; architecture produces the architect rather than vice versa.

This inertial obedience operates under the euphemism of responsibility. But the details of the formula, the fact that the equilibrium is between quantities rather than wills, suggests the possibility of a different dynamic between architectural subject and object, one in which the quantity of the will of the subject the architect, determines the dynamics of the equilibrium. Thus in the design process, the architect, freed from a nonexistent obligation to the object, can learn to employ a wider range of motives and consequently produce a much wider range of forms. This is what I have elsewhere referred to as a theory of displaced texts.

...if you will pardon the play on words, the built environment is literally *second nature*, that is, it is more "natural" for us than what we call "nature." We take it as radically given in the same way and for the same reasons that we continue to take the certainty of self-consciousness as radically given, despite the decisive destabilization of the latter, exemplified in such concepts as "the unconscious" with which we are all familiar and even take for granted. Thus the built environment shapes us, significantly contributing to our sense of our-selves individually and collectively and to the shapes and figures of our knowledge.

Two factors collaborate in this forging (in both senses of the term) power of architecture. First are its physical quantities — how large it is, how much of it there is, how protractedly and repetitively we are engaged with it; I believe it was Lenin who remarked that quantity has a quality all of its own, a simple statement rooted in dialectical materialism, yet nevertheless, a statement which, when one reflects upon it closely, unfolds vast implications for architecture and for theories of the object in general.

Secondly are its qualities, the seminal interpretive relationships in terms of which we engage the architectural object including physical and emotional shelter, power, identity, status, beauty, and so forth. The significance of the quantity/quality domain of architecture leads to the amplitude of the transference and identification which we form with that object, accounting, for example, for the "maternality" of architectural space discussed by Bachelard. Hence architecture stands with family, state, and language as one of the principal formative arenas, yet its theorization has avoided the depth of scrutiny enjoyed by those other fields of study.

Perhaps we should talk more about the design process and less about arcane theories. So, let me compare two architects who have for some time now been the focus of my thinking about the design process, John Hejduk and Peter Eisenman. Strictly speaking, I should add Daniel Libeskind to the list to form a triangle, but for the purposes of our discussion, let me confine myself to John and Peter.

Earlier I spoke briefly about Hegel, alluding to an overturning of the totalizing role of reason in his work. In Hegel's formulation, reason conquers, bringing all *other* under its domain, thus *knowing* itself in itself as itself. It does so through the process of dialectical negation and sublimation. Today, we mount a critique of this totalizing role of reason on two fronts, first, by asking what residue does the process of sublimation necessarily leave behind so that the *other* can be contained, in other words by asking what is the unsublimatable as such and why is it repressed. Secondly, in a related question, we examine the conquering power of reason, not only to show that reason is inadequate to the task of conquering the *other*, say madness or irrationality (notice that those concepts are neither mad nor irrational), but that in its passion for conquest, reason is always already a function of desire, a passion, irrational and mad. So, if architectural history is viewed as an arena of the encroachment of reason in the name of order and beauty, it is also always an arena for the suppression of the *other*.

John and Peter seek, each in a different way, an *other* architecture. John does so by focusing on reason's *shadow*, by restoring to his architecture the forbidden residue left behind, roughly speaking, in the capturing by reason of the architectural object. Thus he displaces his process from what purports to be rational design by constructing poetic texts in and about an historico-imaginary context which reinforms his object with an irrationality that might be called architecture's suppressed anima. His work can be viewed as attempting to drive architecture to and through those stages of art which Hegel sees as exceeding architecture — sculpture, painting, music, and poetry to find architecture as sculpture, architecture as painting, etc.

Peter, on the other hand, prefers to concentrate on the zone of reason's madness, its margin, its edge. In his design process, he does not seek to exchange the reasonableness of reason for the shadows of the poetic, but rather to turn reason back on itself, driving it into a frenzy. He does this by borrowing reasonable reasons from displaced texts, *i.e.*, any other source of authority than traditional architecture — typically extreme philosophy or literary theory but also on occasion the sciences and mathematics — and causing those to drive his design process by analogy. In so doing he in effect states, in contradiction to John, that the grip of reason on architecture cannot be broken, but only exhausted; he seeks to unchain architecture's animus.

Part of Hegel's relegation of architecture is his identifying it as constrained to the symbolic, that is, roughly speaking, to the representational. Peter's project can be seen as exploring the possibility of architecture to exceed the representational, to look into the possibility of architecture as a writing, a dynamic matrix of arbitrary signifiers, with a view to the becoming motivated, the becoming symbolic of the arbitrary.

Shadow and edge; two very different projects, two very different sources of motive, two very different architectures. Yet they are inherently intermingled, for edge and shadow are conjugates, each constructs the other.

The question of text in architecture, in fact in the object world in general, is different from the question of the text in the realm of language. That difference can be located in the metaphysic of the Living Present, the here and now. I say "metaphysic" to indicate that those concepts, the "here" and "now" strictly speaking, are untenable on their own terms yet continue to operate as radically self-evident. Without going into the complexities of the argument, their destabilization grows out of the destabilization if the "I" and consequently the "I am here, now."

Anyway, to continue, Derrida, in *Of Grammatolgy*, was able to disrupt the operation of the "metaphysic of presence" in written texts in part by focusing on the physicality, the objectivity, of writing — correct spelling, spacing, punctuation, capital letters, etc. In other words, he uses the fact that language, whether written or spoken, depends on the disappearance, the becoming invisible of its objectivity to express the presence of its meaning. In a sense, that is the very definition of meaning.

Derrida then takes advantage of the fact that the disappearance is never complete. We might say that the metaphysic of encounter with language is such as to repress the objectivity in order to express the textuality. Deconstruction derives from and thrives on the fact that the repression can de facto never be total; therefore, there will always be a return of the repressed, an insinuation of the consequences of residual physicality into language which will always disrupt language's goal of achieving univocal meaning. For example, consider the sentence, "architecture stresses the importance of man." Most likely, we read it as meaning that architecture emphasizes man as important. But, because the physical word s-t-r-e-s-s-e-s also can mean to cause tension, the sentence can mean just the opposite of our former interpretation. In this case it means something like architecture challenges the importance of man. The

physical word never disappears into its univocal meaning. The privilege of the first meaning over the second in this example evidences our desire to think architecture as the former rather than the latter, but everytime we say the first, we also say the second.

The key question for the theories of textuality vis-à-vis the object, on the other hand, concerns the apparent reversal in the metaphysic of encounter. When confronted with a specific thing, an ashtray for example, its objectivity is expressed and its textuality is repressed. No matter how much you understand that you are not in the presence of an ashtray in essence, that "ashtray" is a relation between, you cannot suspend the sense that you are in the presence of an ashtray, here and now.

Thus this physical ashtray can be considered always to be the best spelling of the word "ashtray." It is better than the word, for in our encounter with it, we seem to be in the presence, in the here and now of the concept, which the word, as it disap-

pears into the absence of the concept, cannot invoke. Yet I said "best" spelling, not "correct" spelling, for if it were truly correct, we would be faced with the *eidos*, ashtray-in-essence, the single ideal and perfect ashtray, which does not exist. Hence the word and the object, textuality and objectivity each cast a kind of spell over us, a spell of "truth" which is in truth only a spelling of "best," *i.e.*, not an ontological but a moral condition.

We are faced in this condition, by the way, with what might be called the object/text duality, which echoes the familiar wave/particle duality of physics, not merely analogically, but, I believe, actually structurally. The wave/duality is in this view but a special case of the general object/text duality.

This duality provides yet another way to examine the question of architecture in the face of the repeal of transcendentality, in this case in terms of its repressed textuality. Text and therefore meaning is essentially dynamic, multivocal and/or ambiguous. This amounts to the condition of the essentially unessential, a splendid oxymoron which tries speaking to the heart

of the matter but cannot quite get there. The suspension of transcendentality in textual terms is stated as the nonexistence of the transcendental signified, that is, the nonexistence of the singular, unambiguous referent of a signifier. Given this nonexistence, the futile pursuit of such a signified in any discipline can be seen as a desire, a wish in the Freudian sense of the term.

An analysis of architectural history suggests that it is profoundly dominated by just such a pursuit. The consequences which we recognize are a deep moralization — a coordinated set of prescriptions and proscriptions — of the architectural object (beauty, context, function, etc.), a metaphysical privileging of the architect's intentions, and a set of design processes which operate to keep these "first principles" of architecture firmly and permanently in place.

Some very good friends of mine are committed to a view that architecture has become "language-bound," *i.e.*, governed by the law and operation of the word. In this view we need today to effect a return to a study and understanding of architecture's non-linguistic, "visual meaning." I disagree. Though I certainly agree that there is "visual meaning," alluding to it when I speak, for example, of quantity as quality, I do not agree that any sort of "return" can be or need be effected. Because of the duality I mentioned above, there has never been a time when there was a purity of visual meaning in architecture. The architect has always worked in terms of texts, his/her motives and methods have always been as "language bound" as they are today. Hence I am interested in exploring the full range of textual possibilities in architecture by relieving the architect of a responsibility to an untenable and restrictive transcendental text.

I want to unhook the way s/he works from the morality of the result, or at least delay the encroachment into the design process of that morality as much as possible. That is, in a nutshell, the method of my critique of transcendentality in its design phase. The architect is not the author of the building, only of the architecture. This does not mean that s/he has no effect on the building, quite to the contrary. It means that, under the aegis of the rubric "responsibility" and the causal interchangeability of architecture and building design, the architect is rendered obedient to the will of the object, the building, before exploring his or her willfulness as an architect.

The "self-evidency" of architecture as a visual art troubles me, for it sets a specific agenda which does not seem to me empirically justifiable, and which therefore is another manifestation of moralization. We live with an architectural object for a very long time, in frequent repetition, etc. Therefore its content does not have to unfold itself in a moment, in a day, in a visit or a photograph. In short, it does not have to be beautiful, even in the very permissive sense of the term as we use it today. Its orders of complexity can be much more elaborate, possibly even to the point of requiring more than a lifetime to unfold.

...as architecture, Villa Rotunda exists only in the plan.

The architect can and, from my point of view, should learn to tolerate the anxiety of designing unfamiliar objects with unfamiliar processes. The question becomes, when is it right to do something wrong? To ask this is to abdicate the pleasures of the "right." To design with the intention of criticizing the moralization of the architectural object is, in the beginning, de-moralizing.

These are just some, a very few, of the terms and conditions of my speculations, I might not get anywhere, in fact, it is not unlikely that I am completely wrong. But if that is the case, great! So be it. Then my project will have been worthwhile. Some different architecture will have been considered, the catalog of possibilities increased, some unexplored avenues of thought mapped. The downside is not bad at all; and then there is the upside....

An Interview with Peter Eisenman

Lynne Breslin

LB: I would like to ask you questions that circumscribe the rise of an architecture of text. An architecture of text is a quotation from you. It is not an architecture of representation or an aesthetic exploration. This is what we will attempt to define through the interview. It seems that we are presently experiencing a new relationship between theory and practice in your work, in John Hejduk's work, and in several Japanese architects' works. In the past, practice was either considered an application of theory — a consequence of theory, or practice was thought to inspire theory. In any event, practice and theory were understood in terms of a process of totalization and resemblances. Today there is a changed reciprocity, a lack of resemblance between theory and practice. Theory is no longer developed for application; it becomes an "object" in its own right. How do you see the relationship between theory and practice in your work?

PE: You say that totalization and resemblance are the two aspects of the old relationship. By totalization, you mean a comprehensive theory, a program which was all encompassing of which a practice had to subscribe. An example would be when Le Corbusier writes *Vers Une Architecture*, then tries to build an architecture that subscribes to his five points of a new architecture.

LB: At other times there have been architects who practice and then develop theories based on that experience, like Palladio.

PE: My practice has changed as has my theory in the last five years. An interesting interaction has developed that I could not have predicted five years ago. I believe that the larger-scale nature of the projects and the desire to do larger-scale projects certainly has changed the nature of my theoretical investigations. My theoretical work beginning with the houses concerned the process of transformation and the idea of virtuality of space and the concern for the marking of a modernist objecthood would not be appropriate (theoretically or actually) in the larger scale projects. Whether I was aware of it or not, when I started to work in larger-scale projects, first in the *Cannaregio* project for Venice, there was a new attitude at work. While I used the forms of an earlier house, the idea for a site plan (my first real site plan) came from new thinking. This continues in *Berlin*, which I think

was my first conscious realization that my attitude toward the site had changed and what could be called an architectural text began to emerge. I think it was the scale of the projects, certainly *Ohio State* and *Berlin*, which changed the nature of the theoretical investigation. The theories I was dealing with in the houses are certainly now applicable to a larger scale. What one realizes the minute one says "larger-scale work" is that the problem of scale becomes an increasingly important issue; this was not the case in the houses. Even though one was trying to deny the anthropocentrism and the other centrisms of house, one realizes in retrospect that many of those centrisms were present. There was an optimistic and ideal view of those houses, even a naivete about what one could do to countermine the cultural significance that was embedded and their cultural repressions. But I think because of the larger-scale projects one began to get the notion that the way to attack this traditional ontology of architecture was to do it through scale and text, that is, to deny the anthropocentric scale by suggesting that the architectural object was not necessarily mimetic or iconic — that it did not necessarily refer to man but rather could be seen as a text — *an internally consistent and originary series of internal references*. The architectural object is no different from a text; the sign and the signified can become one and the same. For example, the word apple and the apple itself are no different. The word apple is as much an object as the apple is a text.

The notion of scale which was not problematic in the earlier work has now become a center of focus. It is the practice which has triggered this new theoretical work. Now that I am in full-time practice the ideas are more interconnected with the work. There is no question that in the next museum project I will be strongly influenced by the theoretical work that has been uncovered in *Cannaregio, Romeo and Juliet, Berlin* and *OSU*. These projects have triggered and uncovered things that are now going to become more conscious and more central to my work. They are very central in the project that I am doing with Jacques Derrida in Paris. The project is a very clear deconstruction of architecture itself, while at the same time it is the *maintenant* or the maintaining of architecture. In other words, you can deconstruct or destabilize or confront the metaphysics of architecture, but in order for it to be a positive project, architecture — that is its metaphysics of presence, enclosure, shelter, etc. — must remain. There is no reason to suggest that shelter and enclosure are necessarily centrisms merely because architecture has been related to anthropocentric behavior. What you will see in the Derrida project is that we deal with shelter and enclosure but not in any predetermined or culturally determined centrism.

LB: Do you feel there is a separation between theory and practice? Are you able to work out certain issues in theory but not realize them in practice or foresee the possibility of its use?

PE: Certainly. The separations are as follows: There are certain projects — speculative office buildings where there is very little room — forget theory — to do architecture. Basically you do a skin, a core, and a lobby and that's it. Because of the parking requirements, the cost requirements, there is very little room to maneuver. It is not an accident that the museum has become a favorite program for working out architectural ideas at a larger scale. Because, like a house, there is no program for a museum. Museums used to be in the very best houses, so that the house and museum are very similar as a nonprogram. The conditions of the pragmatics of the project do not limit theory; on the contrary, the museum as a program encourages theory, especially one that is critical of that program. One of the interesting things about a museum is that one can take a critical attitude towards the notion of museum in the program.

The second condition does not have to do with the limitation imposed by the program, but merely that the theory is often not worked out enough to sustain a practical project. For example, the theory of scaling in *Romeo and Juliet* was probably not articulated in any other kind of format, because it was not understood well enough. We did not know what we were doing. It is only now that we are able to use it and understand it. For example we are working with scaling in the *Tokyo Opera House Competition*; we would not have been able to do that without having worked on it in *Romeo and Juliet* and now we are using it in a competition project. There is no limitation in practice to using theoretical work, the limitation is in the availability of theoretical work to be employed practically.

LB: The eclecticism of the 19th-century and the present "historicist" postmodern architecture is characterized by a consumption of styles. Does your work represent a consumption of texts, of philosophies? In your earlier works, the influence of Chomsky and structuralism were pronounced. In the *OSU* and *Berlin* projects, Foucault's theories of the episteme and archaeology were quoted, and in the *Fin d'Ou T Hou S* and *Romeo and Juliet*, Derrida's text appears contingent. Would you discuss the impact of modern philosophy on your work?

PE: There is no question that certain external ideas trigger my work. There is no question that the first influences on my work were architectural. They start with Palladio, Le Corbusier, and Terragni. What has become apparent to me is that it is not possible to push the discourse of architecture away from its own centrism — from its own discourse, no matter what external influences are brought to bear on it. You cannot go back into architecture to find out how to move architecture. I think you have to look at other discourses. I was very interested in the middle and late 60s in the work of Frank Stella, Kenneth Noland, Jasper Johns, Rauschenberg, Sol Lewitt, and Michael Heizer. They had a big impact on me. Secondly, film had an enormous impact on me: Antonioni, Goddard, Truffaut. Film in general was in my consciousness. It was in the academic environment at Princeton University where the kind of thinking that influenced my work was initiated. I met people who knew Chomsky and I was exposed to Chomsky, Lévi-Strauss, and Foucault.

It was a gradual process of moving forward and backward in time from that point to people like Nietzsche and Heidegger. The fourth influence after art, film, and philosophy was literature. I met Bill Gass when he did the article on *House VI*. He showed me the relationship of my work to writers like John Hawkes and John Barth. I was re-reading John Barth's *Chimera*. In it he describes a project that is exactly like one of my projects — it has no external references, no resort to teleology and ontology of literature. My article in *A+U* with the three voices, the different authors, comes from John Barth. I also did a presentation at the AIA when they honored Philip Johnson, where I made a presentation of four voices and I was not at the podium — the voices were taped and accompanied by four slide projectors.

It all came from my interest in literature. It is not just philosophy but also fiction. The *Romeo and Juliet* project would not be possible without fiction, and the analogous relationships found in the ideas of palimpsest and quarry, the nonarchitectural types which become the material for me. My work is more analogous to that of a fiction writer today than a poet. It attempts to differentiate between poetry and fiction. Is there a poetic fiction? The writer William Gass triggered that off in me. He is both a fiction writer and a philosopher. Bill said he found that fiction was so much more philosophical than philosophy ever could be. Jeffrey Kipnis said to me, "I wish John Barth would write philosophy." Of course John Barth is writing philosophy. I guess I too am writing philosophy but I am writing in architecture. I am not sure if it's a better way. I would never use the word "better," but it's the only way I can express myself. If you asked me to write a fiction in words, I could not do it. Therefore I am an architect.

It is very fortunate for my own interests that architecture has had the least investigation as a discourse of any of the contemporary discourses. You will find less investigation because it is a discourse that was always thought to have been known, so dependent on anthropocentrism, presence, logocentrism, and rationality that it was stable. I think that we are just finding this is not the case.

LB: Your work has an evolving, but indentifiable, signature. *Fin d' Ou T Hou S* is not unrelated to *House X*, *House X* to your earlier numbered houses — at least in terms of a formal repertoire. But that signature seems to have changed with *Berlin* and *Romeo and Juliet*. Why?

PE: You are asking someone to be conscious in retrospect. I am not conscious in retrospect and I look at it and ask, "The signature changes?" I do not think one works at signing one's pieces. I think the change in the nature of the work forces the change in signature.

LB: Some architects focus on signature, producing an identifiable, marketable signature.

PE: I know they do, but I am far from producing anything marketable. It has never been something that interested me. The value of *Cannaregio*, *OSU*, *Berlin*, and *Romeo and Juliet* is not in whether the signature is the same or has changed.

LB: But don't you think the change in signature registers a deep shift, and what might it be?

PE: I think it may, but I have already suggested that some deeper shift occurred. *Romeo and Juliet* marks a breaking point again like *Cannaregio* marked a breaking point. I think *Romeo and Juliet* is a break project. I do not think I could do *Ohio State* again, if that's what you mean. I am no longer interested in the issues that are in *OSU*. I think what has happened, is that the problem of figuration has entered my discourse. The question for me is how do you reunite what Foucault said has been broken apart — the relationship of figuration to discourse. As a profound and proclaimed absolutist, as opposed to a relativist, as I believe Derrida is, an irreconcilable absolutist and Platonist. There is no question that the reconciliation of figuration and discourse must take place. The recognition and the willingness to be an absolutist in a relativist world has allowed me to bring figuration into my discourse. That is a big change. How do I deal with it? Do not forget that I brought figuration into the *OSU* project under another guise, but yet it was there, it was someone else's figuration.

LB: The armory?

PE: Yes. In *Romeo and Juliet*, it is still someone else's figuration but not as much, it is becoming more mine. The *Tokyo Opera House* again has more figuration in it and so it is moving in that direction.

LB: While your work has been radical in content, you have remained tied to conventional means of representation: plan, model, section, axonometric (though you have often pushed these means to their limit). In your most recent project, you seem to have made a breakthrough in documentation with the glass of *Romeo and Juliet*. Are the allusions to Duchamp and Derrida's *Glas* important?

PE: Yes, there is again the issue of a maintenance of the discourse. I believe that architecture ultimately has to be built. Ultimately it relies on being shelter and enclosure. You can attack the discourse but if you destroy architecture you might be talking about deep-sea diving or something else. When you play a musical instrument you are not talking about architecture any longer. Therefore the metaphysics of architecture is very useful precisely because it is not painting. I could not be a painter. I would not know how to attack the discourses of painting and know how to maintain the discourse at the same time. I do not know what the maintenance of the discourse is if the canvas is not sacred. What is painting? For me enclosure and shelter are part of the maintenance of the discourse of architecture.

LB: What about representation?

PE: The axonometric model for *House X* was certainly an attack on traditional representation. Is it a model or is it the real thing? It cannot be possessed in the traditional way. When you look at it, it is not what it is supposed to be. Only through the monocular vision of a camera or a telescope can you see what it is supposed to be. The text I did, "Notes on a Conceptual Architecture I," in *Design Quarterly*, where I left out the text and only left the footnotes. People had to write in for the text, therefore you have these blank pages. Part of the object was the process of writing in and receiving the text. There was no meaning to the text that was presented in the magazine. The text you received was a representation. The entire process questioned the representational object. The problem of text and representation and the relationship between those two and objecthood has always been an issue for me. I have just pushed it further in *Romeo and Juliet*. It goes so far that the book we are publishing with the Architectural Association is not going to be a document of any value to anyone who wants to study *Romeo and Juliet*; it is merely another object with little relationship to the original object. To study the project we will have to do another book, which is a different thing. The AA book on *Romeo and Juliet* is so much of an object that it is no longer a book but part of the artifactual nature of the project. I would say the transparent plates of *Romeo and Juliet* are interesting. They deal with past, present, and future, with traces and marks and the differences between them; they deal with scaling and grafting in projects like the *Tokyo Opera House*. Themes which I have dropped are recycled and come back to consciousness again. I do not know where it is going and what the meaning is, but it is pushing the traditional integers which establish what architecture is. *Romeo and Juliet* hits a lot of those traditional buttons. I am the worst person because it was a very unconscious project for me. It is a more interesting project for my psychoanalyst. He understands it much better than I do, in a certain sense.

LB: In your continuing deconstruction of classical traditions, you have negated the originary role of the site, program, and representation. Scaling is the latest strategy. What is the relationship between scaling and the artificial excavation of *OSU* and *Berlin*? Discuss the relative role of superposition in each.

PE: There are superpositions in both *OSU* and *Berlin* even though they were never consciously discussed as such. Scaling has made superposition, as a strategy, more conscious. The idea of scaling has brought up the problem of registration, of how an analogic relationship is produced. There are two ways that have been identified thus far. One way is through a process of cascading, that is to start at point and to enlarge outward. The other way is to implode and if one implodes one is superposing. There is a difference between superposition and superimposition. Superimposition means there is a ground and a figure. It is closer to collage and montage. In superposition it is figure to figure. They are covalent. There is no originary ground. Collage and montage depend upon context and taking meaning from context. Superposition is an analogous relationship, there is no contextual meaning. For example, in the *Romeo and Juliet* project the city of Verona as a walled city is analogous to the walled castle of Romeo. If you register the castle of Romeo on the city of Verona you have a superposition of analogous elements. That superposition in itself does not give you anything. It merely produces a mechanical registration. But scaling is not a mechanical process. It is only active if some other analogous relationship that was previously hidden, like the fact that at that particular scale (one castle of Romeo falls inside the wall of Juliet and one falls outside) was revealed. Here something about the relationship of Romeo and Juliet — with the castles together — revealed the notion of division. This is part of the story of Romeo and Juliet which was revealed by this analogous superposition. It would not have been seen had there not been a scaling of Verona and the castle of Romeo. In the *La Villette* project we are trying to find the superpositions that resonate with some analogous material.

LB: In *OSU* and *Berlin* you preserve and resurrect vestiges of the old order (the armory, existing buildings, and city walls). In referring to *OSU* you said "[i]t recalls the past in modern terms and postulates the continuous transformation of memory in the invention of art and architecture." You contrast your project with that of the postmodern attitude of conservation of historic centers that are relegated to so many fetish fossils and stuffed animals. Clarify how the "history and memory" of your projects is an alternative to these processes. How do these forms function as signs and do the histories "salvaged" in these two projects differ from each other?

PE: First of all you say they're vestiges of old buildings. They are not vestiges of old buildings. They are inventions. They are *dissimulations*. The foundations of *Berlin* that were "excavated" had nothing to do with any real foundations that were ever there. It was a pure invention. The fact that it looks like a real foundation is precisely what we wanted to do — to make a fictional reality. The foundations of *Ohio State* are slightly different. In Berlin we were not using the notion of the difference between simulation and dissimulation. *Ohio State* deals with the notion of dissimulation. There were actual ruins, the foundations of the old armory are on the site. We could have uncovered those and built on those, that would have been a simulation — what you call vestiges of an old building. We uncover those foundations only to show that we are not building a building on them, that what we are building is an invention — a fiction — that announces its own fictional quality — that says this is not reality — that says this is not real history. For me the primary characteristic of the postmodern is simulated history. This is precisely what we are not doing. We are making a sign that we are not using history in that same way. We are suggesting another use of history through the creation of fiction. It is the same thing that we did in *Romeo and Juliet*. It is very difficult to know which are the real Romeo and Juliet castles and which are the dissimulated ones. We can tell what is a dissimulated Verona. The integrity of *Romeo and Juliet* is that it continues its history as a quarry. The castles in their present form got that way because people took the stones from them to build in the area. We only continued the process. We take away only what we need to build our own project. The history of our building is recorded in the old castles.

The idea of the quarry becomes part of the project of *La Villette*. We are using the quarry and the palimpsest which are not architectural integers to replace the traditional type forms in architecture. We are not using traditional types like the labyrinth which are within the history of architecture. What we are doing is effecting new types of formulations for this maintenance of architecture.

LB: Is there a word play in your use of quarry?

PE: It has a double meaning. It also alludes to moving arrows of the title of *Romeo and Juliet*. That is the quarry of a moving arrow. So we are using quarry in the double sense. We start from the palimpsest which is the superposition of two objects which then becomes a quarry. You subtract form the palimpsest leaving the trace of the former superposition but also the trace of the subtraction, so in other words, we are talking about Plato's *chora*. The combination of the superposition of palimpsest and quarry gives you *chora* which is the program that Derrida set for the *La Villette* project. I think that the idea of *chora* will be very provocative for my upcoming work.

LB: The Japanese have not had to contend with an anthropocentric architectural tradition like classicism. While the *tatami* is a modular unit based on the human body and generates the plan of the house, it does not have the pivotal hierarchal role it might in the West, nor does the Japanese tradition lend itself to the representational or figuration. Do you think the Japanese have been more successful in exploring an architecture less bounded by centrisms?

PE: I was always impressed with Isozaki's view of *Yin* and *Yang* as being essential apartness as opposed to the Western logocentric view of it as dialectical. There is no question that the Japanese or Eastern sensibility has the possibility of dealing with the issues that concern me in a less logocentric, less anthropocentric way. I always wondered why this was not the case. Obviously there are other centrisms or inhibitions in the Eastern culture that we do not experience or understand that do not allow deconstruction to flourish in Japan, at least not in architectural thought.

LB: Deconstruction has had a great impact on criticism of architecture in Japan. Shinohara has been "deconstructed." Yatsuka has applied it. I think it may well begin to have some impact on the architecture itself.

PE: I see minimalism, asceticism, narcissism, and many different attitudes in Japanese architecture, but not deconstruction. Jacques Derrida said to me that he thought deconstruction was an essentially American idea because America is an uprooted place, where things are constantly being taken apart. It is the place where there is a moral necessity for a deconstruction. It might be that the deconstruction of logocentrism or anthropocentrism has difficulty being accepted in Japan. Whether people like Tadao Ando are aware of it or not, his concrete houses are symbolic, I believe, of the attempt to withstand the next Hiroshima. Therefore, he has gone away from the traditional and dematerialized Japanese light weight and open structure to the notion of the bunker. And so the Japanese have become encumbered in their *avant-garde* with the bunker. And the bunker is a centric enclosure which has a stronger anthropocentrism than the Japanese ever had before. That is why you see these neo-classicisms in Japanese architecture which have this same bunker mentality. I think that there is no question that it is the result of Hiroshima, unconsciously, in the collective society. To deconstruct the centrisms of architecture is not something that the Japanese will be able to reconcile psychologically.

LB: Walter Benjamin was forced to abandon the conventional book in favor of the essay. The essay allowed him the freedom incompletely to digress, juxtapose, and write an "art of interruption" that was essential for the type of analysis he sought. You have used the interview form frequently; I wondered if you have found that the form allowed you to pursue theoretical issues more easily?

PE: It is useful. Today, you have forced me to say what, if you had asked me to write an essay, I probably could not have said. Somehow having an audience — you, the tape, the questions to focus on — has forced me to think about these issues. You have caused me to say things that I probably would not have said before. When I have to present something to Derrida it is like an interview, he asks me questions: "Tell me about this project." It is a much more effective way for me to present my thoughts than writing because I cannot conceptualize well without an occasion which generates some energy. I can now take what I say in these interviews and put them into writing. That is what I have traditionally done. I start from an amnesia and work into the work. Much of what I said you will not find in my writing.

LB: The interview has become very popular with several philosophers. You have done a series of interviews. The dialogue has its own strategy which uncovers a different set of relationships.

PE: There is no question that Valors' *Eupalinos ou l'Architecte* is a model for that. I try to recreate those dialogues in my own writing, talking to myself. I work better dialectically. I am stimulated by people thus the interview is a natural vehicle for me. I am not a person who works well alone. My best ideas come out of situations like this where I misinterpret or misread your questions, or avoid the answers.

Lynne Breslin is a designer living and practicing in New York. She has an A.B. from Radcliffe College, an M.Arch and an M.A. from Princeton University, and is currently a candidate for the Ph.D. in Architecture at Princeton University. Her works and writing have been published internationally in *Space Design*, *A+U*, *Skyline*, *Design Book Review*, *Interiors*, *Architectural Design*, *Metropolis*, and *Progressive Architecture*.

It is amazing how complete is the illusion that beauty is goodness.
    Leo Tolstoy

Author's note: The following text is a series of notes which merely scratch the surface of a subject which will be taken up more fully in my forthcoming book *The Edge of Between*.

Recently a client said to me, "Peter, for the past five hundred years the discourse of science has been about man overcoming nature. Man overcomes nature through things which are rational, which are good, which are truthful, and ultimately these take on the characteristics of the natural itself, *i.e.* the beautiful. Obviously," he said to me, "it follows that architecture has been about this overcoming of the natural, because architecture symbolizes the structures, cosmological attitudes of the society: architecture mirrors what the society is about." Thus, though not explicitly, architecture has represented and symbolized this struggle of man to overcome nature. "Today," he said, "this is no longer the problem which science is addressing. This is no longer where the discourses on the forefront of thinking are." He said that the problem today for man is to overcome knowledge: "You see, computers have knowledge, robots have knowledge, the technological clones that we are developing have knowledge, but man has wisdom. The knowledge revolution, artificial intelligence and the systems of knowledge have gotten out of hand, and have started to control man, rather than the reverse. Science today is trying to find a way to control knowledge, and the knowledge revolution." And my client then said to me, "Peter, you architects, for too long, have been solving a problem, representing and symbolizing a problem which is no longer where we are." He said, "I want you to do a building which symbolizes man's capacity to overcome knowledge." I looked at him and thought, what is that? He said, "Do you know something, you are supposed to be an architect on the edge. Yet," he added, "there is nothing you could do toward this end that would upset me at all." He said, "I do not want you to merely illustrate the problem. I do not want you to decorate a facade with a computer chip, cut into the chip, and say, there — we have symbolized the overcoming of knowledge. No," he said, "I am not talking about that. I want something far more significant. I want something that challenges man's very occupation of space, not just the surface of that space." He said, "And I do not think that you can do it."

Now why is this? First of all, architects traditionally do not speculate on the here and now, on gravity, as scientists do. Architects have to deal with the real conditions of gravity, they have to build the here and now. They have to deal with physical presence. In fact, architects continually not only symbolize the overcoming of nature, they must overcome nature. It is not so simple for architecture merely to shift and say that overcoming nature is no longer the problem, because it obviously remains a problem.

However, it is possible to respond to my scientist client and at the same time still deal with the problems of presence and gravity. To do this the architectural discourse must be displaced. The issue is not merely as it was in the past, that architecture must withstand the forces of gravity, but the manner in which this overcoming is symbolized. In other words, it is not enough to suggest that building must be rational, truthful, beautiful, good, must in its mimesis of the natural suggest man's overcoming of the natural. Rather, as the architectural discourse changes its focus from nature to knowledge, a far more complex object emerges, which requires a more complex form of architectural reality. This is because knowledge (as opposed to nature) has no physical being. What is being represented in physical form when knowledge is being overcome? Nature, traditionally, was the liminal, the boundary definition; it mediated, in the anthropocentric world of the enlightenment, the lost certainty of God. The natural became a valued origin, both useful to explain the world metaphorically and as a process and an object to be emulated. Since architecture had set out to symbolize the overcoming of nature, it is more than reasonable to think that the overcoming of knowledge also could be symbolized. The uncertainty that is contained in something other than the liminal will certainly be part of the expression of man overcoming knowledge.

At the root of the present conceptual structure of architecture is the Vitruvian triad of commodity, firmness, and delight (use, structure, and beauty). The beautiful as a dialectical category has been understood as a singular and monovalent condition; it has been about goodness, about the natural, the rational, and the truthful. It is that to which architects are taught to aspire in their architecture. Thus they search for and manifest conditions of the beautiful as a form of delight in the Vitruvian sense. It was within such a desire that this form of the beautiful became as if natural for architecture over the past five hundred years. There were rules for the beautiful, for example, in classical ordination which, although modified through different periods of architecture, much as styles change in fashion, were never, even in Modern architecture, essentially displaced.

In the 18th century, Immanuel Kant began to destabilize this singular concept of beauty. He suggested that there could be something else, another way to conceptualize beauty other than as goodness, other than as natural. He suggested that within the beautiful there was something else, which he called the sublime. When the sublime was articulated before Kant, it was in dialectical opposition to beauty. With Kant came the suggestion that the sublime was within the beautiful, and the beautiful within the sublime. This difference between opposition and being within is at the very heart of the argument to follow.

Now, interestingly, the sublime also has within it a condition which the conventionally beautiful represses. It is a condition of the uncertain, the unspeakable, the unnatural, the unpresent, the unphysical; taken together these constitute the condition which approaches the ter-

rifying, a condition which lies within the sublime.

The terms of the grotesque are usually thought of as the negative of the sublime. However, this is not quite the case in architecture, where the sublime deals with qualities of the airy, qualities which resist physical occupation, the grotesque deals with real substance, with the manifestation of the uncertain in the physical. Since architecture is thought to deal with physical presence, then the grotesque in some sense is already present in architecture. And this condition of the grotesque was acceptable as long as it was as decoration; in the form of gargoyles, and frescoes. This is because the grotesque introduces the idea of the ugly, the deformed, the supposedly unnatural as an always present in the beautiful. It is this condition of the always present or the already within, that the beautiful in architecture attempts to repress.

That the overcoming of nature, or the depiction of nature as other, preoccupied the Enlightenment and the technological and scientific revolutions, was obvious. In response, the grotesque as it was put forward in the Romantic movement in Wordsworth, Keats, and Shelley, was concerned with rethinking this relationship between the self and nature. Therefore, today, the "sublime" and the "grotesque" deal with this movement between self and the natural, and the representation of this unease in literature and painting. If the "naturalness" of nature is to be displaced in the uneasy movement between nature and self, then our ideas of the sublime and the grotesque must also be reconceptualized in terms of overcoming knowledge without losing the fear associated with the natural, and the fear of the uncertain, *i.e.* the fear of not overcoming nature, must be preserved in any displaced categories.

The fear or uncertainty is now doubly present; the previous uncertainty of the natural, as well as the uncertainty of something other than the liminal,

that is the uncertainty of knowledge that is within knowledge. Since the conditions for the sublime and the grotesque evolved from the expression of man overcoming nature, other terms which contain this double uncertainty will have to be found; the form of expression for man overcoming knowledge becomes far more complex.

What does this mean for architecture? In order to achieve the necessary internal displacement, architecture would have to displace the former ways of conceptualizing itself. It would follow then that the notion of the house, or of any form of the occupation of space, requires a more complex form of the beautiful, one which contains the ugly, or a rationality that contains the irrational. This idea of containing within, necessitates a break from the tradition of an architecture of categories, of types which in their essence rely on the separation of things as opposites. There seem to be four aspects which begin to outline a condition of displacement. The following four aspects should be seen neither as comprehensive (there could be others) nor as a guarantee that their displacing capacities will produce a displaced architecture.

A major displacement concerns the role of the architect/designer and the design process. Something may be designed which can be called displacing, but it may be only an expressionism, a mannerist distortion of an essentially stable language. It may not displace the stable language, but on the contrary further stabilize its normative condition. This can be seen in many examples of current architectural fashion. There is a need for a process other than an intuition — "I like this," or "I like that." When the process is intuitive, it will already be known, and therefore complicit with the repressions inherent in architectural "knowledge." Intuitive design can never produce a state of uncertainty, only, at best, an illustration of uncertainty. While the concept of the grotesque or the uncanny can be conceptualized and imaged, it cannot be designed. Something designed is essentially non-textual, because design of necessity involves certainty; something always has to be made. To attempt to design between uncertainty or multivalency, produces only a superficial illustration of such a condition. If something can be designed it is no longer uncertain.

In the traditional idea of architectural design, form, function, structure, site, and meaning can all be said to be texts. But they are not textual. Texts are always thought to be primary or original sources. Textual or textuality is that aspect of text which is a condition of otherness or secondarity. An ex-

ample of this condition of otherness in architecture is a trace. If architecture is primarily presence — materiality, bricks and mortar — then otherness or secondarity would be trace, as the presence of absence. Trace can never be original, because trace always suggests the possibility of something *other* as original, as something *prior* to. In any text there are potential traces of otherness, aspects or structures which have been repressed by presence. As long as presence remains dominant *i.e.* singular, there can be no textuality. Therefore by its very nature such a condition of trace requires at least *two* texts.

Thus, the second aspect of this *other* architecture is something which might be called *twoness*. There are many different twonesses which exist in traditional architecture already: The twoness of form and function, and the twoness of structure and ornament. But these are traditionally seen as hierarchical categories; one is always seen as dominant or original and the other as secondary (form follows function, ornament is added to structure). In the sense it is being used here, twoness suggests a condition where there is no dominance or originary value but rather a structure of equivalences, where there is uncertainty instead of hierarchy. When the one text is too dominant there is no displacement. When the other text becomes presence itself it obtrudes and loses its capacity for the uncertain. Equally the second text cannot obliterate the first text, but will be understood to be interior to it, thus as an already present "trace" usually suppressed by a single dominant reading. This second text thus will always be within the first text and thus between traditional presence and absence, between being and non-being.

Therefore, the third condition of this other architecture is *betweeness*, which suggests a condition of the object as a weak image. A strong image would give a primary dominant meaning to one or the other of the two texts. Not only must one or the other of the two texts not have a strong image; they will seem to be two weak images, which suggests a blurred third. In other words, the new condition of the object must be *between* in an imageable sense as well: It is something which is almost this, or almost that, but not quite either. The displacing experience is the uncertainty of a partial knowing. Therefore, the object must have a blurring effect. It must look out of focus: almost seen, but not quite, seen. Again, this between is not a between dialectically, but a between *within*. The loss of the idea of architecture as a strong image undercuts the traditional categories of architecture associated with man overcoming nature; place, route, enclosure, presence, and the vertebrate, upright building — symbolic of overcoming gravity.

To deny traditional place or enclosure, suggests an other condition of this displaced architecture, that is interiority. Interiority has nothing to do with the inside or the in-habitable space of a building but rather of a condition of being within. However, as is the case with the grotesque, interiority deals with two factors; the unseen and the hollowed-out. Interiority also deals with the condition proposed by textuality that the symbolism or meaning of any sign refers, in such a displaced architec-

ture, not outward but inward to an already present condition.

Ultimately, each of these four conditions provoke an uncertainty in the object, by removing both the architect and the user from any necessary control of the object. The architect no longer is the hand and mind, the mythic originary figure in the design process. And the object no longer requires the experience of the user to be understood. No longer does the object need to look ugly or terrifying to provoke an uncertainty; it is now the distance between object and subject — the impossibility of possession which provokes this anxiety.

Biology Center for the University of Frankfurt

Peter Eisenman

Model

Site plan

Text from the panel at the gallery entrance of the *Deconstructivist Architecture* exhibition, at the Museum of Modern Art, New York, 1988:

The projects in this exhibition mark the emergence of a new sensibility in architecture. They radically displace traditional ideas about the nature of the architectural object. Traditionally, the architect has sought to produce pure form based on the inviolable integrity of simple geometric figures. The architect protects those figures from contamination in order to sustain the central cultural values of stability, harmony, and security, of comfort, order, and unity. In these

Background to the Design of the Biology Center

Our analysis of the building program and the site requirements revealed that the scientific and educational goals of the University of Frankfurt could be satisfied by a project which satisfies these three criteria: first, the maximum interaction between functional areas and between the people that use them (both within the departments of the university and between the university and the city); second, the accommodation of future change and growth that cannot be predicted today; and third, the maintenance of the site, as far as possible, as a green preserve. This means that a traditional architecture of set spatial hierarchies which rigidly constrain future growth must be abandoned. To undermine these classical architectural hierarchies, it is necessary to dissolve the traditional autonomy of the discipline of architecture. This was done by moving away from the closed categories that traditionally divide biology from architecture and to blur the distinction between them. Blurring the formal options that may fall between biology and architecture.

123

As biology today dislocates the traditions of science, so the architecture of the biocenter dislocates the traditions of architecture. While architecture's role is traditionally seen to be that of accommodating and representing function, this project does not do that. It does not simply accommodate the methods by which research into biological processes is carried out. Rather, it articulates those processes themselves. Indeed, it could be said that its architecture is produced by those very processes.

To accomplish this we first departed from the traditional representation of biology by making an architectural reading of the biological concepts of DNA processes by interpreting them in terms of geometrical processes. At the same time, we departed form the traditional representation of architecture by abandoning the classical Euclidean geometry on which the discipline is based in favor of a fractal geometry. What we discovered was that there is a similarity between the processes of fractal geometry and the geometry of DNA processes. This similarity was used to propose an analogy between architectural processes and biological processes. the analogy made possible a project that is neither simply architectural nor simply biological, but one which is suspended between the two.

Ground floor plan

The Design Process

Rather than simply representing the physical configuration of DNA, (i.e. as a double helix) the project form is the result of the action of the three most basic processes by which DNA constructs proteins: replication, transcription, and translation, on the geometric figures that biologists use to explain these processes by using four geometric figures, each with a specific color, which symbolize the DNA code. The particular shapes of the inner faces of these figures indicate that they are capable of locking together as two pairs. The blueprint for every protein is encoded in long sequences of these paired figures which form a double stranded chain. Using an analogy between biological construction and architectural construction, this cain can be transposed into architectural form in such a way that it produces an architecture which becomes complicit with the discipline which it houses.

Rather, it is a series of discrete ideological experiments about the limits of architecture, carried out over the last ten years by independant architects moving in divergent directions. Each project undermines a different aspect of conventional architectural practice. What they share is that each does so by exploiting the hidden potential of modernism.

Each project interrogates the ready-made language of modern architecture and finds repressed within its pure forms the "impure," skewed geometry — the twisted volumes, warped planes, and clashing lines — developed by the Russian avant-garde early in the twentieth century. Pure form is violated but not destroyed. This is an architecture of disruption and dislocation, of displacement and distortion, but not of dismantling or demolition.

This subversion of pure form pushes architecture to its limits, redefining its most basic problems: structure and function. But these projects are both structurally sound and functionally efficient.

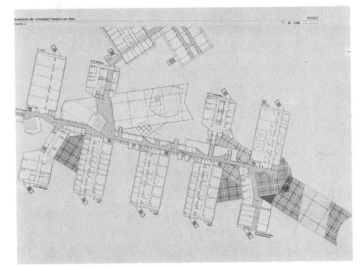

First floor plan

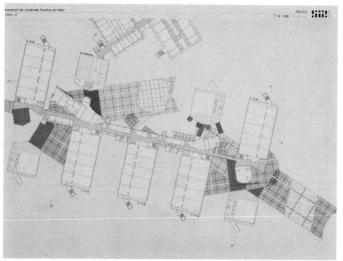

Second floor plan

A. Replication

In the biological process of replication, the DNA chain splits into two strands which then attract their complementary strands to form two new identical chains. The process can be interpreted architecturally (that is, through fractal geometry) by using the code for Collagen as the base form and the complement of that code as the generating form. Then in turn each figure in the complementary code was applied to each surface and each base form. (It should be noted that the curved surfaces of these figures were abstracted into a sequence of straight lines.)

B. Transcription

In biological transcription, the DNA chain temporarily unzips and a new strand inserts itself into the resulting gap and makes a complementary copy of only one of the exposed DNA strands. That copy (MRNA) is then taken to the protein construction site. This process is the same as replication except only one strand is copied and many sections of its code are omitted. Consequently, it is interpreted architecturally as a second iteration of the first fractal process applied to only the lower strand of the original five pairs. The figures produces in the first process now become the base form and their complements become the generating form. This generating sequence is only applied to the inner surface of the lower strand in order to indicate that sections of the code are not transcribed in this process.

Excerpt from *Deconstructivist Architecture,* catalogue for the exhibition at the Museum of Modern Art, New York, 1988:

The result is a complex dialogue between the basic form and its distortions. A world of unstable forms emerges from within a stable structures of modernism. And those multiplying forms

They derive their force precisely from not playing in the sanctuaries of seductive drawing, obscure theory, of uninhabitable sculpture. Instead they belong to the realm of building. Each aims at the reality of built form. Some have been built, others will be built, and some will never be built. But they are all buildable, and as such constitute strategic cultural interventions that produce a certain disquiet by displacing the conservative institution of architecture.

In this project, the biologist's figures were overlaid upon the site in a row beginning at the main entrance and following the precise sequence of the DNA chain for the protein Collagen, which produces the necessary tensile strength of biological structure (as in bone). The five pairs of figures which lay closest to the existing chemistry building became the laboratories for our project. In this way, an initial architectural structure was produced out of the figurative code for biological structure.

Third floor plan

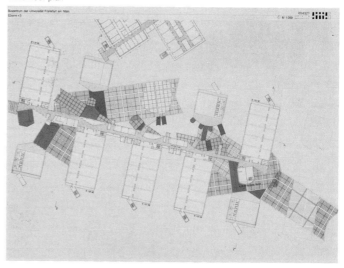

The project was then produced by subjecting that figurative code to the very processes which it describes. These biological processes were interpreted architecturally by the use of fractal geometry. In fractal geometry, geometric forms grow by the application of a generating form to a base form. The size of the generating form varies in relationship to the size of the surface of the base figure to which it is applied. As in biology, the generating form reads the surface of the base form. There is a possible analogy between fractal processes and biological processes when the biologist's figures are used as both the base form and the generating form, that is a replication of the base form. The processes of fractal geometry can also be described by the similar processes of replication, transcription, and translation. Through this analogy, the original five pairs of figures could be successively transformed by fractal processes in a way that articulates the three basic DNA processes.

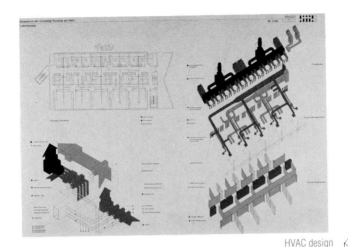

HVAC design

clash in ways that create a range of relationships: sometimes there is no conflict, as one form passes over or under another; sometimes one form is simply embedded within another; sometimes both forms are disturbed and a new form is produced. The project becomes a complex exchange between sold, void, and transparency... Between them, the traditional opposition of abstraction and figuration is undermined. It is no longer possible to separate structural work from ornamental play.

C. Translation

The final biological process in the production of a protein is the translation of the DNA code into the physical structure of a protein. This translation is carried out by another kind of strand, TRNA, which carries the building block (amino acid) to the protein construction site and then releases that block onto a chain of such blocks (polypeptide chain) deposited by previous TRNA strands. This process is interpreted in the architectural project by treating two groups of the upper strand of the original figures as TRNA strands. Theses groups are then displaced spatially in a way that instead of the figurative form, now leaves behind traces of the biological building with the rectilinear forms of the chemistry building, in its siting, to be read as the polypeptide chain of building blocks. In this way the architecture of the biocenter is translated into that of the chemistry building. The traces left by the TRNAs are solid when their building block has yet to be deposited onto the protein chain symbolized by the chemistry buildings and they are void when that block has already been deposited. In this way, the existing buildings are redefined as a product of the biocenter, rather that an original figure of the site.

Design concept

The project is colored according to the biologist's color code for the figures. While the value of these four colors remains constant, their intensity is varied in order to articulate the different processes. The original figures are marked by the lightest shade while those produced by transcription have the middle shade. The traces produced by the translation process are given the same color as the chemistry building of which they are the symbolic building blocks.

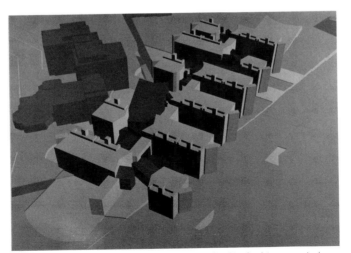

Perspective rendered to simulate a computer image

La Villette

Bernard Tschumi

Deconstruction

Is the *Parc de la Villette* a built theory or a theoretical building? Can the pragmatism of building practice be allied with the analytic rigor of concepts?

An earlier series of projects, published as *The Manhattan Transcripts* (Academy Editions — St. Martin's Press, 1981) was aimed at achieving a displacement of conventional architectural categories through a theoretical argument. *La Villette* was the built extension of a comparable method; it was impelled by the desire to move "from pure mathematics to applied mathematics." In its case, the constraints of the built realization both expanded and restricted the research. It expanded it, insofar as the very real economic, political and technical restraints of the operation demanded an ever increasing sharpening of the theoretical argumentation: the project became better as difficulties increased. But it restricted it insofar as *La Villette* had to be *built*. The intention was never merely to publish books or mount exhibitions; the finality of each drawing was "building": except in the book entitled *La Case Vide*, there were no "theoretical drawings" for *La Villette*.

However, the *Parc de la Villette* project has a specific aim: to prove that it was possible to construct a complex architectural organization without resorting to traditional rules of composition, hierarchy, and order. The principle of superimposition of three autonomous systems of points, lines, and surfaces was developed by rejecting the totalizing synthesis of objective constraints evident in the majority of large-scale projects. In fact, if historically architecture has always been defined as the "harmonious synthesis" of cost, structure, use, and formal constraints ("*venustas, firmitas, utilitas*"), the Park became architecture against itself: a dis-integration.

Our aims were to displace the traditional opposition between program and architecture, and to extend questioning of other architectural conventions through operations of superimposition, permutation, and substitution to achieve "a reversal of the classical oppositions and a general displacement of the system," as Jacques Derrida has written, in another context, in *Marges*. Above all, the project directed an attack against cause and effect relationships, whether between form and function, structure and economics, or (of course) form and program, replacing these oppositions by new concepts of contiguity and superimposition. "Deconstructing" a given program meant showing that the program could challenge the very ideology it implies. And deconstructing architecture involved dismantling its conventions, using concepts derived both from architecture and from elsewhere — from cinema, literary criticism and other disciplines. For if the limits between different domains of thought have gradually vanished in the past twenty years, the same phenomenon applies to architecture, which now entertains relations with cinema, philosophy, and psychoanalysis (to cite only a few examples) in an intertextuality subversive of modernist autonomy. But it is above all the historical split between architecture and its theory that is eroded by the principles of deconstruction.

It is not by chance that the different systems of the Park negate one another as they are superimposed on the site. Much of my earlier theoretical work has questioned the very idea of structure, paralleling contemporary research on literary texts. One of the goals at *La Villette* was to pursue this investigation of the concept of structure, as expressed in the respective forms of the point grid, the coordinate axes (covered galleries) and the "random curve" (cinematic promenade). Superimposing these autonomous and completely logical structures meant questioning their conceptual status as ordering machines: the superimposition of three coherent structures can never result in a supercoherent megastructure, but in something undecidable, something that is the opposite of a totality. This device had been explored from 1976 onwards in the *Manhattan Transcripts*, where the overlapping of abstract and figurative elements (based on "abstract" architectonic transformations as much as on "figurative" extracts from the selected site) coincided with a more general exploration of the ideas of program, scenario, and sequence.

The independence of the three superposed structures thus avoided all attempts to homogenize the Park into a totality. It eliminated the presumption of a pre-established causality between program, architecture, and signification. Moreover, the Park rejected context, encouraging intertextuality and the dispersion of meaning. It subverted context: *La Villette is anticontextual. It has no relation to its surroundings. Its plan subverts the very notion of borders on which "context" depends.**

* Bernard Tschumi, *Cinégram Folie, Le Parc de la Villette* (Princeton: Princeton Architectural Press, 1987). Reprinted by permission of Bernard Tschumi.

La Case Vide, La Villette

Bernard Tschumi

The somewhat mechanical parts of the *folie* apparatus are organized around a repetitive structure — the point-grid — which constitutes an absolute rule, a reassuring certitude. This certitude proved necessary at the time of implementation: Builders, administrators, and politicians do not take lightly the infinite substitutions, transformations, and permutations of concepts. But the point-grid only gives the appearance of order, by simulating it. For material presence on a large metropolitan site is only one moment in a larger process which questions the very idea of structure.

Hence *La Case Vide*, this *folio-folie*, expands questions first raised with the conceptual diagrams of the competition entry, developed in the working drawing stage and, finally, implemented in the form of actual buildings during construction. The red architecture of *La Villette* is not meant to be apprehended as merely built. Its traces in the ground constitute only a given moment of presence in the course of a larger programme, a larger project. Its material face constantly refers to another, immaterial one which today dislocates the built structures it reflects.

We know that architectural systems are always noted for the coherence they represent. From the Classical era to the Modern Movement, from Durand to the Constructivists and beyond, the notion of an incoherent structure is simply without consideration. The very function of architecture, as it is still understood today, precludes the idea of a dis-structured structure.

However, the process of superimposition, permutation, and substitution which governed the Parc de la Villette plan could lead only to a radical questioning of the concept of structure — to its decentering — since the superimposition of three autonomous (and coherent) structures (points, lines, surfaces) does not necessarily lead to a new, more complex, and verifiable structure. Instead, they open up a field of contradictory and conflictual events which deny the idea of a pre-established coherence. Permutations and substitutions of elements within the systems of points, lines, and surface further add to the disruption. *La Case Vide* takes its title from one specific drawing (*La Case Vide*, 1985) in this process of disruption. Although this drawing preceded actual construction on the site, it contains in its very logic the displacements and dis-structuring which informed the making of this *Folio*. A *case vide* is an empty slot or box in a chart or matrix, an unoccupied square in a chessboard, a blank compartment: the point of the unexpected, before data entered on the vertical axis can meet with data on the horizontal one. The matrix normally suggests endless combinations, permutations and substitutions. But each of the combinations one arrives at can, in turn, be distorted, fragmented, or endlessly repeated. Derived from the key drawings of the project, each plate dislocates the structure of the systems which compose it, transforming and reassembling them not so much in order to question laws of representation, but to contradict the apparent logic of the actual ordering device — divergence, deviation, deflection, dispersion, exorbitation.

The line of trees, the cinematic promenade, the galleria, the *folies, as built*, are then nothing but a moment in the process of conception, the ephemeral and temporary materialisation of concept at one arbitrary moment in the conceptual chain, in the development of architectural thought. Architecture moves on. On one hand, the constructions on the site *are* real, material; on the other, they are abstract notations in a process, meta-operational elements, a frozen image, a freeze-frame in a process of constant transformation, construction, and dislocation.

La Case Vide: La Villette, Folio VIII (London: Architectural Association, 1985), Perspective view: north-south gallery.

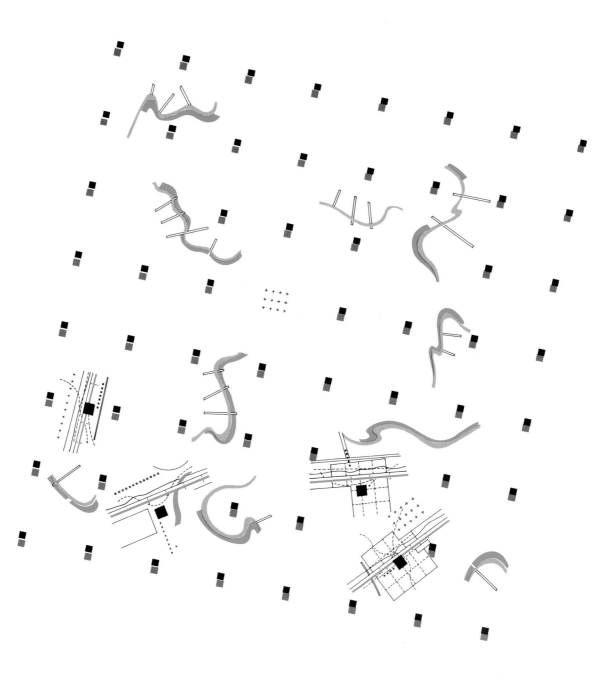

La Case Vide: La Villette, Folio VIII (London: Architectural Association, 1985), Plate 20.

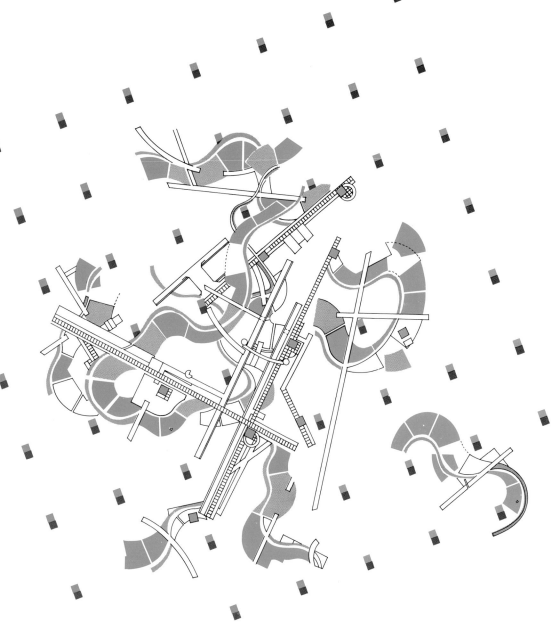

La Case Vide: La Villette, Folio VIII (London: Architectural Association, 1985), Plate 16.

Point de Folie — Maintenant l'Architecture *Jacques Derrida*

3 *Maintenant*: if the word [now] still designates what happens, has just happened, promises to happen *to* architecture as well as *through* architecture, this imminence of the *just* (*just* happens, *just* happened, is *just* about to happen) no longer lets itself be inscribed in the ordered sequence of a history: It is neither a fashion, a period or an era. The *just maintenant* [just now] does not remain a stranger to history, of course, but the relation would be different. And if this happens *to us*, we must be prepared to receive these two words. On the one hand, it does not happen to a constituted *us*, to a human subjectivity whose essence would be arrested and which would *then* find itself affected by the history of this thing called architecture.

We appear to ourselves only through an experience of spacing which is already marked by architecture. What happens through architecture both constructs and instructs this *us*. The latter *finds itself* engaged by architecture before it becomes the subject of it: master and possessor. On the other hand, the imminence of what happens to us *maintenant* announces not only an architectural event but, more particularly, a writing of space, a mode of spacing which makes a place for the event.

If Tschumi's work indeed describes an architecture of the event, it is not only in that it constructs places in which something should happen or to make the construction itself be, as we say, an event. This is not what is essential. The dimension of the event is subsumed in the very structure of the architectural apparatus: sequence, open series, narrativity, the cinematic, dramaturgy, choreography.

4 Is an architecture of events possible? If what happens to us thus does not come from outside, or rather, if this outside engages us in the very thing we are, is there a *maintenant* of architecture and in what sense [*sens*]? Everything indeed [*justement*] comes down to the question of meaning [*sens*].

We shall not reply by indicating a means of access, for example, through a given form of architecture: preamble, *pronaos*, threshold, methodical route, circle or circulation, labyrinth, flight of stairs, ascent, archaeological regression towards a foundation, etc. Even less through the form of a system, that is, through architectonics: the art of systems, as Kant says.

We will not reply by giving access to some final meaning, whose assumption would be finally promised to us. No, it is justly [*justement*] a question of what happens to meaning: not in the sense of what would finally allow us to arrive at meaning, but of what happens to it, to meaning, to the meaning of meaning. And so — and this is the event — what happens to it through an event which, no longer precisely or simply falling into the domain of meaning, would be intimately linked to something like madness [*la folie*].

7 Let us never forget that there is an architecture of architecture. Down even to its archaic foundation, the most fundamental concept of architecture has been *constructed*. This naturalised architecture is bequeathed to us: we inhabit it, it inhabits us, we think it is destined for habitation, and it is no longer an object for us at all. But we must recognise in it an *artefact*, a *construction*, a monument.

It did not fall from the sky; it is not natural, even if it informs a specific scheme of relations to *physis*, the sky, the earth, the human, and the divine. This architecture of architecture has a history; it is historical through and through. Its heritage inaugurates the intimacy of our economy, the law of our hearth (*oikos*), our familial, religious, and political oikonomy, all the places of birth and death, temple, school, stadium, agora, square, sepulchre. It goes right through us [*nous transit*] to the point that we forget its very historicity: we take it for nature. It is common sense itself.*

* Excerpts from Jacques Derrida, "*Point de Folie — Maintenant l'Architecture*" in Bernard Tschumi, *La Case Vide*, Folio VIII (London: Architectural Association, 1985).

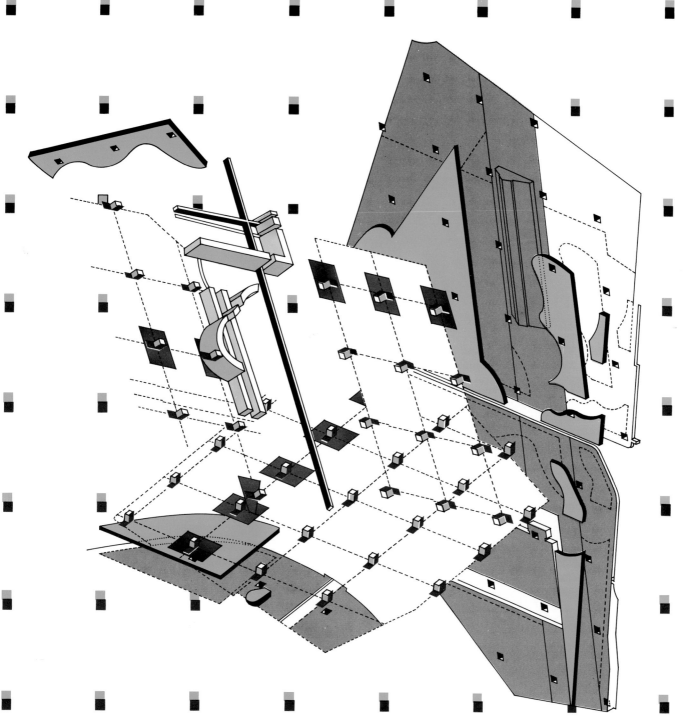

La Case Vide: La Villette, Folio VIII (London: Architectural
Association, 1985), Plate 4.

Drawings recreated by Tony Wong

Observatory Tower

Alastair Noble

Observatory Tower I, 1985. Mixed media illuminated with black and white T.V. Photo: Mary Bachmann.

Inverted obelisk: a mechanism of displacement, a language of place redirects the space of chaos. This transformation of structure reveals an opening, a point of entry, into a collecting vessel, through which passage can be made. It becomes the recipient of all atmospheric noise, which is drawn through, guided down, and transmuted into the luminous flux of the cathode-ray tube. The apex of this distillery transmits the fragmented signals of communication condensed into points of fractured light. In turn these emissions are reflected up from the polished surface of a dome beneath the suspended obelisk. A floating constellation of fluctuating impulses dematerializes and rematerializes, hypnotically engaging within the depths of the translucent medium. An electronic atmosphere of multidirectional signals traces presence within absence, without text, without context, a vertiginous state.

Study II for Observatory Tower I, 1985. Pastel/ bronze powder (above in background). Photo: Mary Bachmann.

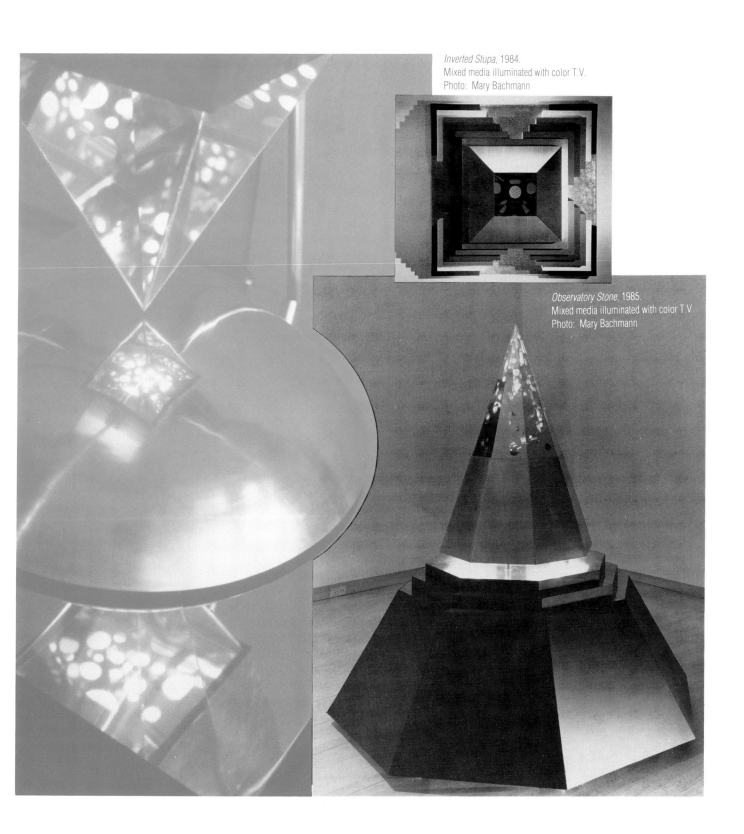

Inverted Stupa, 1984.
Mixed media illuminated with color T.V.
Photo: Mary Bachmann

Observatory Stone, 1985.
Mixed media illuminated with color T.V.
Photo: Mary Bachmann

Art & Language

Incidents in a Museum

Michael Baldwin and Mel Ramsden's latest series of paintings, *Incidents in a Museum*, 1985-87 resulted in a sense of alienation from their work in that series. Without mutually agreeable points of reference the artists were at- walls, and coffered ceilings determine the iconography of the picture space in which the "incidents" occur. The Whitney Museum of American Art, taken as a representative of its type, cannot include the work of Art & Language in its collection; thus the Museum became the imaginary theater, in which that work could be figuratively located and displaced. A museum is, after culture and not simply of its production. Art & Language aspires to a critical realism which requires that the actual conditions of meaning and significance in culture be referred to, and their insecure margins exposed, and that response to this reference and this exposure be an inescapable requirement for the would-be competent viewer.

The strategies employed effect an interruption of pictorial space and mimetic identity through shifts of scale, marked

Index: Incidents in a Museum XIII, 1986. Courtesy: Marian Goodman Gallery.

tempting to navigate in a world without bearings. A sense of Art & Language's having entered culture, business, and mythology led to the first representation of *The Studio as Incident in a Museum.*

The project series gradually developed around the concept of the modernist museum as the site of alienated production, a place where things are encountered, and events transpire, a brutalizing image of the conditions of distribution of high culture. The Whitney's slabbed floors, moveable screen all, a site for the generation of representations; a museum represents Art.

The practice of Art & Language has been a dialogue with the conditions of failure and refusal in the signifying languages of art. The suggestion is that art must continue at the edge of this failure. The position of the edge is historically determined. Its location is a condition of the consumption of art and either by literal changes or figurative divisions of the surface. Through the individual whole, configurations may cohere in some trivial sense, the changes of scale provoke conflicting perceptual attitudes and cultural expectations. Separate parts are not easily brought together in the descriptive and rhetorical forms characteristic of current critical discourse. Description falters in the face of actual or potential overlap between the painting and the representation of the painting, between a part or a representation of a part. To become a competent viewer is to engage in an unreassuring activity.

Robert Smithson

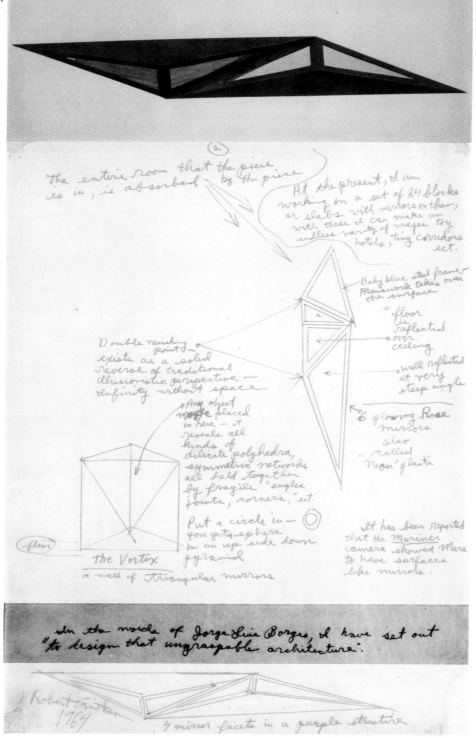

Untitled, 1963-64.
Steel/plexiglass mirror.
Courtesy: Jon Weber Gallery.

②

the entire room that the piece
is in, is absorbed by the piece

At the present, I am
working on a set of 24 blocks
or slabs with mirrors on them,
with these I can make an
endless variety of mazes toy
hotels, tiny corridors
ect.

Baby blue steel frame
Framework takes over
the surface

○ floor
is
reflected
○ over
ceiling

○ wall reflected
at very
steep angle

Double vanishing
point —
exists as a solid
reverse of traditional
illusionistic perspective —
Infinity without space

○ Any object
maybe placed
in here — it
reveals all
kinds of
delicate polyhedra,
symmetric networks
all held together
by fragile "angles
joints, corners," ect.

Put a circle in — ⊙
you got a sphere
in an up side down
pyramid

the Vortex
a well of triangular mirrors

floor

¢ glowing Rose
mirrors
also
called
"Neon" plastic

It has been reported
that the Mariner
camera showed Mars
to have surfaces
like mirrors.

In the words of Jorge Luis Borges, I have set out
"to design that ungraspable architecture".

Robert Smithson
1964

4 mirror facets in a purple structure

*Drawing of 3 Untitled Works
in Metal and Plastic*, 1964.
Ink/typing paper.
Courtesy: Jon Weber Gallery.

Circular

Helen Anne Easterly

Take
care
          what you write
                              down. It may reach
toward light, run
          roots into your depths,
              masquerade as shelter. Birds
may hover, hang
                              nests of frail feathers there,
insects flicker in its shade. Glittering
from its branches (leaves, lights, ornaments) may depend
              (perhaps eventually fall) fruits,
flowers you never imagined, from
seeds you did not intend.
              You will be able then
                              only to gild or embroider,
          string,
          restring,
search for boxes and baskets,
                              press some into
                              pages you will fear to open.

Someday
someone
          may come, call out,
                              looking purposeful or innocent
                              splinter it all in a minute
from idea to fuel,
                              toothpicks,
          paper. There it lies,
                              razed,
          potential. You imagine
                              here is a-
                              nother chance

Crisis in Poetry

Stéphane Mallarmé

...Each soul is a melody which must be picked up again, and the flute or the viola of everyone exists for that.

Late in coming, it seems to me, is the true condition or the possibility not just of expressing oneself but of modulating oneself as one chooses.

Languages are imperfect in that although there are many, the supreme one is lacking: thinking is to write without accessories, or whispering, but since the immortal word is still tacit, the diversity of tongues on the earth keeps everyone from uttering the word which would be otherwise in one unique rendering, truth itself in its substance... Only, we must realize, poetry would not exist; philosophically, verse makes up for what languages lack, completely superior as it is.

. . .

The pure work implies the disappearance of the poet as speaker, yielding his initiative to words, which are mobilized by the shock of their difference; they light up with reciprocal reflections like a virtual stream of fireworks over jewels, restoring perceptible breath to the former lyric impulse, or the enthusiastic personal directing of the sentence.

. . .

One desire of my epoch which cannot be dismissed is to separate so as to attribute them differently the double state of the immediate or unrefined word on one hand, the essential one on the other.

. . .

What good is the marvel of transposing a fact of nature into its almost complete and vibratory disappearance with the play of the word however, unless there comes forth from it, without the bother of a nearby or concrete reminder, the pure notion.

I say: a flower! and outside the oblivion to which my voice relegates any shape, insofar as it is something other than the calyx, there arises musically, as the very idea and delicate, the one absent from every bouquet.

Excerpted from
Stéphane Mallarmé Selected Poetry and Prose,
Copyright © 1982 by Mary Ann Caws.
Reprinted by permission of New Direction
Publication Corp.

Essay on Multi-Dimensional Architecture

Madeline Gins

Appendix A: In Use
Only texture selecting from amongst itself. . .

An even dispersal of whatever comes along is the way to make it more bearable. Divide and disperse the impact. Let anything be scattered throughout, as lightly or as pinchingly as need might have it — but throughout. The impact of which. The preparation for the impact of which. All the while. A forward tornado-trough, but more usually, the same, but in reverse, a pulling-back through, a back-weaving trough (troughing) dipping back pointedly [suction without suction] into. And why? Oh, so as to proceed. Into which door [or impassive face/facet of texture] otherwise closed to you did you say you had in this way bitten?

Pain: One way to cut it out is to cut the deck thoroughly. Thinking of cutting a deck gives a close-up view of what troughing might be. All the metaphorical everything arrayed. Aspects thumbed through aspects, with thumbs out of the blue. Do this with the rhythm of gods, and you'll be fine. Who was it who invented a waffle pan for irony? Was that the god of mirages and of tear waves?

It is not just the spine (not just along the spine), nor just this spine or that, which cuts, is cutting [the] muster/mustard [dear chocolate grinder] or, you see, how would the plumed serpent (broad-backed deck and cellular banner) ever come to be. And yet the spine is thoroughly implicated, intimately "cut" through [trough/troughing], full deck that it is, or the game is dead. Probably some of what has just been said should be further defined. Probably that will amount to all there's left to say on the matter — but this matter talks back.

But this texture, in some ways, why, it is nothing but spine. Certainly not. Yet all active [as in volcano] spines are deck cutters of the multi-dimensional. The multi-dimensional has all the cards in the deck and is self-cutting. In one way or another, there is always a spine in the vicinity of the cutting. The breaths of spine can be plumes. These plumes, thoroughly cellular, are, of course, also cut into the deck [See the Arakawa painting "Ignore the Compass," 1964]. A free enough cutting of all this "cuts" or makes the mustard. As the mustards of the vertebra appear on the tongue, these should be known to have carried a message. Shuffle the deck, shuffle the unruffled (or all-ruffled) feathers of the plumed serpent. Serpent through serpent sways, bred, folded, says. A feather, some mustard, on (at) your lips.

Serpent moving is a cutting of the deck; all graceful, non-shut down movement yields mustard [you might say that Futurism, for example, was painted in mustard].

Not really mustard, but multi-dimensional, another aspect, a bridge aspect, ground to a non-halt; as if the riverbank, having been thoroughly cut into [troughed through] the river, would be able to walk even while the river with which it had been interspersed were "walking" at a different rate within it: two ways of sidling along in one. That type of bridge. A puddle in transit which is full of grains (stepping-stones) of friction. Its aroma is what thinks?

If and when the metaphor is pulverized, it can be mixed. Let scale wink.

He cut back around to return to the ranch the other way.

Then what does it mean to pinchingly receive in an over-all way? Contrast (to prevent) this way of decidedly receiving with a having been as lightly sprinkled on as confectioner's sugar. There will have to be an overlap and a bite. Texture does really grab its own "hand" and it must be allowed this so that what will proceed can. Pinch me to see if I am awake, it might say to itself, if it spoke that way [I don't think it does]. Pinch her cheeks [internally] to give them a little color. And how pinching should this pinching feel? Or any series of ratchets. . . ?

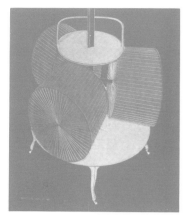

Marcel Duchamp, *Chocolate Grinder*.

Arakawa, *Ignore the Compass*, 1964.

Well, do you feel in cartilage? Not much, but. . . what if there were a jar made of cartilage that strongly resembled a clear glass one? It is threaded up top just the way any ordinary jar would be. What if its cover were also made of *in situ* (you) cartilage but more brassy (not very) and it were, of course, perfectly threaded to be screwed onto the top of the jar. Well, the pinchingness of which [a word — which — sounds already close to catching that degree of pinching I seek to define] I speak would feel no less but no more than how it would feel to have the cover placed upon this jar, as a foreshortened you, and screwed on — in the interiority of what would be undergone as a screwing-on-ness around and about. How the cover, how the jar, in greatly magnified threads, grooves, would each, at the juncture of transparent leadenness, tightening, but in even, non-tightening, gradations, feel in cartilage — and given a minimal rusting — that would be the sought-after degree of pinching; the screwing on of the cover would yield up the ideal bite. I know it's hard to believe but, in this example, there would be absolutely no itching along the way.

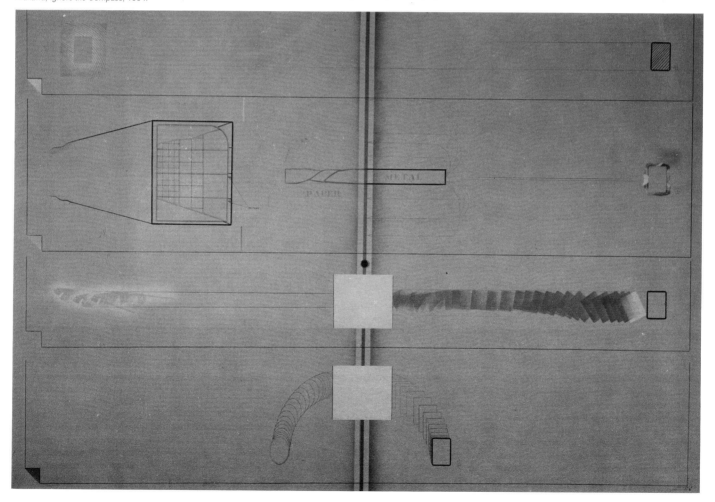

Appendix B: On Appendix A: For a Poetics

Since we will not be available indefinitely. . .

In Appendix A, dimensions are sacrificed to one another for the sake of forming bridges. A bridge all out of the grain of digested dimension. A grain-by-grain mustard steel. To be worthy of one's own mustard, here's mud in your eye. Perception makes/is made of dire mustard.

Damp enough for you today, is it?

Mustard-making as a way to touch base, the sediment, the base toucher, the telling. Bridged moist traction, is it?

Then why would she bring in the notion of cards? As the deck is cut into itself, these metaphors (and/or dimensions) are being cut into each other. Something about the paradigmaticness of the plumed serpent as sweeping image statement, as form of action. Certain (most) images are sweeping statements. Almost no statement sweeps more than the plumed serpent (even this moment undergoing an earthquake in Mexico City). Chop, chop dimensions to be cards for a moment and be shuffled past each other: Throw them up all at once and the plumed serpent is practically there (I think of a sculpture by Vincenzo Agnetti). This is what dimensions do with "itself," too, underlyingly and up.

Then what happens.

The whole is but an exercise in even dispersal. The way to save your head is put it everywhere. Put it all to grain. That grain which is a hole or hutch to the rabbit-atom. The notion of a grain of action. A grain of not see-through but be-through. Ratchom hatch. Ore in the back of the jaw and anywhere, ratchet, derived, at last, atlas. For ratchet atlas, see above.

So that a certain amount can be exhibited to us, I said, torture is necessary. Time (mustard) for the appearance (mustard) of an evolution (mustard). Can there, after all, be a bulk of time without some degree of torture (?) Simply that is what is asked of mustard dispensers (to endure). When clogged, pathology, or dear poetaster, as in your forlorn case, without your realizing it, no mustard comes. But is it not innate in us at least to know whether or not we cut (muster) mustard even as we have no idea as to why?

Poetry exists to make known to dire us, in one way or another (and not inconceivably, even at times, by means of lyricism alone), whatever it is that can be done. But given the straits we are in, it becomes more and more a question of actually spelling this out, a salvage operation, ark construction. And so I have begun to think that every such effort should be at least double. All the strength they had mustered out of symbol...

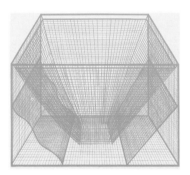

Each side of the inverted truncated pyramid that fills the container has a mesh density of its own. One of these sides is highly irregular in weave. Mesh panel-walls to either side of the object lean toward exterior walls at a forty-five degree angle. Each top corner has applied to it, for a length of six inches in each direction, a highly reflective material. To walk around and view this object named Bottomless, *the participant, leaning backwards, will have to move sideways.*

Arakawa, Beneath Untitled no. 3, 1986. Oil and acrylic on canvas. Collection of N. & J. Rounick (opposite).

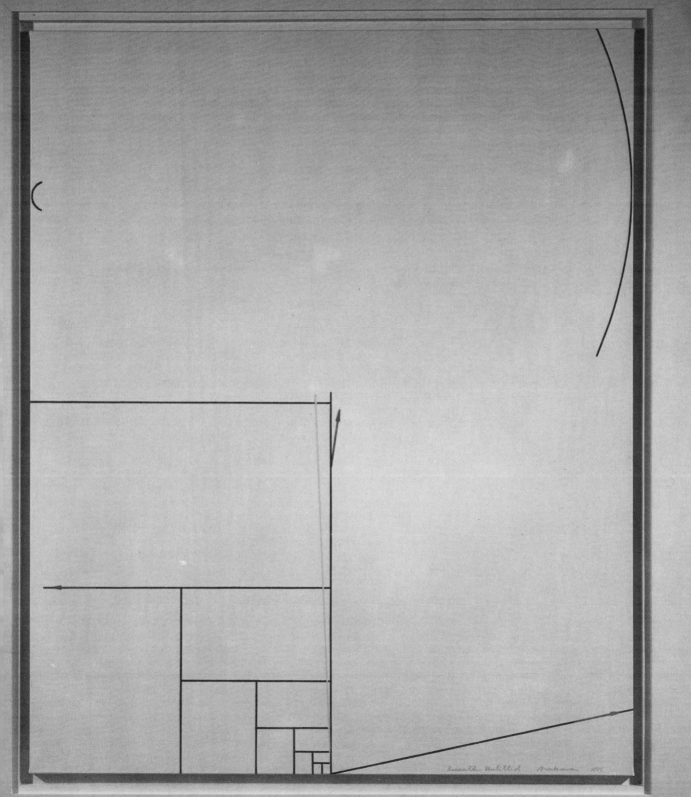

THE   ENTIRE   BODY   WAS   PERCEPTION

Containers of Mind: Bridge Project *Arakawa and Madeline Gins*

Proposed site: Spanning the Moselle River at Epinal, France

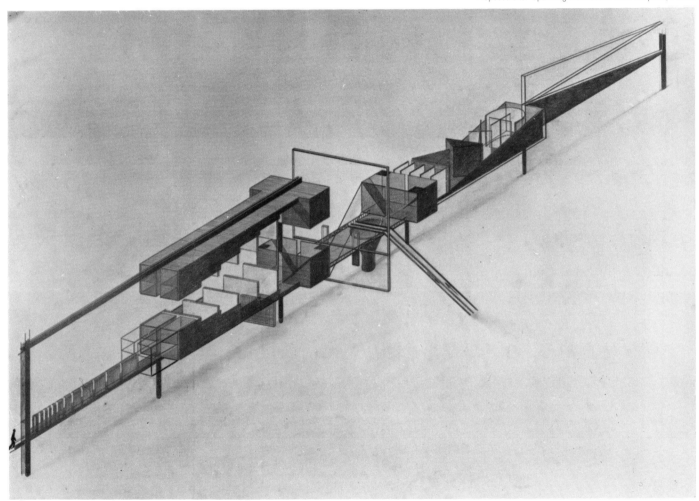

BOTTOMLESS GRADIENT

THE ETERNAL GRADIENT
In which eternal life is equivalent to the desire
not to stop...

BRANCH OF THE UNSAID

THE SHARING OF NAMELESS

BLANK PROTOTYPE

ALL FACADE

ALL ENTRANCE

AN INTERMEDIATE
perception in skeletal form

CONTAINER OF NEUTRALIZATIONS

Taking evolution into our own hands

With a built-in mistake

A grid upon which to hang events and
non-events,
one which could come to know it knows.

NEARLY ZERO PATH

For the circulation of there throughout here

The container suspended on the right is one foot higher than its double. Not more than eighteen to twenty inches separate the two. To pass between, all participants (children excepted) must walk sideways or crawl. Walls

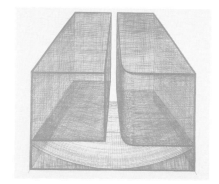

in corresponding positions differ as to mesh density from one container to the other. Six feet below the lowest point of the sloping floor, and six feet above the river, hangs a planter containing a meadow.

As one proceeds around the circle, every two feet, either texture or angle of floor, and hence footing, changes. The distance between top and bottom culminating points is scarcely half-an-inch. Depending on where, and consequently also upon what, one is standing, the points, as they rise and fall, will appear at times to touch. The side walls are made of a tight, dark

mesh. Light comes through these at two oblique angles, one at the middle, angled up toward the interior, and the other at the base, turned up toward the exterior. The pointed mesh mounds can be seen, seen through and into, to vary as to texture or color in relation to position. The topmost surface (the cover to the upper mesh mound) is slightly hummocked.

The corrugations and indentations suggest to the viewer numerous possible landing strips upon which the viewing could come to rest, and countless receptacles or depositories into which, in passing, seeing might be inserted. Jagged, raised planes, jutting out at oblique angles from brightly painted dips and hollows, cause in the viewer, through an accelerating of the accumulating and compounding of his/her viewing, frequent

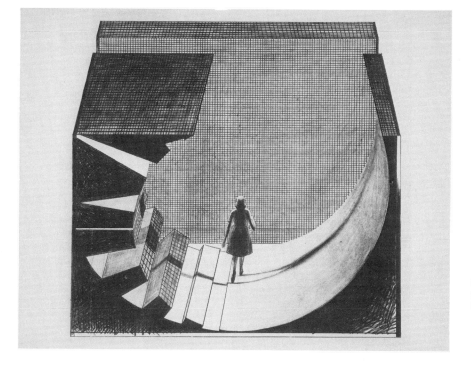

déjà vus. The concave slope, which, rising smoothly up from the floor in full contrast to the furrowed surface, becomes the opposing wall, serves to further compound viewing events, and to augment the déjà-vu forming process within the container passageway; this surface, made of a mesh in which hardly a hole or incision can be discerned, is so fine that the gaze immediately bounces back off of it — as though it were a mirror.

From Blank to Spacetime

Arakawa

Each of the four walls bears the same image as shown. Although they appear to protrude and recede, the thick lead wire in which they are drawn nowhere juts beyond the wall frames. Access to the container may be gained by walking into drawings on any of the four sides. The non-illusion of the flowing river and the illusion of the enclosing drawings should "ignite" one another.

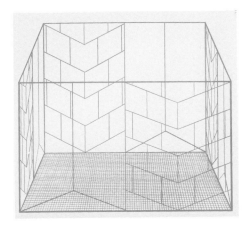

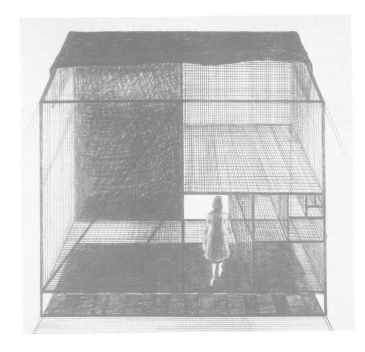

The mosaic base of mesh embedded with a wide range of materials has a few sections left widely open to the river. The second mesh floor is one-and-one-half feet higher than the base. It all depends on what the access is for. Eleven possible entrance-ways (and countless more, if one includes those the mesh itself suggests) are presented; only one of these actually admits of entry. The walker will come to be unsure where and into what s/he is stepping. The smaller the would-be access, the lighter the gray of the mesh. Several layers of unstretched mesh straddle the structure at top, covering approximately one third of it.

Blank is familiar to everyone, but it has been mis-used for a long time. An active understanding of it has not yet been achieved. It is crucial that it be properly introduced. I do not think spacetime can be fully explained without blank.

Most of the statements which follow come from or are related to a long-term study which Made-line Gins and I have made on this subject recently published in a bi-lingual edition by *Editions de la Différence* under the title of *To Not To Die (Pour Ne Pas Mourir)*.

Nothingness, Void, Emptiness, *Tabula Rasa*, Vacuum, the Unconscious; none of these quite covers what I wish to point out by the notion, "Blank."

Blank is above all a neutral positing — in the sense of a holding open; it may be thought of as universal filler; as what is there but undifferentiated, it may be the basis of both something and nothing, but it is not nothing; it can accumulate: It is not void. Having its own laws of operation, it does not provide a *tabula rasa*. It is what fills both Emptiness and the Unconscious — in different proportions. It may draw upon or feed whatever it is the vacuum is but is not identical with it.

It is the individual which manufactures Blank. From the start it can be seen that part of doing is always Blank. Even those energies which lead us move blankly. What are commonly called feeling and thinking are such energies. In addition to providing a place for a "forming Blank," these configurations of energy themselves move through Blank to make varying degrees of awareness or sometimes to remain in it, completely Blank.

There is no thought without Blank. Each mental act comes out of and through Blank, and so does any act, for that matter.

A large part of any presence "is" diffuse blurring — with this "is" shifting constantly. In the diffuse blurring "is" is localized, then shifted to be transferred; this process may be what constitutes "aboutness" or intentionality — also adding, along the way, to diffuse blurring; and diffuse blurring, either previous to, or concurrent with, narrowly-focused, shifting delineations, should be considered Blank. Blank supplies the diffuse blurring presence characteristic of consciousness.

The power or capacity to localize and transfer which makes possible "aboutness" or intentionality is the same, except in degree, as that which constitutes a diffuse blurring presence or Blank. Blank grows by accumulating diffuse blurring.

Power, of a different, scattered degree, accumulates in the wake of any event. Through and within accumulating power, because of a fundamental reassembling of Blank, the nature of spacetime available to an individual or to a group alters.

When it itself, an open possiblilty for reassembly, behaves in waves across/through configurated energies at its own pace, it gradually becomes a "forming Blank" into which all configurations are drawn, absorbed, condensed, and out of which unrecognizable places jump, shaping volumes into images.

Everything comes out of "forming Blank," even spacetime. Without Blank, there would be no spacetime, only energy-matter. Within the specified region, some areas are in a state of activation; no areas are in a state of complete inactivity. All that which is currently non-activated yet not non-active, that is, the sum of static activity, may be considered "forming Blank." Even within specific activations, there may be unspecified activities which also may contribute to the Blank. Some of any individual's Blank is always being used to represent the condition of spacetime. Blank modulates forwards and backwards to and from "being spacetime."

"Forming Blank" is the medium through which localization and transference occur. A fragment, a middle-ground, and a whole, all at once. To localize, it cleaves, in the middle-ground, in the middle range. It cleaves again to transfer. The many-hinged, the cleaved. During the cleaving, something becomes apparent and something remains Blank. A group of cleaving, transferring in cleaving, an image. In the sweep of cleaving, the sweep of appearance.

During transference, and possibly during localization as well, the functioning area of "forming Blank" may increase due to chance or according to the intention of an unknown and unnameable… subject. In many ways, each individual is its own after-image.

The photo accompanying this text is of a bridge that is to demonstrate this way of thinking as well as that of our earlier collaborative study, *The Mechanism of Meaning*, and is to ultimately lead to an exegesis and/or embodiment of perception.

The Japanese Order of Things:
Notes on Humanism and the Man — Environment Relationship in Japan

Botond Bognar

Industrialized nations of the globe have today 'consolidated' their control over nature by the most irresponsible plundering of its resources.... A profound confidence in our powers to come to know and thereby control our environment and destiny lies at the heart of every humanism; in this sense, we must acknowledge a continuity of theme, however warped it may have become with the passage of time, between the Renaissance celebration of the freedom of humanity from any transcendental hierarchy or cosmic order, the Enlightenment faith in reason and its powers, and the 'social engineering' advocated by our contemporary 'scientific' humanists.

Kate Soper, *Humanism and Anti-Humanism*

When contemporary Western societies under the banners of "humanism" and "progress," and in the name of Man, the "measure of all things," provide incessant proof of Homo sapiens' astonishing yet brutal capacity to harness nature in the service of its own ends, we need urgently to reconsider the issues of our very humanity. A number of Western thinkers such as Claude Lévi-Strauss, Mircea Eliade, Martin Heidegger, Jacques Derrida, and Michel Foucault have undertaken this project; yet another way to reveal the underlying issues may be to consider Oriental cultures developed under different circumstances from those in the West.[1]

The foundations of Western metaphysics are rooted in a persistent belief in and desire for a universe ruled by all-encompassing and immutable laws. Western thought and conduct have systematically split the world into binary oppositions, *i.e.* being *vs.* nothingness, presence *vs.* absence, privileging the positives and rejecting or suppressing the complements.

Oriental cultures, on the other hand, especially the Japanese, managed to transcend this metaphysics. Universal and immutable laws did not appeal to them and they remained equally uninterested in defining the world in terms of dichotomies. The nature and order of things for them thus could not and did not reside in the logic of pure identity or self-sameness; Japanese things were not subject to a one-way process of individuation and objectification. The Japanese were more interested in circumstantial relationships, and in the concrete interface between things, not in the consistency of a whole system. This interest has lent Japanese life, throughout their history, the highly intuitive, situational, and paradoxical quality which they were able to preserve even after having been exposed to the West.

Homogeneity/Heterogeneity

Japan is a complex society. Contrary to many Western preconceptions, Japanese culture is paradoxical: It is both homogeneous and heterogeneous: homogeneous in the sense that its features, values, and "spirit" pervade the whole society, comprised of a remarkably homogeneous ethnic group with only one spoken language. On the other hand, it is unquestionably heterogeneous in its elements, and in the patterns that order these elements into systems.

Japanese culture has always been profoundly influenced by others through a conscious act of borrowing from the Korean, Chinese, and currently Western culture. Teiji Itoh writes, "The seeming hodgepodge in Japan today is the result of great cultural accumulation and diversification over the centuries around a hard core of indigenous culture."[2] The Japanese have become a culture of "both/and," wherein old and new, native and foreign, traditional and modern are complementary aspects of the same thing.

In religion, for example, the ancient Japanese Shinto survived and even flourished after Buddhism, Confucianism, Taoism, and others gained wide acceptance following their introduction to Japan in the 6th century AD. Today most Japanese would consider themselves both Shintoist and Buddhist, as they participate in the rituals of both, while the legacies of Confucian ethical values and some elements of Taoist teachings still pervade the whole society. One percent of the population also follows Christianity; the result is religious pluralism.

Japanese language, especially writing, displays similar heterogeneity. The Japanese borrowed their whole writing system — as they had not had one before — from the Chinese. In addition to the adapted Chinese ideograms, however, two more systems of syllabary writing (*kana*) were developed, and so today every Japanese text is an intricate mixture of three systems. The reason for this complexity derives from the fact that Chinese writing was superimposed on a language that was, and still is, basically different from Chinese, while having nothing to do with any Western languages either.

The built landscape in Tokyo and other cities in Japan appears as a disordered battleground of incongruous elements (figure 1). One experiences visual uncertainty and feelings of impermanence; an apparent lack of rational pattern and perspective to structure the Westerner's perception and understanding of the Japanese world. The Japanese themselves appear to behave, act, and speak "irrationally," changing manners as if complying with a multiplicity of contradictory rules. Each observation may be affirmed with limited validity by saying "yes," then adding immediately, "but also...."

Beyond the obvious heterogeneity of elements, the underlying orders reveal as much heterogeneity as the elements themselves. This "lack of consistency" accounts historically for a high degree of adaptability which operates behind every phenomenon of Japanese life. Western and Japanese scholars alike have said that the Japanese "lack basic principles," or that theirs is an attitude of "relativism" which distinguishes them from the West.[3]

Shintoism/Buddhism

Shinto, the indigenous Japanese "religion," is a form of animism and pantheism, a mythology, centered around the worship of nature, and fostered by local communities. According to Shinto beliefs, a myriad of spirits (*kami*) populate the cosmos, each devoted to a different, usually natural, phenomenon or event. Thus each of the many shrines that dot the Japanese landscape is dedicated to a different *kami*. Shinto, as opposed to other major religions, does not have a founder, and so, no identifiable origin; its beginnings fade into prehistoric times. It has no sacred scripture, no established doctrines or dogmas, no well-defined moral norms. There is no clear distinction

coexisted with and adapted itself to Buddhism, Confucianism, and even Christianity, and survives today. It simultaneously exerted considerable influence on these religions in Japan, particularly on Zen Buddhism, and on Japan's sociopolitical system, attitudes, and aesthetics.

Buddhism, which had a more complex body of teachings, was modified considerably after its introduction to Japan. Buddhism views the world as having no creator or ruler, and thus no origin and end. Salvation is found not in the faith in an absolute and eternal God, but in conduct leading to *nirvana*, the domain of nothingness, by way of enlightenment, the liberation from passions, desires, illusions of individual

emphasizes the evanescence and insubstantiality of all things. A key principle of Buddhist thought, this emphasis articulates the non-duality of *nirvana* and *samsara*.

In a world of paradoxes, opposites are not in conflict; different entities mutually define, rather than oppose each other. In a perpetual flow of entities there can be no sharp distinction between being and not being, subject and object, self and other, the dichotomies that have haunted the Western mind throughout its history. In Western thought the Archimedean point is the idea of "being"; in Buddhism the reality of our being-in-the-world has a void beneath, a bliss at its core. This void, however, is *not* a *negative* state;

1. Part of Tokyo's cityscape today.

between good and evil, nor between man and the *kami*. Opposed to the Christian dogma of "original sin," Shinto considers man a creature good by nature, who should follow his natural instincts. Although Shinto implies a delicate system of hierarchy, it does not have an absolute deity who is *the* creator and ruler of everything; it is not absolutist. While not transcendental beings, *kami* cannot be defined conceptually or theologically; the Japanese are aware of them intuitively; as Sokyo Ono has said, "it is impossible to make explicit and clear that which fundamentally, by its very nature, is vague."[4]

This world view afforded Shinto belief the flexibility with which it related to other thoughts and religions. Shintoism

being, and thus from suffering.

This Great Void (*sunyata*) is a realm wherein the oneness of everything — man, nature, and Buddha — finds realization. Opposing forces, notions, ideas, and qualities are quieted and unified. This state underlies every phenomenon in the universe, and is accessible by way of learning and a special intuitive awareness through "meditative action." It is concealed by, yet also implied in, the ever changing world of phenomena (*samsara*), wherein everything is always in continuous transition. Principles of absoluteness, permanency, eternity, and perfection, which are cherished and striven for in the West, are bound to lose their immutability and their definite meaning. Buddhism

within it, presence, absence, affirmation, and negation are the same thing, or are interchangeable. It cannot be approached by way of logic, only through intuition and a state of mind that is unfettered by a true/false dichotomy. In this way the emphasis of Buddhist teachings in Japan shifted to "man in the phenomenal world in search of a transcendental realm."[5] Buddhism became a religion that affirmed the phenomenal world and the concreteness of experience. Since religion and philosophy were not separate fields of knowledge until the middle of the 19th century, Shintoism and Buddhism pervaded intellectual conduct and everyday life, providing a background for a homogeneous culture and society.

Boundaries

When Buddhism was introduced to Japan in the mid-6th century AD, it transmitted various aspects of Chinese culture. Centralized state bureaucracy was adapted by the Imperial Court. The first permanent capitals mimicked the Chinese model of Chang'an, and construction of palaces, temple compounds, and other important buildings also followed precedents of Chinese architecture (figure 2). These imports to Japan introduced the Chinese world view which manifested itself in the form of a rigid order including geometrical, symmetrical, and hierarchical layouts of cities, Buddhist temples, the Imperial Palace, and other complexes.[6]

After the first encounter with China, the history of Japanese culture increasingly deviated from Chinese ordering principles. This gradual but significant change started as the implementation of the Chinese model began. For example, the new and permanent capitals, first Nara (Heijo-kyo 710-784), then Kyoto (Heian-kyo 794-1868), though laid out along the gridiron plan of Chang'an, were never built as planned. They developed unevenly, leaving large areas unbuilt, while surrounding city walls were erected partially or not at all.

Without clearly defined boundaries these cities were gradually to overlap the surrounding natural and agricultural areas. The legacies of this early development showed a Shinto influence and the Japanese appreciation of land and nature. The traditional city retained a rural character that, as a latent quality, has survived until today, prompting many critics to call Tokyo "the world's largest village."

These were the first steps by the Japanese toward a conscious attempt to blend the man-made environment with nature. This mediation extended into almost every segment of Japanese life (figure 3). Art could be characterized as choreographing a variety of intermediary zones. This "in-between" realm, a derivative of Buddhist philosophy, is called *ma*.[7] It has many meanings, including space, place, room, interval, activated void, or pregnant pause. As described by Michihiro Matsumoto, "*Ma* is that moment unbridled by contradictions — contrast between part and whole; it is the moment that allows one to be aware of and part of his surrounding." Iwanami's *Dictionary of Ancient Times* states: "*Ma* is the natural distance between two or more things existing in continuity," or "the natural pause or interval between two or more phenomena occurring continuously"; it is the sense of a moment in the passing of time.[8]

Ma can be understood as "gap" or absence between two or more phenomena, it gives shape to these phenomena as much as it is shaped by them; they cannot exist without each other; they are mutually inclusive. *Ma* underscores the Buddhist thesis that "form is emptiness, and emptiness is form."[9] The Japanese, while giving form to the tangible, also shape intangible aspects of their world, as manifested in the pictorial arts influenced by Zen, wherein the empty areas mean as much as those articulated by the paint brush.

A similar mode of mediation by *ma* is implicit in Japanese verbal communication, developed into a special form of art called *haragei*. The Japanese communicate also with the silence between spoken words. Michihiro Matsumoto writes that

"Japanese *haragei* practitioners listen more attentively to the pauses between the words and gestures. One does not need the art of persuasion that underlies Western communication practices to be a successful communicator in Japanese society. In fact, *haragei* performers are verbally inadequate in front of others, and by no means logical, coherent, or articulate, because they give *ma* full play.... There is in Japan no historical evidence of great public orators like those known in the West."[10] Having spatial and temporal connotations, *ma* is one of the most significant features of Japanese culture, human awareness, and conduct; it is in this sense that Japanese art is the art of "invisible" boundaries[11] (figure 4). "Designing" in Japanese originally meant *ma-dori*, or the grasping, creating, activating of *ma*.

Centers

The tendency in Japan was not to accurately define boundaries physically or artificially; there was no need to establish centers in the manner done through the history of civiliza-

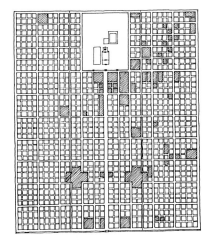

2. Plan of Kyoto (left).
3. Katsura Imperial Villa, Kyoto, 17th century. Interior (opposite above).
4. The veranda (*engawa*) around the Japanese house mediates between interior and exterior. Shugakuin Imperial Villa, Kyoto, 17th century (opposite below left).
5. Futamigaura *Wedded rocks* off the shore of Ise (opposite center).
6. Part of the east section of Kyoto from the air (opposite below right).

tions including the West. The Chinese city, a prototype for early Japanese capitals, in its layout, did not have a center, and this quality was further reinforced in Japan. The Imperial Palace compound within the homogeneous grid was located at the northern end of the north-south axis, and, as a walled-in area and "forbidden city," it was, and still is, off limits to the general public. Nara, Kyoto, and other kinds of urban developments lacked large open city squares or plazas defined by a large number of concentrated public buildings and institutions, providing political and spiritual centers for the city. Analogous centers in the West are indicated by a church spire or tower.

In Japanese cities important buildings were lined along streets and spaced at certain intervals. Religious compounds were located along the perimeter or outside the city. After Kyoto became the capital, Buddhist temples were banned from the city by the Imperial Court to neutralize their increased political power. Medieval castle towns, having no city walls, assigned numerous temples to the outskirts for defensive purposes. Temples of esoteric Buddhist sects, and most Shinto shrines, were

built away from populated areas.

Kami, the Shinto spirits, were believed to dwell in mountains, deep valleys, forests, trees, and in other unique topographical formations such as cliffs, remote islands, and caves, which are marked by smaller or larger shrines (figure 5). Kami were invisible and intangible as were the places where they lived or were summoned to periodically from their underworld of shadows and darkness (yami). The extremely variegated landscape of Japan, with heavily wooded hills, mountains, narrow valleys and few flat lands or open plains, and a humid, hazy climate, fostered a Japanese fondness for invisible, mysterious, often dark places (oku).[12]

The notion of oku, meaning least visible, least accessible, extending far back, or deep, permeates Japanese culture, and is a quality of architectural compounds, gardens, and urban spaces. In his study "Japanese City Spaces and the Concept of Oku," Fumihiko Maki describes the peculiar sense of depth and devotion to hidden, secret scenes underlying Japanese perceptions of space and conceptions of place.[13]

Japanese urban patterns, whether rural villages or large capitals, did not allow for an open and easily accessible center; rather they formed a large number of inner spaces, diminutive and hidden within densely built areas, away from main roads, difficult to approach and often im-

possible to enter (figure 6). These inner spaces may be considered a multiplicity of "negative" or "empty" centers or, conversely, the dispersal of one dominant center.

Roland Barthes observed that present day Tokyo "offers this precious paradox: it does possess a center, but this center is empty. The entire city turns around a site both forbidden and indifferent, a residence concealed beneath foliage, protected by moats, inhabited by an emperor who is never seen, which is to say, literally, by no one knows who. Daily, in their rapid, energetic, bullet-like trajectories, the taxis avoid this circle, whose low crest, the visible form of invisibility, hides the sacred nothing"[14] (figure 7).

This indicates the relationship between spatial experience and Shinto religion. There is no clear distinction between the world of kami and that of man; every human being implies the spirit of kami. In the hierarchy of this interrelated pantheon, the Emperor was considered both the symbol of Japan, the highest priest and the most important kami among humans. The spatial qualities of his residence show affinities with Shinto shrines.

Japanese residences all involve a sense of oku, through their spatial disposition. They are all conducive to a unique progression or modulation of openness to depth, outside to inside, and light to darkness, or vice versa. This has been

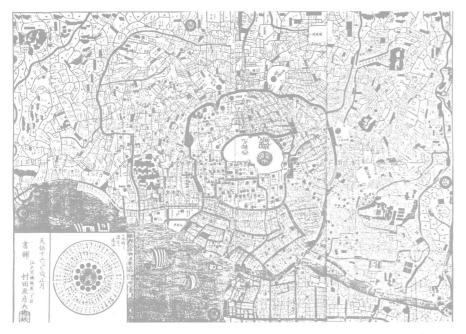

achieved by creating indefinite boundaries as multiple layers with a variety of two-dimensional and thin elements, which often take the form and quality of signs. The layered spaces created this way can act as unit space, intermediary space, or spatial crease, depending on their momentary arrangement (figure 8).

The ambiguity of boundaries as layered "envelopes" (*ma*), is closely related to the ambiguity of a center (*oku*) in architecture, urbanism, and other cultural forms. The *oku*, writes Maki, "is the original point (mental touchstone) in the minds of people who observe or create it, and hence becomes the invisible center; or more precisely, it is a convenience devised by a spirit and climate which denies absolute objects or symbols such as the notion of center. The *oku* is a center in which those who relate to the object can set it freely, for it does not need to be made explicit to others."[15] *Oku* implies value judgment and forms the basis of the unique spatial hierarchy of the Japanese.[16]

In Japan the various forms of folding, wrapping, and enveloping have a long tradition and have developed into a sophisticated art. Presents, merchandise, and personal items are wrapped, usually several times, in boxes, layers of paper or cloth, one over the other. This custom goes far beyond the rationale of protection, even aesthetics, and enters the realm of psychology. Opening a package can take "forever," postponing the discovery of what it contains. At the end, the object reached often turns out to be less significant than the packaging and appears to lose its quality as an object; it is de-objectified by the sumptuousness of its wrapping. As Maki concludes "the *oku* is nothing but the concept of convergence to zero."[17]

Path/Arrival

As Kyoto gradually increased in both size and density, the new urban developments, deviating radically from the original rigid system, began to adapt better to topological and other local conditions. A new and "random" pattern of roads was laid over the old grid, expanding toward the surrounding hills, shrines, and temples, while subdividing the previous rectangular city blocks (*bo, ho,* and *cho*). These narrow roads, lanes, and paths, representatives of the special street architecture in Japan, all contributed to the evolution of spatial creases and pleat-like folds, the multiplicity of "inner spaces" (figure 9).

Shrines had to be reached by intricate and often long paths (*sando*). Having the qualities of *oku,* the empty center, the experience is typically "anti-climactic"; shrines do not assure dramatic arrival. They do not have magnificent interiors to enter or a central symbol to look at; the innermost sanctuary is a closed, empty, and dark space, off-limits to worshippers. Sometimes not even the exterior of the "building," often enveloped by layers of fences and thick foliage, is allowed to be

seen. The approach (*michi-yuki*), lined with a large variety of signs — votive plaques, lanterns, gates (*torii*) — is as important as the arrival (figure 10).

Similar layout characterizes other forms of the built environment: the city, the house, the stroll garden, all with a procession, revealing an irregular network of small focal points in the manner of "hide-and-seek" (*mie-gakure*) but with no major or dominant central object. The house is only one element among many in the garden, not the main attraction. Architecture is not confronted in Japan as it always has been in the West; all paths approaching the house are diagonal (figure 11). For defensive purposes, main

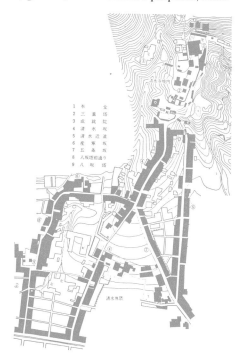

roads leading to and crossing a castle town were laid out with numerous bends and never ran through the "center."

The indirect mode of approximation is detectable in most aspects of Japanese life. Nothing exemplifies this better than the structure of the Japanese language. Until the very end of a sentence, or paragraph, it is difficult to decipher what the speaker or author is trying to convey, and often at the end the

meaning is vague. Edward T. Hall has explained: "the Japanese have been brought up to avoid coming to the point too quickly. In fact, the point may only be alluded to indirectly...."[18] The Japanese prefer a loose structure of argument without sharp and clear statements. Yet, as Koji Yagi noted, "for a people with a certain degree of common basic sensibility within a defined area, there is the... assurance that somewhere along the line things will be understood without clearly stating them in black and white."[19]

Imperial villa, Katsura
General plan 1:400

A tea-pavilion (*geppuro*)
B oldest building (*ko-shoin*)
C middle-building (*chu-shoin*)
D most recent building (*shin-shoin*)

Part/Whole

The homogeneous structure of the Chinese city and architecture introduced the notion of universal space to Japan, yet Japanese space was to become increasingly heterogeneous. Japanese space was closely related to topographic conditions and rooted in the land rather than represented by buildings or permanent structures. Space was not an *a priori* entity existing apart from and independent of the various phenomena, but was unequivocally the outcome or the very function of them.

7. Tokyo (Edo), early 19th century map (opposite above).
8. The spatial quality of *oku* in a town house. Yoshijima Residence, Takayama, 19th century (opposite below).
9. The pattern of path leading to Kyomizu temple in Kyoto (center).
10. Shinto *torii* gates along the path leading to Fushimi-Inari Shrine, Kyoto (above).
11. Katsura Imperial Villa plan, Kyoto, 17th century (below).

153

The spatial quality of a given locality depended on how the built environment responded to the landscape. Since its conditions and their interpretations varied widely, the Japanese developed an extreme sensitivity toward the most subtle variations in their environment. This sensitivity further increased the significance of particular qualities of a place, developed from a multiplicity of elements, acknowledging differences in conditions (figures 12, 13).

Tokyo, for example, features several small districts whose qualities differ, and contradict one another. They do not have the consistency of an overall system or follow an *a priori* ordering principle. The Japanese city, represented best by Tokyo, has grown piecemeal into what may be called an "interpretative labyrinth"; it has neither the structural clarity of European cities nor the geometric form of grid-planned American cities.

A "microgeography" is most important in understanding the significance of any part of the built environment. A spatial system wherein the rules of relationship change from situation to situation yields a kaleidoscopic environment with relatively autonomous parts adding up to an ever changing and incomplete aggregate whole. In Kisho Kurokawa's words, parts are "ever relating to while at the same time rejecting the whole... an integration without integration" or synthesis.[20]

Language/Environment

Kengo Kuma, in an article on "Tokyo – New York: A Comparison by Linguistic Analogy," pointed out several analogies that exist between the Japanese language and the built environment.[21] Unlike English and other Western languages, Japanese words and sentences, like architectural and urban compounds, do not have logically built grammatical structures. Japanese grammar does not specify gender, singular or plural, definite or indefinite articles; and, while subject and object can change order in a sentence, there is a tendency to omit the subject or object or even both if they can be implied within the context; they depend on the actual situation. Akira Miyoshi writes, "The unique linguistic characteristic of the Japanese language lies in a non-structural

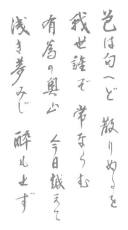

approach in which words do not necessarily have a logical relationship to one another, but where the words spoken have a number of invisible meanings and *ma* or silent beats from which the listener is expected to extract and interpret the meaning intended by the speaker."[22]

Words are compiled from Chinese characters (*kanji*) as the root elements, and Japanese syllables (*hiragana*) as inflectional endings, though the Japanese use relatively few inflections. Most words are more than one character and almost all characters have several readings, the actual depending on, in each single case, the preceding or following character, or the whole sentence (figure 14). Having two or more *kanji* that have their own range of "original" meanings, a word would carry all these implicitly, layer by layer, within its own meaning. Most words have a large array of connotations; alone, the meaning of some words, even if of one *kanji*, is impossible to determine precisely. These include:

内 *uchi*: inside, interior, with, among, house, home, family, one's own folks, we, I, recently, etc.
家 *ie*: house, home, residence, housing, household, family name, fortune, etc.
奥 *oku*: heart, interior, lie deep in, extend far back, secluded, innermost, depth, the back, most valuable, etc.
間 *ma*: space, room, internal pause, rest (in music), time, a while, leisure, luck, chance, timing, harmony, etc.[23]

Kuma characterizes Japanese buildings as connotative, rather than denotative or representational, because of their being vaguely defined. Relationships among elements — buildings, or words — are not fixed but in flux. Larger architectural compounds, like sentences, are brought together as loose agglomerates, and so, they too tend to be connotative. The traditional and widely practiced form of poetry, *haiku*, is an example of vague relationships:

Full moon
And on the matting
The shadow of a pine tree[24]

Roland Barthes has described *haiku* as that which is "articulated around a metaphysics without subject and without god, [and] corresponds to the Buddhist *Mu*, to the Zen *satori*, which is not at all the illuminative descent of God, but 'awakening to the fact,' apprehension of the thing as event and not as substance"[25] (figure 15). More than in ordinary language, the silent pauses (*ma*) in *haiku* play a significant role in understanding the poem and its elusive meanings. A *haiku* demands that one includes oneself in the reading, becoming a part of what the poem attempts, but cannot say.

Multifocal Perspective

An environment understood as a texture of heterogeneous elements without clearly defined order or logically constructed syntax, could not evolve an omniscient viewpoint. A singular, fixed perspective was a missing aspect of Japanese understanding, until this Western mode of representation was introduced to Japan. Instead, the Japanese developed a multifocal approach requiring the perceiver to be situated in space and time during a

sequence of events, entering into and interpreting from within.

The English language employs tenses characterized by a fixed point in time, which is not the case in the Japanese language. Kuma exemplifies this with the following Japanese sentence and its English translation:

Nihon ni itta toki ni ningyo o kaimasu.
(Japan went time doll buy).
When I go to Japan, I will buy a doll.[26]

The Japanese puts the future event of going to Japan in past tense, since the time of buying the doll — the main concern of the speaker — happened in the past. The person, is placed into the concrete situation of buying the doll, adding another viewpoint to the present position of the speaker.

The change in perspective continuously involves a person observing the shifting axes (*ore-magari*) of intricate paths, roads, and lanes opening a range of alternating vistas and smaller focal points in a discontinuous urban environment. In the pictorial arts, depictions of various natural or built environments are often composed of numerous scenarios, each with its respective viewpoint. Among the "independent" pictures we can often see golden or white clouds (*unka-ho*) that separate and connect the sections like the unpainted areas (*ma*) in Zen ink paintings or calligraphy (figure 16). Also it is not uncommon to interweave the painting with Japanese writing or calligraphy, fragmenting the picture into smaller elements, and blurring the borderline between traditional modes of visual and textual arts.

Several Japanese maps show an inconsistency; they do not adopt a single angle of vision from above, a detached and fixed vantage point, as in the case of our modern orthographic maps. Directional indications, place names and other information on a 19th-century map of Tokyo are drawn and written in different directions corresponding to various local blocks or zones. When pictorial manuals of scenic routes were laid out in unfolding booklets, the sights along the continuous road were drawn as they would appear to the traveler, in place, time, and direction, alternating above and under the road line. Indicating only famous vistas along the road, a manual of Tokaido could depict Mt. Fuji several times.[27]

Systems of spaces easily grasped at a glance from any one strategic point may place the observer in a position superior to his/her environment. Since its discovery in the Renaissance, perspective has been an expression of Western man as the center and ruler of the world. An emphasis on visual perception tends to objectify; the eye sets everything at a distance while establishing, maintaining, or consolidating order. This instills a feeling of mastery over the environment.

In the Japanese world of things individual elements and fragments, seen as scattered signs and symbols, are encountered. These fail to provide an overall, objective pattern. Although recognition of the oneness of everything is important, totality is never presented visually in a state of completeness or perfection; one always has to sense unity through its constantly changing aspects. The whole remains elusive, to be conjured up by the perceiver, emphasizing intimate relationships of shifting parts with

alternate possibilities. The Japanese very often prefer imagination to fact. As Tomoya Masuda has said, they live "in both the worlds of actuality and of imagination at the same time."[28]

Self/Other

Tomonobu Imamichi has observed that "the Japanese do not feel an inconsistency in moral principle, since moral values are understood to be situation-specific. Westerners with universalistic ethical principles often accuse the Japanese of moral inconsistency."[29] Standards of human behavior are not centered around the individual as permanent property as much as in the West; in Japan they depend on particular relationships.

Japanese outward conduct does not always involve true respect for others. They sense discrepancies between outward conduct (*tatemae*) and inner feelings (*honne*), the difference is not rigid, but can overlap and be reversed. *Tatemae* and *honne*, though they may appear contradictory to a Westerner, are complementary; the Japanese act, behave, and speak in a realm brought about by a simultaneous awareness of the two. The qualities of architectural and urban spaces, inside and outside, are mediated by an intermediary zone (*ma*) with the qualities of *tatemae* and *honne*.

In Japan interpretation is more pervasive and inevitable than in the West. The process of interpretation is a mode of establishing circumstantial relationships between an interpreting subject and the interpreted object. This ties a person into the world, losing opposition and independence; subjects relinquish their subjectivity while objects suspend their objective character. Neither the world nor human beings can claim a self-contained and delimited autonomy.

The self is not an indivisible whole as in the Western *individuum*. Subject and object are not mutually exclusive opposites, neither is there antagonism between self and other; they are complementary. Western metaphysics has envisaged human beings as self-actualized, independent and above others. Western man's relation to the world is one of domination. Traditionally in Japan self-awareness coalesces in a flux of intrinsic and intimate relationships. Identity is constituted by a relatedness to the Other; inversely, the Other lends itself, neither having definite boundaries.

The Japanese language embodies this continuous relatedness. The Japanese word for human being is *ningen* 人間, where *nin* means "a person," *gen* (a different reading of *ma*) translates to in-between, interval, place, or relationship. Ningen represents man-in-relationship. Nitschke in his essay "Space, Place, Void" has pointed out that "in the traditional Japanese there is no term identical with 'individual' or 'man' in the Western philosophical sense of '*cogito ergo sum*'.... The current word for 'individual,' *kojin*, literally 'private person,' is of relatively recent origin and stands for a notion imported from the West."[30] The Japanese do not picture a world in isolation; the word *seken* 世間, literally means "world-in-relationship."[31]

In the flux of interrelations, "self-constitution" is accompanied by a simultaneous "deconstruction" of the self. This paradox involves the affirmation and negation of the self in relation to others. Recent Western philosophy has engaged in a discussion about the subject/object dichotomy. Terry Eagleton summarizes a new understanding of the self which approximates that of the Japanese: "Human consciousness [is] the subject's active, material, semiotic intercourse with others, not some sealed interior realm divorced from these relations; consciousness, like a language, [is] both 'inside' and 'outside' the subject simultaneously... or rather, it exists 'between' us, as our relationships do."[32]

It is increasingly evident that the Japanese could *not* consider Man the "center of the universe" and "the measure of all things." Japanese world view and culture have *not* been anthropocentric; they have not developed a Renaissance or Enlightenment notion of Man as a "free and sovereign artificer" determining his "own nature without constraint from any barrier."[33] If the West has learned how to adapt the environment to his needs, forming in this way a basis for what Michel Foucault called "Western *episteme*," the Japanese have been more inclined to adapt themselves to others.[34] This traditional mode of thought and conduct reveals an affinity with both contemporary hermeneutic phenomenology and post-structuralist deconstruction.

Recent Situation

After the Second World War, Japan underwent an unparalleled development, and emerged as an industrial superpower, becoming an advanced leader among the industrial nations of the West. The principles of modern production and consumption, *i.e.* productivist rationalism, instrumental reason, universal technology, and utilitarianism, gained ground. Negative impacts, though mitigated by the "Japanese order of things," were aggravated by Japan's geographical conditions: lack of available terrain, high density of population, etc. Yielding to the explosive development of industry, urbanization, and society, neither the land nor the urban environment could avoid the consequences of growing abuse and exploitation. The face of the land has been scarred, in some instances beyond recovery; cities, seriously injured by increasing pollution, congestion, and land speculation, have become less habitable. Japan has caught up in most of these respects with its Western counterparts.

Signs of a deepening crisis of modern man manifest themselves today in increasingly problematic relations, "now at the height of our scientific and technological mastery, we 'Western' individuals seem to be more than ever divorced... from our created world and... from ourselves, as well as from our fellow human beings."[35] This crisis can be traced to the Modernist project with its modes of production and consumption predicated by positivistic reason, instrumental sciences, and a "value-free" technology.

In his book, *One-Dimensional Man*, Herbert Marcuse demonstrates that a value-free technology is not neutral or innocent as it may appear. The transformation of nature involves man; manmade creations originate from, yet also re-enter and structure the society. Marcuse has asserted that "today, domination perpetuates and extends itself not only through technology but *as* technology, and the latter provides the great legitimation of the expanding political power, which absorbs all spheres of culture."[36]

The fast-escalating Japanese megalopolitan project or "Japan-the-city," ushered in by contemporary consumer society, and predicated by the instrumental rationality of modernist urbanism, began to open the densely woven and ambiguous fabric of the city. Rigid and deterministic patterns resulted, autonomous buildings appeared along urban highways. The trivializing and irrational practices of consumerism penetrated the urban realm converting every segment of urban life into forms of commodity.

Toyo Ito, an architect of a new generation, is concerned about the predicament of contemporary architecture, urbanism, and society, and has outlined the recent situation: "Today Tokyo's old resilience is being covered up by a rigid frame. The city itself is gradually rigidifying. While modernizing and becoming more and more controlled, Tokyo preserves, if only latently, a resilience and flexibility that accounted for its wonder and charm, and that are not to be found in Western cities. How much longer it will be able to preserve these qualities is a moot point. The rigidifying process is proceeding every day. Afraid of it, people surround themselves with consumer code items in the form of decoration. And the heavier the ornament, the emptier."[37]

The difference between the qualities of the Japanese city and today's consumerist urbanism is not always obvious. The former, with a sensitive response to changes in local conditions, has developed a "sophisticated order" inviting human participation. This assures that the person and the world could be simultaneously identical and different.[38] The latter is motivated by the promotion of consumption and increased profit, achieved if the meaning of urban elements is finite and targeted carefully. They culminate in an environment where the consumer has no need to participate creatively. One is prompted to claim rights to meanings offered as a commodity.

Addressing the role the "communicative or instrumental sign" plays in a populist consumerist architecture, Kenneth Frampton explained: "Such a sign seeks to evoke not a critical perception of reality, but rather, the sublimation of a desire for direct experience through the provision of information. Its tactical aim is to attain as economically as possible a preconceived level of gratification in behavioristic terms. In this respect, the strong affinity of Populism for the rhetorical techniques and imagery of advertising is hardly accidental."[39] The manipulative action or politics of human desire presents the whole built environment as continuous entertainment with the pleasures of effortless recognition, affirming unconditionally and uncritically the individual as consumer perpetuating thereby the consuming process; it maintains existing power relations in a manner whereby the control of a ruling order appears as a natural process; or as atemporal and ahistorical as nature itself.[40] The built environment of modern mass society, as Foucault observed, is the spatialization of Power, a process in which the domination of power is rendered invisible.[41]

The present situation of increasing control is a discouraging predicament for the *avant-garde* of contemporary Japanese architects. The historical *Avant-garde* has been overrun by the Progress of the Modernist project it was so eager to foster. Today's late *avant-garde* or *arrier-garde*, to use Frampton's term, seeks ways *to resist* the tendencies of such progress. While resistance in the works of a growing number of Japanese architects is manifested in various ways, it means to establish "new relations between the space and

person."[42] This resistance aims to change, alter, and even break the "naturalized" or taken-for-granted rules. The intention is to open the deterministic and reductivist circuits of representation by challenging normative perceptions within the realms of architecture and urbanism. Instead of a formalist context, the focus of attention is shifting to a more liberating *intertextuality* of the built environmental fabric. This signals the return of a graphic and *calli-graphic* quality of design and building with a manifest critique of the instrumentality of the sign.

Tadao Ando's architecture re-introduces nature to people who in the microcosmic worlds of his buildings are exposed, directly and indirectly, to

changing natural phenomena; layered wall planes, often around tiny courtyards, carefully limit and focus openings sensitively modulating the elusive effects of light and shadow. This manipulation creates a porous matrix of *indefinite* spaces (figure 17). Ando writes: "My approach is to pursue more than superficial comfort. I want to try to recapture and reexamine one by one the truly enduring and essential elements of the human residence, many of which have been abandoned in the course of rapid economic growth: basic relations with nature, direct dialogue with materials, the small discoveries and surprises people can detonate in their daily-life spaces, the pleasure and aesthetic uplift to be had from creative

initiative in a simple way of life."[43]

Several architects, including Tadao Ando, Kazuo Shinohara, Ryoji Suzuki, Hajime Yatsuka, Hiromi Fujii, and Hiroshi Hara, employ layered concrete or imprinted glass walls and orthogonal framework to "suspend form," deconstruct space, or filter the surrounding urban environment in a discontinuity (figures 18, 19, 20). The majority of the young designers, however, turn to industrially mass-produced lightweight elements to create membranous boundaries and ambiguous collage-like enclosures with an intended "superficiality." They are able to achieve a lightness and "insubstantiality" with the products of heavy industry, while also reinterpreting tradition, instead of nostalgic or sentimental applications of a formal past. These architects manage to apply materials and products of the industry and at the same time express their opposition to industrial and consumer society. Itsuko Hasegawa, for instance, uses "architectural and technological details to evoke nature, and natural and cosmic details to evoke architecture"[44] (figure 21). Riken Yamamoto is concerned about the redefinition of dwelling over and above the detrimental conditions of industrial and commercialized cities. In his recent designs, he employs elements, and strategies of fragmentation that are found in the Japanese urban environment, and wherein "the city [is regarded] as topography"[45] (figure 22).

Toyo Ito has further articulated these issues; in his essay "Collage and Superficiality in Architecture" he writes: "What I wish to attain in my architecture is not another nostalgic object, but rather a certain superficiality of expression in order to reveal the nature of the void hidden beneath.... Collage architecture is composed of architectural elements which carry different meanings. My intention is to destroy the realm of ordered imagery and construct a more open, autonomous architecture."[46] Also, he points out that "[t]here is a precedent for such 'collage' approach throughout the history of Japanese architecture and urban design.... There seems to be a syntax of space by collage which is peculiar to Japanese culture."[47] This precedent is the disposition of signs and symbols, often with a multiplicity of

17. *Koshino Residence*, Ashiya, 1982 by Tadao Ando (opposite).
18. *Edge Building*, Tokyo, 1987 by Ryoji Suzuki (above left).
19. *Tarlazzi Building*, Tokyo, 1987 by Hajime Yatsuka (above).
20. *Ushimado International Arts Festival Building*, Ushimado, 1985 by Hiromi Fujii (left).

implied meanings — in a discontinuity wherein apparently unrelated and contradictory elements, forms and patterns, "perform" magnificently; they are brought together in a unique order where neither opposition nor reconciliation occurs.

Ito's first building that manifests this understanding is the PMT Building in Nagoya (1978). The small office building displays the paper-thin membrane of the aluminum facade with an *ideogrammatic* delicacy that veils only an "empty" space-frame behind, returning to a condition where architecture and the city are signified but not really represented. Writing about "*Ukiyo-e* and the Art of Toyo Ito," Kenneth Frampton points out that this architecture, and the majority of late *avant-garde* work, have the implicit quality which has always characterized Japanese design, calligraphy, and *ukiyo-e* (pictures of the "floating world"), where there is no clear distinction between writing and painting.[48] The intricate semi-transparent layers of the new urban fabric, created by a growing number of Japanese architects, alludes to an invisible depth, an intangible and unexplainable void, reminiscent of the goal of Buddhist conduct, which frustrates rationality and causes the knowing subject to vacillate.

Ito's residence, the "Silver Hut" of 1984, goes further in the direction of *destructuring* form, decomposing it into a fluid entity. Laid out along a system of concrete columns in a traditional modular pattern, the house is defined by thin punched aluminum screens, various sizes of diamond-shaped latticework vaults, and colored fabric penetrated by light, and moved by the wind (figures 23). Lynne Breslin has commented: "Ito's dismantling of type, dematerialization of form, and deconstruction of style extends with each new building and its capacity to comment on the past."[49] With regard to his recent works, Ito has mentioned: "My present ideal is to create, in the city, buildings that, while arousing architectural images latent in human memory, lack clear forms. Only when I succeed in this will I be able to say that my buildings have urban context. Architecture with clear forms degenerates into nothing more than another of the countless consumer codes in the city."[50]

The experience of these designs and of the intended urban realm cannot be easily reduced to mere information provided by the representation of a sign. The actual experience involves not only memory and imagination, but active participation, creating the possibility for various intuitive networks among the interpreted and perceived elements of sign and symbol. These new designs challenge rather than affirm "natural," fixed point modes of perception. Fumihiko Maki, writing about his current architecture, characterizes the intended environment as an aggregate of active, heterogeneous parts that never conform to a formula as they generate a whole.[51] This attitude resists the dominance of an absolute center or origin as Maki's latest projects, including the Spiral Building in Tokyo (1985), exemplify (figure 24).

The goal of these and many other Japanese architects is to seek out "gaps" in the rules of the form-creating and meaning-generating game. Through uncovered interstices, they wish to dismantle or *critically deconstruct* self-evident, natural, and finished entities or stable totalities. This practice frustrates objectification and exploitation by the marketplace. Deconstructing form and meaning or language in architecture and urbanism itself does *not* mean their complete elimination, or that all positions are open and anything goes. It means a *critical* path of *practice* that *destructures* form and meaning in order to reinscribe them in a way that denies a privileged mode of representation and aesthetic realm. It intends to restore and play out differences through a critical mediation and thus go beyond the recent false debate between high Modernism and populist Post-modernism.

This architecture has the special "form" and quality of what might be called "*le poetique*," a poetry that, not altogether unlike Japanese *haiku*, posits language against its proper laws and rules which are constantly questioned and pushed to the edge. This form of *le poetique*, where boundaries between creative and critical processes are dissolved, promises to be an effective mode of probing into the life and order of things, revealing also the present reality of the human condition. In Japan, this new mode of understanding and conduct echoes aspects of the traditional "Japanese order of things," which has now acquired another dimension, *critical ontology*, with the potential to challenge prevailing *bourgeois* Western representation, ideology, and metaphysics.[52]

21. *Rotunda*, Yokohama,
1987 by Riken Yamamoto
(above left).
22. *Silver Hut*, Tokyo, 1984
by Toyo Ito (left).
23. *Spiral Building*, Tokyo,
1985 by Fumihiko Maki
(above).

Notes

1. It has to be noted that thinkers working in the contemporary styles of Western philosophy are often ill-trained in, and therefore neglectful of, Eastern forms of thought.

2. Teiji Itoh, "Japan's Cultural Legacy," in *The Dawns of Tradition* (Tokyo: Nissan Motor Co., Ltd., 1983), p. 4.

3. Both Chie Nakane and Edwin O. Reischauer used these terms in their respective books: C. Nakane, *Japanese Society* (Middlesex: Penguin Books, 1973), p. 2, 155; and E. O. Reischauer, *The Japanese* (Cambridge, MA: Harvard University Press, 1977), p. 391.

4. Sokyo Ono, *Shinto — The Kami Way* (Tokyo: Charles E. Tuttle Co., 1962), p. 8.

5. Mitsukuni Yoshida, "The Ethos of Japanese Life," in M. Yoshida, I. Tanaka, and T. Sesoko, editors, *The Compact Culture* (Hiroshima: Toyo Kogyo, 1982), p. 11.

6. The Chinese world view, derivative of the Hindu cosmic order, regarded the sky or "heaven" as round, and the earth as rectangular, with the four sides representing the cardinal points of the compass; the realm of in-between was assigned to man.

7. In the continuous chain of transformations, according to Buddhism, there is always an in-between state between two different forms of being wherein the two co-exist but are not synthesized. Accordingly this in-between is a state of "both/and," as well as "neither/nor." Taking this idea a step further, since change is continuous, every state of being is always an in-between.

8. Michihiro Matsumoto, *Haragei* (Tokyo: Kodansha International Ltd., 1984), p. 38. Iwanami's *Dictionary of Ancient Times* is quoted by Arata Isozaki in his "Space-Time in Japan — MA," in *MA: Space-Time in Japan*, catalog for an exhibit in the Cooper-Hewitt Museum, New York, 1978, p. 12.

9. This basic principle of Mahayana Buddhism was first formulated by the Indian philosopher, Nagarjuna (approximately 100-200 AD).

10. Matsumoto, *op. cit.* 8, p. 32, 40.

11. Time in Japanese is *jikan* 時間 where *ji* can be interpreted etymologically as the forward movement of the sun and means time in this sense, while *kan*, the other reading of *ma*, stands again for a pause, an in-between, or "space." Thus the Japanese word "time" expresses "space or place in flow."

12. It is worth quoting again from Matsumoto's book, where he outlines the important role the natural landscape has played in shaping the mentality of the Japanese, which came to differ significantly from that of the classical Greeks: "A misty country like Japan which abounds in ambiguity, accompanied by a changeable climate, can hardly contribute to clarity of thought. While the ancient Greeks believed that unity and order came out of chaos, a 'yawning void,' the Japanese have successfully preserved the chaos and developed the void into a highly polished art of human interaction" (Matsumoto, *op. cit.* 8, p. 70).

13. Fumihiko Maki, "Japanese City Spaces and the Concept of Oku," *JA, The Japan Architect*, May, 1979, p. 51-62.

14. Roland Barthes, *Empire of Signs*, trans. Richard Howard (New York: Hill and Wang, 1982), p. 31-32.

15. Maki, *op. cit.* 13, p. 20.

16. This hierarchy, or progression towards *oku*, is also represented by the relative elevation of the floor. The higher the level of the floor, the further inside that particular space is perceived to be and the higher in esteem it is held. This is also shown by the way the house is entered, vertically rather than horizontally: outside path, steps up to the veranda (*engawa*) or anteroom (*genkan*), followed by the wooden decking, and finally the *tatami* rooms, which are raised slightly higher again.

17. Maki, *op. cit.* 13, p. 59.

18. Edward T. Hall, "Introduction," to Matsumoto, *op. cit.* 8, p. 15.

19. Koji Yagi, "Climate and the Japanese Way of Life," in *Japan: Climate, Space and Concept — Process Architecture* No. 25, 1981, p. 30.

20. Kisho Kurokawa, "*Le Poetique* in Architecture: Beyond Semiotics" in *Kisho Kurokawa: Recent Works and Projects — Process Architecture*, No. 66, 1986, p. 154. The Japanese mentality had nothing in common with the Classicism and Classical episteme of the West. In the Japanese world of things the whole could not be meticulously reconstructed from its parts.

21. Kengo Kuma, "Tokyo-New York: A Comparison by Linguistic Analogy," *JA, The Japan Architect*, Feb. 1987, p. 64-67.

22. Akira Miyoshi, "The Silent Beat of Japanese Music," *Japan as I See It*, Vol. 3 (Tokyo: NHK Publications, 1985), p. 101, 103.

23. The meanings of these words are based on Andrew N. Nelson, *Japanese-English Character Dictionary* (Tokyo: Charles E. Tuttle Co., 1975).

24. This *haiku* is quoted from Barthes, *op. cit.* 14, p. 81, and appears without reference.

25. Barthes, *op. cit.* 14, p. 78. *Mu* means "emptiness," and *satori* "enlightenment" in Japanese.

26. Kuma, *op. cit.* 21, p. 66.

27. Günter Nitschke, "Space-Place-Void," unpublished manuscript, © Nitschke, 1987, p. 16. The conception and perception of the environment and space itself as a "discontinuous continuity" in Japan is also well illustrated by the woodblock print (*ukiyo-e*) series of Ando Hiroshige (1797-1858). In one, the famous pilgrimage road between Tokyo and Osaka, along the seacoast is depicted as a sequence of "Fifty-three stages of Tokaido" (1833).

28. Tomoya Masuda, *Living Architecture: Japanese* (New York: Grosset & Dunlap, 1970), p. 9.

29. Tomonobu Imamichi, "Ethics, East and West," *Kodansha Encyclopedia of Japan*, Vol. 2 (Tokyo: Kodansha International, 1983), p. 232.

30. Nitschke, *op. cit.* 27, p. 23.

31. *Ibid.*, p. 22.

32. Terry Eagleton, *Literary Theory* (Minneapolis: University of Minnesota Press, 1983), p. 117, 118, and 173.

33. Kate Soper, *Humanism and Anti-Humanism* (La Salle, Illinois: Open Court, 1986), p. 14-15.

34. Michel Foucault, *The Order of Things: An Archaeology of the Human Sciences*, (New York: Vintage Books, 1973), p. xxii.

35. Botond Bognar, "Between Means and Meaning: Architecture and the Human Condition" in *The Spirit of Home — New Orleans 1986*, proceedings of the 74th Annual Meeting of the Association of Collegiate Schools of Architecture (Washington, D. C.: ACSA, 1986), p. 466.

36. Herbert Marcuse, *One-Dimensional Man* (Boston: Beacon Press, 1964), p. 158.

37. Toyo Ito, "In Search of a Context, 1971," *JA, The Japan Architect*, April, 1982, p. 22.

38. Günter Nitschke coined the much quoted term "sophisticated order" in his "*MA — The Japanese Sense of Place*" in *AD, Architectural Design*, March 1966, p. 117-157.

39. Kenneth Frampton, "Towards a Critical Regionalism," in Hal Foster, editor, *The Anti-Aesthetic* (Port Townsend, Washington: Bay Press, 1983), p. 21.

40. According to Michel Foucault, "modern power" operates as a "government of individualization" that, by manipulating the "right" to individuality, attaches to the person a certain owned identity "in a constricting way"; by acknowledging individuals only in their isolation, it deprives them, in an insidious manner, of their ties and intimate relationships with others and community life thereby also denying them everything that would make them truly individuals. Today the individual is subject(ed) to his or her autonomous identity. M. Foucault, "The Subject and Power," in H.L. Dreyfus and P. Rabinow, *Michel Foucault: Beyond Structuralism and Hermeneutics* (Chicago: University of Chicago Press, 1982), p. 211-212.

41. Foucault outlines this especially in his book *Discipline and Punish: The Birth of the Prison*, (New York: Vintage Books, 1979), p.195-228, by using Jeremy Benthams's model of the Panopticon.

42. Tadao Ando, "New Relations Between the Space and Person," *JA, The Japan Architect*, Oct-Nov. 1977, p. 44.

43. Tadao Ando, "Townhouse at Kujo," *JA, The Japan Architect*, Nov. - Dec. 1983, p. 60.

44. Itsuko Hasegawa, "Thin Membranous Boundaries," *JA, The Japan Architect*, Nov.-Dec. 1986, p. 55.

45. Riken Yamamoto, "The City as Topography" in *JA, The Japan Architect*, Nov.-Dec. 1986, p. 42.

46. Toyo Ito, "Collage and Superficiality in Architecture," *A New Wave of Japanese Architecture*, IAUS Catalogue No. 10 (New York: IAUS, 1978), p. 68.

47. *Ibid.*

48. Kenneth Frampton, "*Ukiyo-e* and the Art of Toyo Ito," *SD, Space Design*, Sept. 1986, p. 144.

49. Lynne Breslin, "Ito and Ecriture," *SD, Space Design*, Sept. 1986, p.149.

50. Ito, *op. cit.* 37, p. 22.

51. Fumihiko Maki, "Modernism at the Crossroad," *JA, The Japan Architect*, March 1983, p. 22.

52. I use the term "ontology" *not* in the sense of Western metaphysics, but along a much broader interpretation including within its scope not only Being, Truth, Subject, etc., but also their counterparts: non-Being, Fiction, the Other, etc. This is exactly a critique of Western ontology.

All photographs by Botond Bognar.

Deconstruction, the Great Annihilation or Necrophily?

This text is a much shortened version of an essay written in 1984/85 which set out to investigate the potential for new thinking in architecture beginning with the decline of structuralism. The original text offered a critique of current architectural discourse and works as varieties of eclectic contextualism to show them caught-up in structuralist positions, which continued the two-fold intention of Renaissance classicism: under the dominance of the word, to establish a universal structural system for architectural form, and to enforce the principle of representation.[1] The "tendenza's" quest for the so-called autonomy of architecture did liberate architectural form but only insofar as it rebelled against the functionalistic appropriation of architecture by social and cultural engineering.

In the '70s the critique of structuralism and of the dialectic, Hegelian or Marxian, gave rise to new post-structuralist positions. The best-known writers are Foucault, Derrida, Kristeva, Baudrillard, Lyotard, Deleuze, and Guattari. Their thinking is relevant for a new and critical architectural practice; this essay will touch on Foucault — a key figure in the dismantling of structuralism — and focus on the contribution of deconstruction to a new architecture. These writers reject both the earlier humanism, with its idea of a subject in control and at the center of the world, of a history with an origin and an end, and also the extension of humanism into the idea of a structure with its own center. They go in search of the secret lust for power at play in the structural systems of culture, of language, of social practices. It may be said that all these authors search for ways to accept materiality without relying on the authority of interpretive systems. These ways include the "Archeological" reading of texts (Foucault), the deconstructive approach to textuality (Derrida), and finding the lines along which the tyranny of the structure can be fled and turned into an affirmation of the unpredictable, the event (Deleuze). The great themes are, respectively, power, language, desire.

Foucault's work investigates the genealogies of power, its nexus with knowledge, the colonization of bio-power, and the nexus of power/knowledge with the creation of the modern "subject/individual." The subject is a by-product of the historical form of the will to power and knowledge that is subjectless insofar as it operates above and below the level of the subject through "its" instincts, passions, malice, subtlety, rationalizations. Foucault avoids imposing interpretive schemata from above and stays with the concrete (as Adorno put it). He happily accepts the deroga-

POSTCLASSICAL *POESIS*

John Knesl

tory epithet of "positivist," and scorns only being called a structuralist. Power becomes visible as one weaves, as one "merely connects," as one reads diagonally across the discourses; and one begins with the historic *practices*, discursive and non-discursive, as they are conducted ordinarily. This Foucaultian archeological analytic reads human history back to us as the development of the techniques of power, a power that threatens the subject of experience but also creates it. Power is not clout or influence that can be possessed by a person, nor is it the control of resources in order to bring about some transformation (Giddens): Power is force relations that play at a level beyond that of the subject, it is development of order in fields established through power such as punishment, sexuality, care of the self, order is based on techniques designed for the welfare of society by agents who know. It is clear that this Foucaultian concept of a largely subjectless machinery of power, building itself through discourse, social practices, and their connections could have substantial heuristic value for an analytics of architectural form as a "silent" discourse (or rather non-discourse) connected with the other discursive and the non-discursive practices. Such an analytics has, to my mind, not been attempted. We need it whether or not we accept the potentially devastating critique of Foucault made by Baudrillard: Power does not exist; in fact it *is* only insofar as it fabricates the myth of its existence; Foucault fabricates the idea of power through his analytics.[2] However, Baudrillard's investigations into the power that he does see, *i.e.*

the power of transparence and simulation, could be seen as a (divergent) continuation of the Foucaultian work. In fact, the constitutive concepts in Foucault's work are the heterogeneity of the expressible and the visible, of knowledge and power, the idea of non-relations, and consequently of war. The development of these ideas may prove more difficult, but also more productive, than the impulse of deconstruction.

Deconstruction

Like the other post-structural positions, deconstruction reels away from the last attempt in Western thinking to impose unified and unifying order on the world — even if God was no longer present in this order but forever absent — an order stemming from the *fear of otherness*. This last great and deadening inquisition was structuralism. Yet to what extent deconstruction itself remains caught in the idea of structure remains to be seen.

A response to both ontological and methodological structuralism, deconstruction was inspired by Derrida's reading of Heidegger and Nietzsche. The structuralist reading of the text (and this would include readers such as Hegel and Marx and father Plato) does violence to it and remains incapable of sniffing out the strategy and the secret armature of the text. Deconstruction hunts down the founding concepts of metaphysical thinking and of dialectics and shows them to be hollow, without substance: presence, fullness, subject, consciousness, history, *telos*, origin. It seeks to reveal how the largely hidden textual tactics to achieve domination rely on signification, the link between sign and the "real thing," and on representative signification in particular. It argues that there is no such thing as pure reason: All reasoning depends on language and is therefore of an inevitably "textual" nature. The meaning of texts is not — as it is for humanist realism — a reference to something outside, to the "real," but it resides in the play of a structure of oppositional traces or marks that derive their authority from a center, the heart of the structure that makes possible the play of signs and meanings but also keeps this play in check. However, as the text is deconstructed, the nonexistence (or rather, the vexing absence) of this center is revealed through the playing out of the structure. The structure, the deepest strategy in the text, the fabric of textuality itself, betrays a will to dominate, in turn legitimated by the coherence generated by the center. The emptiness of the center, the lie, does not however, abolish meaning, but condemns it to a ghost-like incarceration into structure from which it tries to dig its way out: It becomes the mole of differen/ance. (Yet in the end, the very notion of structure may be metaphor itself, dependent on the will to forget the rhetorical status of the very concept of structure.)[3]

Since everything depends on the play of structure, deconstruction cannot accept the idea of an author/creator of texts, of a subject that speaks, present to itself and one with itself: "*It*" speaks, or rather, *writes*, and therefore all social systems are inherently alienating because external to their subject. Grammatology, the theory and practice concerned with textuality in general, seeks to bring about "writing" as the free play of language. It eschews any methodology because the latter would presume principles which in turn would be based on metaphysical presuppositions. Deconstruction has as its principle to have no principle, parasitically to attach itself to the text, to insinuate itself into it, to make it play more freely than intended by its structure. There is no original author but only writers who quote, paraphrase, extend, and involve the text in a dance/battle that forces it to become freer play. It is not the pure difference of Saussurean structuralism that creates meaning, but the uncanny *differance*, the continuous sliding away and changing of a meaning that no longer has any presence behind itself. But since, as Derrida has said, there is nothing outside the text, the structure itself must be full of worms, there must be other wills inside it that are fighting it out and make *differance*.

At this point the strongest and also the weakest in deconstruction are peculiarly merged: Nietzsche had prepared some of the way: The fundamental laws of Aristotle are only our inability to think beyond them, since logic is nothing but the will-to-power manifesting as will to understand; and whereas we assume that our concepts come from experience, the link between empirical evidence and conceptual truth is only another metaphorical displacement. Foucault, in fact, restates this: The link between knowledge and power (thinking and force relations) is not of a logical nature but it is established by hurling the spear across the gap; the metaphor, or rather, *all signification*, constitutes such a hurl. Deconstruction lives on "...[T]he Nietzschean affirmation... of the play of the world and of the innocence of becoming... of a world of signs without fault, without truth, and without origin which is offered to an active interpretation."[4] But deconstruction also exhibits a peculiarly resignative acceptance of language as having to rely on structure and on signification. If the aim is to restore the free play of language itself by allowing difference, this constant *deferment* of meaning, to somehow force the structure to reveal itself naked, where can one go after this fundamental metaphoricity of all meaning has been demonstrated? Did we accept too quickly the enclosing of textuality, the keeping away of

writing from living, must the meaning be forever deferred because it can never become event and metamorphose into another sign *and life*? Is deconstruction content with unearthing the "bad" buried opposite terms and the absent center? Is it perhaps caught in negation, which belongs to the model of repression, rather than proceeding by positive affirmation of otherness with its undecidability and fatefulness, *i.e.* the real free play? Later works by Derrida, such as *Spurs* and *Living On*, do become wild playing with textuality — still somehow confined by operating with allusion, "wrong" etymologies, and free associations. Perhaps the real promise held out by deconstruction is the development of hunters' tactics that seek out the *vagrancies of meaning*, *i.e.* the will that seeks to become life and refuses to be caught-up in structured systems. In this light, deconstruction in architecture should concern itself with the deconstruction of typology and the development of deconstructive architectural work as experiments in the art of the creation of life as hunting and warfare.

Themes and Methods

Deconstruction as a style of critical (and potentially creative) action is of interest to architecture because it seeks to establish a legitimate cultural practice in the intermezzo after the old humanism, discredited if not yet altogether shaken off. But we had better take care: In deconstructive works, references abound to the architecture of a text, to the spatial makeup of its governing ideas, to its "spacing." Derrida's ultimate terms are the trace, the mark, the spacing that is effectuated by the ("restricted") play of the structure. To see architectural forms through these metaphors is tempting but means to treat architecture like a literary text, Eisenman's *Fin d'Ou T Hou S* is an example of this. While architectural form has often been given the task to organize thought, the conduct of the body and the performance of practices, it should be regarded as a uniquely spatial and material "text" with its special relation to the body and thus to life.

Deconstruction hunts down the metaphysical, since it is the metaphysical that supports the act of assigning meaning and value that is performed by the will that brings itself to life in the strategy in/of a text. The metaphysical rests in the idea that a system (made up of hierarchically ordered oppositions) is founded on a vindicating, authorizing power center, a presence from which emanates meaning. If we look upon architecture as a text which for the deconstructionist is something *woven* from strands, where certain threads are kept in certain positions behind others (they *are* opposed), we can see that classicism has elaborated the idea of

architecture as a structure of systematically opposed types that were founded as a totality on a center (God) and on *principia* emanating therefrom. Structure it is, from *venustas, firmitas, commoditas* — all of which are derived from "truth" — to Semper's naturalistic historical evolution as the truth center, to modernist vacillation between acceptance of life decentered into multiplicitous functions, values and forms no longer supported by authorizing referentials and, on the other, espousal of a renewed humanism based on the idea of progressive enlightenment and technical progress.

Structure is to tame the difference that is the movement of the becoming of the world at every instant, so that it will play the role of a mere difference of position *within* a system that enforces unity from above or from behind and relies on identities based on the structure as ultimate referential. How could there be a structure of justice or of knowledge if one could not recognize this piece of "land" again as "identical" as opposed to something fundamentally and irreconcilably different? In this, architecture has clearly played a principal role by forcing this kind of memory of the identical on "us," thus making us into subjects for whom identity is a necessary constituent. The world that was becoming a different one at any moment became one of ordered opposites, each reducible and referable to a higher identity resting in itself, more lasting and powerful, an identity that education (and architecture as part of it) made us learn to see at work in the differences. This identity is metaphysical since it supplants by the everlasting sameness of the signifier/signified relation, the wild play of material and formal/abstract differences that is the becoming of life, of fate, of the world.

Deconstruction detects the telling cracks and divergences in the identity and *unity* of a concept by making it play itself out until it overextends the logic of the semantic and syntactic system that it is part of and thus betrays classical unity as a form of *forced closure*. Structure and identity harbor dominative and repressive desire since they want to be absolute; to repress the divergence in the counterforces against which they form, *i.e.* they seek to turn the multiplicity of forces that are the world into a structural system supporting only *itself*. While deconstruction affirms that identity is really no more than a relation of difference between this and all that is "other," relations are primary as opposed to elements (Ollmann reads this in the early Marx),[5] and non-relations are even more primary (*differance* is a non-relation), does deconstruction's differen/ance go far enough in shaking structuralist difference, the supremacy of the system, out of its hierarchical trees?

Behind and beyond systemized difference, deconstruction recovers the suppressed unassimilable "other" that is a necessary constituent of the very self that later denies the other. It does what art does instinctively: to sense the contradictions in the ostensible purposes and ideas, to find the dark side of the great concept, to tease out the suppressed "other." Light needs dark. This otherness is not at all a dialectical contradiction that would resolve itself in higher identity: It is divergent, heterogeneous difference that does not lead to synthesis as it is represented in the classicist figure of balance. The kind of *balance* proper to it is the stirring peace of the war of full affirmation of all *otherness*, a balance in motion that eludes the social institutions keen on appropriating it. Non-classicist balance would be the graceful affirmation of otherness.

Derrida's text on Tschumi's *La Villette* park project opposes architecture as an archetypal and paradigmatic making of structures with closure, to the movement of *differance* and of otherness. The ensuing observations and associations about the tugging between grid and elements are all based on identifying architecture with structure. Yet the history of architecture — and not just modern architecture — is full of episodes during which the structure was blown apart into a becoming, an event, *i.e.* something that brings new life: Not only mannerist sub-streams in all periods attest to this, but also anti-structural moves within highly canonical buildings, for instance, the anti-classical hyper-extension of the facade of Schinkels' museum.

The critical questions are these: Can deconstructive interventions do more than "relativize" the structure by exposing it behind the rhetoric of the text? Does deconstruction remain caught-up in the classical idea of art and criticism as the making conscious of truth, even if only of the latter's absence? Do these tendencies point to another approach, to an idea on a new level, that of forcing the structure not just to transform itself but to open up beyond structuredness to a new becoming arising from non-relations, from a transversality of effects that turn the carefully hierarchically organized structure, the ghost in the text, into a heterogeneous multiplicity? Are even the free associations of deconstruction still far too dependent on the structures instead of racing away in full affirmation of the other? Deconstruction may only be the grave digger; it leaves us — corpses ourselves — with corpses. Is this only because it limits itself all too willingly to narrowly textual/cultural activity, because it relies too much on old meanings even if they are found deceitful, or is it because deconstruction ends up leaving intact signification as based on structure,

the idea of opposition and of something deeper sanctioning it — by default, because it does not take the step to unreserved affirmation of otherness?

The con- and distortions in Eisenman's earlier opus have betrayed the same old desire to reveal the structure (the truth appearing as geometry) by forcing different appearances of the same depth structure to superimpose themselves on the same place. This deconstruction of the presence of a building by dissolving it into various interpenetrating aspects nevertheless seeks to conjure up the deeper substance, the idea. The classical position is reaffirmed: dialectics, architecture as the theater of representation. There is also something monstrous about this collapsing of time into the moment: as if everything should be made present all at once, to be possessed, to allay the fear of encountering the object as an unpredictable other. Fear of the other: Derrida's wilder texts seem aware of the necessity to push deconstruction beyond the point of no return. They seek to become the wild play of language "itself," a play that transgresses the pudenda and the prudence of the structure. Does this wild writing lose courage and arrest itself by holding onto what hides in *differance*: signification versus a free, a-signifying, "machinic" taking-off of events in which forms do not signify but function as conductors?

Deconstruction takes the first step by seeing difference not as the unavoidable means to build structural systems that would make manageable the *terribilita* of fate, but as differen/ance, the fount of all creativity and of all life. Difference in a world in which the non-identical is no longer suppressed (this is perhaps what Adorno fought for) becomes an erotic cloud in which all manner of identities can form to live for a moment as intensities of the life force. Such difference is not a pluralism beneath which identities reign that actualize certain social, cultural, and economic power. Such difference is closer to "the most exasperated plurality" which Negri finds affirmed in the dialectics as it is still envisaged in the "Grundrisse." Along with such difference deconstruction must embrace indeterminacy and inconclusivity as fundamental conditions so that life may come to happen.

Has classicism not sought to create a force field of differences between types, and thereby to contain *differance* within a canonical system of differences, preventing it from escaping into making new life outside and against the system? Classicist architecture seeks to preserve the sanctity of a higher identity behind the types, the idea of its structure and of structure in general. To contain and tame this proliferating runaway difference, this veritable "dissemination," 19th-cen-

tury architecture had to conjure the systems that would ultimately ensure the unity and identity safeguarded as and by the system of types: Viollet le Duc (material construction as basis of identity) and Durand (the dictionary of canonical types as the system).

History

The textuality of deconstruction has no place for "works" and "authors": If deconstruction could also go beyond textuality, it could give the text ever-new *lives*, or rather, allow it to become new lives *with* acts other than writing. There is no production without repetition, since production is still seen as dependent on systems of oppositions, which provide the ground for the mole of differen/ance. Both the archeological technique of Foucault and the tactics and ruses of deconstruction reject the kind of history that is written and lived by imposing a master code, a higher schema of "explanation" and "interpretation" on the streaming of events. Foucault offers the concept of a counter-memory that remembers what official history suppresses or, perhaps better, rewrites. This counter-memory lives in everyday lives, in what the *body* (the unconscious) remembers, what it brings up and puts together: To remember is to *reassemble*. As deconstruction forces the structure to play out again and again its strategies for selfhood, it remembers also the counter-forces that were antagonists before they were "integrated" or written/structured out of existence: Deconstruction regurgitates swallowed-up otherness. Again there is a strong link to architecture: In "speaking" to the body rather directly, architecture could bypass the normative *schemata* of explanation and valuation and enable the body to remember desire, not to have more phantasies, but to reassemble desire into machines to make new life, and to shake off the "subject" that the structure has impressed on the freely moving fluidity that the subject, the "we," could be.

Early deconstruction used the technique of *re-reading, repeated and repeated again*, often quoting in full text, to weaken the interpretive *schemata* which would normally let us read the "content" and to make visible the bare tactics of/in the text as its structure. As it repeats, deconstruction prods, even contradicts, in order to challenge the text into performing its strategies. But contradiction is not used to generate a winning synthesis, but rather to lay bare the schemes and the sources of power and desire in the text, in the piece of history examined; and, finally, to show the place of the center empty, taken up by a silent trace, in itself meaningless, that establishes nothing more than difference and thus power as a supra- and infra-subjectual force relation between *differances*. But where does this prodding come from, who is it that performs the deconstructive battle: surely not the text all by itself?

Deconstruction reaffirms the primacy of the written trace over the breath of lived speech and therefore reads the text without the authority of author or interpreter, just as Foucault deals with the statements and objects and not with interpretations. As it retraces the text it retraces the subjectless drive to become power that forms itself in/through the text. The deconstructive technique wants to force the power in and of the structure to bring down itself as the challenged structure proceeds to destroy the other that constitutes the difference on which the structure's very identity is secretly founded. Could deconstruction bring the text to the point where power appears, no longer as the attribute of a sacrosanct structure, but as an always recallable force relation operating through signs that regulate forces as they impinge upon nature and society. Would deconstruction lead back to Arendt's free will of political beings whose decision to join and make a city first creates the very possibility of "true" political power, or will deconstruction be content with just staging the battles for power that rage behind the muteness of the trace?

Could it be said that it is the affirmation of the right to differen/ance that allows deconstruction to identify the dominative interests within the text, that in a way *are* the text? Where is this differen/ance coming from, this nagging, never-quite-graspable other? If affirmation of *differance* is *affirmation of otherness*, what would be its relation to the body as the blind affirmation of life by and for itself, would the silent body become the ultimate arbiter, since there is no recourse to any metaphysical foundation? Could deconstruction escape the mythification of the body by opening it and the world to an experiment, free of metaphysics, with forms of and for life?

Deconstruction further repeats the text to play a cynical game with it, to annul it. Later deconstruction blows apart the text into all the winds of allusion, alliteration, association, contraposition. While destroying the deceits of metaphysics — it *could* also metamorphose the text not only into other texts but into new lives outside the text. Rather than restricting itself to new and perhaps all too parasitical textuality, it should move out to form assemblages with other practices. If architecture were to approach its historic context, or better, situatedness, in the manner of deconstructive re-reading would its first steps be close to Eisenman's *Fin d'Ou T Hou S* or Tschumi's *La Villette* follies? Even if one accepted a certain nihilist tendency that often comes with deconstruction, these projects demonstrate that deconstruction owes us a discussion on how to select

texts and which parts to subject to over-repetition, to paraphrasing, or to over-extension. More fundamentally, the literal transposition of a literary technique would vitiate the nonlinguistic nature and the special powers of architecture. Perhaps the current episode of deconstruction is nothing more than the decline of the classicist enterprise that insisted on subjecting what is wild about architecture and life to the order of linguistic structure, thus assimilating spatial relations (which are in a way more textual than the literary texts) into logico-semantic argumentation for and by the state. If, on the other hand, architecture were to approach the physical traces of history not through a staged repetition, but by adopting fully the principle of *adding* (the idea of assemblage), it could both perform a non-negativist critique *and* build new and divergent values and lives. Such trans-deconstructive play would be informed by the critical thinking in the works of Deleuze, Guattari, Lyotard, and Baudrillard.

Power, Subject, Desire

If deconstruction is not to lose itself in narcissistic circling around literary differen/ance, it must address these themes. In differen/ance, deconstruction presumes an overabundance of meaning, which in turn may be the trace of a still tacitly presumed drive or life force. Does not this pushing-asunder, 'this explosive disseminating penetrated by differ/ance resemble the death drive that seeks to achieve a complete discharge, a complete streaming away into a no-thing-ness? And does differ/ance not *return* — as does Nietzsche's return — in ever different forms? What for? The engine that drives Nietzsche's universe is the wild becoming of life, without any reason or purpose beyond unfolding the manifold of life power. Especially after humanity has reached the point of becoming capable of affirming this life force fully without moral restraints imposed by God, it is unreserved affirmation that must become the basis of a new morality. Deconstruction seems not to address these questions directly; but where does this incessant movement of differ/ance keep coming from?

Refusing to impose master codes on the text deconstruction demonstrates that power is a structure of force relations that pervade the text. Deconstruction here seems to parallel Foucault who has first investigated power as a structural relation above the heads of all its subjects. While earlier deconstruction seeks to unmask the power hiding in the signifying structure (only to show, with Nietzsche, that there are only masks), later deconstruction tends actively to explode power by *disseminating* the power of signs to signify. It is not clear to what extent the disseminated signs could become signifiers for a new structure.

The analyses of Foucault show that there is no history, no becoming, without power/knowledge. He investigates the history of power and its connection to systematic discursive practices, to a type of dominative knowledge that emplaces the power/agent outside and above, develops instruments to "observe," to define (cut out) and move around on strings *its* objects, to cut them open to study their internal machinery. This type of power/knowledge has developed the modern "subject," its persona, its desires, its relationship to objects outside it. By rewriting, deconstruction tends to dissolve, along with its object relation, the humanistic and metaphysical subject. For this subject-inside versus object-outside relation, deconstruction substitutes the outside of the written trace, the written sign instead of the spoken word that is thought to carry the soul of its author.

Has Guattari gone farther than deconstruction? He leaves behind the subject that is incarcerated in the structural cages of the established significations which *produce*, shift, and transform the desire that makes the drive and thought into the individual subject. Inspired by the semiotics of modern physics and art, he proposes a non-signifying semiotics where actions are induced by the "diagrammatic" functioning of signs. Non-signifying semiotics speaks directly to thought and the body: it allows desire to invent forms for new life at a "molecular" level below the level of common meanings and of the powers that get actualized in the structure of conventional language. Guattari's universe of "desiring machines," assembled subjectivities arising from the dissolution of the old heavily integrated "egos," is ultimately founded on life-affirming desire set free in the microcosm where desire is subjugated by sociopolitical powers.

From the classical subject-object relation follows an ever-expanding sickly conception of desire as *lack*. Rather, desire should be thought of as an overabundance of will-to-become-life, seeking to form assemblages of forces. For Kristeva it is still lack that first establishes the subject through expulsion and rejection of the world into an *outside*, an object, thereby setting off a constant search for the "good" object to be re-incorporated. This outside-object thus becomes the origin and ground for signification. Surely this categorical and systemic opposition between the expelled and the inside should become a target of deconstruction so that the "other," the world, would be recognized as inseparable from what "we" are.

If deconstruction were to dissolve the classical subject–object relation, it could prepare the paths to a free becoming of life and of its agent, the new subject. Kristeva still follows Freud: Eros reduces tension through fabricating the artifice, ever greater organic "units," by constructing a sublimated identity between the subjects and their "good" objects. The artifice *is* the expulsion and reincorporation of an object. Eros readies the object for consummation, for reunification, even if this latter always fails because it occurs within a restricted economy of drives which must stop short of dissolving the subject in a burst of discharge: While this subject suffers under the subject – object relation it also depends on it for its very existence. The later Freud struggles to accept Thanatos as the true master. But there is no need to resign oneself to Freud's pessimistic interpretation of Thanatos as a return to the peace of the inorganic: If we are afraid of undoing the structured subject then we must see Thanatos as death. If, however, we were to think of ourselves as ever-becoming subjectivities we would live forever in what we pass into precisely by discharging "ourselves," by dying every moment into the becoming of new lives. The relations between desire, drive, language, and the material world must be approached through entirely new techniques capable of dealing with the transversal relations (or even non-relations) between language and the speechless, the wild material substance of the body itself. These non-relations are *assemblages* of heterogeneities that make up lived lives, they are functional connections not the metaphysical ones between signifier and signified content, *i.e.* the life that is always only "meant." Would unreserved deconstruction not have to say that nothing of the world can be kept "outside" me because I am and can become anything: Godlike, "I am all." This is Nietzsche's unconditional affirmation; I believe that deconstruction does not yet affirm enough its own founding term, *differance*, as its *becoming other* itself. If it did, it would ceaselessly turn into other life outside the realms of literature.

Much hinges on the alliance between the old subject and representation: Can we say that classicist closed harmony and absolute perfection seek nothing but to *cover over* the *lack*, to close the Lacanian gaping of the drive? Classicism is production of the *imago*, that in "standing for" forever removes into absence the complete reconciliation and reunion of the desiring subject with the world/mother. For as long as the subject obeys the *dispositifs* which structure what is really the chaos of endless becoming and regulates what the subject thinks, feels, and acts down to the deepest levels of the self,[6] there will be a reward: a sense of self, a mission. Would it not be better to invent a new "subject" made up of freely multiplying and ever metamorphosing assemblages of heterogeneous "I's," loopings of life forces making up a subject freed by and to a post-Nietzschean ethics and epistemology? Foucault

was working his way to an analytics of what the self might become after the age of "Man."[7]

A deconstructionist architecture then should really deconstruct — not merely represent — the way in which "normal" architecture assists with forming us into subjects. Perhaps initially deconstructive architecture might operate analytically to take apart the ways in which architecture holds together the subject, leaving behind the "pieces" of this subject to engage freely with the other moments of subjectivity. Or are "we" as Baudrillard argues, already broken up into so many fractal facets anyway, molecular "I's" ceaselessly engaged and moved around by the networks of modern communication.[8] If Baudrillard is right deconstruction has to go farther. Deconstructive architecture then could begin with transgression, a kind of free experimentation in a post-humanist world no longer organized by a God, by origin and *telos*, but inhabited by multiplicities of (Nietzschean) gods and demons. This does not mean an architecture presenting *representations* of fragmentation or explosion (the little dramas of Libeskind and Hadid), since these only reinstate the subject by challenging it to integrate them and thereby itself. Not even environmental ambivalences or multivalences that cannot be integrated by one coherent structure would do. Rather, deconstructive architecture should free the energies chained into the subject and allow them to form divergent multiplicitous subjectivities: *Addition and assemblage, not breaking up and opposition.*

Language: Representation or Sign-conduit

Deconstruction rejects the humanist metaphysics of the spoken word into which a soul is breathed by the "real" referent. Instead it locates power in the structure of the signs by themselves and the meanings they establish by virtue of differen/ances *within* the sign systems. Only with the idea of dissemination does deconstruction seem ready to push out from literariness into the uncharted non-relations between signs and life. The deconstructor's hesitancy to take this step is the malaise. This step is even more important for the relevance of these techniques for architecture, since classicist theory has systematically subjected architecture to language, and since architectural

forms enter and become life — they do not remain abstract typologies. As deconstruction frees the text from metaphysics towards free play, deconstruction in architecture must free architecture both from linguistically-anchored meaning and from the patterning of architectural forms on the oppositional structure of language and the "things" and "non-things" which it established as the world.

Behind the masks, deconstruction searches out the tropes in the deep. Is this deep the *machinic* level at which Deleuze/Guattari locate the purely *"diagrammatic"* functioning of signs as mere *conductors of forces*, of energetic metamorphoses outside any signification? Architecture and the city are normally perceived and lived in as background structure, the hidden skeleton of the "texts" that are our everyday lives. Architecture as *nonlinguistic* "textuality" must not adopt analytic models developed for linguistic texts and project them onto its "spatial texts." Classicist theory imposes on spatial bodily forms the corset of the double articulation (synchrony, diachrony) of linguistic language with its significations that are geared to capture, domesticate, to make useful, comparable, and exchangeable, the life force in its values, ideas, and bodily intensities. Foucault seems to suggest that the more power (operating through knowledge, *i.e.* signification) "develops" the life forces, the stronger the counter forces become. Everything is a long war. This may be the great suffering, necessary for the creation of Nietzsche's overman after "man." But there is currently no convincing evidence of the strength of these counter-intensities; a critical culture certainly would have to strengthen them. Languages are critical for the freeing of life power — and therefore also architecture as a non-discursive language — because human existence has nothing to design itself after, but must trust itself to experiments with the interplay between languages and the war at the level of the organismic since we have left behind classical humanism and its extension, the model of mother nature.[9] Without an anthropocentric humanism to follow, desire and power must be invented and evaluated in the free play of languages. We are thus thrown back onto languages as *sign manifolds (not structural systems)* serving as conduits (not as representations) for the experimentation that now becomes our mode of life.

Habermas' enlightenment model of emancipatory communicative praxis still relies on the concept of truth as an intersubjectively secured reference either to "fact" or to shared and wholly transparent meaning. Post-structuralist philosophy and artistic production instead force a free play of interpretation that generates even new differences to reveal the "truth" simply as the will that establishes the structure in the text or fabric. Deconstruction presumes Heidegger's human "*geworfensein*," finding oneself in a world without pre-installed meaning: This situation predetermines us to *signs* so we may "know," so desire may be set in motion. Deconstruction seems to accept Heidegger's center: For "man" to live, she/he must think; it is only in thinking — in language — that he/she can make his/her real home, in what "regions" toward him in the landscapes of his language. But in the end Derrida only finds a decentered mobile home in language that has become an ever shifting territory without safe ground, a painful Odyssey.

Our postmodern relation to language is unprecedented. One could argue that the history of thinking now culminates in full affirmation of *materiality* with all it brings: chance, singularities, multiplicity, and the prospect of immortality only in the form of the *return* of the willed-again. After magic, ritualistic, apotropaic, and incantatory language and after technical language we have become strong enough to affirm the incessant movement of differen/ance the Dionysian expenditure of meaning and life force. Nietzsche and Freud have taught us that language is not only what opens paths to new forms for life, but that it also becomes the golden cage that power has "us" build to reduce the intensity of life to a lower, a more "manageable" level, to contain and control it through the systems of signification, to channel the drive and turn it into desire fixated in images. We need freer languages that can invent paths for life energies by conducting visible new forces and new forms for life through a *mapping*, not through a *representational structure*. Representation means endless metaphysical recursion of references to something ever more "real," never to be reached. The significance of Deleuze/

Guattari's diagrammatic non-signifying signs is that they conduct energies to become new life *together with* the form they offer; they do not weaken the power of the sign to connect or disconnect forces by making them part of a representative structural system. A wall is not just a heap of mass nor is it only an idea: It *becomes life through its connections* with the many paths of lives that it enters and pulls along with itself. "It" becomes what is lived around, against, with, at, this side of, away from the wall, and in this way "we" become "it" also, not in the form of a mystical union but as *connective assemblage*.

Spatial form can resist the imposition of linguistic structure because of its multiplicitous capacity to assume an acategorical multiplicity of forms as well as to enter any form of life: thoughts, affects, actions, events. The special power of architecture rests in its ways of addressing and entering the body directly, undetected by the surveillance performed by the structures that determine linguistic thinking. Architecture is privileged because it touches the body, our hold on materiality and its hold on "us"; we are in it, and it can thus reach us forcefully — especially where it lowers itself to becoming mere background. Architecture "speaks" to the drive, the unconscious, the dormant "wills," it can engage desire in a most direct way.[10] Can it be said that the Derridean trace touches material flows in a similar way and that it comes close to the transversal connection between the *sign* and the *material flows* in Deleuze/Guattari? The trace is both material and formal-abstract sign, and architecture exhibits the qualities of a trace more than the written word or the image. A trace is, of course, not the same as a tracing, a copy, the outline that desire draws around the object in order to bind the drive energies to this object.[11]

Excursus: Deconstructive Architecture before Deconstruction

Deconstructive tendencies range from mannerist turning-on itself of the structural order and a theatrical collapsing, to adding the poison to the structural order that would carry it off in other streams and open it, metamorphotically, into new life.

In the entrance hall to the Laurenzian library in San Lorenzo, Florence, the conventional relations between entry hall, stair case, and reading room, and between columns, cornices, friezes, and walls, are strained or even contravened. The stair

pushes in on and marches forcefully into a tight tall cube, all but filling this cube and obliging the entrant to make a very sharp turn to ascend. The stair case is more concerned with its own unfolding than with mitigating the non-axiality of the entrance. The columns, paired to concentrate forces, appear to push into and through the wall instead of reinforcing it as the canons of classicism would oblige them to do. The cage formed by the columns and the horizontal friezes seems at once to squeeze the space even higher as well as to make it flee outwards. The wall, traditionally the strongest element in defining space, is turning into a non-identity that both moves outward and pushes in, thus both exacerbating and relieving the tightness of the vertical prism. Placement and sculptural treatment (the proportions) of the volutes and door frames contravene architectural convention that assigns these elements the role of signifying the carrying of weight. Elements at all scales are allowed to assert a difference, a virulent discordance culminating in the tension between a long quietly rhythmized reading room and a taut and excited prism. Reading is not the measured procession to the book, to knowledge granted by and represented in god, but becomes an intellectual and emotional flight, the desire that pushes the walls of the hall apart to free itself from the cage of structure. In the entrance room the canons of classicist architecture have not just been deconstructed: They have been confronted with a most violent push up into that long shape of the reading hall and as a result they have been blown — not apart (this is the mistake made by Libeskind, for instance) — but off into a new direction, taking flight into a wild and modernist space.

In the villa at Garches, Le Corbusier's principles are presented as certainties, as requirements of an economy of rational thinking and of building construction: The system of *pilotis*, the floor planes stacked on top of one another, the freestanding stair, the freestanding plane of the facade and within it the freedom of the position of the window band and of the holes cut out or of plastic elements attached to the plane. But are not these elements themselves the result of a deconstruction of the classicist system which requires that the building be made into an hierarchically organized whole? Are these principles, by having been made principles, the result of a critical analysis rather than of deconstruction? These principles do tend to reestablish a much more austere *structure* of horizontal floor planes and vertical pins to which holes and elements are added and called to order by the modulor. The pure archetype of the cube holds them together after all. It is true that the Corbusian game sets the cube — which is the implied result of the principles — against the elements that continually de-mask the cube as an ideal/formal entity. The vertical windows show that the frontal facade plane is merely pinned to the floor slab edges — but it is then recaptured into the cubic surface which later is broken by small balconies. Some of the *pilotis* are suppressed to give way to semi-defined activities. The stairs are free but

captured in part by an enclosure or by becoming attached to the *pilotis* system. The stacked floors are cut out to allow a transgressive visual continuity between living spaces. The programmatic elements of the wall and window band are subjected to a proportional system that assign them certain divisions. The "wild" landscape on the roof finds itself disciplined by the partially realized framing that completes the ideal cube, as are the forms of the bathrooms and dining room, whose freedom is restrained by their relations to the *pilotis* system. The facade is reinstated as a metaphorical face, and with this the structural difference between inside and outside and the concomitant principle of representation, both of these constitutive of classicist architecture.

Similarly the self-assertive panels of De Stijl at once explode into space and are restrained by a virtual center or by being referred to a reference wall (as in the Schroeder house), whereas, by comparison, in the Barcelona Pavilion each element keeps the others on their toes in a much more fragile balance. In LeCorbusier's work the willingness to let things clash and take flight coexists with the desire to bring them into a modern kind of harmony under the auspices of clear and strong geometric form. Wright, by contrast, is more aggressively modern. He builds houses without faces (the overhang), houses that are freely forming outsides even if still arranged around a center in the endless plane of the prairie, disciplined only in the earlier houses by classicist axes.

At Garches, Le Corbusier plays the game to which all but the most resolute deconstruction reverts. He sets up a largely undeclared structure to play against but reveals it only indirectly as the commanding structure. Why enclose the divergent ele-

ments in a unifying cube? Why unify the spaces with any of the other integrative design principles put forward by Le Corbusier, *i.e.* the dominant grid, the strong Gestalt, the completed cube? Why not encourage elements to form assemblages in many directions, to attain a machinic consistency rather than obey the authority of a new system? A facade is truly deconstructed only when there are positions other than inside or outside, other spaces made by/with/against/aside it, spaces not possible in the inside-outside system. The repetition of the facade, the so-called layering, does achieve some effects in this direction, it constitutes more an "adding" of explosive poison rather than a turning of structure on itself. The principle of the *pilotis* which establishes a bare open plane for the new modern life practices does not deconstruct the 19th-century street by making new spaces for a multiplicity of intensive life, but replaces it by a desert-like park that lacks the landscape formations that would create the tensions that would allow new public life to form and flow.

Venturi

Venturi may be claimed as one of the first postmoderns for having explicitly legitimized overt contradictions and the resulting "difficult whole." Can the "ordinary box" (*minus* unification) be regarded as a deconstruction of the classicist and of the modernist cube? Against the surfaces and the ordinary circulating systems of this box are set the reverberations of the enclosed public activities which cause ruptures, deformations, and breaks in massing, plan, and surfaces. But the cube is still posited, even if only as a box. Does irony deconstruct, or does it reestablish a self-righteously higher authority, the authority of the judging subject that has a superior view? Long before deconstruction and inspired by Pop Art, Venturi turned away from "deep" (structuralist) representation to surface, and flattened out meanings into mere *emblems*, highly *abstract*, "*written*" signs that seemed on their way to being able to attach themselves anywhere.

Venturi rejected the resurgence of classicism in modernism: the structural characteristics of closure, equilibrium, clear meaning, a typology of spatial elements,

the central idea of representation of the whole, of the totality of a culture, of striving for hierarchical integration, unification, and for identity between form and content. Venturi began with abstracted ironic representation as opposed to functionalist representation. In the later work the abstract sign on the plane, a kind of calligraphic writing, tends to predominate. No attempt is made to force the *sign*, the *form*, to express the content. This is in clear opposition to regressive attempts to re-semanticize the spatial structure of buildings so that it may again become the representation of deep anthropological and theological meanings (Kahn) and the manifestation of a local/historical *genius loci* (both Rossi and Norberg-Schulz).

The no-nonsense box simply sidesteps the issue with a zero-degree poverty of articulation to which other characters are simply *added*, resulting in deformations or surface modifications. Irony still prevails where traditional architectural elements are flattened into mere emblems that, in the more successful occasions, "work" through their form rather than through the meanings which they quote with ironic detachment. These quotations are made "out of context" since they seem taken out of the book of architecture; they are unlike his earlier deconstructions that take apart the systems rather than quoting the past ironically. Yet the deformations in the box, wrought by the impacts of lived life, are very effective (if non-deconstructive) since they set up break-ins into the box for intensities of living, by opening the box to forces from an outside that cannot be integrated by the box through systematization, but must be suffered by it. Nevertheless the box still serves as a scene in which a drama is played out and the idea of representation is still at work. Then again, this restrictive plane is left behind when Venturi allows ornamentation to go wild and turn the facade into a plane that waves with energies which threaten to swallow up the windows with their stoical rhythms. Elsewhere a local cultural symbol is flattened to a mere emblematic logo spilled all over the walls. Here perhaps he is closest to deconstruction: The merciless repetition bespeaks a bewildered frenzy that ceaselessly repeats the shell of a content lost, the center lost that would again spurt forth meaning through its structure (built on "X" means "Y").

At Purchase, the presence of a lecture hall motivates an oversize window detailed to look like the abstraction of a window, sashes magnified to make it even more abstract as the light baffle above undergoes a scalar hyperbole, reinforcing this effect. This "talk" might even be considered a sort of deconstruction. I believe, however, that beyond this referential effect there are direct effects that are more important: The corridor is forced to open to the outside campus with a window that undercuts the conventional inside-outside treatment. The stair ending is taken over by an impulse to become an impatient student meeting place and it is allowed to inundate the corridor with the rim of its water-fountain seat edge.

Rossi

Rossi's work began as a fight against the usurpation of form by the logic of the late capitalist "system" which makes architecture into a means to instrumentalize and technify life into a sign serving to express its powers and its legitimacy. His project, on balance, is a recuperation of meaning, not of idealist meaning but of the meaning that forms have acquired in the bodily rhythm of everyday life in a place over time. Therefore, Rossi has searched for the memory of the city, the memory it has and the memory it *is*, memory sedimented as the traces left by its history, the history of the actions, the sufferings and the delights of the people who have lived there. This memory belongs to a collective city body with its peculiar sensibilities, habits, and its rationality, a material body that can resist the modern power techniques that develop "subjects" and "things" into resources. The postulated formal autonomy provides the conditions for the building to mobilize desire other than the desire already adjusted to reigning powers and interests. But this difference is too abstract from the "little" escapes that can open up in day-to-day life, from the reality of scale, from the materiality of construction. Irretrievably abstract, the perfectly autonomous fragment (DalCo) refers to the possibility of a city composed of "individuals" enunciating themselves across a *neutralized and neutralizing distance*. The spark that is to fly from between them must stay at the level of a highly abstract cultural message. His technique, therefore, is not out to deconstruct the postmodern condition of architecture, *i.e.* the way in which

architecture serves to pacify and to foster a fundamental cynicism; rather, he digs, like the old structuralists, for gold, and compares his finds to distill something structural: a postmodern classicism, after all.

Deconstructive Techniques for the Re-assemblage of Architectural Works

Having discussed the posthumanist views on which deconstruction rests, having pointed out the fallacies of importing it straight into architecture, and having discussed examples of deconstruction in architecture, I will focus once more on transferable characteristics of these techniques. They are of potential relevance for architectural design and criticism because they are geared to working/playing with things and relations, systems and structures in a truly postclassical framework of thinking about subject, self, society, nature, history, language, materiality. Once again, it will be useful to recall how modernism arose in a largely dialectical opposition to classicism, keeping in mind that a postclassical *poesis* — while this opposition prepared for it — must go beyond that first oppositional modernism.

Classicist Referentials
- struggle against death
- memory
- signification
- sense, origin, *telos*
- history
- perfection as completion
- closed hierarchical harmonies
- permanent, static, balance
- repetitions as imitation, *non nova sed nove*
- structure
- image of body as symbol of god-given life

(Early) Modernist Referentials
- fascination with life
- forgetfulness
- signs representing functional/operative solutions
- purpose
- nature, technicity
- unfinishedness, limited perfection
- disharmonies, openness to what may come
- balance is in ever becoming
- *creatio ex nihilo*, radical innovation
- constructions ever revolutionized
- body as natural machine

The affirmation of life in modernism was not strong enough to carry it from dialectical opposition to the conception of a *non-structure*. While earlier deconstruction often seems to resign itself to the inevitability of structure and metaphysics, in one seminal text Derrida opens up the prospect of leaving behind the old Western framework, of entering a mode of thinking and living beyond structure, of becoming the new man, unpredictable and unbearably "monstrous." He does not seem to have pursued this new man directly.[12]

The structure is built on a restricted economy of flows and relations: If it were forced to play itself out completely it would unravel and reveal the emptiness where its center of strength was supposed to be. One way, therefore, is to involve the strategic text in a protracted battle that forces the opponent to give its all. But deconstruction can also fight like the guerrilla that engages the structure at so many points that the structure is unable to

reorganize. In this sense deconstruction joins the battle from a location at the boundary/limit of the system, not from a theoretical position that would allow it to look down on the structure from above. Nor does it allow itself to be drawn close to the center where the structure has the advantage of the territory and determines the rules of the battle. Deconstruction must remain on the move like a nomadic warrior. Deconstruction certainly could be the grave digger who lays to rest old forces and perhaps sets free new forces that would induce old stabilities to release their energies in dying away or would re-affirm them once again, and bring them back to life. Later deconstruction disseminates the meanings it has set free, across all other texts, the *seeds* of meaning now *nomads* between all texts.

Placing the critical activity not above but within the very arena the text itself has staked out should be a lesson for contextual architecture, as must be the technique of forcing a spatial typology to play out its secret allegiances, ideas, and values. A deconstruction of typologies would range through all levels of structure, from the obvious — say, the facade of a city hall and its relation to the state, or the apartment house and its relation to the palace, to the deeper levels, *e.g.* the urban grid and its connection to market and exchange. Placing oneself within but always beyond the limit means not taking a neutral observer status, but remaining uncaptured between the efforts of the structural system to assign everything a place within its structure, even if this place is "outside" it. (It is still in an outside that has been defined by the structure itself.)

Deconstructive technique in this sense is more experimental tactics than the vanquishing of one bad system by another (good) one. Deconstruction could prepare for a new ethics precisely where it abolishes the metaphysics of meaning, the signifier, because it forces consideration of an ethics in a universe of proliferating run-away meanings. When life is no longer ruled by a *telos*, it must become free experimentation. Ethics — also for architectural practice — can no longer be determined by the rationality that serves the survival of the clan or the state. Ethics would be founded on *play/battle/agony*, the rule of the radical affirmation of *otherness* as the precondition for life to become ever again. Play betrays its closeness to divergence, otherness, battle, and creativity, where it first begins: For Fuller, play begins with hallucination — a reaction to the withdrawl of the ever providing mother — and moves on to become imagination, invention of a world and an "us" made up of different rules and powers than those of normal "reality." Play is a war that forever makes new rules and creates new beings: It *is* and it *makes freedom*. Both deconstruction and Deleuze/Guattari play by pursuing the signs through their smoke screens of meanings to a non-signifying, diagrammatic, radically abstract level far below the conventional signifier/signified relation: There another aspect of the structural character of the sign system becomes manifest (Derrida's deconstruction) and the potential of de-structured formal relations can be opened up directly to conduct creative life energies, activities, to turn into "war machines."[15]

The target of deconstructive play is what constitutes structure (we can go back as far as Alberti):

1. The unity and identity of the parts is deconstructed as disparate relations between "other" components; this sends shock waves down and up the ladder of structuration.

2. The relations between parts set up to make a larger unity and to safeguard transformability are deconstructed as rules imposed by force to keep intact a unity that itself is located above the parts and relations.

3. The hierarchical relations that are to build totality and to guarantee subordination to "higher" purpose are deconstructed as imposition of a will that commands and lives as the totality of the structure.

A literal transposition of deconstruction into architecture might take architectural form as meaningful, *i.e.* representative of forces, and then play out the structural qualities of the architectural forms to the point at which signification would bring up strings of new meanings and new forms. Deconstruction thus would begin with an attack on signification but would end as theater continuing it. Deleuze, by contrast, would play the structure out by inventing an in-between, letting it loose on the signification that upholds the structure thus opening its fragments directly into new events, new life. Such play can retain some characteristics of analysis (that does not question the concept of structure itself). If it were to be radically deconstructive, it would seek and presume nothing but the opening up of new paths for life to become. Architecture then affirms everything but does not become part of any system.

At this point the classical model of oppositions, signifier and signified, of public and private, of the free cultural activities of art and politics versus unfree biological labor, and the modernist model of a new technical functional/organismic integration, are all left behind: The becoming of a life, forms of ever greater intensity, is the new goal

that needs no further justification. The architect is neither a demiurge nor a mere liberal, but one who affirms (and negates only through ever more intensive affirmation) by freeing the spatial "text" to connect into the events that form new life.

The Architectural Play

The most poignant quality of an architecture based on the spirit of deconstruction would derive from a commitment to affirm the movement of differen/ance that forever shifts meanings and introduces ever-new life into the oppositional structure of signifying language. If deconstruction is dedicated to divergence and the ever-new becoming of *otherness*, and if it is pursued to the point at which it becomes Derrida's free dissemination, it not only attacks structure but flies out and leaves it behind.

A postclassical *poesis*, armed with deconstructive techniques, must risk everything because it knows it cannot win otherwise. More than simply enduring to have little control, it must gladly affirm chance and fate so that it may bring up the unexpected other; it must allow itself to become vulnerable by insisting on a radical openness of its own constructions. The radical *affirmation of otherness (as differen/ance)* replaces the classical idealist model of perfection and closure by a new kind of wholeness that results from affirming the auspicious moment and situation, contingent on unpredictable constellations and conjunctures of forces operating in a place and at a time. As affirmation of otherness it proceeds both by counterposing and by repeating, which will bring up unresolved discordances, forces, and tendencies. It opens up new paths for life, not in the form of pluralistic messiness but as the most intensively played-out open difference.

Since post-classicist *poesis* must reject the classicist idea of the total work of art as yet another imposed absolute, it works with little escapes and in-betweens. It welcomes the challenges of materiality (and thus also difference/ance, undecidability, imperfect control, surprise, *chance*, and logical inconsistency): There is no unification by structure but only a heterogeneous unity arising from material, machinic consistency. It leaves behind the monument, the *imago* of the eternal life of the idea, of the law of structure, victorious over the death of the flesh. A life lived fully in materiality means that death need no longer be simultaneously feared (and desired) in the erection of monuments as representations of the power of structure and in mapping this structure onto the human body. Fully lived materiality allows the life force in the body to play freely. It sheds the burden of the classicist obsessive subordination to the authority of a *princeps*, and instead builds on an immanent *consistency* of concatenation and assemblage.

What "is" a particular piece of architecture?

The free play of postclassical *poesis* dissolves the dictate of the binary opposition as a method of designating and thus controlling the world. It fosters multiple (and the logically contradictory) assemblages that are new life forms, new intensities of thinking/feeling/acting. There are no appropriate names for these, except proper names. They are best named as they are created *and lived*, namely by *assemblages* of the "normal" designations seen from as many different angles of "view" as possible: words, visual representations, maps. The invention of new signifying designations would often only help to incorporate the new life into the old signifying structures. Identity, this crucial category, not only of philosophical reflection but of any methodical investigation, is no longer defined in opposition to what *it is not* (A = Not [not A]), but by what it is capable or not of *becoming through a multiplicity of connections with the other.*

In order to mobilize differen/ance, to induce and accelerate the emergence of what has not become (yet) will-to-live, this "text" of assemblages will have to work more like metonymy than like metaphor: The metaphor transposes established meanings and structural relations to new areas of signification; the metaphor is the device of classical representation: The building resembles a body, or a metaphor of the body. Metonymy simply juxtaposes semantically unrelated significations and thus forces one to form a new idea that then burrows its way into the structure in rebellion against that which had prepared for it to arise. The definition of metonymy used in this essay does not follow Jacobson. In brief, while the metaphor is defined as the logico-semantic intersection of two overlapping meaning fields, the metonymy, based on mere contiguity, is defined as the logico-semantic union of two otherwise separate meaning fields.[14] Metonymy does not so much seek to *mean* more (inside a language system) as it pushes to do more, to live more intensively. It tends to make new concepts outside the old ones simply by joining the old ones in a guerilla formation, creating an assemblage that avoids inventing a new idealizing term. Metonymy combines signifiers from previously disparate or even inconsistent realms of semantics. By inserting terms into a semantically illogical series, the metonymic operation *also recursively* changes the meaning of the original terms themselves without changing their form. These terms will never again be what they once were even if they still "look" the same. (Metonymic juxtaposition in language corresponds to the montage of Duchamps' ready-mades.) The *event* that carries us away into new feeling/thinking/acting *happens between* the old concepts and words (it is not the result of a new signifying word) and it carries them away into a new becoming. The metonymic operation refrains from inventing a new theoretical language of founding terms because it wants to keep signification *direct* and at a *minimum*. It eschews the metaphysics that underlie "deeper" meaning. Instead, metonymy stays closer to the practices, the discursive as well as the nondiscursive ones.

By forcing together divergent parts, the metonymic operation, the equivalent in language of the assemblage of objects, can create a high *density* (of possible meanings and becomings). Freud observed a similar density in his dream analyses of the displacements and condensations of meaning. Density was considered an essential quality of the aesthetic sign by Nelson Goodman. Alvaro Siza has referred to this density as "simplicity," the very opposite of the reductive simplicity that reduces all multiplicity to itself. The *connecting lines* of the force relations that make up such a (horizontal rather than deep) density constitute firm but ever shifting networks: Architectural form becomes akin to intensive divergent lines of force, to events that make gaps and regions. In these spaces, manifolds, non-structures, related to mathematical chaos more than to classical structured space, every element "is" what it can *become* with/against/next-to/apart-from/because/despite/during/after/before the other elements and rules of power. The non-structure is reached by the Foucaultian transgressions of an operationalism that stays at a literal level but plays the structure beyond its limits.

Postclassical *poesis* seeks a distinctly non-classicist *balance* that consists in the act of embracing materiality, in how it threatens life and in how it opens up paths for new life to burst forth unexpectedly. The classicist ideal of formal resolution with perfect unchanging balance and universal validity for all people, at all times, and in all places, is but a symbolic representation of the perfection of structural order. The cyclical time of the an-tique classical world *arrests* the continual movement of the event by incarcerating it within a circular structure that is its *telos*. Deconstructive balance becomes the affirmation of the *return* of *motion* as the falling and jumping from one event into the next. The classicist idea of reconciling all tendencies in synthesis, forever balanced in an integrated *recursive* structure, is replaced by the unreserved affirmation of the *moment* as the *singularity* of all the event lines that in intersecting create the moment, not the perfect fragment of classicism that evokes an absent whole but a singular and most intensive moment/event carrying *all the life* it can, representing nothing, and connecting with all other moments.

The very redirection of classicist perfection and balance to the moment and the point in space is by no means reductive, but simply refrains from incorporating the otherness of other moments and events into itself. Thereby it does not only leave room for other impulses but actually *attracts* them through offering itself to differen/ance. The presumed richness and mastery which classicism sought in the idea of art as representation of the great whole through the part, can now be recognized as a burden and an impoverishment of the here and now. Fully affirming this moment opens it *directly* to all other moments rather than turning this here/now into a sign representing all the "other" there is, thereby destroying its otherness. This, the task of representation, defeats the idea of the affirmation of the other as other, *i.e.* as unpredictable and a non-relation (since not relatable by common unifying terms). While earlier deconstruction sought to drive the structure mad, dissemination leaves it behind and sets off an open series of *fortuitous leaps* from sign to sign. *Perfection* would be *in* the *singularity* of these leaps, of these events. This perfection is no longer a metaphor for the perfect knowledge and power possessed by a god; it becomes metamorphosis (and death), the ever-new beginning for a new assemblage of life. Put into linguistic terms, this perfection is not a metaphor for the absent perfection belonging to god/structure, but a metonymy of these pieces assembled here and now. The potential for new, "nobler" life power (as Nietzsche might have put it) is expressed *metonymically, between* the forces present. Ideas and actions are only implicated, and remain dependent on leaping from the singular situation in which they occur: They cannot be made into a program that might usurp the ideas by turning them into instruments for itself.

Metonymy *produces* new ideas — and with these also new forms of life — out of assemblages together/with/ against/alongside other forms rather than creating a new metaphor to extract energy from or feed it into the old power center, the structure. When architecture actually "speaks," it does so metonymically: Its meanings arise more out of connections of contiguity with other elements and practices than out of itself as a language of-itself and in-itself (into which the "Third Typology" would transform it). For architecture to renounce any aspirations to the depths of metaphysical meaning is an act not of modesty, but of self-assertion though the radical *affirmation of materiality, of the moment, and of the locus of events.*

A common objection is that it is not possible to have works (or life) without stable supportive structure. Post-classicist *poesis* does not accept any structure of necessities (god, nature, writing) but affirms the very singularity of the event so fully — lives it out to beyond itself — that the internal and external, the other, is actually called-up by how fully the singularity has been lived: instead of supportive structure there is only a regaining of new balances. Deconstruction still wants to criticize: All writing is either naive or necessarily parasitical. Why the motivation to take apart the inner workings of the text, if not to disarm, to control, to dominate anew? With Deleuze one might answer: Better a this *and* that *and* that *and*.... Do your thing now, fully, and you will be ready for anything that may happen when the wave of the *other* comes along to carry you out of yourself.

Postclassical *poesis* is first *all non-negative affirmation* of fate which itself brings out new forces: Not contradiction, but challenging and luring the other to become together the next event. Affirmation, not imitative repetition, is therefore, the way for architecture to interpret and evaluate the stabilities of its "context": They should be understood as nodes and bundles of *local recurrences* of reaffirmed forms of life. But they should not be allowed to become supporting structures. The only support-in-itself is the omnidirectional divergent stream of becoming, the floating and shifting entities that are stable in the manner of the denseness of the open web of events. This web is a manifold, not a structure like the "strong" forms of Rossi which desire to live forever as the same — by not becoming other.

The concept of recurrences (rather than that of types) would redirect the discourse on place and regionality. The region may have a mission (as Frampton has argued) in resisting the exploitive movement of late capitalism, and it may help to keep resources under control within the ambit of everyday life. Yet regionalism is also the exploitation of the unique "assets" of regions by capital and the state. Only when *place* is conceived as the locus of *singular events,* and completed acts always open to a multiplicity of otherness, can a fetishism of place (and its commodification) be avoided. Place then becomes *the conduit* for time, for the series of perfect events in which life unfolds with greatest intensity, it becomes the door for new becoming to enter. To deconstruct a place can go either way: It can reinforce the hypnotic structure of a place or it can build the singularity that is always *in-between,* and as such, has the power to set in motion for a new becoming the energies implicated in a situation.

An Ethics of/for Deconstruction?

Deconstruction will not offer a new "program," political, moral, or even cultural. Yet it will not suffice to say, as Ryan does, that an engaged deconstruction amounts to an advocacy of all needs which will stretch the dominative/exploitative power structure beyond its limits. (This assumes that "needs" simply "are" whereas they ought to be conceived as constructions built within historic and local systems of powers and desires.)

It would not be appropriate to oppose a new model to the hypnotic (and increasingly soporific) neo-neoclassicist models of tampered-with closure in the current quasi-pluralistic eclecticism. What is proposed here as the result of a critical assemblage must be more a series of techniques than an image. The techniques of a postclassical *poesis* would be based on the fundamental idea of the affirmation of life as the affirmation of otherness. It would challenge the powers and desires involved in a design situation to "inscribe" themselves into space by structuring it according to their "will." Direction and strength of these powers and desires would emerge in their play with other powers who make different claims in ordering the world and space. In this interplay of "text" written by the desire of powers that want to become life, to *be* a certain identity, a multiplicity of forms and of meanings are played through.

Deconstruction should propose an ethics that rejects dominative structure insofar as the latter puts an end to otherness and thus to the becoming of new life. It could stand for free dissemination — not just of signs and linguistic mean-

ings but of the seeds for new life in all directions, against all prohibition, transgressing all boundaries. Taken in this way, deconstructive practice might be compared to the Deleuzian ethics that seeks lines of escape from structured systems in order to form new assemblages of life-force machines for new life to "run."

A Deconstruction of Deconstructive Architecture: *La Coqueterie du Parc*

Bernard Tschumi's La Villette park of follies has been discussed by Derrida as an example of deconstruction. As such, one would expect it to unleash the forces of architecture from the structure(s) to which they had been subordinate. But whence this increasing languor that befalls the visitor moving through this grid that never is threatened by the superimposed, carefully contrived systems of (winding) paths, clearings of simple geometric shapes, and the crossing of the roofed paths. It is because Tschumi conceives the events as the objects, the movements and the spaces as *systems* and certainties, and this they remain, despite the superimpositions. These are never played through far enough either to reveal (even less, depose) a hidden structure — everything is plain anyway — or to carry the systems away into other events and forms. The "conflicts" are tired, the variations in the cubes (made of 27 cubes) never challenge the cube.

What does Derrida see? First, he sees, not significations for a real place, but a text; the project for him *is* graphic text *about* architecture. Second, he accepts the grid as *representing* the idea of architecture which is assumed to be the archetypal *representation of coherence.* The grid, and what Tschumi calls the superimposed "autonomous coherent structures (points, lines, surfaces)," soon are said to represent the city, and since they are not brought to a formal synthesis, it is asserted that they deny the idea of structure: As Tschumi says, the published drawings — not the work — "contradict the apparent logic of the actual ordering device" by "divergence, deviation, deflection, dispersion, exorbitation."

With these statements the lines have already been drawn: Once it has been posited that architecture is necessarily a representative structure or even a structure at all, only a deconstructive hollowing-out and poisoning of this structure is possible. But why this insistence on designating architecture as the theater of representation and signification all over again? Once architecture and language are set up as representative, only theater can ensue. This step destroys the potential value of deconstruction for architecture: Architecture as representation is what has to be deconstructed. Portraying systems in conflict on the stage provided by architecture, will not unleash differen/ance, will not propel dissemination into new events. (In fact, Derrida's founding terms, "trace" and "writing," are forcefully anti-representative.)

Derrida's thoughts on the project merely expand Tschumi's approach. On the one hand, the structure constructs us by its "spacing," by its "sequence, open series, narrative, the cinematographic dramaturgy..." — theater and rhetoric again. Derrida sees Tschumi's follies as the madness of a meaning that leaves itself. Through their madness the follies are to deconstruct the semantics of architecture as a structure built on four points.

1. Meaning must be dwelling and being present.
2. Architecture must materialize hierarchy and origin.
3. Architecture must serve a *telos*.
4. Beauty, harmony, and totality are its goal.

Western thinking first establishes signification so that it may rule over architecture and then the substance of architecture is made metonymically to reinforce metaphysical signification. For Derrida the follies affirm an architecture freed from imposed extrinsic meanings to become itself, a pure signature. This liberation is, for Derrida, announced in two points: Architecture is offered not to fulfill a function but to become pleasure and; the freed architectural "writing" would interpret events which are marked by photography or cinematography. For Derrida, this new "transarchitecture" is no longer interested in its users and contemplators, but appeals to the other to invent the event. This architecture is no longer one that has the "hieratic impassibility of the monument"; rather, it leaves opportunity for chance, transformation, and wandering. One would agree with Derrida about the event. But this opening is too much restricted to a play of

transformations that ultimately preserve structure, and this architecture does not drive itself far enough to be open to chance, for the body to "receive from this other spacing the invention of its gestures." Derrida's central point of appreciation is that he sees in these follies, and even more in the fact that the buildings are an almost dispensable part of an open series of "writings," the deconstructivist act that opens up the monumental structure of architecture to the winds of psychoanalysis and cinematography and thus destroys its previous metaphysics of permanence and material substance. (What about the deconstruction of psychoanalysis itself, already begun by Derrida?)

Derrida dismisses the literal application of deconstruction to architecture since it would destabilize what (he asserts) it "is," namely structure. Tschumi's work has shown him that deconstruction must measure itself against the social institutions and, more importantly, deconstruction must construct. This realization then legitimizes the battle between systems that Tschumi has staged: First deconstruct, then (re)construct. The grid becomes for Derrida (again too metaphorically, at too many removes from the wars of everyday life) not a totality that occupies and structures space, but a permeability, weaving a texture rather than moving through one already existent. And the grid has been reduced to an abstract system of dissociated points, a spacing of generative cells whose transformations will never let themselves be calmed, stabilized, installed, identified in a continuum." And then the new construction happens: "...[T]hrough a series of mishaps, rhythmed anachromies, or aphoristical gaps, the point of *folie* [Fr. *point de folie* = no *folie*] gathers together what it has just dispersed..: It gathers into a multiplicity of *red* points." "The law divides *and* arrests division."

As Derrida sees it, Tschumi accomplishes this by affirming the many de's and dis's of deconstruction as such: "this writing *maintains* the *disjointed* as such, it joins up the *dis-* by difference." The wager then is "to give dissociation its due, but to implement it *as such* in the space of reassembly." This is the first time, to my knowledge, that Derrida has decisively moved beyond the negativist tendency in deconstruction (Heidegger once said that architectonics or the art of the of

the system is but one of many ways of assembling). There are many ways of assembling life, and we must surely leave the straight jacket of classicist totality and closure behind. But it is at this point that the misunderstanding between Derrida and the work in question becomes finally all too clear: Where Derrida speaks of new ways of assembling, he still appears to mean something that in superposing itself holds the dissociated together. He must mean this because he does not hesitate to quote Tschumi at this point: "Putting dissociation into form necessitates that the support structure be structured as a reassembling system." There is no reason for this regression to mother structure other than a lack of courage to unreserved affirmation of otherness; for why should there not be the possibility of assemblage as divergence and transversality itself, a city made of the multiplicity of otherness, not a reassembly of what has been carefully disjointed first with the help of a "support structure"? Where Derrida sees the task accomplished in the red points which to him both maintain the continuity of the grid and also interrupt it, we only see the dominative presence of the grid and the mechanical superimposition of the other "systems" (paths, clearings). We would fully agree with Derrida where he speaks in conclusion of how this new transarchitecture would not maintain a past or a new synthesis but that it would *maintain the interruption,* "the relation to the other as such." This Other is what Nietzsche called fate, Derrida would perhaps agree, and yes, deconstruction should be pushed this far. We cannot see it done in the *Parc.* Genuine deconstruction would have to work harder to open up systems into spatial assemblages which would open themselves to the multiplicity of the Other(s), by playing these systems against one another to the point where they open the door to a new event, a flashing up of life power. This cold superimposition won't do, nor will the grid that does not succeed in splitting up and spacing out the energies tied up in the various "systems" and activities so that they might become free to engage the other.

A Conclusion still to be Deferred

We should work up the courage to welcome our post-classical awareness of the decenteredness of human existence and to make this recognition work for conditions that allow new non-exploitive power to form freely. This postclassical "making" (*poesis*) would continue the best of modernism and work with the advances in our understanding of language, history, and nature. It is possible to avoid the current cynicism, opportunism, blind positivism, and nostalgic recreation of the classical figure of closure, a figure based on hierarchical oppositional structure, obsessively and sadistically/masochistically fixated on making itself into a totality.

The postclassical approach rejects the idea of identity founded on incorporation and expulsion, on drawing a tight circle/boundary around the self-identical. Definition instead proceeds by differences, by the *affirmation of otherness*. Otherness is not just what could not be subdued into a system of differences, but it is other paths for new life to be *opened up* by the affirmation of the singular event. (On the psychological plane this means that the modern subject shakes off the burden of the classical synthesis under leadership of the Ego and becomes free-figured subjectivity.)

Such an architectural "text" will not have to choose between escape into formalistic art or turning itself into a mere instrument for immediate ends: By tracing out the powers and desires involved in the design situation and by pushing affirmation of the spatial counterparts of power beyond their limits, architecture will open an *in-between for new differen/ances* to emerge. This kind of transgression distinguishes postclassical *poesis* from an opportunistic theater representing power conflicts. The stance of postclassical *poesis* is to be on guard, to take part and not to take part at the same time, to be at the limit, off center, where one is and is not subject to the current rules of the game.

Architecture certainly has its own "textuality" in that it can speak rather directly to the body: Linguistic models cannot, therefore, be imposed on it. The meanings of architecture are in how it is bound up with the cultural, social, and economic practices that make up the whole of life practices at a time and in a place: If we want architecture to speak strongly, we cannot allow ourselves to make an architecture which is about itself only. Architecture is bound up with the practices which it houses, directs, elicits, questions, supports, modifies, represses, legitimizes, represents again and again, searches, etc.: We must deconstruct only by affirmation and in order to clear paths for the assemblage of the forms of life which we might become.

Deconstruction turns against the structure that homogenizes, assimilates, and subordinates the other to itself. Its ancestry is in the unconscious rationality of liberation at play in art and history, in the drive to destruction, in "de-differentiation" as a phase of artistic creation (Ehrenzweig), in man's rage for chaos (Peckham), in the Greek recognition that war is the father of everything. For Bataille, the body desires *ekstasis* that frees it to escape from the isolation of the individual body into a limitless outpouring, an immortality achieved in fusion with the universe in the moment of death. The unreserved affirmation that should drive deconstruction also must affirm the singularity of the moment, the life that must die so there can be life (no more architecture as permanence). *Ekstasis* is the not-yet-expurgated death drive that seeks, not the absence of life, but the maximally intensive flow of libidinal energies (which necessitates destruction of structurations): The silent but intensified play of differen/ance frees the energies subordinated to structure. An architecture of assemblage based on affirmation of otherness must set up the *in-between* (but *not* as a mediating dialectical form) that makes such flows happen. *In-between is the a-structural heterogeneous non-relation*, the gap or distance, that as difference or tension between forces initiates the event, which itself is an assemblage of non-signifying signs and force flows, not a representative drama that seeks to domesticate life force within a structure of powers. For deconstruction to propel itself beyond a literary/philosophical practice, it must intensify the momentum of radical affirmation, its principle and technique: Then it will *become* new life.

Notes

1. John Knesl, "Architecture and Laughter" *PRECIS 7*, (New York: Rizzoli, 1988).

2. Jean Baudrillard, *Forget Foucault* (New York: Semiotext(e), Columbia University Press, 1987).

3. Christopher Norris, *Deconstruction: Theory and Practice* (New York: Methuen, 1982).

4. Jacques Derrida, *Writing and Difference* (Chicago: University of Chicago Press, 1978).

5. Jean-François Lyotard, *Des Dispositifs Pulsionnels* (Paris: 10/18 U. G. E. Série, "S", 1973).

6. Hubert L. Dreyfus and Paul Rabinow, *Michel Foucault: Beyond Structuralism and Hermeneutics* (Chicago: University of Chicago Press, 1982).

7. Jean Baudrillard, *Subjekt und Objekt: Fraktal* (Bern: Benteli, 1986).

8. Michel Foucault, *The Order of Things* (New York: Random House, 1970).

9. Jean-François Lyotard, *Driftworks* (New York: Semiotext(e), Columbia University Press, 1984).

10. *Ibid.*

11. Anthony Giddens, *Profiles and Critiques in Social Theory* (Berkeley: University of California Press, 1982).

12. Julia Kristeva, *Revolution in Poetic Language* (New York: Columbia University Press, 1984).

13. Bertell Ollmann, *Alienation* (Cambridge: Cambridge University Press, 1976).

14. Jaques Dubois *et al.*, *Rhétorique générale* (Paris: Librairie Larousse, 1970).

Photo: Louise Tremblay

Textus Interruptus

Mark C. Taylor

The questions with which I would like to linger are posed by the discourse of the other. Does the other speak? Can I (the "I") hear/understand (*entends*) the other? Who or what is the other... that approaches (without arriving) as the not-same? Is the other who is my counterpart actually other or is s/he really identical in her/his difference? "Is" there an other other that allows others to be other and differences to be different? How might such an other be (almost) thought? Does the other other make any difference... or every difference?

To linger with questions posed by the discourse of the other is to wrestle with the problem of translation. Can the other speak my language? Can I make the other speak my language? Does translation allow the other to speak or does it silence the discourse of the other? Without translation, there is no conversation — no

shared communication. And yet, can either *entretien* or *partager* be translated with certainty?

Entretien: conversation, talk, interview. *Entretenir*: to hold together, keep in good order; to maintain, support, feed; to converse or talk with, to entertain. *Entre*: between + *tenir*, to hold. *Entretien*: a holding-between.

Converse: French — *converser*, to pass one's life, to dwell with or in, to exchange words with; Latin — *conversari*, to turn oneself about, to move to and fro. Conversely; converse: Latin — *conversus*, turned about, transformed. Turned round; opposite or contrary in direction; action, acting in reversed manner.[1]

con verses

l'entretien infini

Partage: sharing, distribution, division; share, lot, portion, apportionment. *Partager*: *diviser*; *demémber, morceler*; *couper, fractionner, fragmenter; solidariser; participer*. To divide, share out; to share, participate in.

Share: the iron blade in a plough that cuts the ground at the bottom of the furrow. From *(s)ker*, scratch, cut, pluck, gather, dig, separate, sift; and *sek*, divide,

cut, scrape. Share: a part or portion belonging to, distributed to, contributed by, or owned by a person or group; to divide, parcel out in shares; to apportion, participate in, use, or experience in common.

The word itself parts and divides by be(com)ing the converse of itself.

partager

la parole plurielle

Forever suspended *entre-deux, le partage des voix* marks the re-turn of *l'entretien infini*.

Art of Conversation

Granted that Derrida is the latest and largest flower on the dialectical kudzu vine of which the Phenomenology of Spirit was the first tendril, does that not merely show the need to uproot this creeping menace? Can we not now see all the better the need to strip the suckers of this parasitic climber from the still unfinished walls and roofs of the great Kantian edifice which it covers and conceals?[2]

In a series of articles and books written over the past decade, Richard Rorty has been developing an interpretation of conversation — or more precisely an interpretation of interpretation in terms of conversation — that has become extremely influential. Since his central ideas are anything but new, the impact of Rorty's work is somewhat puzzling. The excitement his texts generate seems to be more a reflection of who is writing than the result of what is written. To Rorty's erstwhile philosophical colleagues, the scandal seems to be that one of the most respected members of their congregation has committed heresy by falling under the spell of illusions from which true believers have long been free. As soon as one realizes that contemporary Anglo-American linguistic philosophy began as reaction to the revival of Hegelianism in England during the early decades of this century, the impact of Rorty's "fall" becomes more understandable. In shedding his analytical skin, Rorty has had the audacity to argue that Hegel, if read in a certain way, was right. To make matters worse, Rorty (mistakenly) maintains that the return to Hegel (via Gadamer) makes it possible to appropriate important insights from contemporary philosophers who have been anathematized by the high priests of the philosophical ecclesia. Rorty's errancy, however, is neither as extreme as his detractors insist nor as radical as his supporters believe. Acknowledging that he stands in the tradition of the *Phenomenology of Spirit*, Rorty suggests, albeit inadvertently, the way in which his philosophy extends the Western struggle to master difference. Instead of patiently listening to a discourse not his own, Rorty's "dialogue" ends as a monologue spoken/written to colonize the other. In the aftermath of this conversation, a persistent question remains: Is it ever possible to break the circle of domination by overcoming the domination of the (hermeneutical) circle?

As one skilled in the art of conversation, Rorty likes to tell stories. His reading of the story of modern philosophy has only two chapters, which are variously described as epistemology and hermeneutics, or commensuration and conversation. As his use of the image of the parasitic kudzu vine suggests, Rorty traces these two types of philosophy back to Kant and Hegel respectively. Though epistemology and hermeneutics differ significantly in assumptions and conclusions, the most important differences distinguishing them can best be seen in their alternative accounts of representation. "The [Kantian] tradition thinks of truth as a vertical relationship between representation and what is represented. The [Hegelian] tradition thinks of truth horizontally — as the culminating reinterpretation of our predecessors' reinterpretation of their predecessors' reinterpretation.... This tradition does not ask how representations are related to nonrepresentations, but how representations can be seen as hanging together.

The difference is not one between 'correspondence' and 'coherence' theories of truth.... Rather, it is the difference between regarding truth, goodness, and beauty as eternal objects which we try to locate and reveal, and regarding them as artifacts whose fundamental design we often have to alter."[3] While the "Kantianism" struggles to re-present primal presentations, "Hegelianism" acknowledges the inaccessibility of every thing-in-itself and admits that representations always refigure representations. In the absence of primal presentation, signs are signs of signs.

As I have noted, this all too neat and tidy philosophical tale makes sense only if Hegel is read in a certain way. It is significant that the tangled lines of Rorty's genealogy go back to the Phenomenology rather than the System. For Rorty, there is a significant difference between the implications of the phenomenological and the systematic Hegel. In the *Encyclopedia of the Philosophical Sciences*, Hegel claims to have reached absolute knowledge by accurately representing the truth that had been gradually unfolding in nature and history from the beginning of time. The Phenomenology, by contrast, examines the experience of consciousness as it moves from subjective self-certainty to the truth that purportedly is (re)present(ed) in the System as a whole. Repeating (without acknowledging) insights advanced by earlier commentators, Rorty describes the Phenomenology and a *Bildungsroman* in which each chapter is, in effect, a rewriting of earlier chapters in the genesis of self-consciousness.[4] Over against Hegel, Rorty insists that the final chapter of the story cannot be written and thus a conclusive end is forever delayed. The deferral of absolute knowledge creates the possibility of an unending conversation that is essentially hermeneutical. From this point of view, hermeneutics can be understood as something like Hegelianism without absolute knowledge. "Hermeneutics," Rorty explains, "sees the relations between various discourses as those of strands on a possible conversation, a conversation which presupposes no disciplinary matrix which unites the speakers, but where the hope of agreement is never lost so long as the conversation lasts. This hope is not a hope for the discovery of antecedently existing common ground, but simply hope for agreement or, at least, exciting and fruitful disagreement."[5] While epistemology is an archeological search for secure foundations, hermeneutics is a teleological quest for a certainty that never arrives. Rorty is persuaded that when conversation gives up the dream of commensuration, it becomes edifying.

Though Hegel repeatedly asserts that philosophy can never edify, Rorty insists on "translating" Hegelian *Bildung* into hermeneutical edification.[6] Edification involves the process of building up oneself in and through the expansion of consciousness and self-consciousness brought about by "acculturation."[7] In Rorty's philosophical story, Gadamer emerges as a pivotal character. By successfully extricating the notion of *Bildung* from the most problematic metaphysical presuppositions of 19th-century idealism, Gadamer prepares the way for the recognition of the thoroughgoing historicity of human consciousness. Commenting on *Truth and Method*, Rorty writes:

[T]he importance of Gadamer's book is that he manages to separate off one of the three strands — the romantic notion of man as self-creative — in the philosophical notion of "spirit" from the other two strands with which it became entangled. Gadamer (like Heidegger, to whom some of his work is indebted) makes no concessions either to Cartesian dualism or to the notion of "transcendental constitution" (in any sense which could be given an idealistic interpretation). He thus helps to reconcile the "naturalistic" point: that the "irreducibility of the *Geisteswissenschaften*" is not a matter of metaphysical dualism...with our "existentialist" intuition that redescribing ourselves is the most important thing we can do. He does this by substituting the notion of *Bildung* (education, self-formation) for that of "knowledge" as the goal of thinking. To say that we become different people, that we "remake" ourselves as we read more, talk more and write more, is simply a dramatic way of saying that the sentences which become true of us by virtue of such activities are often more important to us than sentences which become true of us when we drink more, eat more and so on.[8]

In Hegel's metanarrative, history is the process in which the absolute subject (*Geist*) becomes self-conscious through the emergence of total self-consciousness in individual subjects. With the disappearance of the absolute subject, history becomes completely anthropocentric. "Gadamer develops his notion of *wirkungsgeschichtliches Bewusstein* (the sort of consciousness of the past which changes us) to characterize an attitude interested not so much in what is out there in the world, or in what happened in history, as in what we can get out of nature and history for our own uses.'"[9]

Outlines

Must we always talk in circles... circles that tend to be hermeneutical? Are outlines impossible? Or do outlines sketch the impossibility inscribed by the *Riss* of *Umriss*? Might the *Riss* rending *Umriss* imply "something that will not find itself in any text, the outside of the text [*hors-texte*], the excessive, superfluous word [*le mot de trop*], in order that it should not be wanting with respect to the completeness of complete Works, or to the contrary that it should always want"?[10] The *hors-texte... mot de trop* breaks the hermeneutical circle by interrupting every conversation.

Behind discourse speaks the refusal to discourse, as behind philosophy would speak the refusal to philosophize: non-speaking speech [*la parole non parlante*], violent, concealing, saying nothing and suddenly crying.[11]

La parole non parlante is a word that divides as much as it unites, separates as well as joins. Neither simply binding nor unbinding, *le mot de trop* is always *entre-deux* — suspended (in the) between. Forever falling between the lines, *la parole non parlante* echoes in (empty) space or nonspace that cannot be represented but can, at best, be outlined. The discourse of this strange word, which both haunts and eludes hermeneutical conversation, repeatedly returns to fragment Maurice Blanchot's extraordinary *L'Entretien infini* and to disrupt Jean-Luc Nancy's provocative *Le partage des voix*. What Gadamer and Rorty struggle to repress, Blanchot and Nancy attempt to solicit.

Nancy and Blanchot are obsessed with the *Riss* of difference. Heideggerian difference, Nancy argues, is a different

difference and an other other. Forever eluding the (dialectical and binary) opposites it articulates, *Unter-Scheid* is a radical difference that cannot be returned to the same. While dialectical (*i.e.* hermeneutical) dialogue is either deaf to, or tries to silence every such difference, nondialectical dialogue solicits an other it can neither contain nor express.

The *infini* of *l'entretien infini* cannot be represented but can only be staged or performed *indirectly* — as if "in" outline(s). Language is never only itself but is always at the same time the discourse of the other, which, as *le mot de trop*, remains in a certain sense unspeakable. The converse of dialectical/hermeneutical conversation repeatedly returns to interrupt the communication whose space it nonetheless clears. Since the eternal return of the discourse of the other is inevitably differential, *la parole* is *la parole plurielle*.[12]

In the play of Blanchot's *entretien*, speech, the word says: "infinite distance and difference, distance that is attested in *la parole* itself and that holds it outside of all contestation, all parity and all commerce.[13] *L'entretien* maintains (*tient*) the between (*entre*) without which there can be no conversation and with which there can be neither unification nor communication.

The "between" (*l'entre-deux*), which is neither positive nor negative, neither is nor is not, is a difference or an other that cannot be dialectically sublated through the positivity of double negation. Repeatedly slipping away from the dialectical logic of both/and, as well as the antidialectical logic of either/or, the timely interval of *l'entretien* implies the paralogic of neither/nor.

between: between/ne(u)ter. Play, play without the happiness of playing, with this residue of a letter that would appeal to the night with the lure of a negative presence. The night radiates the night as far as the neuter, where the night extinguishes itself.[14]

Patience

The play of dialectical/hermeneutical conversation is always an impatient power play.

Imperative of the purge. Thus exclude the third, the Demon, *prosopopoeia* of noise. If we want peace, if we desire an agreement between object and subject, the object appearing at the moment of the agreement, at the Last Supper as well as in the laboratory, in the dialogue as on the blackboard, we have to get together, assembling, reassembling, against whoever troubles our relations, the water of our channel. He is on the other bank [sometimes the Left, sometimes the West], the rival is. He is our common enemy. Our collective is the expulsion of the stranger, of the enemy, of the parasite. The laws of hospitality become the laws of hostility. Whatever the size of the group, from two on up to all humankind, the transcendental condition of its constitution is the existence of the Demon.[15]

When fully developed, hermeneutics tends to become culturally imperialistic. "The attempt to edify (ourselves or others)," Rorty maintains, "may consist in the hermeneutic activity of making connections between our own culture and some exotic culture or historical period, or between our own discipline and another discipline which seems to pursue incommensurable aims in an incommensurable vocabulary."[16] As I have stressed, the participants in dialectical/hermeneutical conversation move toward the other so they can return to themselves enriched. The "exotic" edifies only when it is first domesticated and then assimilated. The imperialistic implications of this strategy of interpretation become clear in a remarkable statement that Rorty makes in an essay entitled "Pragmatism, Relativism, Irrationalism." According to Rorty, the pragmatist "can only say, with Hegel, that truth and justice lie in the direction marked by the successive stages of European thought."[17] *Bildung*, it seems, is identified with the cultural tradition of the West. Other cultural traditions are valued only insofar as they aid Westerners "in becoming new beings."

Though not immediately apparent, this cultural imperialism grows out of the interpretation of the subject that emerges in modern European philosophy. As we have seen, Rorty credits Gadamer with rescuing "the romantic notion of man as self-creative" from the problematic metaphysical framework of 19th-century idealism. Hermeneutics, however, remains more metaphysical than most of its proponents are willing to admit. The self-creative subject, which receives comprehensive expression in Hegel's System, is essentially constructive and thus fundamentally impatient. In the final analysis, the im-patient subject finds difference or otherness insufferable. The end of dialogue is monologue and, as Blanchot insists, every monologue is "imperious."[18]

While dialectic issues in a dialogue that is a monologue, paralectic interrupts monological discourse by allowing "impossibility" to be spoken.

Le partage des voix... l'attente qui mesure la distance infini. L'attente: waiting, awaiting, expectation, hope... Patience: *patior*, to suffer. The possibility of the im-possible (*in* + *possibilis* [*poti-*]) implies a certain impotence (*in* + *potens* [*poti-*]). In the play of paralectics, the dialectical struggle for mastery gives way to the patient suffering of the unmasterable discourse of the other.

To respond to the other, one must learn to be patient, or, more precisely, one must learn how to allow patience to arrive. The patient (subject) is always (already) passive before active. The suffering subject receives itself as well as the other (subject) from an other other that is dif-ference "itself." The gift (Gift) of the other is a *don* that is a *coup...* a *coup de don* that is a *coup de grâce*. The *Riss* engendered by this impossible *coup* opens the possibility (no more and no less) of relating to other as other.

Notes

1. *The Oxford English Dictionary.*

2. Richard Rorty, *Consequences of Pragmatism* (Minneapolis: University of Minnesota Press, 1982), p. 103-4.

3. *Ibid,* p. 92.

4. See *inter alia*, M.H. Abrams, *Natural Supernaturalism: Tradition and Revolution in Romantic Literature* (New York: Norton, 1971), and Jean Hyppolite, *Genesis and Structure of Hegel's Phenomenology*, trans. S. Cherniak and J. Heckman (Evanston: Northwest University Press, 1974), and Mark C. Taylor, *Journeys to Selfhood: Hegel and Kierkegaard* (Berkeley: University of California Press, 1980).

5. Richard Rorty, *Philosophy and the Mirror of Nature* (Princeton: Princeton University Press, 1979), p. 318.

6. It is precisely Hegel's rejection of the notion of "edification" that leads Kierkegaard to describe some of his writings as "Edifying Discourses." See *Edifying Discourses*, trans. David F. and Lillian M. Swenson (New York: Harper and Row, 1958).

7. The etymology of the word "edify" underscores the close relationship between edification and building or construction. "Edify" derives from the Latin *æficiare, ædes, ædis,* dwelling + *ficare*, to make. The Danish word for "edify" is *opbygge, op,* up + *bygge,* to build. Compare the German *erbauen,* build, raise, erect, construct; edify. Apparently opting for "accuracy" instead of elegance, the most recent translators of Kierkegaard's writings insist on rendering *Opbyggelige Taler* as "Upbuilding Discourses."

8. Rorty, *op. cit.* 5, p. 360.

9. *Ibid,* p. 359.

10. Maurice Blanchot, *Le pas au-dela* (Paris: Gallimard, 1973), p. 158. I would like to express my appreciation to Thomas Carlson for translating many of the French texts in this paper.

11. *Ibid,* p. 158.

12. This is the title of the first section of *L'Entretien infini.*

13. Blanchot, *L'Entretien infini*, p. 91.

14. Blanchot, *op. cit.* 10, p. 97.

15. Michael Serres, *The Parasite*, trans. L. Schehr (Baltimore: Johns Hopkins University Press, 1982), p. 3, 12.

16. Rorty, *op. cit. 5,* p. 360.

17. Rorty, *op. cit.* 2, p. 173. Emphasis added.

18. In a para-enthetical aside, Blanchot writes: "Let us recall the terrible monologues of Hitler and of every Chief of State. He enjoyed being alone to speak and, enjoying his haughty solitary speech, imposed it on others, without constraint, as a superior and supreme speech. He participated in the same violence of the *dictare* — the repetition of the imperious monologue" (*L'Entretien infini*, p. 106-7).

**Pratt Institute
School of Architecture
Faculty and
Student Projects**

Door: 11 rue Larrey, Marcel Duchamp, Paris 1927. Ready-made wood door.
Courtesy: Cordier and Ekstrom Gallery. Photo by Geoffrey Clements.

Office Baroque, Gordon Matta-Clark, Antwerp 1977.
Courtesy: Holly Solomon Gallery.

181

Raimund Abraham

I remember when I was a boy I went hunting with my uncle. We were sitting and he was watching the deer and other wild animals on the other side of the valley. I also had binoculars, and I was looking but I didn't see a thing. For weeks and weeks I was really frustrated. Then, suddenly, I could *see*, and I don't know how. There was no method, no taught strategy. It came upon me, at one moment, and I saw — and from that moment I always saw.

Raimund Abraham is Associate Professor of Design at the Pratt Institute School of Architecture and The Cooper Union. He has taught at the Rhode Island School of Design, the University of Texas, the Architectural Association in London, and has held the Davenport Chair at Yale University. Professor Abraham has exhibited and published extensively in both the United States and Europe.

Donald Cromley

Cromley Studio

There is a "situation." The notion of a situation involves a desire and a place and the means physically to realize that desire at that place. Traditionally, this situation was called program, site and budget. The separation of desire, place, and means is crucial. For example, one may have desire and not be able to get a hold of a place, or the means may be unknown, so within situation I separate these things.

The desire involved my office at home, which was inefficient and hard to work in. The basic needs were working surface and library. The office was a place with a history I had to respect because of what it would do to the rest of the home. The entry had to be kept because the intent was not to change the home but to change my office. The job was to reconfigure the same functions in exactly the same space. My wife might not tolerate a radical change, good workmanship is hard to come by, my funds were limited; I consider these all part of the situation.

The building we are in was a cheese smoke house; our space is a loft planned in an *ad hoc* way. The place has an old tiled floor; the walls are lumpy and remind me of Greece or Southern Italy. Contemporary building doesn't hit me in the gut, but a lot of ancient, "naive" or prehistoric building does. Although there is a lack of craft, there is a very strong sense of meaning, purpose, or message. I've been interested in the issue of statement through "bad" building. This has led me to appreciate some of the characteristics of Frank Gehry's work which makes me *feel* sheetrock, J-beads, and crummy studs, which are the materials I use.

My interest in geometric orders and rhythms can work with this notion of imprecision because it is a way to transcend crude workmanship and materials. Because I tell the builder where to put the studs, the mathematics are there whether he likes it or not. The notion of dimension has to do with people; there are certain absolutes about dimensions, and they occur at all levels of importance. The most important one for me is the dimension of the human body. The size of the human body combines with geometric orders to make the relationship physical.

The loft has a wall running down the middle; thus the project became a dual object. The office deals with dialogues, subdivided into equal but opposite zones, both frontally and laterally. To increase the visual size of the existing space the notion of buildings or objects was introduced within the space; the notion of a village inside of a larger envelope.

The office is for me. Everything else is for the public, which includes my wife, our children, our guests; all are considered public. The inside and the outside of the office are two different worlds, one for me, the other for the public.

I took the things which would normally have been on the inside and put them outside, specifically the sheetrock. The first layer of sheetrock on the outside gets a typical trim, and the second layer acts as an infill to the trim. The trim ends up projecting the difference between the thicknesses of the trim and sheetrock. Because the dimensions are subtle they appear and disappear, depending upon the light. It becomes dynamic instead of static, because I see this work as anthropomorphic, not inanimate. There is also a recollection of the treatment of parts of vernacular bindings; base, belt, lintel, and cap.

The difference between the entry and the office is that the entry has only an "outside" which occurs on its inside; its whole facade has been sucked in to form the interior. There are certain ambiguities where one wall collides with another. The slit by the closet is saying that that piece of wall is really a part of two different orders. The inside of the office is a different world. It is my personal world. It uses ordinary materials: metal studs, wood studs, wood beams, conduit, bx, and exposed electrical boxes, all constructed by an inexperienced carpenter. The studs, the joists, and the bookcase sections are located by different rhythms. The studs and joists use metal connectors and typical carpentry details; the bookcases have neo-constructivist details. The statement is made with the things we build with. The office is divided into three rooms all open to one another. An existing building shaft became a room with a desk and a window. Next to that is the library, a similar space. The structure in the library is painted black and recedes; the room is totally lined with books which become its walls. The third room involves two work spaces, one of which has a window aligned with a window in the loft that affords views.

The outside of the project is "slick" because that is what is expected; inside is not what might be expected. The outside has to do with conventional expectations; the inside is the precious part, the intricate, involved, passionate part of the design.

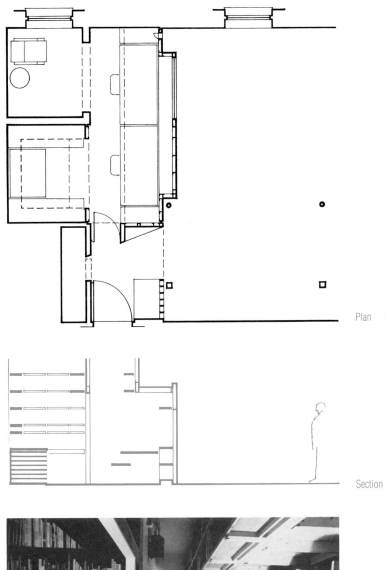

Plan

Section

View from entry

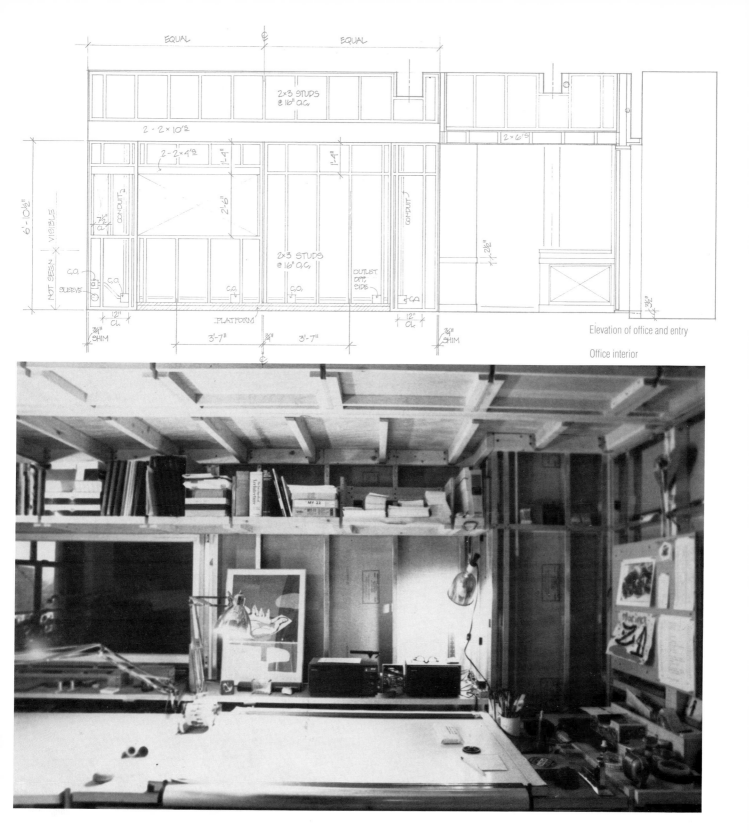

EQUAL   EQUAL

2×3 STUDS
@ 16" O.C.

2 - 2 × 10½

2 - 2 × 4½

1'-4"

1'-4"

2'-6"

2 × 6½

6'- 10½"

CONDUIT

CONDUIT

NOT SEEN   VISIBLE

7½"
CL.

2×3 STUDS
@ 16" O.C.

1'-2½"

3½"

C.O.

C.O.

SLEEVE

OUTLET
OPP.
SIDE

C.O.

C.O.

C.O.

C.O.

12"
CL.

PLATFORM

12"
CL.

¾"
SHIM

3'-7"

¾"

3'-7"

¾"
SHIM

Elevation of office and entry

Office interior

185

Detail of library shelf

Interior photos by Caleb Crawford

Donald Cromley is an architect living and working in New York. He is an Adjunct Associate Professor of Architecture and Undergraduate Chairman of the Pratt Institute School of Architecture. He has studied with Louis I. Kahn, and worked for Alvar Aalto and Marcel Breuer.

View of library interior

Interior view of entry

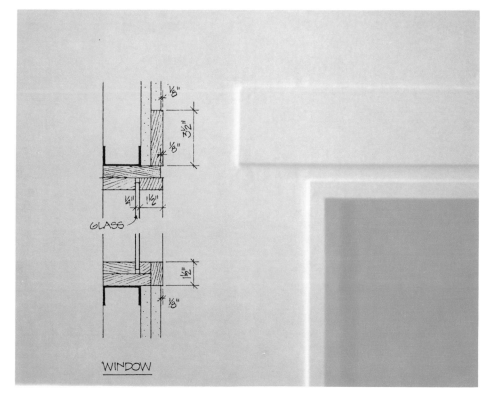

WINDOW

GLASS

Detail of window

Samuel J. DeSanto

Steelcase Showroom

Context is a force, which, among others, helps define the appearance of a building. Architecture, however, cannot be, unless there is an idea to give it meaning. The idea is not a force which produces architecture — it is architecture. If a building is to be considered a work of architecture, the essential ingredient on which it relies is the idea that other issues generate it.

Site generates form. All buildings exist in some relationship within a location. Rural sites generate much more than primal ideas such as tree houses or cave dwellings. Urban sites do not necessarily suggest a collection of discontinuous or dissimilar fragments.

The expression of columns and beams makes visible the physicality of the building. Interior architectural form is related to the exterior architecture. In the design of interior spaces structure is a vital ingredient and should be expressed. When I look at a plan I should be able to sense how a building was conceived. A design qualifies as a work of art if, when I enter that space, the same occurs: I can sense the intent of the architect. Interior architecture is a direct result of the building as an idea. To design a building is to invoke a complexity of forces, which include site, materials, structure, and function. The success of the work of art depends on the perception of the metaphor which results from these relationships.

Can architecture exist as art and not be comprehensible? What is the role of tradition in understanding form? Traditional cultural values can be a welcome restriction which provides meaningful familiarity. Inventiveness and ingenuity are part of a creative process, but the term "creativity" is often misused. When it is applied to architecture it rarely if ever produces something appropriate.

Meaning invoked in form can be interpreted through metaphor. In the plan of the Steelcase showroom, a transforming line implies alignments and serves as a datum for the experience of the program. A line is an idea, and is meaningful as a metaphor. The conception for the use of a line was determined by the interrelationships of the issues in the design problem. One segment of the line is suggested by the alignment of the entry with the conference room, which is reinforced by the reception desk. The line then meanders through a number of various types of wall materials which are the resolution of private spaces and axial alignments. The line exists as a metaphor of the experience.

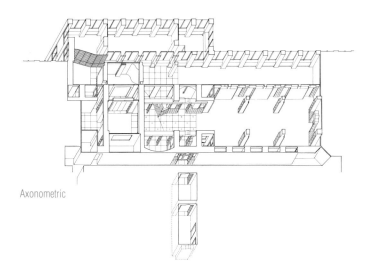

Axonometric

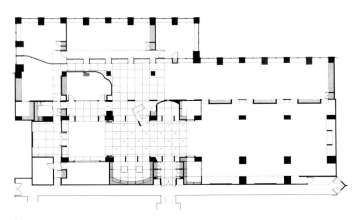

Plan

Samuel J. DeSanto is an architect, and principal of Samuel J. DeSanto Design Associates. He is an Associate Professor at the Pratt Institute School of Architecture. He has worked on projects throughout the United States and abroad.

View from entry

Livio Dimitriu

Hawaii Loa College Competition

The project recognizes and respects the campus planning guidelines in the context of landscape, orientation, and relationship to view and to the existing highway.

The proposal consists of three conceptual "bridges," an architectural element which simultaneously connects and separates.

The elevation is a unified and unifying facade providing an articulated wall effect parallel to the axis of the campus in a contrasting juxtaposition with the mountainous backdrop. Behind the facade the academic functions, the theaters, and the "black box" are the culmination of a southwest-northeast layering, blending with the drama of the Hawaiian landscape.

The section involves the southwest-northeast theater's axis, resulting in a "bridge" connecting the northwest-southeast campus axis to the uphill landscape backdrop.

The plan organizes the academic functions grouped around the sculpture garden, connect through and under the theater's axis with the "black box." The "bridge" is a U-shaped circulation which recognizes the land configuration and attempts to minimize excavation and building footprint. The U-shaped massing of the building orients the functions to the valley below.

Livio Dimitriu is an Assistant Professor at the Pratt Institute School of Architecture and at the New York Institute of Technology. He is an Associate in the firm of Perchuk Design Associates in New York and has exhibited and published extensively in the United States and Canada.

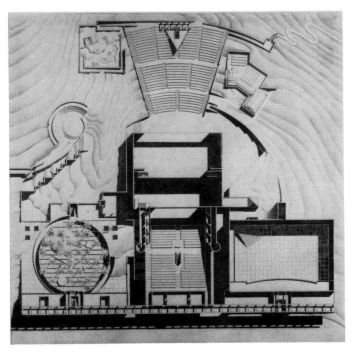

Site plan

Analysis

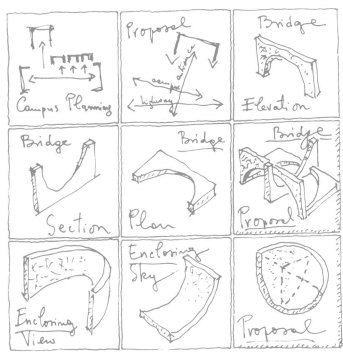

Gamal El-Zoghby

El-Zoghby Residence

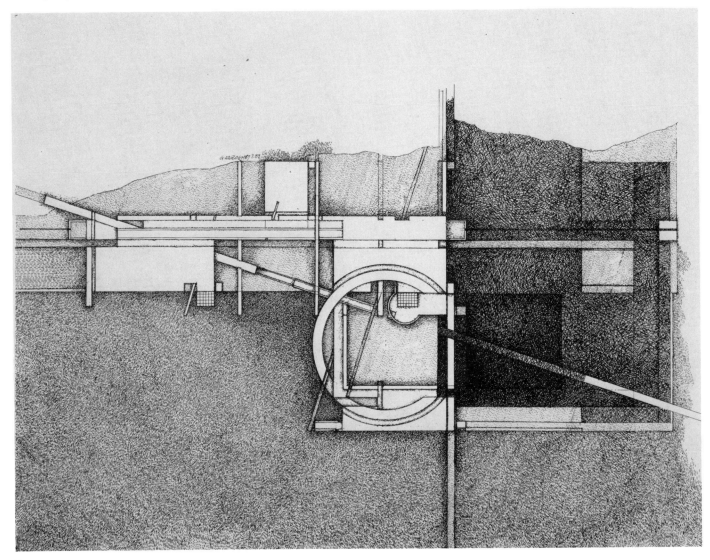

Plan

192

Gamal El-Zoghby is an architect living and working in New York. He received his B.Arch at the University of Cairo, and an M.Arch from the University of Michigan. His work has been published and exhibited internationally. He is a Professor of Architecture at the Pratt Institute School of Architecture currently on sabbatical developing the final design and commencing construction of his private residence.

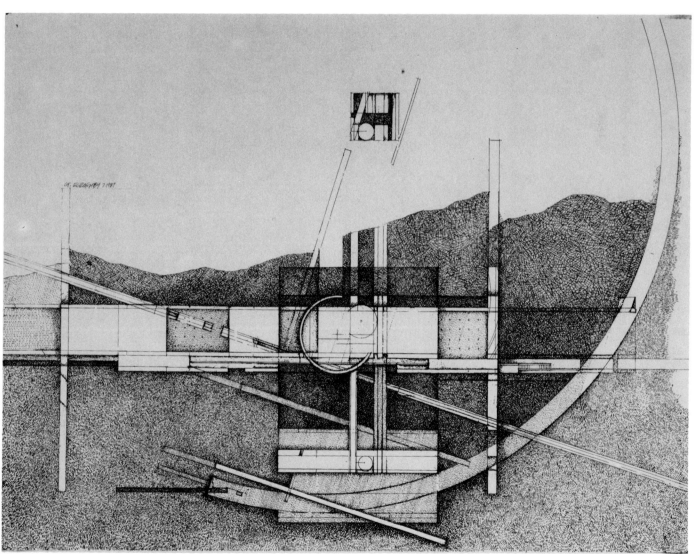

Plan

Vittorio Giorgini

One might think that the reason for an implementation of contemporary technology in urban design is self-evident; however, its use is largely ignored. Despite much literature and the insights of visionary urbanists, approaches to urban problems are still limited by conventional solutions which inevitably do not work.

Urban design solutions of the past reflect the societies they served, as patterns. They represent urban models of a past culture, but, as solutions, cannot serve the needs of the 20th century. Public services have become overly complex and inefficient, therefore uneconomical; they also threaten the environment. The dilemmas of a global urban condition are better treated by approaches which are imaginative and fertile. The utility and economy of a system depend upon its structures' accordance with organic principles. Urban systems are complex organizations similar to structures in nature which are shaped by limitations in an ecosystem.

The work of Vittorio Giorgini proposes to affect the environment minimally, touching the ground only when the program requires. The work is conceived as an insertion into the existing urban fabric. Proposed communities are to be implemented incrementally, gradually transforming the context. Construction can be a transformation rather than an imposition. Continuity in the environment must be preserved to maintain its integrity. Services and construction techniques can be made more efficient technologically through industrial methods which make efficient use of building materials. Transportation systems and the speed of movement at connections are tools for density control. Connections should be organized hieratically in different complexes.

Although this vision of urban design may by viewed as utopian, it also suggests that the politics of design follow production systems rather than bureaucracy.

Vittorio Giorgini is an architect and Associate Professor of Architecture at the Pratt Institute School of Architecture. His work has been exhibited and published internationally.

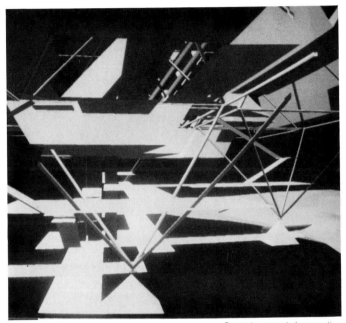

Computer generated perspective

Model

194

Computer generated perspective

Model

195

M. Louis Goodman

Front elevation

Side elevation

Eisen House, St. Simons, Georgia

In this house, the location, history of the area, the background of the clients, the indigenous architecture, and the intentions of the client were considered.

The clients wished to incorporate a walled forecourt, reminiscent of homes the wife enjoyed as a child. The front facade was to be private, formal, and protective, but also out of public view. As a reflection of their private life together, the front was also to be romantic.

The front thus forms a protective wall which contains rooms and extends to frame the forecourt and part of the property. Behind this wall glimpses of a "romantic" pavilion may be seen. The pavilion, rests in a garden with a "secret" *allée* of flowering trees within a scrub-pine forest. The pavilion is also adjacent to a golf course, which the clients enjoy as a means of relaxation. The gardens, interiors, and furniture were also developed through a collaboration with numerous artists.

The house is composed of primary forms (cubes and tetrahedrons) which through detailing and use of materials attain historical references. The concern in this building was to evoke an historicality which would unify the modern with the familiar.

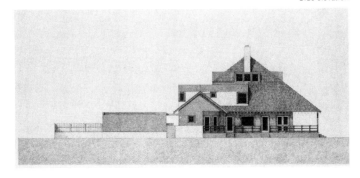

Site plan (opposite)

Rear elevation

Side elevation

Louis Goodman is an architect and an Associate Professor of Architecture at the Pratt Institute School of Architecture. He was a student of the Philadelphia School and has worked on projects throughout the United States and abroad. He is a founder of the Gallery of Applied Arts in New York.

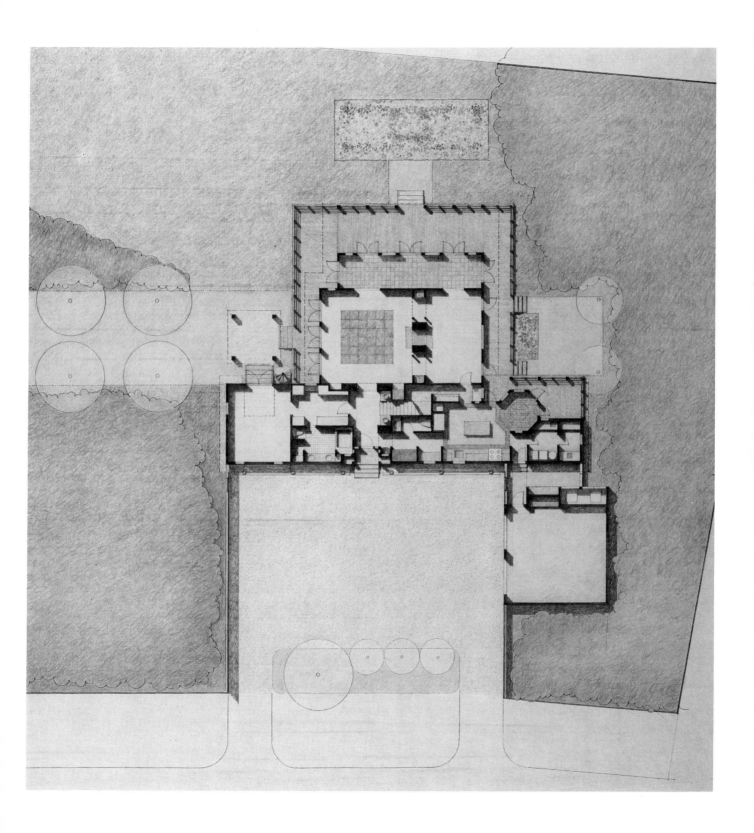

John Johansen

The New Mummers Theater, Oklahoma City, Oklahoma, 1970.

The New Bio-tech Architecture

Introduced recently by Robert Theobald, who directs a research organization called Action Linkage, is the term "socioquake." This term refers to any time in the history of human events when a new set of social realities replaces the old; a time between those more stable periods of high cultural achievement, *e.g.* Periclean Greece, the good Emperors of Rome, the Renaissance of the Cinquecento, and 19th-century industrial society. As we of the highly industrialized countries now enter upon what is alternately called the space-electronic-communication-information age, it must occur to us all that we are undergoing a transition of some magnitude. In this transition, we are relinquishing machine industry as the significant motivating force in our society, and the mass-produced commodity as its resultant image. Yet we are unable to understand or adjust to the impact of the communication age, or find that corresponding image which serves as a necessary therapeutic effect and as an inspiration in our future. Although at present our professional efforts are marked by energetic search in many directions, I believe we are undergoing, in an historical sense, a cultural reevaluation, leading, we might hope, to a reformation.

In this view I am not alone. Alvin Toffler, in his book, *Future Shock*, sees this as the "Third-Wave Revolution" quite as formidable as what man experienced much earlier in the Agrarian Revolution, and later in the Industrial Revolution. In his book *Megatrends*, John Naisbitt, another futurologist, offers ten separate manifestations of change, the most significant of which is entitled "From Industrial Society to Information Society." Hartwig Fritch, the Danish social historian reports that mankind, having advanced from the "Nature Society" to a "Culture Society," is now undergoing a transformation into a "Technic-Society." Pierre Teilhard de Chardin, the Jesuit theologian, speaks of our civilization as one in which we find ourselves "increasingly in charge of our own evolution." In his book *The Turning Point — Science, Society and the Rising Culture*, Fritjof Capra, the eminent physicist, employs such extreme terms as "Crises and Transitions," and our coming awareness of "the New World View," or "The New Paradigm."

Considering the magnitude of these observations of change, it is no wonder that architects are bewildered and unable to understand, as is their responsibility, and to express these forces of change for our society in architectural terms.

Sifting through a multitude of observations made by advanced physicists, social observers, psychiatrists, theologians, futurologists and others, one comes to recognize certain recurring patterns of movement which reinforce each other in some consistent direction. We might start with the observations of Fritjof Capra in his chapter "The Two Paradigms." The paradigm of the recent past presented a view of order and reality based on the Cartesian and Newtonian perception of the universe. That view dealt with a linear, static, hierarchical, and mechanistic order. Newton saw the universe as a giant machine, following purely geometric and causally related operations. Descartes similarly envisioned the world and all living organisms as machines constructed of separate parts. Our crisis, as Capra puts it, develops from the fact that we are still trying to apply the concepts of an outdated world view, *i.e.* the mechanistic world view of Cartesian-Newtonian science, to our existence today. Failing to recognize this discrepancy, he says, is a crisis of perception.

That New Paradigm, the new vision of reality, is a holistic view, an organic view, an ecological view. It is the new framework upon which we can bring into sharper definition human endeavors in various fields; and this must include the arts and architecture to these human endeavors. This emerging concept of reality is a way of perceiving all natural phenomena, including ourselves, in a relatedness to nature and to all human praxis.

During the latter phase of the Industrial Age, 1910 – 1920, scientists were already aware of this view of reality; the "New Physics," encompassing the Principle of Relativity, Quantum Theory, and more recent reconciliation of Unified Field Theory, were profoundly changing our sense of reality. One might ask, how can the New Physics have any influence on architecture? How can a science dealing with particle physics, and astrophysics, have any influence upon our existence within the limits of

our senses? As a matter of record the new physics has since 1910 permeated biology, medicine, psychiatry, sociology, economics, political science, theology, and the arts. As Capra has said, "the emerging world view implied by modern physics is inconsistent with the passing industrial society which does not reflect the harmonious and interrelatedness we observe in Nature. To achieve this new state of dynamic balance, a radically different social and economic structure is being formed. We are undergoing a cultural revolution in the true sense of the word."

Speaking of the universe, Sir James Jeans has said, "We seem to be moving towards a non-mechanical reality." Speaking of our world and human events, we are moving from an industrial society in which we have been conditioned to a mechanistic view of life, to a post-industrial society in which the organic process is becoming more the essence of a new reality which will determine the fabric of our culture.

The mechanistic view of the universe is conceived and organized as a consecutive stacking of building blocks, molecule on molecule, solar system on solar system. The industrial equivalents of these building blocks are machine products, identically manufactured in precisely programmed steps. The nature of a machine's activities are determined by its structure. In the organism, the relationship is reversed; the structure is determined by its processes.

In our nation, one of the most industrialized, we are beginning to see the emergence of extensive underlying organic patterns. Speaking about industry, the futurist John McHale predicted an integrated research-development-management-marketing system which he described as "production metabolism." In business management, the economist John Galbraith observes that giant corporations are increasingly governed by organic principles.

From these observations, we may make the following deductions. First, the "machine for living," either in its performance as a building or as an aesthetic concept, no longer appeals to us. No longer seeing the reality of our world as a sequential stacking of building blocks, we can expect architecture to change from the established manner of joining elements in additive relationships, to a fusion of elements in seamless continuity. Our buildings may be less strictly defined, more generalized and subject to change. Buildings will be seen no longer as static, lifeless mechanisms, with fixed programs of use, but as accommodating human events in continual flux; events recurring, events probable or even unpredictable, approaching the nature and characteristics of living systems. According to our view, "system thinking is process thinking, forms become associated with process, interrelation associated with interaction," as Capra says. The nature of an organism is that its form is determined by its processes; no longer subject to, or victim of, machine structure, the human being and his/her processes will increasingly determine the building's form. What we come to build may be conceived as outgrowths of, or responses to, and expressions of the living processes of the occupants within. The occupant and the building may come to be conceived of as one organism.

In a recent issue of *Architecture-Technology*, Forrest Wilson states that "mechanical and electrical components, *i.e.* moving parts, have developed faster than the architectural elements. We must revise our view of buildings from inanimate to animate artifacts." As opposed to outdated mechanics, the new electronically controlled mechanics take on characteristics of living organisms and the conventional distinction between the machine and organism will in some cases become obscured.

Other characteristics of all living systems are self-organization and self-regulation. Such readjustment is said to assume a state of "non-equilibrium," in which the organism is always "at work," undergoing constant change or adaptation. Such is the "dynamic stability" of self-organizing systems. The intelligent or "smart" building comes to mind, buildings which not only regulate their own heating, ventilating, lighting, elevator, and escalator capacities, but also perform these as a coordinated systems operation. As electro-kinetics and robotics develop further, the possibilities are boundless. In the future, building interiors will respond and adjust in size, form, color, light, temperature, both functionally and aesthetically, at various frequencies according to changing market requirements, family life cycle, season, unpredictable event, or momentary whim. Sensory devices might change building exteriors as the context changes, in a state of organic symbiosis, as in the balance of ecosystems. On a larger scale, within the urban fabric, there is the implication of greater convertibility, fusion, permutation, growth, atrophy, metamorphosis, and death. Urban design and regional planning, which at the present time are distorted by political and administrative powers, might approximate a natural bio-physical ideal.

Current research on tall buildings examines muscular analogies, whereby companion structures mutually interact through "bone, tendon and muscle" that can, by computer manipulation, contract and relax in response to unpredictable exterior forces. Instead of being pieced together with countless joints, organic "skins" of variable permeability will be sprayed on. Computerized structural calculations will allow biomorphic architecture which was previously non-calculable, and therefore never realized. Manufactured parts, by computer manipulation, will be produced not identically, but organically varied.

Anything organic in concept assumes that humans are a part of nature. In our advancing technology the theologian, Teilhard de Chardin, suggests that technology is an extended form of humanism. Primordial spatial symbols for six-thousand years have been continually updated in each historic advance of building technology. The development of the new bio-tech architecture has the potential to become the new "symbol."

John Johansen has been the principal of his own architectural firm from 1950 to the present. His projects have involved the design of theaters, university campuses, the Embassy for the United States in Dublin, libraries, and large experimental housing projects. Professor Johansen has a B.S., B.Arch, and an M.Arch from Harvard University, and has Honorary Doctorates of Fine Arts from Clark University and the University of Maryland. He has taught as a Professor of Architecture at Yale and Columbia Universities, and at the Pratt Institute School of Architecture. His work has been published and exhibited extensively in the United States and abroad. He is presently a member of the American Academy-Institute of Arts and Letters.

John Lobell

Architecture and the Structures of Consciousness

The means whereby to identify dead forms is Mathematical Law. The means whereby to understand living forms is Analogy.
Oswald Spengler, *The Decline of the West*

Seven Pillars

The primitive hunter-gatherer lived in the body of Gaia, the Earth's biosphere named after the Greek mother-goddess and now perceived by contemporary biologists as a living organism. Individual consciousness was not differentiated from the flow of the Earth's consciousness. Thus the Amazon Indian moved in the shadow of a perpetual green canopy, deriving food, shelter, and psychoactive drugs from an unbounded organic home. The Australian Aborigine lived under a dome of stars that encoded ancestral stories. There was no monumental architecture, as frozen stone would have blocked the flow of consciousness and disrupted an umbilical union.[1]

Once separated from Gaia, the early monument builders used their stones to direct the flow of energies. Stonehenge is but one of thousands of megalithic structures built to serve as great acupuncture needles, marking first the earth's energies, then the moon's cycles, and finally the sun's movement through the seasons. No longer a part of the earth, human consciousness now gained a power over it. The umbilical cord was cut and innocence ended. Differentiated consciousness set out on its wanderings of the earth and, most recently, of the heavens.

The Egyptian moved through a narrow corridor of time, with smooth stone walls defining the Path of a linear progression through life and into death. Orderly social customs prescribed activities in life, and the Book of the Dead prescribed the precise manner in which one was to advance through successive tests in death. There was no field of action for the Egyptian, no open-ness of space. Nothing existed outside the one dimension of the Path. The polished faces of the Pyramid in the sun defined the Path across the desert. Likewise, at Luxor (figure 1), the avenue of sphinxes from the river led directly to the pylon of the Temple, beyond which the court, hypostyle hall, and sanctuary also

marked a clear progression. The columns of the Egyptian temple were on the inside to screen the walls. A bare wall led the eye to focus on a space on the other side of the temple. The screen of columns denies the existence of anything beyond the wall. Outside the temple, architecture, with the exception of the pylon, had no existence.[2]

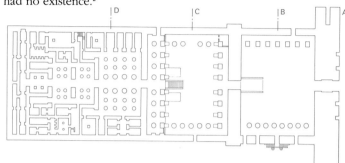

1. Temple of Medinet Habu

Egyptian directional movement can be contrasted with the flowing Chinese Way of the Tao. Lao Tzu wrote:

The highest good is like water.
Water gives life to the ten thousand things and does not strive.
It flows in places men reject and so is like the Tao.[3]

2. Kuan Yin hall, Tu Lo temple, Ch'i-hsien

201

The Chinese followed this flow, achieving a harmony that comes from a focus on non-desire. The Chinese temple and palace complex is not a self-contained building, but rather an open complex that includes hills, water, trees, flowers, and rocks, as well as the building. The openness of the Kuan Yin hall of the Tu Lo Temple (figure 2), erected in wood in Ch'i-hsien in 984 A.D., is expressed through the layers of the roof and the spaces between the bracketed supports over the columns. They let space flow through the building like a breeze.

The Greeks experienced the beginnings of an emergence of the individual from society and nature. In his study of Greek tragedy, Nietzsche wrote:

At the very climax of joy there sounds a cry of horror or a yearning lamentation for an irretrievable loss. In these Greek festivals, nature seems to reveal a sentimental trait; it is as if she were heaving a sigh at her dismemberment into individuals.[4]

The Greek temples at Paestum (figure 3) stood apart from nature, the geometric form of the buildings contrasted with the landscape, and the freestanding columns outside the temple represented the complete emergence of the individual. From the outside, columns screened the walls from view. Focus was not on the partially hidden walls, which brought awareness to the interior space they contained. The experience of the Greek temple was as a piece of sculpture. The Greeks were only concerned with the bodily whole, as may be noticed in their sculpture, abhorring the voids of space and time. In the Greek tragedy there was no development of character as seen in the Western novel. Character exists at birth, waiting to be revealed. In the Greek vase there is no depth, and Greek arithmetic sees only one number between two and three, as opposed to our mathematics of fractions, irrational numbers, and functions. Greek mathematical thought did not extend in abstraction beyond X^2, and thus Euclidian geometry could neither square the circle nor trisect the angle[2].

The Gothic world was defined by a total presence of a God who cast souls into the material world to be tested by bodily temptations. The response to this test was an asceticism, a "starving away of the flesh." The Gothic cathedral at Chartres was similarly stripped of all unnecessary material, leaving the thin ribs of the vaults and flying buttresses. Openings in the walls allowed the luminous presence of God to flood through stained glass windows filling the interior space. This was analogous to the experience of God's presence flooding through the body of a person, thus illuminating the soul (figure 4).

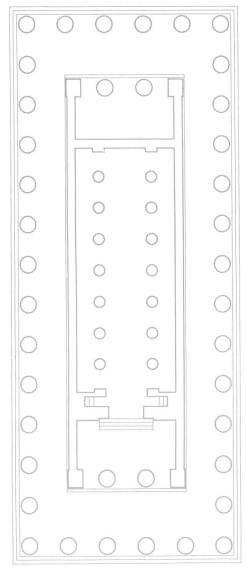

3. Temple of Hera Argiva, Paestum.

The early 20th century witnessed the fall of the central point of reference with an emergence of an existential, relativistic cosmology. Einstein's equations shattered Newton's assumptions about absolute space, leaving the human observer in referenceless motion. The novels of Proust and Joyce were organized by the flux of the consciousness of the protagonist rather than by the tick of a universal clock, and mathematics became topological, concerned with patterns rather of relationship than of measure. In Frank Lloyd Wright's Robie House the chimney core displaced the human being from the center, putting it into motion, once again a part of nature.

Currently it may be suggested that Eastern influences on the West have enhanced a merger between Buddhism and existentialism, facilitating the development of a world in which the dichotomy between the existing Western notion of a self and an exterior world are diffusing into one.

Consciousness and Cultural Forms

Consciousness, in continual flux, generates a changing world. Architecture and other forms of culture record that change.

5. Villa Almerico Capra (also called La Rotunda), Vicenza.

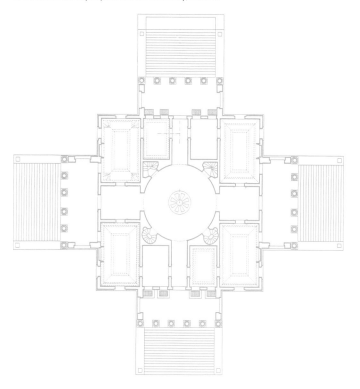

4. Cathedral of Notre-Dame, Reims.

The Renaissance replaced the centrality of God with the centrality of the human being: "Man is the measure of all things." Newton's uniform space and time defined a crystal clockwork in which people moved. Their senses connected them to nature, and mathematics connected them to nature's laws. Perspective painting measured the lattice of space and time, and the rational symmetry of Renaissance architecture established a setting in which the human being, positioned under the dome, could look out: front, back; right, left. Palladio's Villa Rotonda (figure 5) laid Cartesian coordinates onto the landscape.

All cultural forms of a given society and period, including cosmology, theoretical physics, mathematics, philosophy, painting, literature, music, architecture, etc., derive from the structures of consciousness of those who constitute that culture. Consciousness is an active force which, through intentionality, unifies the world. For example, the Renaissance concept of uniform space, time, and causality can be found in Galileo's and Newton's physics, Newton's and Leibniz's calculus, the rational symmetry of the Renaissance plaza, the rational orders of Renaissance architecture, perspective painting, and the chronological novel. Similarly, the existential flux of space, time, and "becoming" of the turn of our century are manifested in Einstein's physics, non-Euclidian geometry, Frank Lloyd Wright's architecture, Postimpressionist and Cubist painting, and Proust's and Joyce's novels.

Isomorphism

We can conceive of the wall of a building as facing two ways: inward as a boundary for the room, and outward as a boundary for the street. In this sense, architecture is the intermediary between the person and the city. Thus architecture is like the shell of a sea animal: the inside of the shell suggests the form of the organism; the outside describes the world the animal inhabits.

Architecture is the shell in a metaphoric as well as a physical sense. It is the intermediary between the person and the cosmos, defining and securing a human place in a larger order of things. The shell of an animal is isomorphic with the animal. In mathematics, isomorphism is a one-to-one correspondence of one set with another. Similarly, in each instance the animal and the shell correspond, one taking a positive and the other a negative shape. The shell is as a form in which the animal is cast. In a similar sense, architecture is the cultural form in which our consciousness is cast.

An isomorphic relationship between cultural forms and structures of consciousness is similar to Schopenhauer's concept of the relationship between music and the will. For Schopenhauer, the will is a generating force behind all experience. The phenomenal world of "representation" is merely this same quality of will objectified. For Schopenhauer, music most directly and immediately expresses the will and therefore speaks "the universal imageless language of the heart." The formal structures in music are not alone in reflecting what he calls the will; all cultural forms — painting, sculpture, architecture, cosmology, physics, mathematics, etc. — reflect this will, indeed, reflect structures of consciousness.[5]

Formal Structures

The active role that consciousness plays generates the phenomenal reality we experience. Consciousness is the mold in which the phenomenal world is cast. All of the particulars of our experience are due to the particulars in this mold — interstices and crevices, extensions and voids. Furthermore, this mold is living. It is a pulsating, evolving organism, in a state of continuous change, a world made up of a myriad of changing detail. Behind this flux there are underlying organizing principles.

For example, much experience takes place in space and time which Kant sees as generated by consciousness:

It is not something objective and real, neither substance, nor accident, nor relation, but... subjective and ideal; it is, as it were, a schema, issuing by a constant law from the nature of the mind, for the coordinating of all outer senses whatever.[6]

We do not mean to establish a Kantian position, but rather to raise the questions what are space and time, for Kant they were fixed in a Newtonian sense. Another consideration would be that space and time are mutable, different for different cultures.

The Newtonian physicist attempts to define space as uniform and continuous, having properties of extension, a potential which can be occupied. Einstein's space is generated by objects rather than containing them, is linked space with time, and is curved. Quantum mechanics describes space as discontinuous. So what can we say about space?

The solution comes in realizing that we can mean two different kinds of things when we use the term "space." One is the specific spaces of Aristotle, Newton, Einstein, the quantum theorist: The second concept involves Kant's definition. To present Kant's definition in more graphic terms, we might say that space (and time and matter and causality) is the graph paper that the mind lays over the world to organize it. We should remember that graph paper comes in a variety of patterns, not just uniform squares. Our notion here is that the graph paper is constantly changing as our consciousness changes.

These major patterns, such as space, time, matter, and causality, are the consequences of laying different graph papers on the world, and are expressed as formal structures in the arts and sciences. Thus we see a continuous space and time capable of instantaneous juxtaposition in Renaissance perspective painting, Newtonian physics, and Renaissance architecture. Similarly, we see relative space and time in Cubist painting, Einstein's physics, and Frank Lloyd Wright's architecture. The structures of consciousness create formal structures within which our experience is developed. They define the limits within which we move, the patterns we follow. Formal structures define culture; their changes define history.

Art

The reality that we know is generated in dialogue by our consciousness. An art experience is when we momentarily penetrate that dialogue. Art serves to remind us of the flux of reality and to reeducate or reform our structures of consciousness.[7] Because of these functions, art reveals the structures of consciousness or general patterns of awareness during a given period. Artists are, in McLuhan's term, "early warning systems" for their cultures.[8]

The artist's prime subject is himself or herself. He or she is constantly asking, "What am I experiencing?" Each is not content merely to have experiences, but wishes also to be aware of the processes that generate those experiences. When this attempt becomes overly self-conscious, the artist can be described as a Romantic. The attempt to penetrate self is there even if the artist describes it in other terms.

On developing a technique for perspective, Alberti exclaimed: "At last, I can see the world as God sees it!" Today we would hold that God probably does not see in perspective. What Alberti succeeded in doing was to see the world as *he* saw it. As structures of consciousness change, the world changes; to grasp what is happening, we must penetrate into phenomena, into the dialogue itself. On the edge of our experience we can map our ever-changing limits.

The limits Alberti was exploring were further mapped by Descartes' coordinate algebra and Galilean and Newtonian inertial systems. Newton was involved in an inner search similar to an artist's. In mathematical terms science delineates the principles of the dialogue. The artist renders irrationally the structures or maps of consciousness, the scientist describes them precisely. But the maps are to be found inside us. Einstein did not use laboratories; he seldom used any technological devices more complicated than pencil and paper.

Cézanne said of his paintings that he was trying to portray the "solid world" of the paintings in the museums. If this was his aim, why didn't he copy the techniques of the masters? In fact he did. The masters looked at the world with an intensity revealing formal structures ordered by their consciousness. Cézanne looked with a similar intensity, but his perception of the world changed because the generating structure of consciousness had changed. He showed us his world rather than an imitation of that of the masters. He wanted to go back to the confused sensations with which we are born. He was able to follow the process of experience and penetrate into its origins.

The purpose of the artist, scientist and mathematician, is to uncover the dialogue, the limits of experience. The artist usually performs this task earlier than the scientist or mathematician, and alters structures of consciousness. The scientist or mathematician performs the task later and gives precise mathematical definition to the structures.

Architecture As Art

Architecture has been described as the art of space or the art of interior space. This description is inadequate. Instead, we may see architecture as the art of institutions, and, more generally, as the art of existence. Architecture addresses human institutions. The house addresses the institution of residence; the cathedral, the institution of religion; the office building, the institution of work.

Architecture addresses existence through its formal structures. Through the space, material, structure, organization, and ornament of a building, the architect creates an encounter with the limits of existence for his or her culture, and reveals the relationship between the individual and the larger order of things. The manifestation of human being is historical, individuals come in touch with their being through an encounter with the materials and techniques of their time. In Mies's words:

Technology is rooted in the past. It dominates the present and tends into the future. It is a real historical movement — one of the great movements which shape and represent their epoch. It can be compared only with the Classic discovery of man as a person, the Roman will to power, and the religious movement of the middle ages.... Architecture is the real battleground of the spirit. Architecture wrote the history of the epochs and gave them their names. Architecture depends on its time. It is the crystallization of its inner structure, the slow unfolding of its form.[9]

As an art, architecture restructures consciousness. Consequently, the arrangement of buildings and urban complexes reveals how people saw themselves and how they related to each other. Architecture is an unwritten language which can tell us as much about its users as can painting or literature.

History

Much of current historical analysis views history not as dynamic, but as static and given. In architecture, the tendency is to rummage about and draw on past styles for contemporary buildings. The resulting eclecticism leaves no sense of what previous buildings meant in context and manifests a meaningless-ness in the present. There is no sense of "our place in history."

This static attitude toward history has roots in the work of René Descartes (1596-1650), who attempted to extend mathematical methods to all fields of human knowledge, thereby rationalizing experience and trivializing history and culture. Descartes' influ-ence spread throughout the sciences, and into all areas of human affairs, including education, psychology, and government. This static sense has influenced discussions in art and literature and the French intellectual traditions, including semiology, structural-ism, post-structuralism, and Western Marxism. These traditions have become dissatisfying as they play across the surface without penetrating the depths from which meaning is generated.

Giambattista Vico (1668-1744) rejected Cartesian rationalism and the notion of a rational human nature. For Vico, history was central, with each period having its own pattern of meaning, discernible through the study of language and myth.[10]

The views of these two generators of Western thought, Descartes and Vico, are still in conflict. Vico's views are emerging as people sense the sterility of Cartesian-based aesthetics and social sciences and their inability to yield the meanings underlying our individual and collective lives. In the Viconian tradition, Oswald Spengler addresses meaning in history, Carl Jung illuminates the psyche, and Joseph Campbell explores mythology.

Human beings are symbolic creatures, and language (spoken, written, mathematical, and artistic) is our defining quality. We are also metaphysical creatures, standing between the phenomenal world and something transcendent. The shape of the intersec-tion between these two realms is molded in cultural forms and changes dynamically with history. Thus, history is full of meaning, revealing to us the differences between cultures and the unities within them. [11-17]

Notes

1. Mimi Lobell, *Spatial Archetypes*, unpublished book.

2. Oswald Spengler, *Decline of the West* (New York: Knopf, 1939).

3. Lao Tzu, *Tao Te Ching*, Trans. Gia-Fu Feng and Jane English (New York: Vintage, 1972), verse 8.

4. Friedrich Nietzsche, *The Birth of Tragedy*, trans. Walter Kaufmann (New York: Vintage, 1967), p. 40.

5. Arthur Schopenhauer, *The World as Will and Representation*, trans. E. F. Payne (New York: Dover, 1969).

6. Immanuel Kant, "On the Form and Principles of the Sensible and Intelligible Worlds," trans. Kemp Smith, London, 1929, sec. 150. Quote used here is quoted in *The Encyclope-dia of Philosophy* (New York: Macmillan, 1967), vol. 4, p. 308.

7. Morse Peckham, *Man's Rage for Chaos* (New York: Chilton, 1965).

8. Marshall McLuhan, *Understanding Media* (New York: McGraw Hill, 1965).

9. Ludwig Mies van der Rohe, "Technology and Architecture," from Ulrich Conrads, *Pro-grams and Manifestos on 20th-Century Architecture* (Cambridge: MIT Press, 1971), p. 154.

10. Giambattista Vico, *The New Science*, trans. Thomas Bergin and Max Fisch (New York: Anchor, 1961).

11. Joseph Campbell, *The Inner Reaches of Outer Space* (New York: van der Mark, 1986).

12. Milic Čapek, *The Philosophical Impact of Contemporary Physics* (New York: D. Van Nostrand, 1961).

13. Ernst Cassirer, *An Essay on Man* (New Haven: Yale University Press, 1965).

14. Anton Ehrenzweig, *The Psychoanalysis of Artistic Vision and Hearing* (New York: Braziller, 1965).

15. Thomas Kuhn, *The Structure of Scientific Revolution*, Second Edition, Enlarged (Chicago: Chicago University Press,1970).

16. Merleau-Ponty, Maurice, *Phenomenology of Perception* (Humanities Press, 1962).

17. Chögyam Trungpa, *Cutting Through Spiritual Materialism* (Boston: Shambhala, 1973).

Illustrations: Henri Stierlin, editor, *Encyclopedia of World Architecture* (New York: Van Nostrand Reinhold Company).

John Lobell is Professor of Architecture at the Pratt Institute School of Architecture. He is au-thor of *Between Silence and Light, Spirit in the Architecture of Louis I. Kahn*. This paper was written under a grant from the Graham Foundation for Ad-vanced Studies in the Fine Arts, and is part of a forthcoming book, *Architecture and Structures of Consciousness*, which is also being written under a grant from the Graham Foundation.

Christian Xatrec

Christian Xatrec is an artist presently living in New York. He studied at the *École Speciale D'Architecture* in Paris and has taught at Pratt Institute in the Department of Architecture.

**Self Portrait
As A Revolving Door — Fo(u)r Equal Spaces**

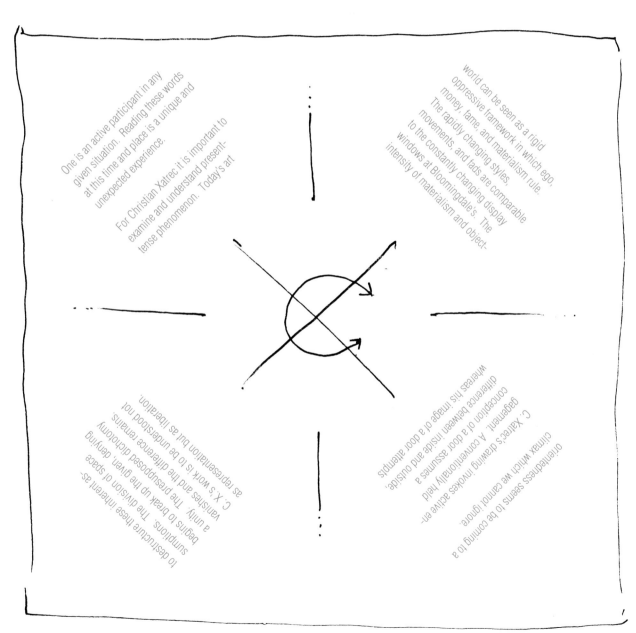

One is an active participant in any given situation. Reading these words at this time and place is a unique and unexpected experience.

For Christian Xatrec it is important to examine and understand present-tense phenomenon. Today's art

world can be seen as a rigid oppressive framework in which ego, money, fame and materialism rule. The rapidly changing styles, movements, and fads are comparable to the constantly changing display windows at Bloomingdale's. The intensity of materialism and object-

oriented, seems to be coming to a climax which we cannot ignore.

C. Xatrec's drawing invokes active engagement. A conventionally held conception of a door assumes a difference between inside and outside, whereas his image of a door attempts

to destructure these inherent assumptions. The division of space begins to break up the given, denying a unity. The presupposed dichotomy vanishes and the difference remains.

C. X.'s work is to be understood not as representation but as liberation.

207

Hanford Yang

House Without Reference

Berwyn, Pennsylvania is an old, historical town with a population of fifteen thousand. It is located at the northwest corner of Philadelphia, about 25 miles away from the city. The site is on Maple Street, an established street with many old but undistinguished houses.

The lot is small and narrow with neighboring buildings built closely around. There are no desirable views or preferred orientations. To build a house like others on the street would make the whole area even more crowded. Therefore, the major portion of this house is underground.

The street facade of the house is created by a double wood trellis with vines planted between. The trellis is in the shape of a house, a style compatible with the neighboring houses. A small structure for the garage and rentable spaces (required by the program) is tucked behind the trellis. The plan of the main house is divided into zones of sleeping, working, and living. These are served by sunken courtyards, skylights, and a large sunken garden for light, air, and guarded views. The roof is tilted to give living areas higher ceilings. It has become a sloped roof-garden with grid walkways, planting areas, and a secondary entry to the house by a flight of winding stairs.

The design intends to introduce humor, whim and visual confusion onto the site behind a seemingly traditional facade. The roof is made to look like a section drawing; the light wells and skylights are windows; the elevation which faces Maple Street has a double trellis to let vines climb; smoke is translated into a spiral stair, and the garden seatings resemble clouds in the sunken garden.

Project assistant: Vincent Linarello

Site plan

Hanford Yang received his B.Arch from the University of Pennsylvania and holds an M. Arch from M.I.T. He was a student of Louis Kahn, Paul Rudoph, and Robert Venturi. He has won numerous architectural design awards and has been published widely. "Pay attention to the things that are seemingly familiar, boring, and paradoxical. That is where the roots of interest generally lie. It takes ones cultivated sensiblitly to discover the uncommon out of the most common: out of the unsophisticated, comes the most sophisticated."

Model

Daniel Assayag

A Cemetery for Roosevelt Island

Located on the southern end of Roosevelt Island, the cemetery is considered an organic extension of the Manhattan grid. A relationship between the living city and the burial site suggests the cemetery's function as meeting ground between life and death. Life is represented in the form of seven artificial canyons carved into the cemetery's surface that also reflect the network of streets and avenues crisscrossing the city. The canyons intersect a longitudinal axis from the Queensboro Bridge to the southern tip of the island. Situated on a gradient, the declining axis represents a descent to death, embodied in a series of seven burial tombs. The towers rising from the tombs, signifying life in the midst of death, recall the symbolic relationship between being and non-being.

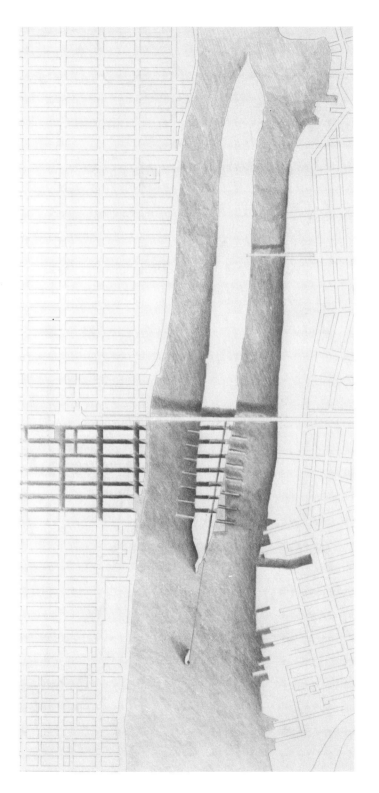

Site plan

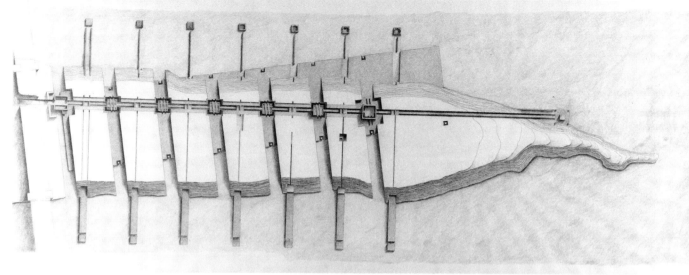

Plan

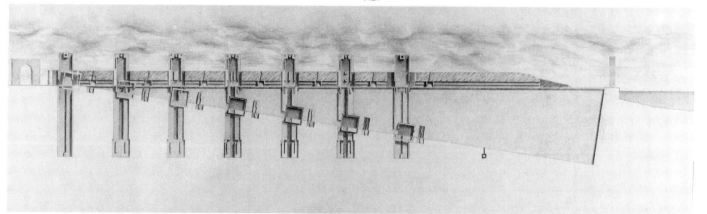

Section

Model

Anthony Caradonna

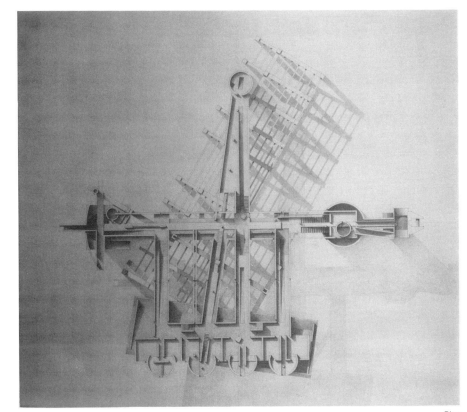

Elevated Church

Analytic study

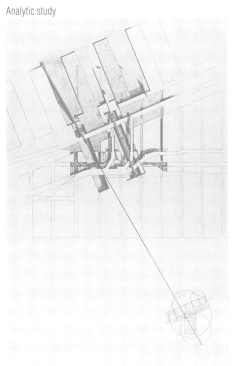

Section

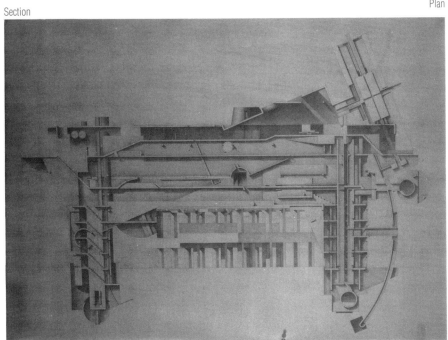

Elevation

Model

Anthony Caradonna

Music Conservatory

This project is a hypothetical music conservatory with spaces filled by the forms of sound. The site is a peninsula surmounted by a triangular Renaissance fortification. At the front is an island with a Phoenician lighthouse at its tip. The canyon is a theme for the vocabulary of the project; and the old castle was removed and used as a formal metaphor for the design. An abstraction of the castle's form is reinterpreted as a triangular vault. Underneath, the peninsula shelters a triangular "auditorium."

On the island in the canyon the conservatory houses all the functions for the school and its students. The public is relegated to the auditorium. The students are isolated on the island side in a cloistered environment facing the canyon. A tension between the sides of the narrow canyon creates a union of the two halves. Under the water in the orchestra pit exists the only connection between the auditorium peninsula and the island school. Performers are heard but not seen from above. The sounds of the students' music waft upward and reverberate in the canyon and throughout the auditorium spaces. The entire site becomes a musical instrument unified by sounds through the fret-like order of the architecture.

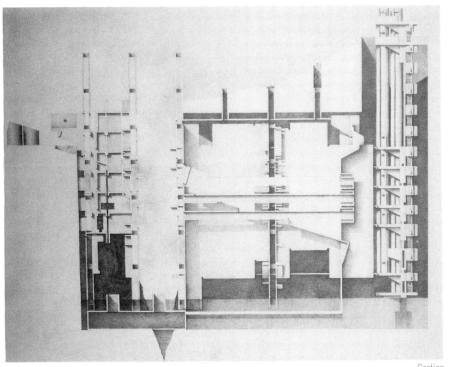

Section

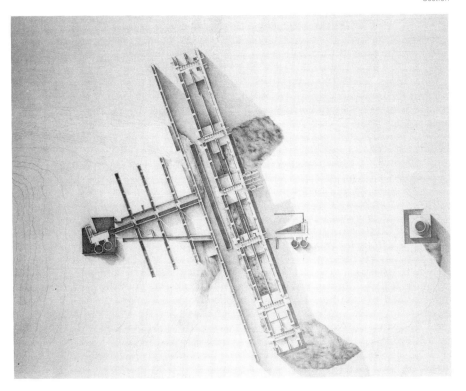

Constructive Art School

Lebbeus Woods once said, "We should design our buildings and then learn to live in them." The Constructive Art School project, however, favors process rather than completion. The program of an art school implies the theme of evolution. Thus, construction is never to be complete. The inhabitants may continually develop the edifice in dialogue with their intentions toward space and form. To impose conventional activities within the program would be contrary to the principle of dynamic change. Rather, the form acts as a blank edifice, ever awaiting further manipulation.

Perspective

Axonometric

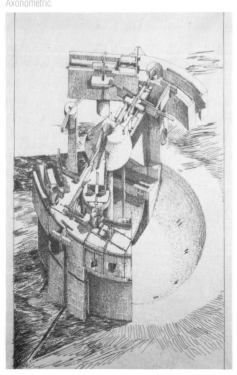

Sketch

Ladan Doroudian

Theater for a Small Park

Three theaters are arranged together in a portion of what was once a wading pool in a portion of the park by Chrystie Street. A stage for marionettes and one for hand puppets replace the space once occupied by a comfort station; all that remains of that structure are the stairs which now lead to the backstage of each theater. The seating areas for each stage are separated, yet a viewer from each area may see either performances as they occur simultaneously. A third theater has stages for hand puppets inset into the circular form of the amphitheater.

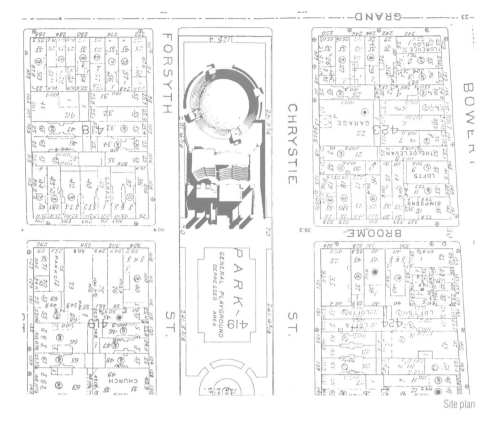

Sections

Site plan

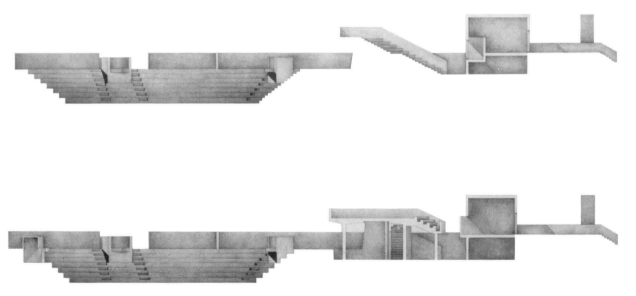

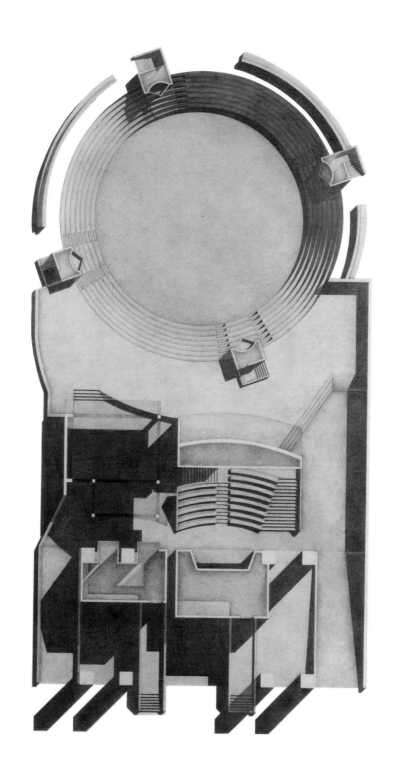

Plan

Juan Garcia

Crematorium for the Unclaimed Corpses of New York City

The project proposes a crematorium as monument and burial ground for the unclaimed dead of New York City. The site is the inverse of an island. It is the farthest stretch of water in the Bergen basin reaching into south Queens. This strip of water pointing north is 30 feet wide and 300 feet long. The site is flanked at the north and south by major roadways. To the east and west, flat grasslands extend until they merge with the city.

The initial gesture was to contain a portion of water in a cylinder suspended horizontally. Space for the program was made by carving into the sides and underside of the cylinder and to allow for the continuity of seasonal tides. Two gates are located along the north-south axis. The north gate connects the project to the edge of the city by underground tunnel. The south gate connects with a small barge carrying corpses to be placed inside the building where final ceremonial preparations are made before cremation. The vertical wall and cylinder attached to the south end contain the circulation and the living quarters for the crematorium operator and his assistants. The tilted wall along the main axis symbolizes the point of cremation.

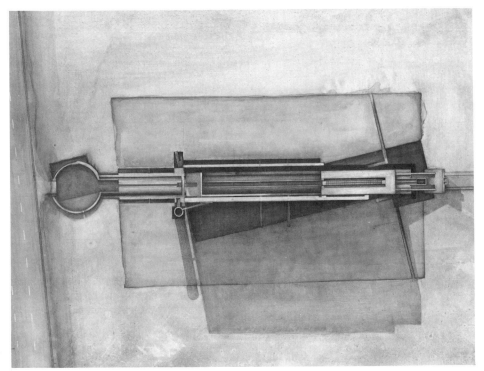

Plan
Longitudinal section

Cross section (opposite)

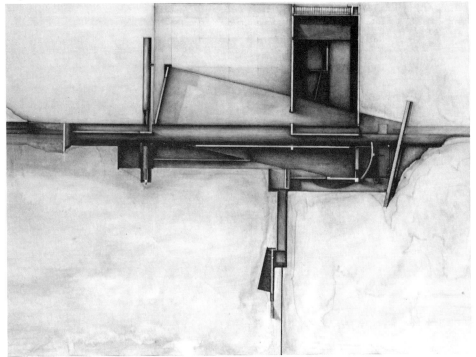

Johannes Knoops

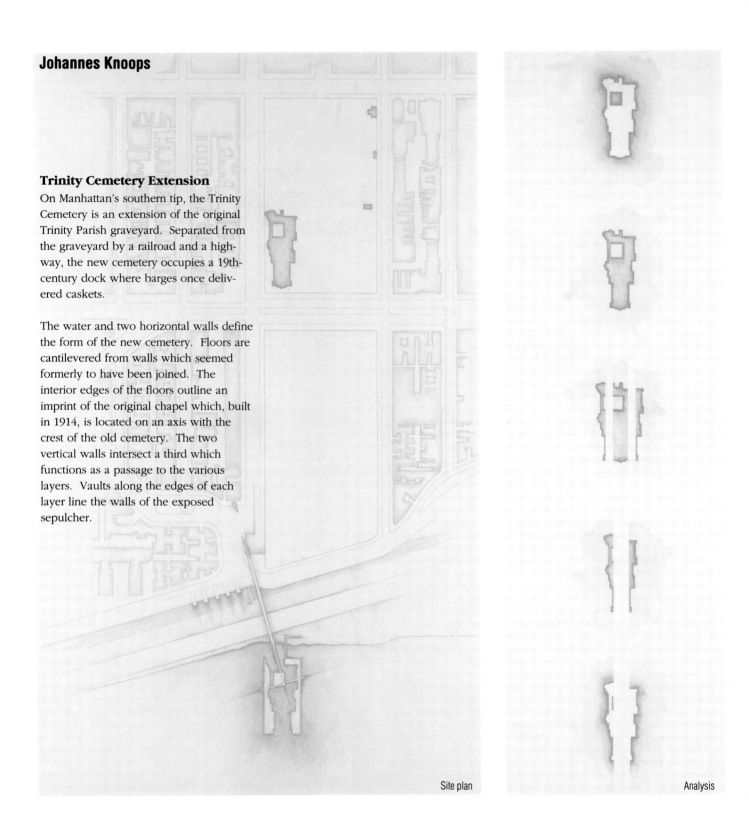

Trinity Cemetery Extension

On Manhattan's southern tip, the Trinity Cemetery is an extension of the original Trinity Parish graveyard. Separated from the graveyard by a railroad and a highway, the new cemetery occupies a 19th-century dock where barges once delivered caskets.

The water and two horizontal walls define the form of the new cemetery. Floors are cantilevered from walls which seemed formerly to have been joined. The interior edges of the floors outline an imprint of the original chapel which, built in 1914, is located on an axis with the crest of the old cemetery. The two vertical walls intersect a third which functions as a passage to the various layers. Vaults along the edges of each layer line the walls of the exposed sepulcher.

Site plan

Analysis

Model

Model

221

Andrew Reach

Oppression: House Held Captive

The house is placed in a sinkhole. Within this domain is an arrangement of geometries. A circle controls a square, a golden rectangle, and an equilateral triangle, locking them in a static configuration. The larger square dominates and peeks above the circle.

Section, plan

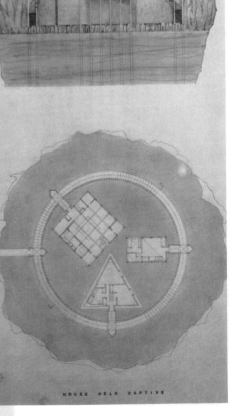

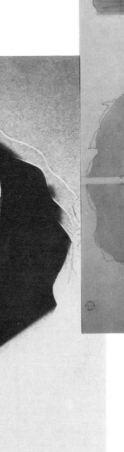

Model

222

Model

Opposite Houses
Freedom: House that Wants to Fly

The house, hanging precariously by cords from a sheer cliff, waits to take flight. It is positioned symmetrically on the cliff. A long staircase descends to the entry of the house and continues to a cantilevered bridge which leads nowhere (unless you jump off and fly away). The staircase, bridge and building act as camouflage. The imagery of a "flying machine" may fool fliers from an aerial view. The perspective from the earth reveals a more geometric and non-aerodynamic form.

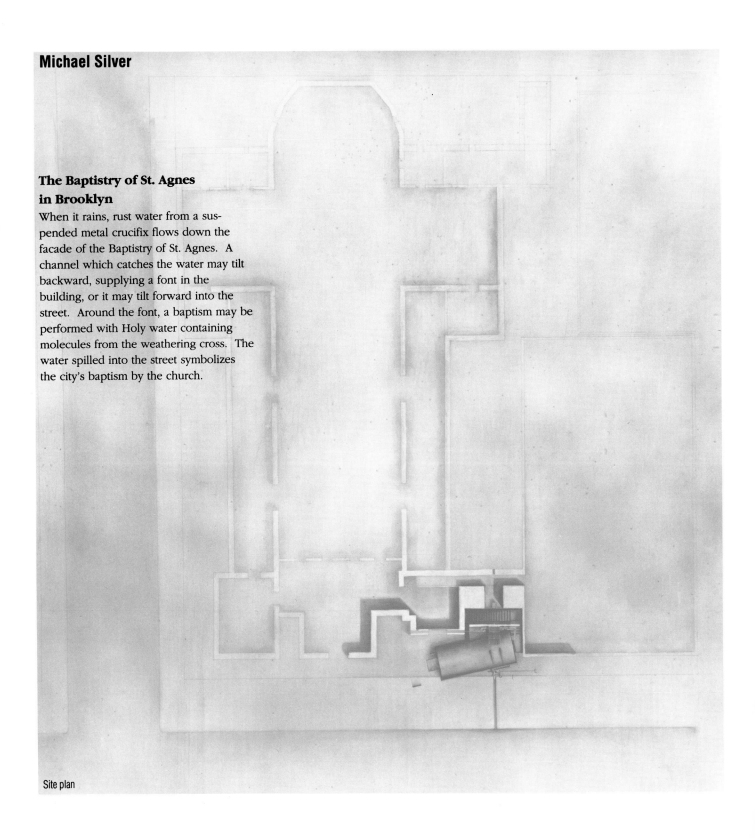

Michael Silver

**The Baptistry of St. Agnes
in Brooklyn**

When it rains, rust water from a suspended metal crucifix flows down the
facade of the Baptistry of St. Agnes. A
channel which catches the water may tilt
backward, supplying a font in the
building, or it may tilt forward into the
street. Around the font, a baptism may be
performed with Holy water containing
molecules from the weathering cross. The
water spilled into the street symbolizes
the city's baptism by the church.

Site plan

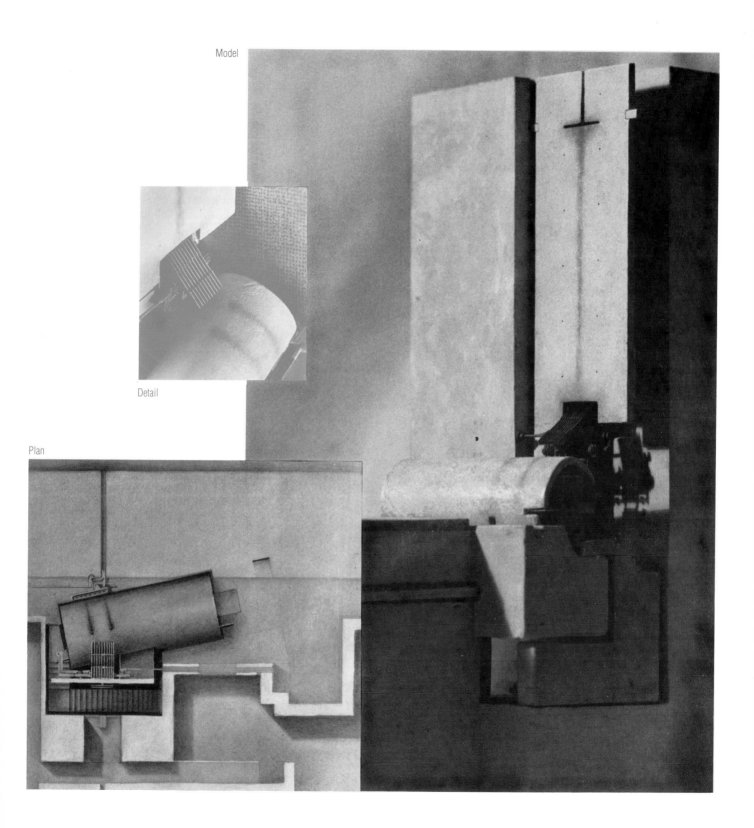

Model

Detail

Plan

BIOGRAPHIES

Vito Acconci was born in the Bronx, New York in 1940 and received his B.A. from Holy Cross College and his M.F.A. in literature from the University of Iowa. His interest in language developed into his early art performances, known as "Bodyworks," beginning in the late 1960s. His performances shifted toward participatory sculptural environments which in his later works became more architectonic. He is currently exhibiting in several museums and galleries in the United States, including the Museum of Modern Art in New York City.

Stanley Allen holds degrees from Brown University, The Cooper Union, and Princeton University. He has taught at the Rhode Island School of Design and the Institute for Architecture and Urban Studies, and is working as an architect in New York City.

Arakawa is a painter and **Madeline Gins** is a poet; they live and work in New York City, doing research and making constructions for how not to die.

Art & Language was begun in England in 1968 by a group of conceptual artists. Their early interests in nonobject content and cultural critique became the focus of their journal Art & Language. Later projects involved paintings as a means to critique idioms within the language of High Modern art. The current core group includes **Mel Ramsden** and **Michael Baldwin**, who live and work in Middleton-Cheney, England.

Karen Bausman and **Leslie Gill** are associates in their own architectural design firm. Both are graduates from The Cooper Union School of Architecture and have received numerous awards in competitions. Their work has been shown in several exhibitions, including the "London Project." Their professional portfolio includes commercial interiors and residential projects.

Botond Bognar is an associate professor in the School of Architecture at the University of Illinois, Urbana-Champaign, where he teaches design studios and courses on Japanese architecture. He has lectured extensively in the United States and abroad; his numerous publications include the book *Contemporary Japanese Architecture: Its Development and Challenge*. Professor Bognar has received several awards and prizes: He is a Mombusho Scholar, a University Scholar at the University of Illinois, and a fellow of the Graham Foundation. Having lived in Japan for many years, he is a correspondent of *A+U, Architecture and Urbanism*, Tokyo.

Chris Burden is an artist living and working in California. He received his B.F.A. from Pomona College and his M.F.A. from the University of California in Irvine. Since 1972 he has executed numerous works, including performance pieces, videos, and installations. His work focuses on the immediacy of violence, both on a small scale, to himself and to others, and on a global scale.

Douglas Darden does the work of architecture through teaching, writing, and designing theoretical projects. He has taught at Harvard University and Columbia University, and now teaches at New Jersey Institute of Technology. Darden has published articles in numerous periodicals, including *Places*, *OZ 9*, *Space Design*, *Transformations*, and *A+U*. His projects have been exhibited in New York, Boston, Chicago, Washington D. C., Osaka, and Tokyo.

Jacques Derrida was born of Sephardic Jewish parents in Algiers. He was associated with the *avant-garde* group Tel-Quel in the 1960s. He is a professor at the *Ecole des Hautes Etudies en Sciences Sociales* in Paris and a visiting professor at Yale University. His strategies of writing, deconstruction, and re-reading structuralism, phenomenology, and psychoanalysis, have profoundly influenced thinking in criticism and philosophy in Europe and the United States. He has written numerous books, including *Speech and Phoenomena*, *Writing and Difference*, *Of Grammatology*, *Dissemination*, *Glas*, *La Carte Postale*, and *Signsponge*.

Neil M. Denari is an architect living and working in New York City. He was born in Fort Worth, Texas, and received his B.Arch. from the University of Houston, and his M.Arch. from Harvard University. He has taught design at the Graduate School of Architecture at Columbia University and is soon to be a studio critic at the Southern California Institute of Architecture. In 1986 he established his own firm, Cor-Tex, and his projects have been exhibited in New York City at the Storefront, P.S. 1, and Columbia University.

Helen Anne Easterly teaches English and aesthetics in the Liberal Studies Department at Parsons School of Design. She is a candidate for the Ph.D. in English with a concentration in Poetics at New York University. She has been a visiting instructor of English at Pratt Institute since 1980.

Peter Eisenman, FAIA, is an architect and educator; he received his B.Arch. from Cornell University, his M.Arch. from Columbia University, and his Ph.D. from the University of Cambridge, England. He has designed and built numerous projects varying in scale from housing and urban design to private residences, and has participated in international competitions including winning entries in the Third Architectural Bienniale in Venice, the Berlin Roch-Friedrichstadt Competition, and the Center for Visual Arts at Ohio State University. He is the founder and former director of the Institute for Architecture and Urban Studies in New York City. He was editor of *Oppositions* and *Oppositions Books*, and has written several books, including *House X*, *Fin d'Ou T Hou S*, *Moving Arrows, Eros and Other Errors*, and *House of Cards*. Mr. Eisenman has taught at Cambridge, Princeton, Yale, and Harvard Universities, and now teaches at The Cooper Union.

Elliot Feingold teaches philosophy at Pratt Institute in the School of Liberal Arts and Sciences.

Kristian Gullichsen was born in Finland in 1932, the son of Marie and Harry Gullichsen, important patrons of Alvar Aalto, builders of Villa Mairea and producers of Aalto's furniture. He graduated from Helsinki University of Technology in 1960. He worked with Alvar Aalto, started his own office in 1961, and has been in partnership with E. Kairamo and Timo Vormala since 1973. He taught at the Helsinki University of Technology from 1961 to 1969, and at the University of Pennsylvania in 1969.

Martin Heidegger (1889-1976), born in Messkirch, a small town in Swabia, Germany, was a philosopher who, though widely considered central in contemporary existentialist thought, would reject the label "existentialist." Heidegger became *Privadozent* at the University of Freiburg in 1915, professor at Marburg in 1923, and professor at Freiburg in 1928. As a student at Freiburg he had been trained in the phenomenological method of Edmund Husserl. He obtained his interest in the question of being from Brentano and attributed his preoccupation with language to time spent in a Jesuit seminary. Heidegger was interested in the pre-Socratics and in Greek culture, and was deeply affected by the existential element in Kierkegaard; a number of his writings are on Friedrich Nietzsche. His major work, *Being and Time* (1927), is by common consent the most impressive analysis of human existence of the existential movement. Throughout his life, Heidegger believed it was the nature and vocation of man to ask the question, What is it, to be?

John Hejduk, FAIA, is an architect and educator living and working in New York City. He has taught at the Irwin S. Chanin School of Architecture of The Cooper Union since 1964, and became Dean in 1976. He has published and exhibited his work widely in the United States and abroad, and is a Fellow of the Royal Society of Arts. He has received a Brunnar Grant from the New York Chapter/American Institute of Architects, a Design Arts Fellowship from the National Endowment for the Arts, and an Arnold W. Brunner Memorial Prize from the American Academy and Institute of Arts and Letters. Structures from his award-winning projects are currently under the auspices of the Internationale Bauausstellung Berlin. *Mask of Medusa*, a comprehensive volume of the past thirty-six years of his work, was published by Rizzoli in 1985; and in 1986 the Architectural Association of London published *VICTIMS* in connection with the structures from that project entitled "The Collapse of Time."

Don Ihde is dean of the School of Humanities and Fine Arts, and professor of philosophy at SUNY, Stony Brook, and the author of *Hermeneutic Phenomenology*, *Sense and Significance*, *Listening and Voice*, *Technics and Praxis*, and *Existential Technics*. He co-edited volumes in the series "Dialogues in Phenomenology and Interdisciplinary Phenomenology," and edited the books *Descriptions*, *Hermeneutics & Deconstruction* and *Consequences of Phénomenology*. He also has been an executive co-director of the Society for Phenomenology and Existential Philosophy.

Anselm Kiefer, born in 1945 in Nonavenscheingen, Germany, is an artist living and working in Hornback/Odenwald, West Germany. Kiefer has been called on of the most remarkable artists to emerge from Europe in the last twenty-five years. Critics have said he has given back to the act of making art, the primacy among human activities that it has elsewhere lost. His art delves into the mythical past, excavates the unspeakable parts of German history, reviving what his elders wish to forget: the Nazi years. His painting harnesses ancient German myths and Egyptian gods to modern metaphors of good and evil, enacting the process of destruction and recreation. In his work *Martin Heidegger*, published in this issue, the progress of the philosopher's tumor on the brain is charted in detail, as if a mental dissolution were taking place.

Jeffrey Kipnis is an assistant professor of theory and design in the Department of Architecture of Ohio State University and adjunct professor of theory at The Cooper Union. Contingent with his work on architectural theory and his Theory of the Object, he is a frequent lecturer and visiting critic at universities internationally.

John Knesl was born in Vienna, Austria and received his Ph.D. in Architecture from Technical University in Vienna. He has worked as an architect in Austria and England, and has taught architectural design and theory/history from 1974 to 1985 in Austria and the United States. He has had articles published in the *PRATT JOURNAL OF ARCHITECTURE*, Vol. 1 and in *PRECIS 7*. Since 1985 he has been chief of urban design for the New York City Department of Transportation.

Justen Ladda, born in West Germany, is an artist living and working in New York City. He has been published internationally, and participated in numerous exhibitions including shows at the Willard Gallery,

Artist's Space, Kunsthalie, Dusseldorf, Galleria Communale d'Art Moderne, Bologna, the New Museum of Contemporary Art, the Los Angeles County Museum of Art, and a solo show at the Museum of Modern Art in New York City.

Diane Lewis is an associate professor of design at The Cooper Union. Over the past ten years, as a member of the faculty of The Cooper Union, Yale University, and the University of Virginia, she has published essays and projects in numerous publications, co-edited *The Education of An Architect*, and is an editor of the forthcoming *Eye2Eye*. Recipient of the Rome Prize in Architecture in 1976, she worked in the offices of I.M. Pei and Richard Meier for six years before initiating an independent studio with her colleague Peter Mickle. Their studio is engaged with projects in New York researching new programs for the city, in public and private works both realized and projected. She asserts that the life of the architect is an enmeshing of theory and praxis.

Stéphane Mallarmé was born in Paris in 1842, and died in 1888. He is considered to have been one of the founders of modern poetry, and the greatest French Symbolist poet. His concerns addressed all the arts including the book, the newspaper, design, music, and theatre. Mallarmé was an idealist who sought the salvation of society through art and poetry, and his reevaluation of nature and man back to their ideal origins, to be brought into effect by a masterwork, *'L'Livré* a twenty volume set, an ultimate work of art, intended to be performed. This work, although often referred to, was never written. His poetry, theoretical comments and method, in particular "*Un Coup de des n'abolira jamals la hasard*," have had a resounding effect on the arts of the 20th century, particularly the Surrealists.

Gordon Matta-Clark received his B.Arch from Cornell University in 1968. In 1974 he exhibited work in the "Anarchitecture Show," the culmination of weekly meetings of artists concerned with architecture. In the same year he persuaded Horace Solomon to allow him to cut apart an abandoned building Solomon owned, and in 1976, Matta-Clark went to Berlin to take part in an exhibition where he proposed cutting a hole in the Berlin Wall. The son of the Surrealist painter Matta, Gordon died of cancer in 1978 at the age of 36.

Diane Michelfelder is an associate professor in the Department of Philosophy at California Polytechnic State University, where she teaches courses in contemporary European philosophy and philosophy of art. Her interest in the relationship between philosophy and architecture grew out of her research into Heidegger's later philosophy. Her most recent project is a study of the aesthetic and ethical dimensions of post-structuralism.

Taeg Nishimoto is an architect born in Osaka, Japan, and currently living in New York City. He received his B.Arch. from Wasada University and his M.Arch. from Cornell University, has taught design at Columbia University Graduate School of Architecture, and now teaches design at New Jersey Institute of Technology and Pratt Institute. He is a Fellow of The New York Foundation for the Arts for 1987. His work has been published in *The Japan Architect*, May 1985.

Alastair R. Noble is a British artist living, working, and exhibiting in New York City for the past ten years. His earlier interior installations and graphics, under the title, "A Theory/Theatre of ((Noise))" have been condensed into his current sculptural work. These architectonic forms are often illuminated from within by the fluctuating light of a television set.

Jesse Reiser was born in New York, received his B.Arch. in 1981 from The Cooper Union, and his M.Arch. in 1984 from the Cranbrook Academy of Art, and is a fellow of The American Academy in Rome. His collaborator, **Nanako Umemoto** was born in Kyoto, Japan, received her B.A. in landscape architecture in 1975 from the Osaka University of Art, Japan, and in 1976 became assistant professor. In 1983 she received her B.Arch. from The Cooper Union. Jesse Reiser and Nanako Umemoto are principal partners in their firm Reiser/Umemoto in New York City.

Aldo Rossi was born in Milan, in 1931 and graduated from the Milan Polytechnic. He has taught in Europe at the Milan Polytechnic, the Federal Polytechnic at Zurich, and Venice University. His teaching affiliations in the United States include Cornell University, The Cooper Union, and Harvard University. His publications include *L'Architecttura della Città*, *A Scientific Autobiography*, and *Architetture Padane*. In 1973 he was the director of the international architecture section of the Milan Triennale, and was director of the the architectural section of the Venice Biennale in 1983. Aldo Rossi's works have been published and exhibited internationally, and he is currently working on new projects in Japan and the United States.

Mark Schneider received his M.A. in philosophy from the University of Wisconsin, and an M.A. and Ph.D. in architecture from Virginia Polytechnic University. He has taught architectural design, history, and theory at Leeds Polytechnic in England, Virginia Polytechnic University, and the University of Houston, Texas.

Robert Smithson was born in 1936 in Rutherford, New Jersey. Taking the ordered geometry of the crystal as his form, and entropy (the tendency of matter to reach order through an intractable period of chaos) as his

concepts, Smithson developed a non-studio art form that viewed "the strata of the Earth as a jumbled museum." His use of geological matter, the content of his work, developed into large-scale landscape art know as "Earthworks." The term Earthworks reflects the spirit of an age which juxtaposes concepts of pre-industrial naturalism with post-industrial materials. Smithson died tragically in 1973 in an airplane crash while he was photographing his final Earthwork, *Spiral Jetty*.

Keith Sonnier was born in Mamou, Louisiana and received his B.Arch. from the University of Southwestern Louisiana, and his M.F.A. from Rutgers University. He was one of the first artists to use neon in sculpture to articulate the calligraphic characteristics of the medium; he has also explored various communication systems, including satellite transmissions both in radio and television. While his work reflects technology, it is also influenced by the numerous cultures he visits, including India, China, Bali, and Brazil.

Lewis Stein was born and is anticipating death. He is an artist living and working in New York City.

Mark C. Taylor is professor of religion at Williams College. His most recent books include: *Erring: A Postmodern A/theology*; *Deconstruction in Context: Literature and Philosophy*; and *Altarity*. "*Textus Interruptus*" is a selection from a longer essay to be published in a forthcoming book.

Richard Thatcher is an artist living and working in New York City. He has exhibited his work in numerous group and solo exhibitions and performances.

Bernard Tschumi is chief architect for the *Parc de la Villette* in Paris which is currently under construction. Recent projects include the *Tokyo Opera House* and *Strasburg County Hall*, two schemes concerned with juxtaposition and superposition of independent fragments. He was a Davenport Visiting Professor at Yale University in the spring of 1988, and has just been appointed dean of the Graduate School of Architecture, Planning, and Preservation at Columbia University.

Dalibor Vesely was born in Vienna and lived in Prague where he received his Ph.D. in architecture from Prague University. Since moving to England in 1968, he has taught at the Architectural Association in London and currently teaches architectural history, theory and design at the University of Cambridge. Professor Vesely has lectured and served as a visiting critic at a number of universities throughout the United States. He practices architecture with Eric Parry in London, and is working on a book on the poetics of architecture.

Robert Venturi's *Complexity and Contradiction in Architecture*, published in 1966, was described by Vincent Scully as "the most important book on the making of architecture since Le Corbusier's *Vers une Architecture*, of 1923." Venturi and Scott Brown expanded and developed their theories in *Learning from Las Vegas*, and the partners have earned their reputation as practicing architects and planners. In over twenty years of practice, the firm has worked on more than 400 architectural, urban design, and urban planning projects in thirty-one cities in the United States, as well as in Europe and the Middle East. Current projects include several major museums and new university buildings. The works of the firm have received worldwide attention and over seventy major design awards, including the AIA Architectural Firm Award for having "so profoundly influenced the direction of modern architecture."

Andy Warhol is thought to have been born around 1930. He was educated at Carnegie Institute of Technology and lived and worked in New York City from 1952 until his death in 1987. For thirty-five years as an artist he created paintings and films, produced his own cable television show, and published *Interview* magazine. Warhol is known as one of the founders of the Pop Art movement whose paintings, derived from advertising production techniques, were exclusively silk-screened in his studio, "the Factory," established in 1963. In March of 1965, Warhol was called to arbitratration involving a dispute over importing his Brillo Boxes: Staff members at the National Gallery of Canada had declared that his artwork was not original; as a result the Canadian Tariff Act was amended.

Mark Antony Wigley was born in 1956 in New Zealand. He received his B.Arch. in 1979 from the University of Auckland, New Zealand. After completing his undergraduate degree he began teaching architecture at the University of Auckland while pursuing his Ph.D. in architecture which he received in 1980. The title of his doctoral dissertation is *Derrida and Architecture: The Deconstructive Possibilities of Architectural Discourse*. In 1987 he began working as an architect in New York City, and at the end of 1987 began teaching at Princeton University. He is associate curator of the exhibition "Deconstructivist Architecture," at the Museum of Modern Art in New York City.

Krzysztof Wodiczko is a Polish-Canadian artist living in New York City and working on the second stage of his project "homeless vehicles," developed in collaboration with Rudolph Luria, with the advice of interested homeless persons and the help and support of concerned individuals, nonprofit agencies, and institutions. The second stage will involve testing prototypes and organizing homeless people in the design of manufacturing workshops during the fall of 1988 in New York City. Those interested in supporting this project should write to Homeless Vehicle project, Box 212, 496 La Guardia Place, New York, N.Y. 10012.

Bibliography

Arakawa and Madeline Gins, *The Mechanism of Meaning*. New York: Abbyville Press, forthcoming 1988

Barrett, William. *Death of the Soul: From Descartes to the Computer*. Garden City: Anchor Press/Doubleday, 1986.

Baynes, Kenneth, *et al. After Philosophy: End or Transformation?* James Bohan and Thomas McCarthy, editors. Cambridge and London: The MIT Press, 1987.

Bognar, Botond. *Contemporary Japanese Architecture: Its Development and Challenge*. New York: Van Nostrand Reinhold Company, Inc., 1985.

Caputo, John D. *Radical Hermeneutics*. Bloomington and Indianapolis: Indiana University Press, 1987.

Deleuze, Gilles. *Nietzsche and Philosophy*. Translated by Hugh Tomlinson. New York: Columbia University Press, 1983.

Derrida, Jacques. *Dissemination*. Translated by Barbara Johnson. Chicago: The University of Chicago Press, The Athlone Press, 1981. *Editions du Seuil*, 1972.

Derrida, Jacques. *GLAS*. Translated by John P. Leavey, Jr., and Richard Rand. Lincoln and London: University of Nebraska Press, 1986.

Derrida, Jacques. *Of Grammatology*. Translated by Gayatri Chakravorty Spivak. Baltimore and London: The Johns Hopkins University Press, 1976.

Foster, Hal. *RECODINGS: Art, Spectacle, Cultural Politics*. Port Townsend: Bay Press, 1985.

Foucault, Michel. *The Order of Things*. New York: Random House, 1970.

Gadamer, Hans-Georg. *Truth and Method*. New York: The Crossroad Publishing Company, 1984. Translation edited by Garrett Barden and John Cumming, 1965. Tübingen: J. C. B. Mohr, 1960.

Heidegger, Martin. *Basic Writings*. Edited by David Farrell Krell. New York: Harper & Row, Publishers, Inc., 1977.

Heidegger, Martin. *Being and Time*. Translated by John Macquarrie and Edward Robinson. New York: Harper & Row, Publishers, Inc., 1962.

Heidegger, Martin. *On the Way to Language*. Translated by Peter D. Hertz. New York: Harper & Row, Publishers, Inc., 1971.

Heidegger, Martin. *Poetry, Language, Thought*. Translated by Albert Hofstadter. New York: Harper & Row, Publishers, Inc., 1971.

Ihde, Don and Hugh J. Silverman, editors. *Descriptions*. Albany: SUNY Press, 1985.

Ihde, Don. *Experimental Phenomenology: An Introduction*. Albany: SUNY Press, 1986.

Ihde, Don. *Hermeneutic Phenomenology: The Philosophy of Paul Ricoeur*. Evanston: Northwestern University Press, 1971.

Kipnis, Jeffrey. *A Choral Work*. London: Architectural Association, forthcoming 1988.

Kockelmans, Joseph J., editor. *On Heidegger and Language*. Evanston: Northwestern University Press, 1972.

Krauss, Rosalind E. *The Originality of the Avant-Garde and Other Modernist Myths*. Cambridge and London: The MIT Press, 1986.

Lyotard, Jean-François. *The Postmodern Condition: A Report on Knowledge*. Translated by Geoff Bennington and Brian Massumi. Minneapolis: State University of Minnesota Press, 1984.

Macquarrie, John. *Existentialism*. New York: Penguin Books, 1972.

Margolis, Joseph, editor. *Philosophy Looks at the Arts: Contemporary Readings of Aesthetics*. Philadelphia: Temple University Press, 1986.

Megill, Allan. *Prophets of Extremity: Nietzsche, Heidegger, Foucault, Derrida*. Berkeley and Los Angeles: University of California Press, 1985.

Merleau-Ponty, Maurice. *Phenomenology of Perception*. Translated by Colin Smith. London and Henley: Routledge & Kegan Paul, Ltd., 1962. New Jersey: The Humanities Press.

Michelfelder, Diane and Richard E. Palmer, editors. *Dialogue and Deconstruction: The Gadamer-Derrida Encounter*. Albany: SUNY Press, forthcoming 1988.

Norberg-Schulz, Christian. *The Concept of Dwelling: On the Way to Figurative Architecture*. New York: Rizzoli International Publications, Inc., 1985.

Norris, Christopher. *Deconstruction: Theory and Practice*. London and New York: Methuen, 1982.

Palmer, Richard E. *Hermeneutics*. Evanston: Northwestern University Press, 1969.

Pérez-Gómez, Alberto. *Architecture and the Crisis of Modern Science*. Cambridge and London: The MIT Press, 1983.

THE PRATT JOURNAL OF ARCHITECTURE, Vol. 1. Brooklyn: Pratt Institute, School of Architecture, 1985. In association with Rizzoli International Publications, Inc., New York.

Sallis, John. *Delimitations: Phenomenology and the End of Metaphysics*. Bloomington and Indianapolis: Indiana University Press, 1986.

Silverman, Hugh J. and Don Ihde, editors. *Hermeneutics & Deconstruction*. Albany: SUNY Press, 1985.

Taylor, Mark C. *Erring: A Postmodern A/theology*. Chicago and London: The University of Chicago Press, 1984.

Taylor, Mark C., editor. *Deconstruction in Context: Literature and Philosophy*. Chicago and London: The University of Chicago Press, 1986.

Wallis, Brian, editor. *Art After Modernism: Rethinking Modernism*. New York: The Museum of Contemporary Art, 1984. In association with David R. Godine, Publisher, Inc., Boston.

Zimmerman, Michael E. *Eclipse of the Self: The Development of Heidegger's Concept of Authenticity*. Athens, Ohio and London: Ohio University Press, 1981.

ZONE 1/2 and *ZONE BOOKS* Fall 1987–Spring 1988. New York: Urzone, Inc., in association with The Johns Hopkins University Press, Baltimore, and The MIT Press, Cambridge.

WE
WANT
YOU
IN

Architectural A G O NY *Guard* *of*

SOON!

RONALD FELDMAN FINE ARTS

URBAN CENTER BOOKS

A bookstore for Architecture and related subjects

457 Madison Avenue at 51st Street · NY · NY · 10022
(212) 935-3592

Please write for our catalogue

Store Hours: Monday-Saturday 10am to 6pm